The History
of
England's Cathedrals

In memoriam

Ernest W. Plowright

William A. K. Hussey

John A. Thurmer

The History

of

England's Cathedrals

NICHOLAS ORME

First published 2017
by Impress Books Ltd
Innovation Centre, Rennes Drive, University of Exeter Campus, Exeter EX4 4RN

British Library Cataloguing in Publication Data
A catalogue record for this book is available from the British Library

ISBN: 9781907605987 (hbk)

ISBN: 9781907605925 (pbk)

eISBN: 9781907605932 (ebk)

Typeset in Dante MT by Swales and Willis Ltd, Exeter, Devon

Printed and bound in England by Short Run Press, Exeter, Devon

Contents

List of Maps, Plans, and Illustrations

Acknowledgements

I am very grateful to Ian Atherton, Sarah Brown, Jon Cannon, Anne Crawford, Ken Eames, Nick Fry, Richard Gem, Derek Gore, Canon Andrew Hindley, Izaak Hudson, Ellie Jones, Dianne Morris, Elizabeth New, Rona Orme, the Right Revd June Osborne, Nigel Saul, Simon Sheppard, Tim Tatton-Brown, Graham Thomas, and John Wolffe for information and advice on aspects of this work. Roger Bowers and John Harper gave me valuable help on the liturgy and music, David Lepine kindly read the whole text, Philip Mansergh generously provided several illustrations, and the staff of the Bodleian Library deserve my thanks for their labours in bringing me books. The responsibility for errors and omissions is wholly my own. I am greatly obliged to my publishers for their care and support in producing the book and procuring the illustrations, and they and I are further indebted for permission to reproduce images from the copyright holders who are listed on pp. 296–7.

Chapter
—— 1 ——

Why Cathedrals?

You are looking towards a cathedral. Almost always it seeks to impress you. It stands apart from its setting, making itself distinctive (Fig. 1, opposite). It is larger than most churches. It usually possesses bold features: an imposing frontage, massive towers, or a tall and tapering spire. If you have come on purpose to see it, you are probably aware that it is special. Churches are numbered in thousands, but there are only forty-three cathedrals in the Church of England (including the Isle of Man) and nineteen in the Catholic Church in England.

Many people who visit cathedrals probably take for granted what they see. To paraphrase Wittgenstein, for them 'A cathedral is that which is the case'. In fact each element of a cathedral, as a building and a centre of activity, exists for a purpose and for historical reasons. There are cathedrals because Christianity came to England in Roman times and again in 597. That nearly all are in substantial towns is also due to the Romans, and that they are in the towns where they are is the result of a lot of history. The Anglo-Saxons built them in certain places; the Viking age caused some to disappear. The Normans moved others, Henry VIII established new ones, and the Victorians and their successors made further additions. So the very fact that there is a cathedral in the place that you have come to see is due not to chance but to the needs and actions of people in the past.

The cathedral sits in surroundings. These may not strike you as significant, yet they are. Some buildings are on main roads, close to everyday life. Nearly all of these are modern foundations, built or adapted in a democratic age. Their makers wished them to be close to people, not in a secluded grandeur like that of a stately home. Others, particularly the medieval ones, still have a degree of seclusion. You find them off the High Street down a side road, and sometimes reach them through a gatehouse or a place where a gatehouse stood. That is because in the Middle Ages cathedrals were staffed by celibate clergy who wished to distance themselves from the outside world and might need to defend themselves in a more lawless era. If there is a grassy space around the cathedral, that is noteworthy as well. It may look like a park meant to enhance the building but it has only acquired that form in the last two hundred years. Before that, it may have been a graveyard and have had its edges fringed with ale-houses or workshops, giving it a more sobering and untidy feel than it has today.

When you enter the cathedral, there too is meaning behind what you see. Architectural histories will tell you when each part of the building was raised and what kinds of designs and decorations were employed. But there are reasons for the shape and layout of cathedrals, which are less often explained. You enter first the nave. This is usually long and narrow, with side aisles. In the older cathedrals it does not allow you to see the whole of the church at once. The building unfolds as you walk through. You pass transepts on each side, you enter the choir which is the central area of worship, you discover aisles alongside the choir, and find small chapels leading off them. Sometimes you reach a larger Lady chapel at the far east end of the building. All these features are here for a purpose. Some have a function in the construction of the building, others in the kind of worship that the builders envisaged inside. But cathedral worship has not always been the same. It was altered radically in the middle of the sixteenth century and more gradually during the nineteenth and twentieth. So as well as the reasons why the building is formed as it is, there is also a history of how it has been adapted from time to time as people's religious and social convictions have changed.

In consequence, an ancient cathedral records more than its own private history. Indeed, it can be read as a miniature history of England. Canterbury, the earliest cathedral to survive, came about through political links between the Anglo-Saxons and the rulers of what would be France. Other circumstances – religious, political, and social – brought the rest of the cathedrals into being, determined where they would lie, and shaped how they would develop. When we visit a cathedral like Canterbury, we are treading in the footsteps of Romans, Anglo-Saxons, Normans, Tudors, Stuarts, Hanoverians, Victorians, and whatever we are going to call the people of the twentieth century. All these societies had something to do with cathedrals. They all left marks upon them and by reading these marks – particularly floor-plans, furnishings, decorations, and monuments – we may learn much of the minds and tastes of our ancestors and how these have changed from one century to another.

If the cathedral you visit is an ancient one, and if you tour it very thoroughly, you will find that as well as the great church there are several associated buildings. These are likely to include a chapter house, cloisters,

1. The grand west front of Lichfield Cathedral, an example of how such buildings have sought to impress their visitors.

a music room, a cathedral library and archives, a cathedral school, and *2. Lincoln* dwelling houses of the cathedral clergy or houses that once served that *Cathedral,* purpose. You may have seen a shop or a restaurant. These too are all here *towering over its* for reasons. They tell us that a cathedral is far more than a church housing *former Roman* worship. It is a community of people: clergy, lay staff, and volunteers. *city in partnership* It is and always has been involved with the production of music, with *with the nearby* study and learning, with the writing and keeping of records, and with the *castle. The city* education of young people. Its shop and restaurant probably date from *had a bishop as* the second half of the twentieth century. They signify that tourism too *far back as 314.* has become important to cathedrals, as a way of reaching out to society and of raising some of the money that is needed to maintain the buildings.

When you have finished your tour of the cathedral and its surroundings, you may feel that you have a fairly full knowledge of both. In fact you have seen as much of them as a ship sees of an iceberg, or even less. You probably did not ascend to the upper storeys, attend any worship, or work in the cathedral archives. You came into contact with only a few of the people who make possible the cathedral's existence and its accessibility to visitors. True, you looked at the building and some original furnishings like monuments. But a good deal of all this consists of repairs and restorations made over the last few centuries: not all of it is original. You did not experience the place as it would have been in Victorian times, when the furnishings and usage of the cathedral were different. They were different again in Georgian England, under Elizabeth I, and before the Reformation. Apart from their monuments, you saw almost no traces of the people who ran and served the church in former times. And you were probably unaware that out beyond the cathedral there were properties that it owned and put its stamp on. These included houses in the cathedral city, landed estates in the countryside, and parish churches on the estates. They carried the influence of the cathedral far beyond its surroundings.

The book that follows seeks to explain these matters and to reveal why and how they came into existence and changed over time. It is not primarily an architectural history, although cathedrals are buildings and this affects everything else. Fortunately, there are several excellent histories of the buildings, both general and individual ones, to which readers may go for further enlightenment.[1] Instead the book aims to provide a history of a broader and more unusual kind. First, it approaches cathedrals as a group rather than one by one, exploring what they had in common as well as the differences between them. Next it tries to do justice to all the major aspects of their life. It asks who founded and staffed them, how their buildings were used, and in what ways worship was done. It examines their involvement in learning and education, their immediate surroundings (cathedral Closes), and their outreach beyond these surroundings. Outreach includes how cathedrals related to the cities and dioceses in which they stood, the extent to which they were visited, what people thought and wrote about them, and how they were caught up in national politics.

The intention has been to produce a concise history that touches on all these major topics and issues throughout the last fourteen centuries – the first time, I believe, that this has been done.[2] One decision has been unavoidable to keep the book to a reasonable size and its story to a coherent one. Foundations are not included except when they were cathedrals, so that Westminster Abbey is omitted as are (say) Gloucester before it was made a cathedral by Henry VIII, or Southwell until it gained this status in Victorian times. Even so, in view of the vast amount that is known and has been written about cathedrals, it is impossible within the compass of one book to do full justice to every relevant aspect. The book seeks to help those who wish to know a little, and to give those who want to know more an idea of what may be known and where it may be found. Expert readers will inevitably find something that has been omitted or abridged. The author can only hope that they will give credit to what is here as opposed to what is not.

Chapter

— 2 —

Romans and Anglo-Saxons

314–1066

Cathedrals are offshoots of bishops. They are the bishop's own church and differ from others in housing his seat: the *cathedra* or chair that he sits on. In most of western Europe they lie in towns; indeed most places in England with cathedrals are known, at least informally, as 'cities'.[1] This linkage goes back to the beginnings of Christianity in the Roman Empire. For local purposes, the empire was made up of city states, each with a territory that it controlled. Christianity travelled through the empire along transport routes from city to city, and made its first substantial groups of converts in these places. St Paul helped to found some of them, and wrote his letters to the Christians of Corinth, Ephesus, Rome, and elsewhere. As Christianity grew and became more organised, each city of the empire gained a bishop. He led its religious life from his chair in the principal church of the city, which thereby became his cathedral church. The city and its territory formed his 'diocese' or area of responsibility. Since he lived locally, and since on the Mediterranean shores – Italy, Provence, and North Africa – the diocese was a fairly small one, he was a frequent presence in the cathedral. There, he presided over the worship and did special tasks like baptising and confirming babies or converts and ordaining clergy.

In 313 the Emperor Constantine gave official approval and toleration of Christianity, and in 391 his successor Theodosius made it the sole allowed religion of the empire. By the early fourth century, at the latest, there were bishops in Roman Britain, who were also located in cities. Britain, like the rest of the empire, was divided into city states, with the difference that they included larger areas of countryside because the land was less populated. Three British bishops attended a Church council at Arles in 314. They were Eborius, 'bishop in the city of York', Restitutus, 'bishop in the city of London', and Adelfius, 'bishop in the city of *Colonia Londenensi*' (probably a confusion with *Lindonensi*, meaning Lincoln).[2] Here too there were bishops in cities and, significantly, cities where their churches would be sited later on. Each bishop must have had a church in his city, in effect a cathedral, and there is no reason to think that these were the only cities with such bishops and churches.[3]

Soon after 400, Roman rule evaporated. The cities fell into decay. Anglo-Saxon chieftains and their followers carved out small kingdoms. Paganism was reintroduced and gradually most of the British inhabitants adopted the Anglo-Saxons' language and customs. Christianity did not completely disappear. It remained strong in the western parts of Britain which the Anglo-Saxons did not reach, but most of the bishops and their churches disappeared along with the cities in which they had been. This was the first of five great crises that cathedrals in England would face in their history. On this occasion they did not survive it.

The Reconstruction of the Church

In 596 Pope Gregory the Great sent the Italian monk Augustine with a group of companions to reconvert the English. They arrived a year later. The spur for this mission was the fact that one of the leading English kings, Æthelberht of Kent, had close relationships with the Christian past and present. The Roman city of Canterbury, or what remained of it, was one of his centres of power and, although he was a pagan, he had married Bertha, a Christian Frankish princess. Indeed she can be said to have started the reconversion of the English because she brought with her a bishop, Liudhard. They held Christian worship in the church of St Martin outside Canterbury, which was either an old Roman church or one rebuilt from Roman materials. To bring a bishop suggests that he may have been meant to preach and ordain clergy if any could be recruited, rather than simply to act as the queen's own chaplain. However, Augustine's mission was larger and more formal. Æthelberht soon agreed to accept the Christian faith and be baptised. Shortly afterwards, he gave Augustine another church, which the historian Bede believed to have been founded in Roman times. This became Augustine's seat, the ancestor of the present Canterbury Cathedral.[4]

3. An early cathedral treasure: the opening page of the Gospel of Matthew from the Lindisfarne Gospels, created in about 700.

When news of Augustine's successful arrival reached Rome, Gregory sent him a letter with instructions to create a framework of bishops in Britain.[5] The island was to consist of two religious provinces. Augustine was designated as archbishop of the southern province with his church in London and twelve bishops under him. A second archbishop was to be placed at York to lead a northern province with another twelve bishops. The pope did not lay down where the other bishops were to be based, but it is likely that he had seen Roman maps, descriptions of Britain, or lists of bishops like those of Arles, and expected that their bases would be in former Roman cities. True, these cities were now ruined, which the pope may or may not have known, but all who were subsequently involved in re-establishing Christianity in Britain had a strong sense that they were restoring Roman civilisation as well as the Roman religion. As we shall see, several of the bishops and their cathedrals were located where there had once been cities, and their presence helped to revive them.

There was another problem besides the ruined cities. Britain was no longer a unity. About half of it was divided into small Anglo-Saxon kingdoms, constituting what we may now call England. The rest consisted of several 'Celtic' kingdoms in Scotland, Wales, and Cornwall which were already Christian and not amenable to coming under the control of archbishops at London and York. It took a long time to re-establish bishops and cathedrals even in England. Augustine managed to do so in Kent, where he founded them at Canterbury and Rochester, as well as London in the nearby kingdom of Essex. But the Christian presence in London was tenuous and lapsed for a time, obliging Augustine and his successors to keep to their original base at Canterbury. This became the permanent seat of the archbishop of the southern province although, later on, he acquired a London base at Lambeth nearby. Paulinus was made bishop (not archbishop) of York in 625, but here again there was an interruption of some years, and although other bishops were appointed to York later on, they did not become archbishops until 735.

Very gradually, during the seventh century, the Church organised itself in all the Anglo-Saxon kingdoms.[6] This happened in a piecemeal unplanned way, but when the Venerable Bede described the situation in 731 the result was a coherent one (Fig. 4, p. 10). There was at least one bishop for every kingdom or major group of people: indeed Bede thought of most of them as bishops of the East Angles, Mercians, or West Saxons, rather than bishops of a specific place.[7] Some had their principal church in a former Roman city or fort. As well as Canterbury, London, and Rochester, these included *Dommoc* (somewhere in Suffolk), Dorchester-on-Thames (now in Oxfordshire), Leicester, Lincoln (the probable base of the bishops of Lindsey), Winchester, and Worcester.[8] Other bishops were based in non-Roman locations with some religious or political importance including Elmham, Hereford, Hexham, Lichfield, Sherborne, and briefly Ripon, while two were on islands at Lindisfarne and Selsey ('seal island') (Fig. 5, p. 11). The major cathedrals, like Canterbury and Winchester, soon became permanent with burials of kings and saints, and it was impossible to

4. *English cathedrals to 800.*

imagine them anywhere else. But in some more rural places cathedrals had less status or permanence. As we shall see, the bishops of Cornwall and Ramsbury in the tenth century may have used more than one church as it suited them.[9] Their colleagues at Elmham seem to have had a second base at Hoxne in Suffolk.[10] In the eleventh and early twelfth centuries there were several movements of cathedrals from place to place, and only then did all the sites become fixed.[11]

This pattern of cathedral locations was partly like that of the Mediterranean world in using Roman cities, even if they were hardly more than ruins. It also had some resemblance with the Celtic world, which based its bishops at monasteries in the countryside or on islands. There was another difference from the Mediterranean, in that the English bishops had to look after larger dioceses, which were based on

kingdoms rather than city states. The bishop of Worcester, for example, ruled two and a half modern counties, and the bishop of Sherborne four. Bishops soon became important in the secular world as well. Once the kings of their kingdoms accepted Christianity, they endowed their bishops with lands which allowed them to employ retinues of clergy and servants and to amass wealth. English bishops were travellers to a greater extent than their counterparts in southern Europe: visiting their estates, touring their dioceses, and spending time with their kings. This meant that they were often absent from their cathedrals and this, in the very long term, would lead to a divergence between the two parties.

5. The island of Lindisfarne, seat of a bishop and cathedral from 635 to 875.

As for Pope Gregory's scheme for grouping the bishops into two provinces, it came into being far less quickly or exactly than he envisaged. Not only was York late in getting an archbishop, but the two provinces which have existed since then have not been equal in size. By the eighth century the archbishop of Canterbury ruled over twelve other bishops south of the Rivers Humber and Trent, making a province of thirteen dioceses in line with Gregory's scheme. North of the rivers, the archbishop of York's domain was limited to the areas ruled by the local kings of Northumbria. It had only four dioceses: York itself, Lindisfarne, Hexham, and (from 681 to the early 800s) Whithorn in Galloway. There was another brief English bishopric at Abercorn west of Edinburgh in 681–5, but the archbishops at York never managed to stretch their authority far into what became Scotland and their province remained far smaller in extent than Canterbury's. In 787 King Offa of Mercia, who was having difficulty in imposing his rule on Kent and hence on Canterbury, tried to create a third province for his kingdom. He got the pope's consent to raise Lichfield to an archbishopric in charge of six other bishops in the Midlands and East Anglia, leaving Canterbury only with London and the four dioceses to the south of the Thames. But this plan did not long survive Offa's death. Lichfield reverted to an ordinary bishopric in 803 and Canterbury recovered its former territory

Cathedrals and Their Life from 597 to 800

'Cathedral' is a familiar word to us, evoking the thought of a great building. But it took many centuries for the word to evolve in this way. The Anglo-Saxons used the Latin word *cathedra* like the modern word 'see' to describe a bishop's seat and the authority and rights that went with it, rather than the building that the seat was in. Much later, in the twelfth century, an adjective *cathedralis* developed and we begin to encounter the term *ecclesia cathedralis* meaning a church where a bishop has his seat, but there was no single Latin word *cathedrale* meaning simply 'a cathedral'.[12] Similarly in English, 'cathedral' is not recorded until the fourteenth century and then only as an adjective like *cathedralis* to put next to 'church'. 'Cathedral' as a noun on its own first emerges in English in the late sixteenth century, which makes a point to which we shall return: cathedrals in the Middle Ages did not have a profile as high as they do today.[13]

How then did the Anglo-Saxons refer to cathedrals? In their own language they had only the general word 'church', meaning any kind of holy building, and 'minster', which was their translation of the Latin word *monasterium*. 'Minster' was used for large churches served by groups of clergy: cathedrals, monasteries, or other religious houses, and it still survives in place-names like Leominster and Westminster. Some minsters were staffed by monks living largely apart from the outside world. Augustine brought monks to England with him and established a monastery for them in Canterbury dedicated to St Peter and St Paul, and subsequently known as St Augustine's.[14] In other minsters the clergy were what historians call 'secular clergy', meaning men who could move freely in the world (*seculum*) and own some personal property. At first the difference between monks and secular clergy was not necessarily very great. Pope Gregory advised Augustine that the clergy who lived with him (in effect secular clergy) should live a common life, which meant that they would live, eat, and worship together, share their possessions, and be celibate.[15] Equally, some of the monks in monastic minsters in the seventh, eighth, and ninth centuries must have engaged in pastoral ministry to the public because there were not yet many parish churches. When such a minster was the only church for miles around, local people would go to worship there, receive baptism, have their funerals, and be buried in its churchyard.

Most of the early Anglo-Saxon cathedrals were staffed by secular clergy, free to travel and do tasks in the world.[16] Only a few such churches in the seventh, eighth, and ninth centuries were in the hands of monks: Hexham, Lindisfarne, Whithorn, and briefly Abercorn, all in the far north where Celtic influence was stronger. As time passed, the differences between monks and secular clergy increased and this was definitely the case by the tenth century, as we shall see. The fact has made it necessary for historians to find a term for cathedrals and churches staffed by secular clergy to distinguish them from monasteries, and the word 'minster' has been adopted for this purpose, even though it was used by the Anglo-Saxons for monasteries as well. The practice can be justified because people have been using the word for centuries to describe important churches in the north of England that were not monasteries. Two were cathedrals and are still known locally as Lincoln Minster and York Minster. Two others, Ripon Minster and Southwell Minster, were communities of secular clergy in the Middle Ages and became cathedrals in the nineteenth century.

Bishops and cathedrals of both kinds, secular and monastic, gradually acquired substantial estates with the rents, food, and power over the inhabitants that went with the ownership of land. These estates were usually given to the saint of the cathedral and his church, which meant in practice that the property was at the disposal of the bishop who was in charge of the church and its clergy. The kings of Kent made considerable gifts over time – 'a landed lordship of phenomenal wealth' – to the church of Canterbury. These were chiefly situated in Kent itself, but came to include outliers in Berkshire, Buckinghamshire, Surrey, and Sussex.[17] Winchester and Sherborne gained properties from the kings of Wessex, Worcester from its local rulers – the kings of the Hwicce, and this was probably true in the other kingdoms.[18] The bishop might use some of these properties for his own use or that of his personal retinue, and allocate others to his cathedral clergy. An instance of such an allocation is recorded at Canterbury as early as 780.[19] But the division of assets between the bishop and cathedral was not permanent until after the Norman Conquest. Even if there was a customary division, a bishop could always ignore it and set up a new one.

Cathedrals were also buildings. Little is known about the earliest ones. York is said by Bede to have originated with a church of wood built 'hastily' by Edwin, king of Northumbria when he was baptised in 627. He then planned 'a greater and more magnificent church of stone' around this first church, which was finished by his successor Oswald.[20] Lindisfarne was first made of wood and thatched with rushes, but was later covered with tiles of lead.[21] On the other hand, Winchester, built in about 648, was of stone, and so was Ripon, founded by Bishop Wilfrid a little later.[22] Stone was probably common because it conferred both status and security. Windows were narrow and difficult to protect. When Wilfrid went to York as bishop in 670, he found that birds got in and fouled the interior, which he solved by installing window glass.[23]

Winchester's cathedral is the oldest to have been excavated, but probably possessed the elements of cathedrals in general.[24] It faced east towards God and consisted of two main parts. To the east was the choir or chancel where services were held, with the principal or 'high' altar at its east end. At Winchester that end was rectangular, but later on a semicircular apse became common in such a location. West of the choir was the nave or 'body' of the church which could be used for processions, burials of important people, and as a place for lay people to watch the worship. There were often other compartments known as 'porches' (*porticus*) which served as additional chapels or burial places. Winchester had two of these, north and south of the nave; Wilfrid provided some at Ripon; and Bishop Acca of Hexham built several chapels there to house altars and relics of saints.[25] When York was rebuilt in 741, it was said to include many beautiful porches and, if one may believe the account, as many as thirty altars.[26] A tower was desirable for bell ringing (Winchester's was detached, and stood west of the nave), and crypts were common beneath large churches, often containing further tombs or housing relics. But the Anglo-Saxon cathedrals were not always single buildings. There was a church of St John the Baptist immediately beyond the east end of Canterbury, which was used for baptisms, and one of St Mary beyond that of Wells.[27] York seems to have had two churches on its site, and Worcester, as we shall see, gained a second in the tenth century.[28] Cathedrals in which everything was under the same roof became universal only after the Norman Conquest.

The early cathedrals were not merely buildings, of course, but centres of worship and repositories of precious objects. Kings and bishops donated books, vestments, church ornaments, and relics. Edwin of Northumbria, the founder of the cathedral at York, was said to have given it a great gold cross and a gold chalice. Wilfrid added vessels and furnishings there, and provided Ripon with a similar gold cross, a gold-mounted gospel book, and a gold shrine to keep it in.[29] Gospel books had a high status because they were read in the principal service, the eucharist or mass, and were treated with veneration on that occasion. They were often richly decorated as well as being carefully written, and cherished for their spiritual as well as artistic value. The Lindisfarne Gospels from about the turn of the seventh and eighth centuries are the most famous of these books for the elaborate beauty of their pages, and their covers were formerly embellished with gold and gems.[30] When the clergy of Lindisfarne left the island in 875, the Gospels were one of the precious items that they took with them (Fig. 3, p. 6). Other such books with cathedral links include the eighth-century St Chad Gospels, eventually possessed by Lichfield; the Hereford Gospels of the same century or a little later; the York Gospels, produced at Canterbury in about 1000 and brought to York afterwards; and the Codex Aureus, an eighth-century gospel book now in Stockholm. When the latter was looted by Vikings in the late ninth century, a nobleman in Surrey paid a ransom to recover it and gave or restored it to Canterbury.[31]

All cathedrals and churches gathered relics of saints which were placed in altars or mounted for display and veneration. Some acquired whole saints'

6. Cathedrals began to acquire their own saints in the seventh century. Here a cripple prays at the tomb of St Cuthbert, bishop of Lindisfarne, later translated to Durham.

bodies, whose presence in graves or shrines was a valuable resource for attracting pilgrims and benefactors. Lindisfarne cathedral held that of the most famous northern saint, Cuthbert (Fig. 6, above), Lichfield that of Chad, and St Paul's (London) that of Erconwald. Others joined them, as we shall see, in later centuries. However, it should be pointed out that Anglo-Saxon cathedrals, and indeed their medieval successors, were not as prominent in relation to other churches as they would become from the middle of the sixteenth century. While cathedrals were being founded, so were monasteries alongside them. Indeed, Augustine, his early successors as archbishops of Canterbury, King Æthelberht, Queen Bertha, and Bishop Liudhard were not buried in the cathedral but in Augustine's other foundation in Canterbury, the monastery of St Peter and St Paul. Some of these monasteries had equally large properties, valuable treasures, and saintly burials, so that although the cathedrals were some of the great churches of the day, they were not the only ones.

The Vikings and Afterwards

In 793 Norse raiders sailed to the coast of Northumberland and sacked the cathedral monastery of Lindisfarne. This began more than two centuries of Viking attacks on much of England. In the north and east they overthrew the local English kingdoms, taking control of large areas of the country and settling there. In the south they raided Canterbury, London, Rochester, and Winchester, threatening if not harming their cathedrals. These events helped to bring about a second great crisis of cathedral history in which several were disrupted or disappeared. The blame for this should not all be pinned on the Vikings. Christian rulers in Britain were not averse to attacking cathedrals. King Æthelred of Mercia destroyed Rochester in a raid on Kent in 676. Hereford was set on fire and some of its clergy killed by an English nobleman and a Welsh prince in 1055. York was 'burnt; its ornaments, charters, and privileges consumed and lost' when William the Conqueror brutally suppressed a rising against him there in 1070.[32]

Indeed, the Vikings were not consistently hostile to cathedrals. The northern archbishops and their church survived at York, and it has been suggested that their library remained intact as well.[33] Even the bishop and clergy of Lindisfarne did not leave their island permanently until ninety years after the first attack on their church. Only in 875 did they forsake the place and take their saint and treasures on a series of journeys that brought them to Chester-le-Street (County Durham) in 883. This was nearer to the areas of Scandinavian settlement, not further away, and may have had nothing to do with escaping from Vikings.[34] Here and elsewhere, disruptions to the Church may have been due less to primary attacks by the Norsemen than to the secondary results of their coming: the collapse of kingdoms and changes in local politics. Still, whatever the reasons, the bishops of Hexham in Northumberland and Lindsey (probably at Lincoln), the two of East Anglia based at Elmham and *Dommoc*, and the English bishop at Whithorn all disappeared in the course of the century, while the bishop of Leicester moved south to Dorchester-on-Thames in about the 870s or 80s. Some of their former cathedrals may have struggled on as minsters but with less status than before. By 900 there were only two full cathedrals (Chester-le-Street and York) north of the line from London to Chester, compared with eleven to the south and the west of that line. This unevenness was to endure for several centuries.

The political fortunes of the English began to recover under King Alfred, who reigned from 871 to 899 over Wessex: roughly southern England from Cornwall to Kent. He beat off Viking attacks on his kingdom and continued a process by which he and his family extended their influence beyond it: at first over Mercia in the Midlands and later further northwards and eastwards. At about this time there were thoughts of creating new dioceses in Wessex. In 870 we hear of a bishop of Wiltshire, and in about the 890s Alfred seems to have placed his Welsh friend Bishop Asser at Exeter in charge of Devon and Cornwall.[35] These arrangements were followed by more permanent ones under Alfred's successors Edward the Elder and Æthelstan. In 909 Edward addressed the problem of the large diocese of Sherborne which covered most of the South-West of England, and split it into three. Sherborne itself was restricted to Dorset, and new bishops and cathedrals were established at Crediton (just outside Exeter) for Devon and Wells for Somerset. At about the same time a diocese for Wiltshire was created or updated with a bishop based at Ramsbury and there was briefly a bishop of Berkshire, but by about 950 the bishops of Ramsbury were in charge of both counties. One of the Ramsbury bishops was described as 'of Sonning' and two 'of Wilton': places at which they had estates but possibly also their favourite principal church, although Ramsbury seems to have held that role for the longest.[36] Finally, Æthelstan added or confirmed a bishop for Cornwall by 936. His seat was at St Germans and maybe also at Bodmin.[37]

Gradually, the Viking colonisers of England became integrated and Christianised. At the same time the power of the kings of Wessex continued to expand until King Æthelstan (924–39) was effectively king of all England. It now became possible to rebuild the Church organisation of the Danelaw, as the Viking lands were known (Fig. 7, p. 18). By the 950s a bishop and cathedral were re-established at Elmham in East Anglia (Fig. 13, p. 29) and a second pair for Lindsey (again probably at Lincoln), although the bishops of Lindsey petered out once more in the early 1000s.[38] In 995 the bishop and clergy of Chester-le-Street moved to Durham (Fig. 8, p. 19). During the following century, however, there was a contrary movement to reduce the number of dioceses in southern England, apparently because their endowments were not wealthy enough. Two were abolished along with their cathedrals. From 1027 the dioceses of Crediton and Cornwall were held by the same bishop, and in 1050 the arrangement was made permanent by uniting the two and returning the bishop's church to Exeter. The old cathedrals of Crediton and St Germans became minsters of secular clergy. In 1058 the diocese of Ramsbury was united with Sherborne, after which the former Ramsbury cathedral kept a group of secular clergy for a time until it turned into an ordinary parish church.

On the eve of the Norman Conquest the English Church contained two archbishops, thirteen bishops, and therefore fifteen cathedrals. The distribution of bishops and cathedrals between the two provinces envisaged by Gregory the Great was still unbalanced, if not more so. Canterbury had all but two, while York comprised only York and Durham, having never managed to extend its authority beyond the borders of the English kingdoms. By the twelfth century there were indeed Scottish bishops and cathedrals which had come into existence independently, and in 1101 Pope Paschal II ordered these bishops to swear obedience to the archbishop of York. But, as before, there was a political frontier between England and Scotland, and the Scottish bishops refused to comply with the order. In 1188 Pope Clement III made the Church in Scotland independent, and since then the province of York and the authority of its archbishop has stretched only from the Scottish border to the Rivers Trent and Humber.

7. English
cathedrals
900–1066.

+ Archbishop's cathedral
O Secular cathedral
■ Monastic cathedral

Chester-
le-Street
O
O
Durham

+ York
O

Lindsey (Lincoln)
O

Lichfield
O

O
Elmham

■ Worcester

O   Dorchester
Hereford   O
       Ramsbury
       O   London
O Wells   O
   Winchester   Rochester O
      ■   Canterbury ■
Sherborne
■   Selsey
CreditonO   O
Cornwall O Exeter
(St Germans)
O

Cathedrals in the Tenth and Eleventh Centuries

Meanwhile developments were taking place in the personnel and functions of cathedrals. During the ninth century, alongside the Viking disruptions, monastic life in England underwent changes. Some monasteries did not survive the disruptions, but in those that did – and in the cathedrals that were not monasteries – community life grew weaker.[39] The clergy tended to move into separate houses, to take personal shares of the income of the church, and even to marry and pass on their posts to their sons. This 'privatisation' of the church was most extreme in the smaller monasteries. At the cathedrals it was probably somewhat restrained by the fact that the

bishop was the legal owner of the church's property and might be more likely to disapprove.

Nevertheless, the practice of living apart was probably common, as was the possession of personal wealth. We hear of private clergy houses at Durham from the beginning in 995, and of married clergy there and probably at Rochester.[40] From the ninth to the eleventh centuries there was a widespread tolerance of clerical marriage in England, even that of priests. Two words were used to describe these more worldly clerics. One was 'clerk' and the other 'canon': canon meaning that the person followed a rule of life, if not as strict as that of a monk. Historians, as has been mentioned, call them 'secular clergy', meaning that they lived in the world and partly according to its values (Fig. 9, p. 20). Cathedral canons, parish priests, and later on vicars choral and chantry priests were all secular clergy, and cathedrals staffed by clergy of this kind are known as 'secular cathedrals' as distinct from cathedrals of monks or 'monastic cathedrals'.

'Every action has an equal and opposite reaction.' The 'worldliness' of cathedral and minster clergy might satisfy them and many other people, but in the tenth century it provoked a contrary view from a new generation of Church reformers. They found the life of the secular clergy unsatisfactory and looked for a solution in a revival of monasticism

8. Durham Cathedral, the final resting place of St Cuthbert after his journey from Lindisfarne via Chester-le-Street.

9. A secular clerk, apparently involved with a woman, from the Bayeux Tapestry. The alleged worldliness of such clerks helped prompt the growing vogue for monasteries.

which would produce more godly religious houses. This reaction began in the middle of the tenth century: a peaceful interlude between the first period of Viking invasion and the second that lasted from the 980s until 1016. The leaders were Oda, archbishop of Canterbury, and his virtual successor Dunstan (Fig. 10, p. 21), Æthelwold, bishop of Winchester, and Oswald, bishop of Worcester, the last three of whom had the support of King Edgar (959–75) and some of his nobility.[41] These reformers saw the monastic life, and in particular the sixth-century monastic Rule of St Benedict, as producing more dedicated clergy and holier services. The secular clergy of the cathedrals and former monastic minsters seemed insufficiently learned and spiritual, badly organised, and guilty of diverting the revenues of the Church to their own families. Monks, now following St Benedict's Rule, would be better trained, more economical in their way of life, and supplied with more books and resources so as to worship more knowledgeably and devoutly.

A couple of dozen new monasteries were founded in the second half of the tenth century, but the reformers had their eye on the cathedrals too. In 964 King Edgar, at the request of the most uncompromising reformer, Bishop Æthelwold, sanctioned the removal of the secular clergy of Winchester Cathedral and their replacement by monks. The other leaders were more cautious. Oda and Dunstan encouraged their clergy to keep the monastic rule but allowed those who preferred to be secular clergy to

10. St Dunstan,
kneeling before the
figure of Christ.
As archbishop
of Canterbury,
he helped
create monastic
cathedrals in
southern England.

continue as such, and the Canterbury community only gradually turned into a body of monks. Oswald left the seculars in charge of the existing cathedral at Worcester and built an additional church for monks in its churchyard.[42] Nevertheless, these three monastic cathedrals, joined by Sherborne during the 990s, brought a new dimension to English cathedral history. Hitherto only the far northern cathedrals had been monasteries, not ones as central and important as these. It was an unusual arrangement by the standards of western Europe, where most cathedrals were staffed by secular clergy, but it remained in being and spread to other churches after the Norman Conquest. From the tenth to the sixteenth centuries there were two kinds of cathedrals in England, monastic and secular, until Henry VIII closed down the monastic ones in the late 1530s.

At the same time another development was in train which would affect all the cathedrals. This was a proliferation of small local churches: those that we now know as parish churches. Some had existed before 900. Canterbury had always had St Martin, and a church of the Four Crowned

Martyrs is mentioned there in about 624.[43] Worcester may have possessed two other churches by the 700s.[44] After about 900, however, they appeared in large numbers in both the countryside and the towns.[45] In places where the cathedral had hitherto been the only or almost the only place of worship, new churches or chapels were founded by powerful lords for themselves and their tenants, by groups of neighbours, or by devotees of a particular saint.

Cathedral clergy had to decide how to respond to this desire for additional churches, and whether to allow it or forbid it. One reason for allowing it was that some of the promoters were people whom it was unwise to offend. In York, for example, the church of St Olave was founded by Siward, earl of Northumbria, and its namesake at Exeter by Countess Gytha, widow of Earl Godwin and mother of King Harold II.[46] Another was that the new churches could relieve the cathedral from having so many people crowding in for Sunday services and desiring baptisms and confessions. This must have been especially attractive at the monastic cathedrals whose clergy were trying to keep themselves aloof from worldly affairs. Funerals and burials were a more contentious matter. These generated money from candles, offerings, and prayers for the dead, which some cathedrals were reluctant to surrender. At least three continued to claim rights over funerals in their cities or to insist that burials took place within their cemeteries. The insistence was hard to maintain as populations grew, but it lasted at Winchester until at least 1331, at Hereford into the fifteenth century, and at Exeter down to as late as 1637.[47]

By about 1100, however, most cathedral cities had at least one other church, like Wells, and sometimes many: Lincoln and York over forty, Winchester over fifty, Norwich about sixty, and London over a hundred. What had once been effectively a single city parish with the cathedral as its church turned into a patchwork of many parishes, in which the cathedral's territory was reduced to its own precincts. This process seems to have happened during the tenth and eleventh centuries. It was complete at Winchester by 1143, and the last recorded instance was again that of Exeter, which was not divided into parishes until 1222.[48] The result was to distinguish cathedrals from parish churches to a greater extent than had been the case in the earlier Christian centuries, yet remains a factor in how they are governed today. Historically, cathedrals have been managed by groups of clergy (aided nowadays by some lay people) acting as what is known as a 'chapter' or governing body. They have not usually been run by a single rector or vicar with churchwardens and latterly a church council, like the parish churches.[49]

At the same time the difference between the two kinds of churches was not always an absolute one.[50] As well as Exeter, Hereford, and Winchester cathedrals with their long role as parish churches for funeral and burial purposes, there was Lichfield which remained the parish church of its city for centuries. Its neighbouring churches were technically its chapels-of-ease (although they had burial grounds), and they were not made independent until 1867. Seven medieval cathedrals actually contained a parish congregation within their buildings.[51] This

arose either because of their original parochial functions or through removing a
nearby church to extend their premises. At Carlisle, Chichester, Ely, Hereford,
Lincoln, and Rochester the parish church was housed in the nave and had its
own altar, while St Paul's had one church (St Faith) in its crypt and another (St
Gregory) against its south-west corner. Ely, Lincoln, and Rochester evicted their
parish congregations to separate buildings by the early fifteenth century, but the
others embraced them until recent times.[52]

A further issue was the cathedral 'Close' or precinct and its inhabitants.
Some Closes lay in the parishes of neighbouring churches while others were
'extra-parochial', forming an area of their own. In the latter case the cathedral
had to be parochial to the extent of providing services, confessions, funerals,
and burials for the Close inhabitants. Salisbury, which was newly built in the
thirteenth century, set up a parish altar within its nave to serve such people.[53]
Baptisms were not usually required in such conditions during the Middle Ages,
because the inhabitants of the Close were clergy and their male servants. After
the Reformation, however, clergy could marry and lay people came to live by
the cathedral, so that their children were christened in its church and some adults
might be married there as well.

Buildings and Worship from 900 to 1066

More can be known about cathedral buildings in the century and a half before the
Conquest, especially about two of the largest: Canterbury and Winchester. The
information in the first case comes from the excavation of the Anglo-Saxon nave
in the 1990s, along with the recollections of Eadmer, a monk of the cathedral
who was born in about 1060. He wrote down what he remembered, or was
told, about the topography of the building before it was ruined by fire in 1067.[54]
Canterbury's plan differed markedly from that of cathedrals after the Conquest
with which we are familiar. The building was nearly 95 metres (300 feet) long
and 31 metres (100 feet) wide, and was 'bipolar' in that it had matching ends
with semicircular apses. It was entered from the middle: by the monks from the
cloister on the north side and by the public on the south. Within it was divided
into two, nave and choir, by three arches and possibly some additional barrier
(Fig. 11, p. 24).

The church, unlike later cathedrals, was not all on one level. At the west end
there was an elevated platform within the apse, accessed by two stair turrets.
It contained an altar of the Virgin Mary at the inner end and the archbishop's
throne at the outer apse wall. The layout enabled the priest at this altar to face
east, yet towards the people gathered below in the nave. At the east end of the
church on both sides were towers, each of which had a chapel and altar in an
upper storey: St Martin in the north tower and St Gregory in the south. A central
tower above the choir is likely as well. The choir area contained seats for the
monks and a 'matutinal' altar where an early morning mass was celebrated, with

11. *Canterbury*
Cathedral, plan.

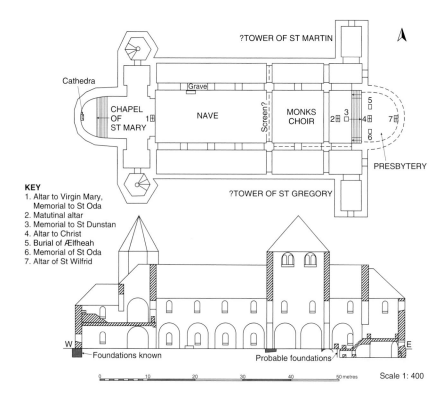

?TOWER OF ST MARTIN

Cathedra

CHAPEL
OF   1⊞
ST MARY

Grave

NAVE

Screen ?

MONKS
CHOIR

2⊞ 3 4⊞   7⊞

5

6

PRESBYTERY

?TOWER OF ST GREGORY

KEY
1. Altar to Virgin Mary,
   Memorial to St Oda
2. Matutinal altar
3. Memorial to St Dunstan
4. Altar to Christ
5. Burial of Ælfheah
6. Memorial of St Oda
7. Altar of St Wilfrid

W

Foundations known   Probable foundations

E

0   10   20   30   40   50 metres   Scale 1: 400

a monument to St Dunstan next to it. East of the choir, steps led up to a
second raised platform in the eastern apse. This held the principal altar at
its centre, dedicated to Christ, and beyond that, at the apse wall, an altar
of St Wilfrid. North and south of the principal altar were memorials to
Alphege and Oda, two other holy archbishops. Stairs north and south of
the choir led down to a crypt which housed a further altar and Dunstan's
tomb.

The other cathedral, Winchester, has also been revealed through
excavation. This, as we have seen, originally included a nave, choir,
two small *porticus* or chapels, and a separate bell tower. Under Bishop
Æthelwold the building was extended to the west between 971 and 974.
The bell tower was joined to the church with a building over the grave
of St Swithin, who had originally been buried in the open air between
the church and the tower. North and south of this building were two
semicircular apses. In a final phase, between 974 and 994, the west end of
the church was further enlarged and four new wings were added north
and south of the nave, two of them as rectangles and two as apses. The
eastern end was lengthened and the altar area was raised above a crypt

(as at Canterbury) in the shape of an apse with a small rectangular cell beyond it. Altogether the cathedral more than doubled its size in the second half of the ninth century. The additions provided space to bury bishops and the later kings of Wessex, for whom Winchester was their ancestral church (Fig. 12, p. 26).[55]

Eadmer's recollections not only assist us in reconstructing a vanished cathedral but provide an early and rare indication of what such a building meant to one of its clergy. Accepting Bede's belief that Canterbury was an old church given by Æthelberht to Augustine, Eadmer felt that the cathedral was very ancient: 'built by Romans' and rooted in that great civilisation. Indeed it was linked with Rome itself because in part it allegedly copied the pope's own church of St Peter's. It was very holy in a physical sense: a gathering place of saints. The easternmost altar contained the body of Wilfrid which Archbishop Oda had brought from Ripon. The high altar in front of it had the head of Swithin, transported from Winchester by Archbishop Alphege. The head of a third saint, Fursey, was in the crypt altar, and that of a fourth, Austroberta, in the altar of the Virgin Mary. Other churches, Eadmer might have reflected, had small bones of saints in their altars; his had their heads, the most precious parts of their bodies. And finally it was a complex building with its barrier between nave and choir, its different levels, its stairs up to the apses, up higher to the towers, and down to the crypt and up again. It is this complexity that Eadmer's description dwells on, not, as some late-medieval successor might have done, on the vista along the vaulting from the west end to a great east window.[56]

The worship in some of the larger cathedrals grows a little clearer when we reach the tenth century.[57] In King Edgar's reign, between 965 and 975, a Church council which met at Winchester agreed a common outline for services in monasteries including the monastic cathedrals: the *Regularis Concordia*, meaning 'Monastic Agreement'. The text, due chiefly to Æthelwold, envisaged a community of adult monks and some boys undertaking a daily cycle of services. The adults were to rise in the early hours of the morning for nocturns or matins, followed by lauds which ended at daybreak. At dawn came the service of prime, a period for reading, and the first of three short day services: terce, followed by a 'morrow' or early morning mass. Next came the daily chapter meeting which included briefings for next day's service and monastery business. Services resumed with sext, after which came the principal mass of the day, then none, and midday dinner. In the afternoon there was more reading time, the service of vespers, a reading from scripture or some other work, the service of compline, and finally bed. Arrangements on Sundays were slightly different. Each day there was only one main meal, and although there were intervals between services, the impression is given of a whole day (and part of the night) spent largely in structured prayer.[58]

In terms of cathedrals, of course, this was relevant only to four. The *Regularis Concordia* was scathing about secular canons ('negligent clerks with their abominations'),[59] but the jibe may be unfair to the cathedrals that were staffed by secular clergy. During the eleventh century, at least, efforts were made to bring the life and worship of some of them closer to those of the monasteries. Leofric,

12. *Winchester*
Cathedral, plan.

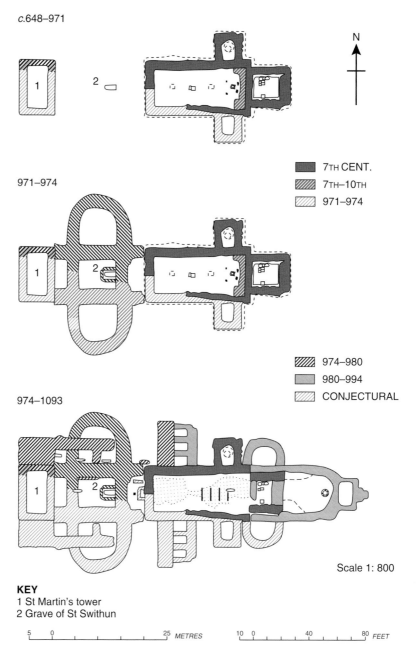

c.648–971

971–974

974–1093

■ 7TH CENT.
▨ 7TH–10TH
▨ 971–974

▨ 974–980
▨ 980–994
▨ CONJECTURAL

Scale 1: 800

KEY
1 St Martin's tower
2 Grave of St Swithun

5   0   25 METRES   10 0   40   80 FEET

the first bishop of Exeter, gave his new foundation the so-called 'Enlarged Rule of Chrodegang', which required the clergy to live a common life with a nightly and daily round of services.[60] Similar arrangements were made at St Paul's, Wells, and York.[61] Smaller cathedrals may not have aimed so high: Rochester was said to have had 'little more than four canons' in the

1060s.[62] The likelihood is that in such places the daily services were simplified in content, performed by fewer clergy, and done in more homely ways. The historian William of Malmesbury, visiting Exeter in the early 1100s, picked up a tradition that Leofric had expelled nuns from the minster that became his new cathedral.[63] There were no nuns at Exeter and it is more probable that Leofric removed the wives of the canons from having seats in the choir. If this was a practice in some secular cathedrals, it would certainly have ranked as an abomination in the mind of a monk.

We know little of the extent to which lay people went to cathedrals for services in Anglo-Saxon England, but the presence of saints was certainly an attraction. As already mentioned, the person to whom the cathedral was dedicated was seen as the living patron and guardian of the place, not as a mere historical figure. Canterbury was dedicated to Christ himself. Peter and Paul were popular dedication choices because they were the saints of Rome from whence the Christian missions had come. One or both were adopted at Dorchester-on-Thames, Lichfield, St Paul's, Winchester, Worcester, and York, while Peter's brother Andrew was chosen at Rochester and Wells. All cathedrals tried to acquire relics of saints – biblical, Roman, or English – and new saints were adopted by popular acclaim, since there was as yet no formal process of canonisation. The period 700–1066 added Ethelbert (d. 729) at Hereford, Hædde (d. 705) and Swithun (d. 862) at Winchester, and Dunstan (d. 988) and Alphege (d. 1012) at Canterbury. These saints drew pilgrims in, and by the eleventh century there was a guide to saints' resting-places in England, which suggests that some people were journeying to more than one shrine.[64] Healing was a particular motive for travel. Splinters of wood from Erconwald's horse-litter cured people at London, while dust from the tombs of Chad and Hædde healed men and animals.[65] But, as has already been said, there were popular shrines in other monasteries and churches, and some cathedrals did not get bodies of saints until as late as the fourteenth century.[66]

Learning and Education

The early missionaries to England needed to gather and teach young people to replace them, and this remained the case for generations. Some of those who passed through such instruction and became adult clergy were stimulated to study and write on religion, history, and science. Again, cathedrals did not monopolise education or learning in Anglo-Saxon England. Some of the greatest Anglo-Saxon scholars and teachers were based at monasteries: Bede at Jarrow, Byrtferth at Ramsey, and Ælfric at Cerne and Eynsham. But at least three cathedrals were important centres in this respect: Canterbury, Winchester, and York, and since it is difficult to separate the training of the young from the studies of the adults, we shall explore them together.[67]

There were probably young people at all the cathedrals, meaning boys and youths, and they fell into two groups according to the two kinds of cathedrals.

Where the church was a monastery, parents – especially the wealthier – would place their son as an 'oblate' or offering. This would have been the case in the early monastic cathedrals as well as the later ones of the tenth and eleventh centuries. At the end of the latter century, Archbishop Lanfranc of Canterbury outlined a ceremony for use on the occasion. A candidate to be an oblate had his hair cut with a bare patch or tonsure. He and his parents attended mass in the monastery church. Then they went up to the altar and the parents wrapped the boy's hands in the altar cloth as a sign that they gave him to be a monk. They promised the abbot – or his equivalent at a cathedral – that they would not remove the boy from the monastery, and the promise was recorded in writing. The abbot undid the boy's cloak and said to him 'May the Lord strip you of the old man.' He gave the boy a monk's cowl, with the words 'May the Lord clothe you with the new man.' After this the boy was taken away to be shaved all over his head and given a full monastic dress.[68] He would remain in the community for the rest of his life.

The secular cathedrals had boys as well: very likely from the seventh century onwards. Here too there was a hope of finding recruits to be clergy as well as to do tasks within the church. The 'Enlarged' Rule of Chrodegang introduced at Exeter after 1050 mentions boys who were evidently the ancestors of choristers.[69] They were fed, boarded, and taught to read, sing, and do what the adults did in the choir. In the later Anglo-Saxon centuries there would also have been the sons and nephews of canons who expected to inherit church posts from their fathers and uncles. But there was less commitment to follow a clerical career than in a monastery. Boys from wealthy families are likely to have come to cathedrals and minsters to learn to read and master Latin before there were any or many schools in the outside world. It was recorded that noblemen sent their sons to Wilfrid to be instructed while he was bishop of York or Ripon, and that this was on the understanding that they could become clergy if they chose or, alternatively, warriors.[70]

We hear in consequence of schools at some cathedrals. Canterbury's was well enough regarded by the mid-600s for Bishop Felix, the apostle of East Anglia, to bring teachers from it to support his mission in that kingdom.[71] It was particularly successful after the Greek scholar Theodore became archbishop in 669. Together with Hadrian, the abbot of the monastery in the city (later called St Augustine's), he gave instruction in the scriptures, the art of Latin verse, astronomy, computation (for calendar purposes), Church music, and even Greek.[72] York had another flourishing school in the eighth century. One of its teachers, Ælberht, became archbishop there in 766–7. He collected a large library of Latin poets which passed to his pupil Alcuin, who taught in the school before leaving England to do so at the court of Charlemagne.[73] Alcuin's major works were written after he left York, but before his departure he appears to have composed a history of its church in verse, and there are indications that he was not the only scholar there.[74] A metrical calendar of saints which seems to have come from York circulated widely in Europe, and

someone compiled annals of local history in the 700s which survive in the twelfth-century chronicle of Simeon of Durham.[75]

Learning at Canterbury may have fluctuated in standard. It has been observed that Latin charters written there in the ninth century have faults in their spelling and drafting. However, it revived in the time of Archbishop Oda (947–58), who invited the Frankish scholar Fredegand to join his household. Fredegand wrote a poem on the life of St Wilfrid to celebrate Oda's bringing of Wilfrid's relics to the cathedral, and helped to educate the archbishop's nephew Oswald, one of the leaders of the monastic reform.[76] This reform included an emphasis on the education of boys, now once more oblate boys, in monasteries. Æthelwold's *Regularis Concordia* laid down rules for their governance. They were only to be ruled by their master, and were never to be alone with him or any monk without the presence of a third person. They spent part of the day in school and part in church.[77] Æthelwold did much to encourage education and scholarship at Winchester, and sometimes helped with the teaching alongside the regular masters. He translated the Rule of St Benedict into English so that it might be understood by monks for

13. A lost cathedral: North Elmham, Norfolk. This former seat of the bishops of East Anglia lay north of the parish church and was later made into a bishop's house and chapel.

whom Latin was still difficult. One of his pupils, Wulfstan the Cantor who became a monk of Winchester, wrote Æthelwold's life in Latin prose and an account of St Swithin in verse. Another, Ælfric, became a famous teacher and writer of schoolbooks, albeit after leaving Winchester.[78] This does not mean that reading and writing at cathedrals was solely religious or scholarly. Leofric, bishop of Exeter, wished his clergy to follow strict lives yet he gave them the *Exeter Book*: an anthology of religious and secular poetry. From it they could have read or listened to heroic and personal verse like 'Widsith', 'The Seafarer', 'The Wife's Lament', and many ingenious riddles.[79]

Today it seems unacceptable to dedicate a boy to a permanent religious life in a monastery when he cannot make a free and informed decision about the matter. To those who parted with their children in this way, there would have seemed advantages: the prayer and prestige that were brought to the family, the relative safety of a monastery, and the possibility of rising to power and status as abbot or (for a girl) as abbess. The attitude that we take stems from the twelfth century. At that time, Church legislators began to define more clearly the boundary between childhood and adulthood. They decided that it lay at puberty and that adult understanding began at that point. It was accordingly improper to expect children to take lifelong vows as clergy or husbands and wives until that age, and better to recruit monks and nuns from older teenagers who would come with real dedication. And so the practice of oblation in cathedral monasteries died out and was gone by 1200.[80] When later they admitted boys again, it was done in another way and without expecting a permanent commitment.[81]

A Strong Foundation

The four and a half centuries between Augustine's mission to Canterbury and the Norman Conquest saw the creation of eleven of our modern cathedrals, including the most important and best endowed. In addition, the period established many of the characteristics that cathedrals would have for the rest of the Middle Ages and, in some respects, down to modern times. There would not be many of them: less than around the Mediterranean or even in Ireland. Within England they would bear the marks of the Viking disruptions for centuries later, with fewer in the north and east than in the south and west. They would be relatively large and well-endowed churches, easily distinguishable from parish churches in both respects but less so from the greater monasteries. Indeed, in some cases, they would be monasteries themselves.

Cathedrals had undoubtedly made an impact on society by 1066. That important people like kings and noblemen valued them and their prayers is evident from the gifts of lands and goods that such people gave. The presence of pilgrims is at least a testimony to the popularity of cathedral saints, if not of cathedrals as such. What people thought of them in this early period is difficult to know, but it is likely that since the cathedrals had long been the principal churches of their districts, they were locally regarded as places of religious and indeed secular importance. Even the secular cathedrals had more clergy and therefore probably more elaborate services than parish churches. All were the churches of bishops, important men in national affairs, and the clergy of cathedrals had spending power of value to the local economy.

One testimony to a cathedral's influence is a list of fourteen religious guilds and their members, written down in the outer leaves of the *Exeter Book* and dating from about 1100.[82] The guilds were based in country parishes within about twenty miles of Exeter and probably comprised the wealthy inhabitants of these parishes. They registered themselves and their members with the cathedral so that they could be included in its prayers. It is a sign that they looked to that church as the centre of spiritual excellence in their region, and we shall see that a similar regard for cathedrals can be traced in the following centuries.[83]

14. *The Lichfield Angel: a rare and beautiful piece of sculpture of about 800 from an Anglo-Saxon cathedral.*

Chapter
3

Normans and Angevins

1066–1250

The Norman Conquest of 1066 began a new era not only for England but for its cathedrals. Norman clerics were appointed as bishops. They had different ideas from the English about where cathedrals should be, the buildings they should have, and the kind of clergy who should staff them. The Conquest helped to accelerate changes in England which were taking place in the rest of western Europe. The Church was becoming more organised and centralised. Reforming popes were striving to extend their power across the European kingdoms by regulating religious matters. Church councils were meeting and enacting canon law – the law of the Church – to define what people should believe and how they should behave. Machinery was being devised to enforce these laws on every person and in every place.

Another effect of the Conquest was to give a boost to monasticism. The Normans came from a country (France) where monasteries were well established. Soon after the Conquest they started transferring some of the lands they had won to these houses to build daughter settlements in England, as well as founding abbeys and priories with an independent status. But the popularity of monasticism was not limited to the Normans. By the early twelfth century, new monastic orders were proliferating throughout western Europe: Cluniacs, Cistercians, Carthusians, Augustinians, and Premonstratensians. Patrons came forward to build them houses and recruits to enter the houses. Monasticism was never more popular in England than between the Conquest and the early thirteenth century. In 1066 there were only about forty monasteries and nunneries; by 1200 there were over 700, and later even more. Many people thought monks superior to the secular clergy of the minsters and parishes, some of whom were still married and hereditary. A monk chose the religious life deliberately. He was trained and disciplined to live in a dedicated way. His worship and his prayers were the most holy and effective within the Church.

The Normans encountered two features of the English Church that were strange to them. One was the fact that some bishops and their cathedrals were based in the countryside rather than in cities. This issue may have come up as early as 1070 when a Church council at Windsor ruled that bishops should have 'definite seats', perhaps prompted by one or two recent movements of bishops to new locations.[1] It certainly did by about 1072 when William the Conqueror got the pope's permission to transfer the bishop of Dorchester-on-Thames to Lincoln. His motive was probably to strengthen the Norman presence in an area vulnerable to an attack from Denmark.[2] Three years later, in 1075, a council of bishops and abbots met at London and considered the matter more widely. They noted various pronouncements by popes and Church councils to the effect that bishops' seats should not be located *in villis*, meaning in rural places.[3] Accordingly, they agreed that three other bishops should move from these *villis* to *civitates*, in other words cities, with the implication that the latter were substantial settlements with walls or castles. Hereman, bishop of Sherborne, was to relocate himself to Salisbury, which was then Old Sarum north of the modern city (Fig. 15, p. 32). Stigand of Selsey was to go to Chichester and Peter of Lichfield to Chester.

These decisions probably reflected the need of the Normans to defend themselves in a conquered land, as well as reflecting their experience in France that a bishop should be based in a town. Admittedly not everyone was worried about this. Giso, a pre-Conquest bishop from what is now Belgium, made no attempt to move his see from Wells, where he was busy reforming his cathedral. Remigius, William's new bishop of Dorchester-on-Thames, was apparently happy to develop the church there until the king told him to go to Lincoln.[4] Nevertheless the current of feeling ran strongly in favour of change. The bishops of Lichfield and Selsey removed themselves immediately. The process at Sherborne may have been slower because of Hereman's poor health, but it certainly took place once his successor Osmund was appointed in 1078. In the same year Bishop Herfast of Elmham

15. A new Norman cathedral in a city: the outline of the church at Old Sarum (upper centre right), which moved to modern Salisbury in the 1220s.

transferred his seat to Thetford, and in 1090 Giso's successor at Wells, John de Villula, did so to Bath. A few years later, in the mid-1090s, Herfast's successor-but-one, Herbert Losinga, abandoned Thetford in favour of Norwich, which was a larger and more flourishing town and had recently acquired a castle. A final change saw Robert de Limesey migrate from Chester to Coventry in 1102. This, the first Coventry cathedral, stood north of Holy Trinity church, and was dismantled at the Reformation.[5]

The other feature strange to Normans was the staffing of cathedrals by monks, notably at Canterbury and Winchester. Although monasticism was now very popular in Europe, it was not thought proper for a cathedral. According to Eadmer of Canterbury, who lived through the decades after the Conquest, those of William the Conqueror's new bishops who were not monks wanted to change the monastic cathedrals back into churches of secular clergy, in other words canons. They got the support of the king, and Walkelin, bishop of Winchester, made plans to turn out the monks and replace them with forty canons. However, Lanfranc, whom William had chosen as his archbishop of Canterbury, was a monk from Bec in Normandy and was determined to keep the monastic cathedrals. To ensure that this was the case, he persuaded Pope Alexander II to confirm his monks as the rightful possessors of Canterbury (Fig. 16, above).[6] In the end, the only

16. Canterbury, England's premier cathedral in age and rank. The building reflects the money and reputation that came to it from the cult of Thomas Becket after 1170.

monastic cathedral to disappear was Sherborne, because its successor at Salisbury was founded for staffing by canons.[7]

Lanfranc was not the only bishop to favour monks at cathedrals. In 1077 Gundulf, another monk of Bec and a close associate of his, became bishop of Rochester and started to turn its cathedral into a monastery (Fig. 19, p. 44). In 1083 a third monk-bishop, William of St Calais, bishop of Durham, got papal and royal permission to do the same, and dismissed (probably with compensation) those of its canons who had no desire to be monks.[8] A fourth, Herbert Losinga, began to build his cathedral at Norwich as a monastery in about 1096. All these bishops were avowed supporters of monasticism, but others of their colleagues moved their seats to monasteries with economic motives as well as religious ones. They wanted wealth with which to improve their incomes. Even before the Conquest, Hereman of Ramsbury had tried to move to Malmesbury Abbey for this reason until the king refused his request.[9] Herfast of Elmham wished to do the same at Bury St Edmunds, and may have gone to Thetford as an interim measure.[10] The other new cathedrals, Bath and Coventry, were based in monasteries for similar reasons.

These changes raised the number of monastic cathedrals from the four of the late Anglo-Saxon period to eight, and the Normans added a further two during the twelfth century. The wealthy Benedictine abbey of Ely lay in Lincoln diocese, but the abbots disliked subjection to its bishop and managed to persuade both pope and king in 1108–9 to create a new diocese for them, covering Cambridgeshire.[11] This still left Lincoln with eight and a half other counties, but a more rational division of its huge territory would doubtless have been controversial. In 1136 the last new English diocese of the Middle Ages was created for Cumbria, with its cathedral at Carlisle. Cumbria was a region in dispute between England and Scotland, and the early history of the diocese was shaky: there was no bishop from 1157 to 1203.[12] Eventually, it was confirmed as part of England and added a third diocese to the province of York. The church in Carlisle that became the cathedral appears to have been served by Augustinian canons before that event. If not, this was certainly so after the arrival of the first bishop, Æthelwulf, who belonged to that order himself. Augustinian canons followed a simpler rule than that of the Benedictines, but one resembling it except in details.

Lands, Churches, and Rights

We have seen how Anglo-Saxon rulers and others gave lands and rights to the 'saint' or 'church' of a particular diocese, which were effectively in the hands of the bishop. He used some of their resources for his own purposes and allocated others to his cathedral clergy. The allocation might change as the bishop wished, and the property was not always clearly in the hands of either party. It might be held from them by a lay tenant or be seized by a king or great lord. After the Conquest there were further complications because Norman kings or their chief followers took

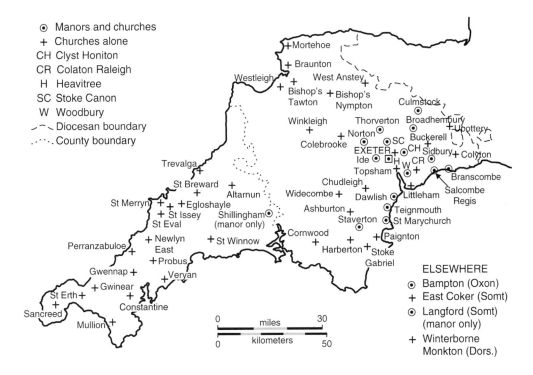

Manors and churches
+ Churches alone
CH Clyst Honiton
CR Colaton Raleigh
H Heavitree
SC Stoke Canon
W Woodbury
--- Diocesan boundary
····· County boundary

ELSEWHERE
⊙ Bampton (Oxon)
+ East Coker (Somt)
⊙ Langford (Somt)
(manor only)
+ Winterborne
Monkton (Dors.)

17. Cathedral property: the lands and churches of Exeter, 1535.

lands from churches. Rochester, for example, lost a good deal of property to Bishop Odo of Bayeux, the half-brother of William the Conqueror. Equally, Anglo-Saxon and Norman bishops were anxious to recover lost estates and frequently did so. Archbishop Lanfranc assisted Rochester to regain its possessions. Some bishops added new properties, particularly at Elmham and Wells, and the unions of bishoprics and their amalgamation with monasteries brought about further increases.[13]

A fresh source of revenue for bishops and cathedrals came from their parish churches. When these churches multiplied in England between about 900 and 1100, it followed that many of them were founded on the properties of bishops and cathedrals. Property owners were normally considered to hold the patronage or 'advowson' of any parish church on their lands. This gave them the right to nominate the clergy ('rectors') of these churches. After the Conquest, when Norman kings, bishops, and lords gained lands and the parish churches and advowsons that went with them, they often presented the advowsons to a religious foundation: monastery or cathedral. The reason for this was that a lay person who owned an advowson had only the right to nominate the rector, whereas ecclesiastical owners could make themselves rector of the church and take the church's income. This income came chiefly from tithes: one tenth of the crops and animals raised in the parish each year, which formed a valuable asset. A monastery or cathedral could not act as rector, of course, because it was distant and otherwise occupied, so it appointed a 'vicar' (meaning a deputy) to serve as the parish clergyman. He received a smaller stipend taken from part of the church's income, while the rest passed to the monastery or cathedral. An arrangement of this kind was known as an 'appropriation' and it brought in substantial revenues (Fig. 17, p. 37).

In 1086 Domesday Book was compiled to list the lands throughout England that were accustomed to pay tax to the king, along with their annual value. The property of bishops and cathedrals was usually tabled under the title of 'The church of . . .', after which it was stated that the bishop held such-and-such estates. Some of these would be specified as for the use of his cathedral clergy. This was the traditional way in which such assets were owned and administered, but during the seventy years from Domesday Book to the 1150s there was a more emphatic division of properties between bishops and cathedrals. It came about for several reasons. Bishops were more involved in royal government and more often away from their churches. These churches housed a substantial number of canons or monks who needed to be able to manage their own affairs. The king now claimed to take over the endowments of bishoprics during vacancies, which meant that some definition was needed in what belonged to the cathedrals. Law and legal documentation were developing, making it more crucial to identify the holders of property and for them to hold charters of ownership to establish their rights. Accordingly, bishops divided their endowments with their cathedrals. The divisions became permanent and were not normally overturned as they had often been in the past.[14]

This was particularly important for the secular cathedrals. First, the change pushed the canons (or was driven by their wish) to become a separate body from the bishop: a 'chapter', which made its own decisions largely without him. Secondly, it enabled each of the canons, who were mostly living separately, to take a piece of cathedral property as a personal endowment. This practice went back to Anglo-Saxon times, but in the twelfth and thirteenth centuries it became more precise and permanent. A canon's share of cathedral property was known as a 'prebend', related to the word 'provender' and meaning a source of support. The prebend might take the form of lands, church tithes, monetary payments, or more than one of these, and its holder was known as a 'prebendary'. The terms 'canon' and 'prebendary' have been in use in cathedrals ever since. They apply to the same person, who is a canon in the sense of following a rule of life and a prebendary through having an endowment and an income.

Cathedrals enjoyed further assets in the form of legal privileges. The most solid of these were exemptions from the authority of the bishop, his diocesan officials, and the mayor and council of the cathedral city. These privileges reached their fullest extent in the thirteenth century and will be dealt with in the following chapter.[15] An apparently greater one was the right of cathedral canons or monks to elect their bishops. In previous centuries bishops were generally appointed at the wishes of kings or on the proposals of archbishops, but in 1215 the fourth Lateran Council of the Church, meeting in Rome, ordered that cathedral chapters should make the choice.[16] This was part of the Church's attempt to make itself independent of lay authority. The Crown, however, had no intention of losing control of such important posts, and the Lateran decree was not effective in practice. The king continued to choose nearly all of the bishops. Cathedral chapters (canons or monks) were expected to endorse his choice and usually did so. In the fourteenth century the system changed to one in which the pope appointed the bishop, but it was still normal for the appointment to be that of the king's nominee. In 1534 Henry VIII restored the right of election to cathedral chapters, subject to the requirement that they should choose only the person proposed by the Crown. This remains the case in the Church of England today.

The Secular Cathedrals after 1066

The creation of more monastic cathedrals meant that they now formed a majority of such churches. Indeed, in the period around 1100 there were only seven that still had a bishop and were staffed by canons: Chichester, Exeter, Hereford, Lincoln, St Paul's, Salisbury, and York.[17] Even here, as we have seen, the first bishop of Exeter, Leofric (1050–1072), tried to make his canons live together, sharing accommodation and meals in a way of life not far from that of a monastery. Similar reforms were introduced at about the same time by Archbishop Ealdred of York, Bishop Giso of Wells, and possibly Bishop Walter of Hereford. Canons, however, disliked being made to live in common. The tendency in all these places was for them to revert to living separately and to receiving personal incomes like their Anglo-Saxon predecessors.[18]

Cathedrals of canons were attractive to some of the first Norman bishops, as we have seen, and developments during the twelfth century tended to increase their attractiveness. First there was the demand of reforming popes, councils, and bishops that clergy should be celibate, and the imposition of this with greater effect than before. Gradually, any married clergy disappeared from cathedrals, reducing any hereditary element and opening up appointments for the bishop. The second was the division of property between bishops and cathedrals, which included arrangements to define how many canons there should be and the prebends that each should have. The prebends were fixed at high numbers, ranging from twenty-four to fifty-four in the secular cathedrals, which produced far more clergy than were needed for worship since their duties in church could be done by deputies. A bishop could now appoint some of the canons to be his administrative staff rather than to serve the cathedral, their stipends coming from their prebends. He could also gratify the king and the nobility by giving others of these posts to their servants and relatives. When universities developed in the late twelfth century, canonries could be used as scholarships to support young men of rank while they studied.

Accordingly, towards the end of that century the preference of bishops began to shift more strongly towards cathedrals of canons, the more so because most bishops were not monks. Henry II (d. 1189) may have been sympathetic to this, as were some of his bishops. Waleran, bishop of Rochester (1182–4), was suspected of planning to remove his monks but died before his plans became clear. Archbishop Baldwin at Canterbury and Bishop Gilbert Glanville at Rochester may have considered doing so during the next few years.[19] However, by this time it was not easy to remove the monks from a monastic cathedral since they had the right of appeal to the pope. The only bishop who tried was Hugh de Nonant of Coventry. In 1189 he came in person to take possession of his cathedral, provoking an affray with the monks after which he expelled them. In their place he put in a group of canons, thus converting the church to a secular cathedral. But this did not last – very likely it was difficult to provide them with prebends – and by 1197 Hugh, by then dangerously ill, had repented. The monks were allowed back and Hugh died in the following year, wearing the habit of a Benedictine monk to be on the safe side.[20]

In two dioceses, Bath and Coventry, the old secular cathedrals at Wells and Lichfield had never been closed and remained communities of canons with prebends. Indeed, Bishop Reginald of Bath started a grand rebuilding of Wells in about 1180. During the thirteenth century, both were restored to their former rank. In 1228 Bishop Stavensby of Coventry secured the pope's consent that Lichfield should be his cathedral alongside Coventry. Both communities would elect the bishop in future, meeting for the purpose at each cathedral in turn. The diocese was usually known as 'Coventry and Lichfield' from then until 1836.[21] In 1245 a similar arrangement restored Wells to cathedral status in addition to Bath, producing the enduring title of the diocese as 'Bath and Wells'. In the other dioceses with monastic cathedrals, the bishops had to make different arrangements for supporting their servants. This was done by using parish churches or founding smaller collegiate churches staffed by similar canons to those of cathedrals.

There came thus to be nine English secular cathedrals alongside the ten monastic ones, as well as four secular cathedrals in Wales which took a similar form in the twelfth century (Fig. 18, p. 41). These were at Bangor, Llandaff, St Asaph, and St David's, and they formed part of the province of Canterbury until 1920. At the same time, these thirteen cathedrals developed stronger administrative structures, sometimes (but not always) in the form of written statutes delivered by their bishops. It used to be thought that the model for these statutes was the so-called 'Institution of St Osmund', which Osmund, the first bishop of Salisbury, was believed to have issued for his cathedral during his period of office from 1078 to 1099. Modern research suggests that the 'Institution', in the form that survives, is a document of about 1200 which represents the practices of the twelfth century as much as those of Osmund's time.[22] Very likely the cathedral constitutions that we shall now discuss grew up gradually during the hundred years after the Norman Conquest and were shaped from more than

18. *English
and Welsh
cathedrals
c.1075–1538.*

Legend:
+ Archbishop's cathedral
O Secular cathedral
■ Monastic cathedral
[ ] Short-lived cathedral

one source. The customs of Rouen and perhaps some other cathedrals in Normandy may have been influential. English traditions would certainly have been so. Each secular cathedral in England was aware of the others, and they all came to share common practices by the 1220s along with individual variations.[23]

Deans and Canons

Before the Conquest, a principal officer, usually known as the dean, had emerged in some cathedrals and minster. He was the chair of the 'chapter', the formal meeting of his fellow canons, and acted in the cathedral as the bishop's deputy. The constitutional developments of the twelfth century kept the dean as the chief dignitary of the foundation.[24] He summoned and continued to chair the chapter, took the most important role in worship unless the bishop was present (which was not usually the case), and had pastoral oversight of all the other cathedral clergy.[25] He came to have three assistant dignitaries. In the usual order of precedence these were a chanter (later known as the precentor or 'chief chanter') in charge of the singing in the choir, a schoolmaster responsible for teaching a grammar school, and a treasurer to look after the precious goods of the church.[26] The schoolmaster soon turned into a chancellor who carried out secretarial and other scholarly tasks. In addition, the archdeacons, the bishop's officers in charge of the parishes, were usually associated with the cathedral but not members of its chapter unless they held a canonry, which they often did.[27]

This arrangement of four chief officers has been called a 'four-square' constitution, evoking the thought of a table or four-poster bed. The analogy is not fanciful because the four officers had seats at the four corners of the cathedral choir. The dean sat at the west end on the south side: the side that is still known as *decani*, meaning 'of the dean'. The precentor was opposite him on the north side (hence *cantoris* for that side), the chancellor at the south-east corner, and the treasurer at the north-east one. Archdeacons were generally placed next to the dignitaries, in descending order of precedence. Then there was the bishop to be considered. In the early centuries of the Church his throne, often of stone, was placed at the east end of the choir to let him preside and be seen. The throne at Norwich is still in that position, but as time went on the increasing importance and use of the high altar at the east end, and the desire to place a reredos (a screen) behind it, caused bishops' seats to be repositioned further west. Canterbury's, as we saw, was at the west end of the nave for a time, but a site on the south or senior side of the cathedral choir, east of the clergy stalls, became the most popular spot. Two medieval wooden thrones at Exeter and Hereford still survive in this location, with stone ones at Durham and Wells.[28]

The dignitaries were expected to keep residence at the cathedral for two-thirds or three-quarters of the year, and each had a house near the cathedral. They also acquired assistants. The most important of these was the subdean, who was usually a canon and carried out the dean's duty of hearing the confessions of the other clergy. The precentor's deputy was the succentor ('sub-chanter'), who did the day-to-day tasks of supervising the choir as well as the choristers who came within the precentor's care. The chancellor appointed a schoolmaster to run the local grammar school, and the treasurer had a sub-treasurer. The succentor and sub-treasurer were not canons but members of the minor cathedral clergy whom we shall encounter presently, while the schoolmaster could be married and usually had little role to play at the cathedral.[29]

The remaining clergy of importance were the canons. They formed the cathedral chapter along with the dean and dignitaries, hence the term 'dean and chapter', and the chapter took decisions about all matters that were not specifically reserved to the dignitaries.[30] These included the administration of the cathedral's property and its income, the management of the building, and the discipline of the subordinate clergy. Each canon's post came with an income: the prebend that has already been mentioned. These prebends were generally known by the property with which they were endowed, and their names are sometimes inscribed on their stalls in cathedral choirs.[31] They were not uniform in value and ranged from rich to poor. At one extreme the prebend of Masham Vetus at York was assessed at about £186 per annum at the end of the thirteenth century and was worth far more than this because the assessment was low. At the other, the prebend of Pratum Minus ('the lesser field') at Hereford was a mere quarter of an acre of a hayfield at Marden in Herefordshire, producing a load of hay valued only at 6*d.* but perhaps somewhat more. At Wells, one large endowment – the manor of Combe St Nicholas in Somerset – was divided between fifteen prebends named from Combe Prima to Combe Quinquadecima.[32]

The small returns from a poor prebend were offset if the canon resided at the cathedral. This entitled him to payments from the 'common fund': those revenues that were not assigned to particular people. Even in the age of prebends, something remained of the older practice of sharing resources together. Some of these revenues came from property, others from fees and donations. The common fund was usually administered by two canons, and distributed to those who were resident at regular intervals which might be daily, weekly, and annually.[33] As with the dignitaries, a canon could qualify as a resident or 'residentiary' if he was present for only a part of the year, varying from a third to two-thirds in different places.[34] Each canon received a house in the precincts of the cathedral. By the end of the thirteenth century these precincts were usually closed off by gateways from the surrounding city, hence the term 'cathedral Close'. The canons' houses bordered the Close, separated from the cathedral by an open space that often served as a burial ground. This gave and still gives the precincts the character of a village around a green. Such 'villages' are a living monument to the separate life-style of the secular cathedral clergy, in contrast to a cathedral monastery where the monks lived in integrated buildings. Their disadvantage was that the canons were obliged to walk to church in all weathers, whereas monks came in by a covered route from their dormitory or cloisters.

Despite these residences, most of the canons did not use them for most of the time and some houses became disused or transferred to other purposes. Many canons never resided and might hold canonries in more than one cathedral, or parish churches elsewhere. The prize for this kind of pluralism and non-residence goes to Bogo de Clare (d. 1294), a younger son of the earl of Gloucester. At the time of his death he was precentor of Chichester, chancellor of Llandaff, treasurer of York, the holder of prebends in Exeter, Lichfield, and Wells, and the incumbent of many parish churches or rather, as someone observed, the incubator. He lived luxuriously in and around London, kept a large household,

19. Rochester, one of the cathedrals converted to a monastery after the Norman Conquest and also rebuilt at that time.

entertained courtiers and judges, and gave sparingly to the poor. When he died it was said that 'God only knows if his life was worthy of praise, but no one thought it worthy of imitation'.[35] Most such clergy, however, had only a few such posts. They were normally hard-working administrators for the king or a bishop, and their canonries were salaries for their services or fees for their advice.

The tolerant rules about residence and the employment of many canons elsewhere caused only a few them to live in the Close at a time.[36] They would attend some (but not all) of the daily services, chiefly the morning high mass and afternoon vespers, sitting in the uppermost rank of the choir. They would come to the chapter house in the middle of the morning to partake in chapter business if this was needed. One could have recognised a canon from the fact that he was attended to and from church by his servants and from his almuce: the hood which most clergy wore. Originally it was a real hood but by the end of the Middle Ages it became a tippet or cape worn round the shoulders. Canons of cathedrals and some other collegiate churches had the privilege of wearing almuces of fur taken from the rarer and finer grey pelt of the red squirrel. These almuces can sometimes be seen on monumental brasses in the form of a fur cape with squirrel tails hanging from its edges.

Vicars Choral and Choristers

The canons' permission to stay away – studying or serving the king or the bishop – required the employment of deputies to do their duties in church. These deputies were usually known as 'vicars choral', 'vicar' meaning a deputy and 'choral' that they attended the daily services in the cathedral choir in place of the canons.[37] Hereford and St Paul's had an additional group of senior vicars called 'petty canons' and 'minor canons' respectively. Vicars choral, of whatever rank, usually occupied the uppermost level of the cathedral choir alongside the canons, to whom at first they were not unlike servants. They could be hired and fired at will, often lived and ate in their canon's house if he was resident, and helped escort him to church. Cathedrals soon found, however, that they needed to bring order into these arrangements. It was laid down that every canon must have a vicar choral and that the vicars must attend all the services and live under the cathedral's discipline. As time went on, the vicars acquired endowments that were independent of their wages, and gained security of tenure so that when a canon left, his successor had to employ his vicar. In the next chapter we shall see how they came to possess their own accommodation and became separate organisations alongside cathedral chapters.

The presence of young people at the secular cathedrals continued as it had done in earlier centuries. Some were choristers, ranging in numbers from five to fourteen.[38] As has been stated, they came under the care of the succentor, who looked after them in a building where they slept and had their school. Like the vicars, each chorister was linked with a canon and often had his meals in the canon's house. They learnt to read and sing and they attended the choir (but not always all together or at all services) where they sang alongside the adults and occasionally read lessons. In the choir they occupied the front or lowest of the three levels of seats on either side. They did useful tasks such as carrying candles and incense, and on two special days of the day they took a chief part in the services. These days were 6 and 28 December, the festivals of St Nicholas and the Holy Innocents respectively, when one of the choristers became boy bishop and the others his retinue. Then they presided in the choir stalls and later went in procession around the city, collecting money after which they enjoyed a feast. At York they even went on tours round the county: visiting monasteries and gentry houses and receiving hospitality and cash.[39]

When the boys reached puberty, at about the age of fourteen, their voices changed and they left the choir. Some left for lay careers because choristers were never obliged to become clergy when they grew up. Others stayed on as 'secondary clerks' or 'altarists', of whom there was a group at most cathedrals. These were adolescents and young adults, some of whom were waiting until they could be ordained priests at the age of twenty-four. A cathedral post was a good way of securing support until that happened. They sang some services in the choir where they occupied the 'second form' or middle rank of the three levels. They assisted in preparing the altars for mass, served the canons or vicars who celebrated it, and carried out other duties such as watching the doors and keeping order.[40]

Buildings

The Normans changed not only the siting and the management of cathedrals but their buildings.[41] Every English cathedral began to be rebuilt between 1070 and about 1120, and by the end of the twelfth century they were all complete in new forms: indeed Canterbury underwent further rebuilding as early as the late 1090s. There was more than one motive for this process. The Normans had no sentimental attraction to the Anglo-Saxon churches and their historical associations. They probably deplored the sometimes modest size or irregular layout of the buildings. Several cathedrals were at new sites requiring fresh structures and there were practical reasons for rebuilding, such as greater numbers of clergy. A wish for security may also have been present. Norman cathedrals were substantial in form and occasionally featured in warfare. In the civil wars of Stephen's reign (1135–54), Geoffrey Talbot seized Hereford and mounted catapults on its tower with which he bombarded the nearby castle.[42] The first cathedral at Lincoln was built for defence at its west end, and Stephen used it himself as a base for besieging Lincoln castle (Fig. 2, p. 3).

The Norman cathedrals shared common characteristics although there were differences too. Let us take Durham as the example (Fig. 20, p. 47). Its west end was flanked by two square towers, between which lay the principal entrance for religious processions and important guests. Beyond this the cathedral followed the shape of a cross. The shaft of the cross consisted of a long nave with aisles alongside it, north and south, and a north entrance for ordinary visitors. The nave and its aisles were separated by an arcade of alternating pillars and columns, with a gallery or 'triforium' above it and a clerestory of windows over that. The arms of the cross were two transepts, each of which held spaces for three chapels on their eastern sides. Above the crossing where the nave met the transepts was a large central tower. The head of the cross contained the choir and sanctuary with the high altar. The choir was flanked by aisles, continuing those of the nave. At the east end of the building the choir aisles ended in chapels capped by small towers, and between the chapels was an apse with a semicircular eastern wall containing the shrine of St Cuthbert. This apse could be accessed from each choir aisle. The choir was planned to have a stone vault, and vaulting was eventually extended to the transepts and the nave.[43]

A cathedral building of this kind provided a large choir for services, usually stretching from under the crossing and halfway up the head of the cross. Greater space was required in the choirs of monastic cathedrals because they were now recruiting large numbers of monks. Canterbury, the largest, had sixty in about 1080 and one hundred in about 1146, but figures of fifty to seventy were probably more common elsewhere. Secular cathedrals too were acquiring more members.

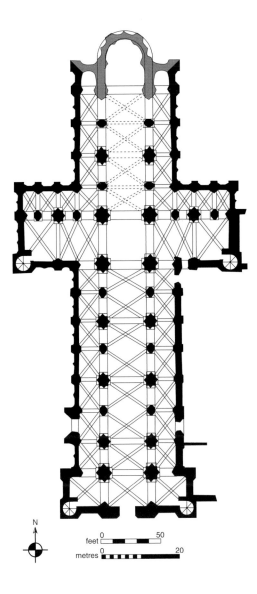

20. *Durham Cathedral, plan.*

N

0   50
feet

0   20
metres

Canons might often be absent, but this was more than offset by the vicars choral, clerks, and choristers. The choir itself was defined with walls to exclude the entrance of the public except for those of noble rank. Room was often required for a saint's burial, and it was becoming more common to place this in a shrine above ground, usually at the east end of the cathedral. Side chapels (which had begun to appear in Anglo-Saxon times) offered space to commemorate other saints and for those of the clergy who were priests to celebrate mass. Finally, the aisles allowed the holding of religious processions for which there were now liturgies of psalms, hymns, and prayers, as well as enabling layfolk to access any eastern shrine.

The Norman cathedrals aimed to create a strong visual impression. Their towers made them look like the stone castles that were rising at the time. Bishop Gundulf of Rochester planned not only his cathedral but its neighbouring castle and the White Tower of the Tower of London. Walls and the piers or columns of the aisles were massive and windows smaller than they would become because of the reliance on semicircular 'Romanesque' arches, which were less effective in bearing heavy loads. Inside there were longer vistas than before. Lengthy naves presented an effect of distance, but one was not meant to see everything at once, at least at floor level, and the building opened up as one proceeded. Height could be emphasised by clusters of colonnettes rising from the floor past the arcades and galleries to the roof or vaults above the nave and choir. Columns and arches could be decorated with dog-tooth patterns, walls stencilled or painted, and windows filled with coloured glass. The effect must have been darker than it became in later centuries and particularly so at the west end of the choir which lay a long way from the windows in the transepts. This concerned monks less because they learnt the daily services by heart, but it may have been an issue in the secular cathedrals and ultimately have been one reason for redesigning buildings.

By the last quarter of the twelfth century, architectural styles and ambitions were moving on. In 1174 Canterbury suffered a serious fire that destroyed the choir. Consultations were held with masons, and William of Sens in France was chosen to rebuild this part of the church. He set out to raise a new choir within the existing choir aisles, and supervised the work until 1179 when he was badly injured by falling from the scaffolding and was replaced by another master builder, William the Englishman. The new work was designed according to the Gothic style of northern France, employing pointed arches. The choir was increased in height by adding a clerestory, and an impression of greater slenderness was achieved by keeping the dimensions of the existing piers but lengthening them. East of the choir a new large Trinity Chapel was built in the shape of an apse with a small circular 'corona' at its east end. This chapel included an ambulatory with arcades, a gallery above, and clerestories higher still, with a crypt underneath. The crypt contained the tomb of Thomas Becket, whose death we shall examine presently. When his tomb became a major centre of pilgrimage, his remains were moved to a shrine in the Trinity Chapel, probably to deal with the huge queues of pilgrims who journeyed to venerate him.[44]

The adoption of Gothic architecture, or more precisely the Early English or Geometrical style, soon spread to other cathedrals. At Wells Bishop Reginald, then based at Bath, began an ambitious rebuilding in about 1180, probably with the idea of restoring its cathedral status. This was the first cathedral to employ pointed arches throughout. The work took until the 1240s and included a striking west front with two towers (Fig. 21, p. 49). Placing the towers outside the lines of the nave created a wide west face which was emphasised by six prominent buttresses and an array of geometrical gables and niches containing statues of saints.[45] The new style reached its fullest expression at Salisbury, where a wholly original cathedral was being planned by about 1198. The bishop and canons,

based in the former hill-fort and Roman site of Old Sarum, found their church and dwellings cramped in area, lacking in water, and hampered by the presence of a castle and its garrison. They resolved to move to a new virgin site on level ground beside the River Avon. The foundation stone was laid in 1220 and the building finished by the 1260s. Here there was plenty of room not only for a new cathedral but for a large Close containing a bishop's palace and ample houses for the canons, protected by walls and gates. Eventually the town deserted Old Sarum as well, and established itself outside the cathedral Close.

21. The great west front of Wells Cathedral, planned to emphasise width and richly decorated with niches and statues.

   Salisbury was built on strictly rectangular lines with a consistent width from east to west, apart from projections (Fig. 22, p. 50). The architecture employed unified and geometrical forms which, as Nikolaus Pevsner observed, convey a sense of 'coolness'; one might say severity.[46] There were three entrances at the west end, chiefly for the clergy and for their processions, leading to a long nave with aisles and a north entrance, probably for the public. Windows were tall lancets without tracery. Beyond the nave was a crossing with wide transepts, each containing three bays for chapels. The choir projected into the crossing and was shut off by a stone screen or 'pulpitum' with images above it: Christ on the Cross (the 'rood'), the Virgin Mary, and St John. The aisles continued beside the choir, and halfway along them were smaller transepts each

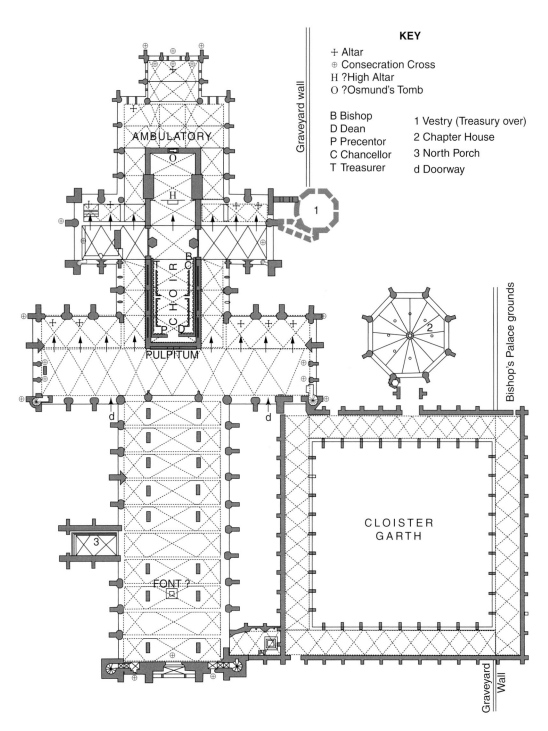

KEY

+ Altar
⊕ Consecration Cross
H ?High Altar
O ?Osmund's Tomb

B Bishop
D Dean
P Precentor
C Chancellor
T Treasurer

1 Vestry (Treasury over)
2 Chapter House
3 North Porch
d Doorway

22. Salisbury Cathedral, plan.

holding two more chapels. Beyond the choir the aisles led into a wide chapel named the Trinity Chapel, as at Canterbury. This had room for three altars at its east end. The west front of the cathedral was built in a grand and emphatic way like that of Wells, and there was a central tower on which a spire was raised in the fourteenth century. Rising to 54.86 metres high (180 feet), it called and still calls attention to the building for miles around.

The layout of Salisbury reflected the requirements of worship in a secular cathedral of the thirteenth century. These resembled those of the previous century but needed to be still more extensive. The long choir accommodated more clergy: not only the handful of resident canons and all the vicars choral but the chantry priests who were coming to be privately endowed to say masses and who were expected to attend the daily services (Fig. 23, p. 52). The availability of many clergy meant that ceremonies could be more elaborate, both around the high altar and in processions through the church. The mass was now more popular than ever. It was seen as a sacrament that created virtue and conveyed it not only to its celebrant priest and his onlookers, but – through his intercession – to other living people and to the dead. Hence the provision of some thirteen chapels and altars as well as the high altar, at which mass could be said. Finally the success of the cult of St Thomas of Canterbury caused Salisbury to seek a suitable setting for its own saint. This was the first bishop, Osmund, whom the cathedral community regarded as holy and wished to be the object of pilgrimage, although he was not formally canonised until 1456. The creation of the Trinity Chapel provided a place, like the east end of Canterbury, where his shrine could lie and where there was space for pilgrims to gather, pray, and depart.

Murder in the Cathedral

It was on Tuesday afternoon, 29 December 1170, that Thomas Becket, archbishop of Canterbury, was hustled by his staff from his palace into his cathedral.[47] There had been an angry exchange between him and four knights from the court of Henry II in France. Frustrated by the presence of his servants, the knights had withdrawn to get reinforcements. Their self-appointed mission was to force the archbishop to remove the penalties he had imposed on certain of Henry's supporters and, if he refused, to arrest him. In the cathedral the monks were singing vespers. Becket stood by a pillar in the north transept, accompanied by his chaplain, Edward Grim. He had forbidden the cathedral doors to be closed, and the four knights and their retainers found him at about half past four. Again they demanded that he remove the penalties, and again he refused. They tried to seize him and he resisted. Then, while Hugh de Morville kept the spectators away, Reginald FitzUrse struck at him, cutting off the top of his head. William Tracy and Richard Brito joined in, the latter breaking his sword with the force of the blow. Becket fell and his blood and brains spilled on to the pavement (Fig. 24, p. 53).

23. Salisbury
Cathedral: the
interior of the
choir looking
east, with the
stalls of the
canons, vicars
choral, clerks,
and choristers.

Thomas Becket had been a close friend of Henry, who had arranged his appointment as archbishop in 1162. Henry expected an ally in charge of the Church. Instead Becket made himself the champion of the Church's claims against the king and became someone with whom it was impossible to compromise. When relations worsened in 1164, Becket went into exile in France and the king confiscated his lands. In May 1170 Henry had his eldest son Henry crowned as his successor, and since Becket was absent the ceremony was done by other bishops. Later that year king and archbishop met and agreed to be reconciled. Henry extended his peace to Becket's supporters and promised to restore his lands. Becket, who had imposed excommunications and suspensions on some of Henry's side, did not reciprocate. Instead, at the end of November, he returned to England where he prepared to take measures against the coronation bishops and even the prior and monks of his own cathedral. When his actions were reported to Henry's court in France, there was general indignation. The king appointed the earl of Essex to lead a mission of remonstrance, but the four knights decided to go by themselves and, as fate would have it, they got to Canterbury before the earl.

Thomas was buried next day at the order of Ranulf de Broc, who had assisted the knights, in a marble coffin in the cathedral crypt. No funeral

24. The murder
of Thomas
Becket in 1170,
as shown on
a boss in the
nave of Exeter
Cathedral.

was held because the spilling of blood rendered a church unconsecrated, and services had to be moved to the chapter house. Almost everyone who had dealt with Thomas found him exasperating but equally many were shocked by the murder of the head of the English Church in his own cathedral. In the next few days local people – and eventually the monks – gathered up the blood and brains in cloths and a basin. On the following Monday, 4 January 1171, a miracle was claimed when contact with some of the blood apparently caused a poor local woman named Brithiva to recover her sight. During the next few months the miracles multiplied.[48] At first they were confined to people from Kent, but by the summer they were spreading to London and to the Midlands as far north as Chester and Lincoln, through people travelling to Canterbury or invoking the saint's aid elsewhere.

The miracles involved men, women, and children from the ranks of knights, citizens, and the poor, and brought about healing from blindness, dumbness, lameness, sicknesses of various kinds, and mental illness. The saint's cult thus began as a medical one but it soon became political. Clergy could represent Thomas as a martyr for the liberties of the Church. Henry's opponents in France, including its king, Louis VII, could use the event to wrong-foot him. Accordingly, Henry was forced to recognise the saint by going to Canterbury and being ceremonially scourged by the monks in front of the tomb. The cult then became a royal asset: an English possession that drew devotees from abroad. By 1300 the name

'Thomas' was even used in the royal family. Meanwhile, within three years, the saint was formally canonised on 21 February 1173.

Pilgrims soon came to the tomb from all over Britain and the adjoining parts of the Continent.[49] In 1220 the body was moved to a new shrine east of the high altar. The shrine became a splendid object embellished with gold and jewels donated by wealthy visitors. In about 1500 it was described as 'entirely covered over with plates of pure gold, but the gold is scarcely visible from the variety of precious stones with which it is studded, such as sapphires, diamonds, rubies, rose-pink rubies, and emeralds'.[50] The pilgrims visited the place of martyrdom, the original tomb, the high altar where the body had lain before burial, the shrine, and the 'corona' chapel where part of the saint's head was preserved as a relic. They bought badges to wear on their hats and small bottles of tin or lead holding water that had come into contact with a tiny trace of Thomas's blood. Large sums of money were offered during the thirteenth and fourteenth centuries: over £400 each year around 1200, £1,142 at the translation of the body in 1220, and £350 to £450 in the 1320s and 30s. Every fifty years from 1220 to 1470 there was a 'jubilee' with special indulgences for pilgrims at which the offerings rose above £600, although it seems that the receipts of the shrine shrank in the sixty years before the Reformation.[51]

In the late 1380s Geoffrey Chaucer used the pilgrimage as the framework for his *Canterbury Tales*. He pictured groups of people meeting at the Tabard Inn at Southwark and agreeing to travel together to Canterbury, telling tales as they went (Fig. 25, p. 57).[52] The original scheme of the *Tales* was highly ambitious: thirty men and three women telling two stories out and two back, but only twenty-four tales were composed and two of them unfinished. Chaucer never brought the pilgrims as far as Canterbury and we do not know how he would have handled their visit except that the final part of the work, the austere 'Parson's Tale' which is actually a sermon, suggests a spiritual and solemn ending. However, in the fifteenth century an anonymous author provided a sequel that rates as one of the earliest portrayals of a cathedral in fiction.[53] He imagined that the company reached Canterbury at mid-morning and took rooms at 'The Chequer on the Hoop', a real inn built for pilgrims by the monks. Then they went off 'to church' (the word 'cathedral' not yet being in use) to make their offerings.

At the church door the issue arose of who went first. The Knight politely invited the clergy to do so. A monk sprinkled the pilgrims with holy water and the Friar tried but failed to get hold of the sprinkler to peer at the face of the Nun. The Knight and his nearest equals walked to the shrine while the Pardoner and the Miller gaped at the coats of arms in the windows and tried to identify them, as if they were gentry. The Host scolded them and sent them away to the shrine. There they all knelt, prayed to the saint, kissed the relics, and offered silver brooches and rings. They stayed until the end of the morning services. Then they bought pilgrims' badges but the Miller stole some instead and shared them with the Pardoner. The company returned to the inn for midday dinner, wearing their badges in their hats, and in the afternoon they viewed the city. The knight and squire inspected the walls, some of the clergy went to a wine bar, and the Wife of Bath and the Prioress walked in a garden. That night the Pardoner tried to seduce the inn's barmaid, but he was trounced by her lover (an echo of 'The Miller's Tale'), beaten, savaged by a large dog, and forced to spend the night in the dog's bed. Early next morning the pilgrims rode back to London.

Returning to Becket's day, a factor that helped him to sainthood was being a bishop. Bishops had a high status as holy men from about the twelfth to the fifteenth centuries: higher than it had usually been before and certainly more than it was in later times. During the period of this chapter, up to about 1250, several other bishops gained popular acclaim as saints in cathedrals although most were not officially canonised. As well as Osmund of Salisbury, they included Wulfstan of Worcester, Anselm of Canterbury, William of York (Fig. 35, p. 92), and Hugh of Lincoln.[54] All were earnestly promoted by their cathedrals but most achieved only local veneration. A few other saints gained shrines who were not bishops. Rochester, always outshone by Canterbury, tried to draw pilgrims with a cult of its own, that of William of Perth. He was a Scottish pilgrim to Becket's tomb who was murdered near Rochester in 1201, and his own grave attracted visitors and offerings on a modest scale. Two other saints of lesser importance were William of Norwich (1154) and Little St Hugh (1255), allegedly and quite improbably child victims of Jewish ritual murder. Each had a shrine, at Norwich and Lincoln respectively, reminding us that cathedrals were not immune to the prejudices of the age.[55]

Culture and Learning

The work of a cathedral, whether monastic or secular, centred on the *opus dei* or 'divine office', meaning the daily, weekly, and annual round of worship in the church. This will be described in the next chapter, when more information survives about its structure.[56] Here it will be enough to say that worship continued to follow its earlier pattern of eight services sung in the choir of the cathedral at midnight or in the early hours of the morning, between dawn and mid-morning, and during the afternoon. Mass or communion was celebrated several times during the second of these periods. In addition to this, the Rule of St Benedict, which was observed in all but one of the monastic cathedrals, recommended that monks should engage in study for up to two hours each day. The Rule did not require high standards in this respect. It talks of monks learning the psalms and lessons that figured in services, with other unspecified reading. Only in Lent was each monk instructed to take a book from the monastery's collection and to read it 'all through in order'.[57] In the secular cathedrals, where attempts to impose a rule of life met with little success, there was not even this requirement beyond the expectation that the clergy should be able to read and sing the material in the daily services.

In practice, however, many cathedral communities included scholars who progressed far beyond the ability merely to carry out services. Before about 1200, when universities had not yet developed, learning was decentralised in the major religious houses of England. This was particularly so in monastic cathedrals. Here the concern to give most monks seclusion from the world established an ambience in which study could flourish along with the copying and illumination of manuscripts and the composition of original works.[58] Canterbury Cathedral was a national leader in this respect. In the twelfth century it was the home of such scholars as Ælmer, Eadmer, Gervase, and Odo – all of whom are surnamed 'of Canterbury' – as well as Ralph of London, Richard Pluto, and Nigel Witeker.[59] All were skilled Latinists who wrote works of theology, history, and literature including letters and poetry. Canterbury's thriving literary culture showed its effectiveness after Thomas Becket's murder in 1170. During the following years the cathedral prior, Benedict of Peterborough, wrote an account of the archbishop's passion and miracles, while his successor Alan of Tewkesbury edited Thomas's letters and prefaced his work with a further Life. Saints owe much to their followers, and the Canterbury writers helped to develop the huge popularity of Thomas's cult.

There were important scholars at some other monastic cathedrals. At Durham, Simeon of Durham revised and continued an earlier history of the kings of England, which Geoffrey of Coldingham extended after him. Reginald of Durham compiled the Life of one local saint, Godric, and wrote in praise of two others, Cuthbert and Oswald. At Worcester, John of Worcester (formerly confused with a Florence of Worcester) compiled another important chronicle of England from the fifth century until his own day, while a monk named Senatus was the author of letters, sermons, and lives of the Worcester saints Oswald and Wulfstan. Winchester was the home of Godfrey, a Latin poet, and Richard of Devizes, who wrote a valuable account of the reign of Richard Coeur-de-Lion and possibly a history of the monastery. One could add Hemming of Worcester and Ernulf of Rochester to whom we owe Hemming's Cartulary and the Textus Roffensis: two major collections of documents relating to the lands and privileges of their monasteries.

The secular cathedrals were less active in this respect. Their way of life was too public, and their canons too involved in administration for their cathedral, bishop, or king, to find much time or incentives for study and writing. Still, they too included some notable individual scholars. Hugh the Chanter, precentor of York, wrote a history of his own cathedral. The dean of St Paul's, Ralph de Diceto, compiled a history of England under Henry II and Richard Coeur-de-Lion, while the archdeacon of London, Peter of Blois, produced numerous works of theology as well as much-admired letters of which collections were made. William de Montibus, chancellor of Lincoln, was another writer of theology, including a poem on penance which became a standard text for study in late-medieval English grammar schools. Finally, Alfred of Shareshill, canon of Lichfield, was deeply attracted by science, writing commentaries on Aristotle's treatises on generation and meteors and translating one of the works of the Arabic scholar Avicenna.

As I fonde · with a ful pale chere
My tale I ganne · anone as ye shal here
❖ Explicit prologus ❖

Prima pars ❖
Here begynneth the Segge of Thebes ful

25. Some of
Chaucer's
pilgrims leaving
Canterbury,
imagined in an
illustration to
John Lydgate's
Siege of
Thebes.

Cathedral Schools

Alongside these exalted studies there was the schooling of young people.
We have seen that the Anglo-Saxon cathedrals were places of education, in
that they had to teach their junior members and may have admitted other
boys to learn alongside them. Such education was not yet independent of
the cathedral; it took place inside the community and was led by men who
were clergy as much as teachers. Schools as we know them – permanent
free-standing institutions taught by professional instructors – emerge in
records in the early twelfth century. This period saw a rising demand for
education in English society, driven by the increase of parish churches
on the one hand and the growth of towns on the other. This seems to
have caused the appearance of schools outside cathedrals and monasteries
which would cater primarily for the general public.[60]

One of earliest recorded examples of such teaching in a cathedral city is
at Canterbury, where the first Norman archbishop, Lanfranc, is said to have
established schools of grammar and music in about 1085–7. Significantly,
these were based not at the monastic cathedral but in association with
a new church of St Gregory nearby.[61] During the twelfth and thirteenth

centuries schools are recorded in nearly all the cathedral cities. They were of two and eventually three levels. All the secular cathedrals instituted a song school to teach their choristers; monastic cathedrals did not have choristers but singing boys, and those only after about 1250.[62] The song school came under the care of the precentor but was deputed in practice to the succentor. Cathedral song schools were on the premises of the cathedral for obvious reasons, and some admitted boys from outside who came to learn to read and sing plainsong. This was at first the case at Hereford and Lincoln. But there was too large a demand for this kind of elementary education, and the fees that could be charged for teaching it were too small to make it worthwhile. Accordingly, most secular cathedrals soon abandoned teaching at this level except for their choristers, and the monastic cathedrals never did so except for their small groups of singing boys. By about the mid-thirteenth century, reading and song in the cathedral cities, as in other towns, were taught privately by clergy, parish clerks, and lay men and women, rather than at or under the auspices of the cathedral.[63]

Once children had learnt to read, they might, if boys, proceed to learn grammar, meaning the Latin language and literature. In the secular cathedral cities, the chancellor, who we have seen originated as a schoolmaster of grammar, soon turned into a grander functionary and appointed a deputy master to teach his school. This school might include the cathedral's adolescent clerks, but it was chiefly attended by boys from the city and the surrounding countryside. It usually stood in the city as well, not in the cathedral Close, and the cathedral merely paid the master a small salary or fees for such pupils as it sent. Most of his income came from charging his external students. In monastic cathedral cities like Canterbury and Winchester the grammar school was even more detached from the cathedral. It lay under the care of the bishop, not the monastery, and its building too was sited in the city rather than the monastic precincts.[64]

Finally, the secular cathedrals became involved in what we would call further education, and more closely so. Some of the leading scholars of the twelfth century were canons of the secular cathedrals and offered teaching to students who were well grounded in grammar. William de Montibus taught theology at Lincoln in the 1190s, when his pupils included the Welsh historian Gerald of Wales. A little later Simon de Fresne, canon of Hereford, urged Gerald to come to his city, claiming that the liberal arts were studied and taught to a greater extent than anywhere else in England.[65] These were individual initiatives, and they faded away after 1200 when universities developed with more teachers and better arrangements for study. During the thirteenth century, however, it became normal for the secular cathedrals to organise lectures in theology or canon law for the benefit of local clergy who could not afford to go to university. These lectures were given by the chancellor or a deputy appointed by him. Chancellors were not always conscientious in this respect and one suspects that their potential pupils were often uninterested too, so that the practice had a somewhat intermittent history, but it continued in principle down to the sixteenth century.[66] Monastic cathedrals did not have chancellors to give lectures, but in 1464 the bishop of Worcester established a library and a weekly lecture on theology in the charnel chapel outside the cathedral. These too endured until the Reformation.[67]

During the later Middle Ages, benefactors slowly began to subsidise the costs of grammar school education. At first this help was limited to enabling a few poorer students to receive bed and board while they attended school, reflecting the fact that many boys had to travel away from home to be educated, which involved the cost of boarding in private houses. Schemes of this kind were set up in Durham, Exeter, Lincoln, and Norwich, usually in hospitals which in those days catered for the poor and travellers as much as the sick.[68] In the late fourteenth century a new idea developed in which education itself was subsidised or made free. The pioneering venture here was Winchester College, founded by William of Wykeham in 1382, although it was not meant to be a cathedral school and the older non-endowed school of the bishop continued beside it for some time. During the fifteenth and early sixteenth centuries, endowments were given to grammar schools in other cathedral cities to provide free education. Durham gained one in 1414, Lichfield in 1495, Chichester in 1497, St Paul's in 1508–12, and Worcester in the early sixteenth century.[69]

Cathedrals, then, played a significant role in education, but there were hardly cathedral schools except for those of the choristers and the theological lectures. Cathedral grammar schools were to be an innovation of Henry VIII; before his time the relationship between cathedrals and such schools was semi-detached.[70] In as far as cathedrals provided education for society, they did so for its upper and wealthier end. Most of the schools in the cathedral cities, elementary and grammar, still charged fees when the Reformation came in the 1530s. The 'poor scholars' about whom we hear in medieval documents were boys and youths who had strong enough links with bishops and cathedrals to gain them the charity they received. Even when the governments of Henry VIII and Edward VI made all the cathedral grammar schools free of fees during the 1540s, pupils who came to a 'free' school needed substantial backing to do so.[71] Their parents had to be ambitious for their advancement, able to release them from working for money, and rich enough to pay for respectable clothes, books, writing materials, and other charges that were not covered by free education. We should beware of assuming that modern cathedral schools have departed from some earlier ethic of helping the truly poor.[72]

Chapter
—— 4 ——

The Later
Middle Ages
1250–1530

The thirteenth and early fourteenth centuries were a golden age for cathedrals. They rose to the height of their material prosperity in terms of wealth, staffing, and privileges. This was not a time of great endowment, since most of their lands and churches had come to them by 1200. Nonetheless money continued to accrue through smaller donations, through the exploitation of lands and tithes, and from the offerings of pilgrims and well-wishers. The period was one of rising population. It grew in England to some six million in about 1300: a figure that would not be surpassed until the reign of James I. There was stable government for most of the time, and the effects of foreign wars were relatively modest up to the 1330s. It was possible for cathedrals to plan building projects on a large scale, and we shall consider these presently.

Disquieting changes began to occur in 1315–17 with a severe famine that led to outbreaks of disease. Worse still was the onset of plague in 1349: the so-called Black Death (a nineteenth-century term). This returned in 1361 and remained endemic thereafter, along with epidemics of other maladies. An intermittent war with France lasted from 1337 to 1453, and the population fell to two or three million during the second half of the fourteenth century. Cathedrals were affected in two ways. They lost clergy through mortality and then found it difficult to replace them. Only four monks are said to have died at Canterbury in 1349, but twenty-five did so in 1361. The sixty or seventy brethren of about 1300 declined to forty-five by 1376.[1] Ely's numbers fell from about forty to twenty-eight, and Rochester's from thirty-five to twenty-three.[2] At Exeter about ten of the canons died in 1349, and at least five of the lesser clergy. Its vicars choral dropped from twenty-four to twenty and its chantry priests from twenty-one to twelve.[3] These reductions were hard to reverse. A smaller population caused wages and prices to rise, while revenues declined from lands and tithes. Even if clerical recruits were forthcoming, it was impossible to pay for as many as before, particularly monks and minor secular clergy, because of the higher costs of supporting them.

A gradual revival of the nation's wealth and population began in the fifteenth century, although it was punctuated by difficult short periods. This was reflected in some but not all cathedrals. Canterbury's monks increased to sixty-one in 1391 and to between seventy-five and ninety between 1400 and 1520.[4] Ely's rose to forty-six in 1379, but were fewer by the sixteenth century.[5] At Exeter the vicars remained at twenty, but new chantry foundations raised the total of chantry priests to eighteen by the reign of Henry VIII.[6] Rochester, on the other hand, never recovered the staffing that it had before the Black Death, and its number of monks remained in the low twenties until the Reformation.[7]

Privilege and Power

During the earlier and more prosperous part of this period, the cathedrals made some solid gains which they would keep for centuries. One that had begun in early times was the enjoyment of financial and legal privileges. Some Anglo-Saxon kings gave cathedrals freedom from taxes and duties on part or all of their lands, although they were not fully exempt from royal demands especially when the Crown was in grave need of money. After the Norman Conquest these privileges began to extend to Church matters as well as secular ones. The twelfth century, as has been stated, saw the Church evolve into a more organised body. Laws were enacted to lay down how the clergy should be appointed and carry out their work, and how the laity should do the duties that were required of them.

Much the same was happening with royal government. It was becoming more effective in imposing its laws on the nation. Once laws existed, systems were needed to enforce their acceptance. Royal officials and the leaders of the Church – bishops and archdeacons – became responsible for monitoring the people in their jurisdictions, and for

26. Ely's ambitious fourteenth-century octagon. In J. M. W. Turner's painting of 1796–7, it dwarfs the congregation of that date.

operating courts that dealt with offenders or civil disputes. This development, however, jarred with a hierarchical society whose privileged members wanted special treatment. The result was that as law developed, so did immunities from it. Kings, ecclesiastics, noblemen, and towns all obtained exemption from the normal operation of the law, and these exemptions – sometimes personal, sometimes geographical – became a part of English life down to the middle of the nineteenth century.

Cathedrals, as rich and powerful bodies, gained an appropriate share of these privileges, shielding them to some extent from the bishop, the diocese, and the surrounding city. It may seem strange that the bishop's church should wish, and be able, to restrict his authority over it. Since the tenth century, however, when Æthelwold brought about the expulsion of the clerks of Winchester by force of will, most bishops and their cathedrals had drifted apart. Bishops ruled for limited periods and were often away. Cathedral communities were permanent, and as their property became regarded as different from that of the bishop, they developed particular ways of running their own affairs. Naturally they ran them in ways convenient to themselves, especially with regard to keeping residence. When, in the thirteenth century, Church law required that every bishop should visit his cathedral at least once to inspect it, the prospect of his arrival with a large retinue requiring hospitality, to enquire into arrangements with which the clergy had grown comfortable, was an alarming one.

In 1239 Robert Grosseteste, bishop of Lincoln, announced his intention to make a visitation of his cathedral. The canons resisted him. Their colleagues in other secular foundations, realising the issues at stake, sent copies of what they claimed to be their privileges to help Lincoln in its battle. The dispute lasted for six years and was finally judged by the pope, Innocent IV. He ruled that the bishop had the right to visit his cathedral and its churches, but might not exact any fees for doing so. This decision did not prevent clashes elsewhere. Chichester kept the bishop out until 1340, Salisbury until 1392, and Hereford until the seventeenth century. When bishops managed to establish their claims, they were forced to compromise and agree limitations on how often they could come. They had to give notice of their arrival, inspect only what was customary for them to see, and might be restricted as to whether they could question the canons individually or merely together in chapter.[8]

Cathedrals also strove to moderate the bishop's rights over their property. He did not expect to involve himself with their lands or finances, but their parish churches lay within his diocese and ought to have come under his rule and that of his local agents: the archdeacons and rural deans. The bishop managed to keep some powers over the churches of his cathedral. He approved the rectors and vicars who were nominated by the cathedral clergy to serve these churches, and formally instituted them for this purpose. By the thirteenth century he insisted on granting permission for the cathedral to appropriate the tithes of any of its parishes and turn them from rectories into vicarages.

But the cathedrals succeeded in withdrawing their parishes from the rest of the diocesan administration. This was the case with all the secular cathedrals and some, but not all, of the monastic ones. By about 1200 their parishes became 'peculiar jurisdictions', 'peculiars' for short. Those that belonged to the cathedral chapter as a whole were controlled by the chapter collectively. Those owned by individual dignitaries and prebendaries were administered by them individually. The chapter or its particular members became responsible for ensuring that the churches in their peculiars were maintained, their clergy conscientious, their laity well-behaved, and the wills made by their inhabitants registered and executed. They held their own Church courts to regulate these matters. Peculiars existed in most English counties until nearly all of them were abolished in the years after 1836.[9]

A third immunity protected cathedrals from their surrounding cities. In some places, like Lichfield and Wells, the city was small and presented little challenge, while new Salisbury was a purpose-built cathedral city where the cathedral was privileged from the beginning. Elsewhere the cathedral was often within the city walls and friction arose with the citizens. The cathedral claimed to be an independent space, exempt from jurisdiction by the city council. Disputes arose when its clergy allowed trading in this space or gave sanctuary to thieves pursued from the city. Outlying tenements of the bishop or cathedral might also be asserted as lying outside the city's control and free of local taxation. There was the further issue that clergy were only subject to the secular law in civil cases such as debt. If they committed crimes and were arrested, they had to be released to the custody of the bishop and judged by him: the process known as 'benefit of clergy'. On their side the cathedral clergy complained of incursions by townspeople into their space, sometimes to steal or do damage. The monastic cathedrals, being monasteries, had long been shut off by walls and gates (Fig. 27, p. 65). The secular cathedrals followed them in this respect during the thirteenth century, closing off their precincts including their cemeteries and canons' houses with gates that were supervised by a cleric and shut from dusk to dawn.[10]

Disputes welled up about these matters in several cathedral cities. In Hereford they surfaced in the 1230s, due to the city's resentment against the bishop's and cathedral's encroachments on its rights.[11] As the clergy acquired more houses and land in the city, they insisted that these passed into their jurisdiction not that of the mayor and corporation. In 1262 the city's bell summoned the townsfolk to arms and they blockaded the cathedral precinct, obstructing access and supplies. This forced the clergy to negotiate, and it was agreed that in future their acquisitions should remain under the rule of the city. There were more quarrels in 1389, 1407, and 1464 over the cathedral's right to fence off its cemetery, incursions by the mayor's officers to arrest people on the cathedral's property, and precedence in religious processions.

Hereford was not unusual in this respect: similar conflicts occurred in Canterbury, Exeter, Norwich, Salisbury, and Winchester. Two of those in

27. Cathedral defences: the Ethelred Gate of Norwich Cathedral, built to protect it and its clergy from the nearby city.

Norwich were particularly severe. In 1272 clashes between the cathedral's servants or tenants and local men escalated into a riot in which the townsfolk attacked one of the gatehouses and set it on fire because it was too strongly defended. The fire spread to the church and domestic buildings, and thirteen people were killed. In 1443 there was another serious rising, led by the mayor, in which the city was out of control for several days although on this occasion the rioters did not breach the cathedral's defences.[12] Violence on such a scale was unusual, however. Most disputes were marked by posturing, in which each side tried to maintain its prestige. And for much of the time a cathedral and its city had amicable relations. Mayors would be given respect when they visited the cathedral; cathedral clergy often came from city families. The two sides needed each other too much to fall out irretrievably.

The Secular Cathedrals

The leadership of the secular cathedrals in the later Middle Ages was what had evolved in the twelfth and early thirteenth centuries: dean, dignitaries, and canons governing together in chapter.[13] As before, not all these men were resident, and the chapter might include only six or a dozen of them. By the fifteenth century residence became formalised. A cleric could not simply turn up as a residentiary canon: he needed to ask permission from his colleagues to come into residence at the start of the following term (or quarter) of the year. This had to be agreed and he was required to hold a feast for his fellow canons and the minor clergy when he started his residence. Eventually the feast was replaced by an entry payment of anything from £40 to £100, emphasising the wealth that one needed to be a canon.[14]

Historically, the bishop had the right to appoint the canons and the dignitaries except for the dean, who was elected by the canons, but this right was a qualified one. On his arrival in his diocese he would encounter a body of canons appointed by his predecessors, which helps to explain the friction there might be over visitations. During vacancies between bishops, their power of patronage passed to the king so that a few canons might be his choices. Once a bishop was in power, he could fill vacant posts (apart from the deanship) with his friends and servants, and needed to do so to staff his administration, but he did not have a fully free choice in the matter. The king and the nobility would press him to appoint their servants and relatives, and some concessions would be essential for his effectiveness as a bishop and his ability to lobby important people himself. Furthermore, during the fourteenth century the popes made a strong and long-lasting attempt to take over cathedral patronage themselves. They argued that since they were the bishop's superiors, they could exercise his powers in the interests of the Church, and that they were better able to give Church posts to deserving and well-educated clerics. These posts included bishoprics themselves, cathedral dignities and canonries, and parish churches in the gift of bishops, cathedrals, and monasteries. Wisely, the popes steered clear of churches belonging to the king and other lay patrons.

Accordingly, for most of the fourteenth century the popes 'provided' candidates to many benefices in England, a practice known today as 'papal provisions'.[15] In the case of cathedral posts such as deans, dignitaries, or canons, a provision might be made to one that was vacant or a cleric might be granted an 'expectation': a document that entitled him to a future vacancy at a particular cathedral. The papal administration accepted applications for provisions, and the English universities submitted lists of deserving scholars, including John Wycliffe: later a leading opponent of papal power. But papal

provisions were unpopular for obvious reasons. Bishops resented losing their right of appointment, and kings and noblemen the chance to ask for favours which were more easily gained from a bishop than from a pope. It was possible for more than one holder of an expectation to turn up to claim a vacant post, leading to litigation and even violence. Popes sometimes provided foreigners to English benefices, and this aroused national hostility. Parliament passed statutes forbidding provisions in 1351 and 1390, and although the Crown did not always enforce them, the practice began to decline. It decreased sharply after 1378 when there were two popes, and the one at Rome whom the English recognised had to be more compliant with their wishes. The papal schism lasted until 1417, during which the papal claims largely evaporated, and by the fifteenth century the bishops were back in control of canonries, subject as before to lay requests.

28. The gate of the Vicars' Close at Wells Cathedral, leading into their college. The buildings indicate the vicars' importance as a property-owning body with legal status.

The small circle of dignitaries and resident canons ruled over a much larger number of minor clergy. These, as we have seen, included the vicars choral, whose number originally equalled that of the canons whether resident or not, smaller numbers of adolescent 'altarists' or 'secondaries', and boy choristers. The adolescents never grew into communities with buildings and assets except at Lincoln where they acquired a common dwelling in the late thirteenth century.[16] The other two groups were more fortunate. The choristers generally lived together in a room or house from early times, and during the later Middle Ages arrangements were made in most places for a master to supervise them, common meals, and education in reading, song, and sometimes Latin grammar.[17] One bishop, Beckington of Wells in 1460, drew up careful statutes to regulate their lives. He laid down the timetable of their day, allowed space for play, told their master to teach them clearly and briefly, and ordered him to warn them twice for any faults before he resorted to corporal punishment. At night they were to sleep three in a bed: two smaller boys at the head and a larger boy between them, facing the other way.[18]

The vicars made more substantial progress. From being mere canons' servants, they grew into independent organisations.[19] The security of tenure that they gained in the thirteenth century was accompanied by the acquisition of endowments in the form of payments and estates, the income of which they shared among themselves. At first they had often lived and eaten with their canons, but in about 1248 the vicars of York were given a communal dwelling, the Bedern College, in which to lodge and have meals. Similar houses were later built elsewhere. These consisted of a cluster of buildings as at Salisbury and York, a street of individual houses with a common hall like Exeter and Wells (Fig. 28, p. 67), or a quadrangle in the case of Hereford and Lincoln.[20] A further development was the constitution of the vicars as a corporate body with a head or heads chosen from their senior members, a code of statutes, and a common seal. This turned the vicars into a college – a word that was often used of their dwelling as well – which formed an autonomous body within the cathedral precincts (Fig. 46, p. 128). It enabled the vicars to protect their traditional duties and customs in a way that the cathedral chapter had to recognise, and the colleges endured until the 1930s.

A further group of lesser clergy emerged at the secular cathedrals during the thirteenth century. These were chantry priests, or 'annuellars' as they were sometimes called.[21] Chantries were private additions to cathedrals, especially the secular foundations. A wealthy patron, generally but not always a bishop or other cleric of the cathedral, gave an endowment of land or money to fund a priest to say a daily mass for the patron's soul at a cathedral side altar. The dean and chapter required these priests to be under their discipline and to be present in the choir at all the daily services. There grew to be large numbers of these priests in the early fourteenth century, ranging from nineteen at Lichfield to seventy-four at St Paul's.[22] The fall in the population and rising prices caused some chantry endowments to become unviable after 1349, and two or three might be joined together so that numbers of priests declined, although they recovered a little in the fifteenth century. As with the vicars, there was a tendency for the priests to be grouped together to live and eat in a common house instead of living in separate lodgings. At York they formed a college, St William's, with corporate status and an elected provost. In the other cathedrals they were less independent, and held their property and managed their affairs under the control of the dean and chapter.[23]

The Monastic Cathedrals

The monastic cathedrals are difficult to characterise in the later Middle Ages.[24] Much is known about them because of the survival of their archives when they were turned into secular cathedrals at the Reformation. But there was little to distinguish a great abbey like Gloucester (later to become a cathedral) from Winchester, which was both monastery and cathedral. Walking around them in the Middle Ages would not have made the difference very clear, and hardly does so even today. Each had a large church, chapter house, cloisters, and residential buildings for the monks and their servants, with a separate house and household for the abbot or prior.

The main distinction was the presence of a bishop. In a monastic cathedral he took the place of the abbot, and the senior monk – the prior – was his deputy, so that Canterbury, Rochester, and the others are correctly referred to as cathedral priories. The monastery church would contain a bishop's throne in the choir, the bishop would be enthroned in it, and he would be buried nearby if he died in the neighbourhood. An abbey like Gloucester would only contain the tombs of abbots and those nobility and gentry to whom the monks were beholden. A cathedral such as Winchester would also house the monuments of bishops and these might be very impressive. There, five late-medieval and early Tudor bishops – William Wykeham, Henry Beaufort, William Waynflete, Richard Fox, and Stephen Gardiner – built magnificent tombs for themselves in chapels within the cathedral. These proclaimed that the church was the church of a bishop, and still do so (Fig. 29, p. 70).

There were other less visible links between a bishop and his monastic cathedral. The monks were his cathedral chapter. He was expected to consult them about diocesan matters such as grants of rights and property, and to gain their formal consent. In three places, Durham, Worcester, and Canterbury, they had wider powers. At Worcester they administered the diocese during vacancies between bishops while at Durham they claimed to and sometimes did so.[25] At Canterbury, when there was no archbishop, they appointed an official to exercise all his rights in his province, including the confirmation of the elections of bishops.[26] At the same time there were potential strains between bishops and monks. Although the monks nominally elected the bishop to office, he was usually the choice of the king. He was rarely a monk and was frequently absent. The prior was the effective local leader, and a monastic community was as jealous as a dean and chapter about preserving its rights against the bishop. It was hard for the bishop to vanquish them in a dispute.[27]

In about 1284 Godfrey Giffard, the bishop of Worcester, felt the disadvantage of not having a cathedral of canons whose members could help him run his diocese. He proposed to remedy this by upgrading the little minster of Westbury-on-Trym near Bristol, which had a dean and five canons all of whom he appointed. More clergy would be funded there by transferring to Westbury a number of the parish churches in his patronage, thereby creating additional prebends for canons. Such a

29. A bishop's presence in his cathedral: the chantry chapel and tomb of William Wykeham at Winchester. He founded Winchester College and New College (Oxford).

change required the consent of the monks of Worcester, and either because they refused or because he anticipated their refusal, he went ahead with the scheme on his own. The monks were annoyed and appealed to the pope. In 1288 the bishop decided to confront them by exercising his right to come into the monastery to hear the new monks make their professions of obedience.

Entering the chapter house, he announced his intention of presiding at the meeting as the abbot. The prior replied 'It does not belong to you, Father'. The bishop said, 'Have you not made a profession of obedience to me?' The prior retorted boldly, 'No, but to God and the Church'. Another monk then read out an appeal against the bishop's actions. Giffard appears to have withdrawn. He tried to enter the monastery a second time, unsuccessfully, and then to make peace with a gift, but the monks responded with further appeals to the pope. In 1290 the bishop came back, carried out a formal visitation (as he had a right to do) and made a further attempt to force the monks to agree to his Westbury plans. He was unsuccessful. Neither the pope nor the king was willing to intervene on either side, and in the end the bishop fell sick and lost the will to fight further. The monks both won the issue and kept the bishop's presence to a minimum.[28]

The monastic cathedrals of the tenth and twelfth centuries tried hard to set themselves apart from the outside world. From the thirteenth century onwards they modified this stance in certain respects. One was by allowing the foundation of chantries like those of the secular cathedrals. Some were operated by the monks who said the daily masses for the dead, but Canterbury acquired at least five staffed by secular priests, including chantries for the Black Prince and Archbishop Thomas Arundel.[29] At Durham Bishop Langley endowed a chantry of two priests in 1414 to say mass for his soul in the Galilee chapel and to teach song and grammar to local boys in the cathedral precincts.[30] Another kind of 'secularisation' was the reintroduction of boys in the thirteenth century, following the end of the oblation of child monks a hundred years earlier. Norwich was a pioneer in this respect.[31] By about 1288–9 it maintained a group of thirteen 'clerks' (meaning boys or adolescents) who lived in the almonry on the edge of the monastery, where alms were distributed to the poor. They received food as well as their lodging, and schooling in Latin grammar from a master who was not a monk. But unlike oblate boys, they were not required to become monks when they grew up, although this sometimes happened, and they remained free to leave and take jobs in the world.

At first these 'almonry boys', as historians call them, came from relatively poor families and were supported out of charity with no returns demanded. Later such desirable places attracted interest. They began to be given to people connected with the monastery, such as relatives of monks or children proposed by local notables. The boys became expected to do small tasks around the church, especially in acting as servers when the monks said private masses. In the fifteenth century this duty was extended, so that some of the almonry boys were chosen for their voices and trained to spend part of their time in helping to sing polyphonic music in the Lady chapel.[32] The almonry boys' school was often opened to outsiders. Boys were taken in as favours to important people, or for the sake of the fees they could pay. At Norwich and Durham the school became popular enough to rival the city grammar school, which was under the control of the local bishop. This sometimes led to ill-feeling, but these monastic

30. *Exeter
Cathedral,
plan.*

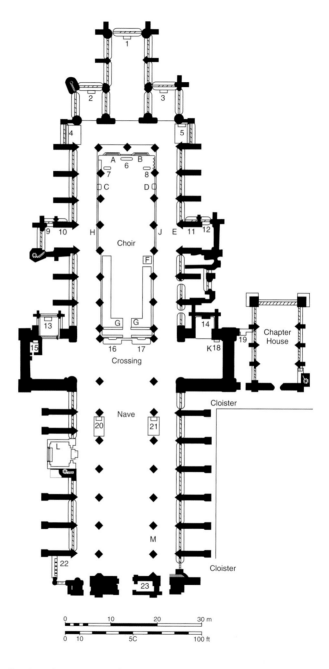

Choir

Crossing

Nave

Chapter
House

Cloister

Cloister

0   10   20   30 m

0   10   5C   100 ft

cathedral schools continued until the Reformation. They represent, in
fact, the chief contribution of the monasteries to public education. This
used to be imagined as a typical activity of a monastery; in fact it did not
emerge until the latter part of the Middle Ages, and then chiefly in the
great foundations that were wealthy enough to afford it.[33]

KEY TO THE PLAN
Altars and Chapels

1. Lady chapel
2. St John the Evangelist
3. St Gabriel
4. St George
5. St Saviour
6. High altar (Our Lady, St Peter and St Paul)
7. St Thomas Becket and St Alphege
8. St Stephen and St Lawrence
9. St Andrew
10. St Katherine
11. St Mary Magdalene
12. St James
13. St Paul
14. St John the Baptist
15. Holy Cross
16. St Mary-in-the-nave
17. St Nicholas
18. St Michael and the tomb of Bishop John
19. Holy Ghost
20. Trinity (Brantingham chantry)
21. Courtenay chantry
22. St Edmund the King
23. Grandisson chantry (? St Radegund)

Images and other Features

A. St Peter (image)
B. St Paul and Our Lady (images)
C. Tomb of Bishop Lacy
D. Tomb of Bishop Berkeley
E. St Mary Magdalene (image)
F. Bishop's throne
G. Choir-stalls
H. Old Peter (image)
I. Choir-screen (*pulpitum*) with cross above
J. St Mary (image)
K. St Michael (image)
L. St Mary (image)
M. Font (in this area)

Collecting Boxes

These were sited by 10, 15, 18, 20, 21, 23, A, B, C, D, H, J, L, and perhaps in other places.

The Buildings of the Later Middle Ages

Although all cathedrals were large and impressive buildings by the early thirteenth century, they did not stay frozen in time. Improvements and adaptations went on for the next two hundred and fifty years. Norman naves were rebuilt at Canterbury, Winchester, Worcester, and York. East ends were extended at St Paul's and York. New towers were raised at Ely, Wells, and York. The architecture of the later Middle Ages is commonly described as passing through two phases. During the second half of the thirteenth century, the geometrical formality of Salisbury gave way to the Decorated style in which the forms flow more freely with elaborate ornamentation. Exeter is one of the largest cathedral buildings to come from this period and to reproduce its fashions. In turn, the second half of the fourteenth century saw the emergence of the Perpendicular style, which lasted until the Reformation. This style is named from its emphasis on strong vertical lines, especially in window tracery, and the flattening of arches towards a more rectangular form. The only cathedral where a complete rebuilding of that kind was planned was Bath, where the work was begun in 1499 by the bishop, Oliver King (Fig. 36, p. 96). It was still not finished when the foundation was dissolved in 1539.[34] On the whole, cathedral building after 1300 was confined to parts of the church, along with additions in the form of a Lady chapel, chantry chapels, chapter house, and cloisters.

Exeter is a good example not only of the Decorated style but of a late-medieval English cathedral and its functions. It survives largely in its rebuilt form and its construction is exceptionally well recorded through the survival of the fabric accounts which detail the income and expenditure involved. Together with other archives, they make it possible not only to chart and date the work and its phases but to envisage the worship, saint cults, and images within the completed church. The rebuilding took from the 1270s to the 1340s. It retained the lower walls of the Norman nave and kept the two unusual Norman side-towers, but otherwise modernised the original work and extended it eastwards. The plan was a smaller version of Salisbury's (Fig. 30, p. 72). There was an aisled nave and a crossing. The towers on either side of the crossing, which had previously housed distinct chapels on the ground floor, were opened up to the interior, given large windows, and turned into transepts. The choir was lengthened and separated from the nave, as before, with a solid stone pulpitum, and from the adjoining choir aisles with open-work screens. Double chapels were built halfway along these aisles, repeating the transepts on a smaller scale, and beyond the high altar were a retrochoir, a large Lady chapel, and two smaller ones.[35]

The decoration of the building was elaborate. The windows were filled with stone tracery in several flowing designs. There was a great deal of fine carving on the corbels of the arching and the bosses of the vaults, with images of foliage, animals, angels, saints, and even the martyrdom of Thomas Becket (Fig. 24, p. 53). The interior was designed for more complex worship than before. Twenty altars in sixteen chapels were provided for the vicars choral and chantry priests to say daily masses, as well as two singing galleries (one interior, one exterior) and plenty of room for processions. There were numerous free-standing images of saints: at least one beside each altar, three at the high altar, and others without altars. The cathedral was finished just before the Black Death, and soon became too large for the depleted number of clergy employed thereafter. One chapel was turned into a Church court and two into vestries. Later still, in the early sixteenth century, finances improved, more clergy could be paid, and three more chapels were added for them to use.

The Exeter fabric accounts allow us to see how the rebuilding of one cathedral was financed and carried out.[36] Money for the purpose came from three sources: the bishop, the dean and chapter, and the clergy and laity of the diocese. At some point, perhaps in 1298, the bishop agreed with the dean and chapter that they would pay £62 9s. 4d. every year, charged on their stipends, and he would provide twice as much, £124 18s. 8d., making £187 8s. This arrangement lasted until the death of Bishop Stapledon in 1326 (Fig. 31, p. 75), after which the bishops were (or claimed to be) poorer and contributed less, but by then most of the building was finished. Once, in 1312, the bishop levied a tax on the diocesan clergy, which produced £90. The rest of the money was contributed voluntarily, from a large donation of £66 13s. 4d. by the earl of Devon down to the pennies

of humble people. Two collection boxes stood in the cathedral to receive contributions, and fund-raising was done in the parishes by means of indulgences. The cathedral paid for the writing of hundreds of copies of these, which were sent out to the parish clergy and announced to their parishioners. The indulgences gave people the opportunity to do the penances imposed on them by their confessors through payments to the cathedral instead of, say, through prayer, fasting, or pilgrimage. This device brought in over £25 a year from 1324 onwards.

These sources produced a predictable income against which to set the expenses. Two men were in charge of the rebuilding. The warden or clerk of the works, a lesser cathedral cleric, handled money and kept records, while the master mason acted as architect and head of the work force. The chief master mason of the rebuilding was Thomas of Witney (1316–42), a well-known expert who was involved with projects at Oxford, Wells, and Winchester. The work force constantly changed in trades and numbers depending on what was needed, and included masons, carpenters, glaziers, smiths, roofers, and decorators of various kinds. The accounts list their names and their wages, week by week. About thirty different men were employed in the course of the year, and from thirteen to twenty-three in any one week. Materials for the rebuilding came from many sources including fourteen known quarries, chiefly in Devon, as

31. The tomb of Walter Stapledon, bishop of Exeter (died 1326), a generous donor to the rebuilding of his cathedral. He lies in a place of honour, north of the high altar.

well as marble from Purbeck and stone from Caen (Normandy) for especially fine work. Timber was needed for scaffolding and for the roof beams above the stone vaulting, iron for fitments, lead for roofing and water pipes, glass for windows, and gold, silver, and colours for decorations. Some of these materials were bought from a fair in Somerset, others from as far away as Boston and Derbyshire, and much of the stone was carried by ship to the nearest port and thence by horse and cart. The enterprise was immensely diverse in its materials, personnel, and geographical links.

The Features and Usage of Buildings

At this point let us take stock and consider how cathedrals had evolved by the fourteenth and fifteenth centuries in terms of what their buildings provided and were used for. The church itself, of course, remained the centre of spiritual life. But a notable disappearance after 1200 was the crypt, unless it already existed. The last crypts to be built lay underneath the Lady chapel of Hereford (made in about 1220–40), and at St Paul's, where the older crypt was enlarged in about 1259 to provide a Jesus chapel. At Canterbury, Becket's tomb was moved from the crypt to the east end in 1220, but the crypt remained in use and was extended in the fourteenth century to include two chantry chapels for the Black Prince and his wife Joan of Kent.[37] Saints' shrines and notable burials of bishops and the nobility were now more often placed above ground in the church, which was one of the motives for lengthening buildings eastwards.

The ground floors of cathedrals continued to include large numbers of chapels or, in some cases, spaces for altars. These had existed back to Anglo-Saxon times, but there were now more of them. They had two purposes. One was to honour one or more major religious cults: Mary, Thomas Becket, the apostles, Katherine, Margaret, and later Anne and the Name of Jesus were especially popular, and their images stood by the altars. The other was to house the chantries whose priests would pray for their founders. The belief in transubstantiation – that the consecrated bread and wine of the mass became the physical body and blood of Christ – meant that chapels and altars had to be screened off from the public to provide a holy space for Christ to appear. Chapels usually had stone screens and other altar places screens of wood or metal, all with lockable doors, so that the priest and clerk who said mass were secluded while onlookers watched through railings or windows.[38]

The largest chapel in a late-medieval cathedral was the Lady chapel, and this was new. There had always been devotion to the Virgin Mary. Her statue stood at the south end of every high altar by the thirteenth century, and there was often an altar in her honour elsewhere in a cathedral. In the twelfth century, however, the wish developed to have an exclusive chapel in which to honour her with distinctive worship. This wish sometimes preceded the existence of a special place for the purpose. The Lady chapel of Canterbury, which was instituted during that century, was based at first in the two eastern bays of the north aisle of the nave.[39] Exeter's, in existence by 1237, may have been contrived beneath the south tower.[40] At Durham the Galilee chapel at the west end of the cathedral was built and dedicated to her in the 1170s, but this had other functions including a place for women to pray, and it came to include the tomb of Bede, a chantry, and a Church court.[41] Even at Salisbury, the chapel that came to be used as a Lady chapel was dedicated to the Trinity not to Mary.

The classic Lady chapel of the later Middle Ages emerged in the thirteenth century, and nearly all cathedrals had one down to the Reformation. It usually lay at the east end of the church, beyond the high altar, although Ely's was an almost free-standing building north of the choir and Canterbury's was on a rather modest scale in the same location, but Canterbury had an additional chapel of the Virgin in its crypt. Lady chapels were sometimes rectangular and sometimes polygonal, but always ambitiously decorated. They were second only to the choir in the importance of their daily worship, because they housed a series of daily services in the Virgin's honour, which will be covered presently.

Another typical building of the later Middle Ages was a chapter house for meetings. This was a normal feature of monastic cathedrals and monasteries by at least the twelfth century, and the secular cathedrals copied it by the thirteenth at latest, which is when most of their surviving chapter houses seem to have originated. These were located at the side of the cathedral, either the north or the south, and joined to it by a passage from a transept or from a cloister. Some were rectangular, but it was stylish to design them in a more intricate shape. Worcester's was round while St Paul's, Salisbury's, and York's were regular octagons, Lichfield's an elongated octagon, and Hereford's and Lincoln's decagons. All were orientated to the east. This was because the chapter house, like the choir, was partly used for prayer, and so that the prior or dean, as head of the chapter, could sit at the eastern end representing Christ. As their shapes suggest, these were meant to be grand buildings. They proclaimed the fact that the chapter of canons or monks was sovereign over the cathedral and its affairs, except on the rare occasions of the bishop's visitations (Fig. 32, p. 78).

The last new feature of late-medieval cathedrals was the building of elaborate cloisters.[42] Monasteries had long possessed them because their domestic buildings needed to be close to the church. It was convenient to arrange the buildings in a quadrangle with cloisters running around its interior to provide a covered walk from one place to another. Cloisters had practical uses too as places to wash, for monks to study, and (at least at Durham) for teaching the novices. The earliest secular cathedral to have one seems to have been Wells in the late eleventh century where Bishop Giso was trying to get his clergy to live together like monks.[43] Salisbury (Old Sarum) had another by the late twelfth century, built by Bishops Roger or Jocelyn to link their palace to the church.[44] Most cathedrals of this kind, however, were slow to acquire them because their clergy lived in separate buildings. Even when new Salisbury was planned in the early thirteenth century, no cloisters were thought of. Later it was decided to have them, and

32. The chapter house of York Minster, the embodiment of the cathedral chapter's independence and magnificence.

they were added in about the 1270s at a slight distance since they were not part of the original scheme. These and the other secular cathedral cloisters belong to the later Middle Ages, and they were built everywhere except for Lichfield and York. They usually led nowhere unless the chapter house was sited next to them, but they served as processional ways, lengthening the route that the clergy could take round the church. In some places a library was built in or off them. Their real function, one feels, was to show that secular cathedrals were as magnificent as monastic ones. And unlike the latter's, the secular cloisters were open to the public and became popular places for people to stroll about.

Compared with the cathedrals of earlier times, those of the later Middle Ages were rich in burial monuments.[45] Bishops were the primary people to be commemorated in this way. By the thirteenth century, they favoured tombs with shallow sculpted effigies, often placed in a recess within a wall of the church. These effigies grew in grandeur to take the form of life-sized images lying on table tombs: sometimes in a recess, sometimes free-standing. Bishops had the right to be buried in the cathedral choir, although as time went on the space there was used up and they were obliged to lie elsewhere in a chapel or aisle. In some cathedrals deans and dignitaries were also allowed raised tombs, but in others not. Canons were generally restricted to flat ledger-stones in the nave, ambulatories, or chapels of the cathedral, and vicars and chantry priests were likely to be relegated even further to similar stones or unmarked graves in the cloisters or the open 'cloister garth' that they surrounded.

At one time kings and queens expected to be buried in cathedrals. In later Anglo-Saxon times Winchester was the mausoleum for the royal house of Wessex, as well as for the Danish kings Cnut and Harthacnut. An exception, Æthelred the Unready, was buried in St Paul's, where his tomb remained until the Great Fire of 1666. After the Conquest three of the Norman and Angevin kings chose burial in France, but two found their way into English cathedrals: William Rufus, who was taken to Winchester, and John, who opted for Worcester. John's son Henry III then developed Westminster Abbey to be the private church of the royal family, and he and most of his successors were buried there. The only important members of the royal family to choose cathedral burials thereafter were the Black Prince in 1376, Henry IV in 1413, and their wives: all in Canterbury. Here the attraction seems to have been to lie near the shrine of St Thomas. One might add two royal princes, William of Hatfield and Arthur Tudor, who were buried at York and Worcester simply because they died nearby.[46]

Burials of noblemen, knights, and their ladies took place in cathedrals, but were not common. Such people were often patrons of monasteries, where they had more power to choose a tomb in a prominent position and could count on monks saying prayers for their souls. There were exceptions, however, both male and female. John of Gaunt lay in St Paul's with his first wife Blanche, while his third wife Katherine Swynford went to Lincoln with her daughter the countess of Westmorland. Hereford had another countess, Joan de Bohun, and Ely an earl of Worcester. Knights occur more frequently, and they and the nobility were often allowed sculpted effigies like bishops or monumental brasses on the floor. Lesser lay people are occasionally found, such as the richer inhabitants of the nearby city or relatives of canons, but they too were rather few in number. The fraught relationship between some cathedrals and their cities tended to lead wealthy citizens to seek tombs in local friaries or parish churches, where they and their donations were warmly welcomed.

One further element of cathedral space should be considered: the Close, the open and usually grassy area around the building (Fig. 37, p. 99). This was a frontier zone between the church and the city, and like many such zones its terrain was disputed.[47] On the one hand it was a public area, crossed by people walking to the church, grazed by visitors' horses, and trampled by young people playing games. The grass was often scarred by use and disfigured by rubbish. On the other it was consecrated ground used for burials or for outdoor worship of various kinds. One common feature was a tall stone cross on steps, known as the 'palm cross' and used in the service of Palm Sunday, the Sunday before Easter. Where there were burials – at Exeter, Norwich, St Paul's, and Worcester – a charnel chapel was built in which mass was said for the dead and where the bones unearthed while digging graves were deposited in a charnel house under the chapel.[48] A third activity was preaching from an outdoor pulpit. Exeter had one attached to its charnel chapel, but the outstanding place for such preaching was St Paul's where it was done near the palm cross. Famous preachers and controversial subjects, especially at and after the Reformation, attracted huge crowds, and a covered external pulpit was eventually built for the preacher with nearby galleries for important spectators (Fig. 51, p. 144).[49]

Cathedral Worship

When we reach the fourteenth century, it becomes easier to reconstruct the format of cathedral worship, especially in the secular cathedrals. This is due to the increasing survival of the texts in which worship – the liturgy – was presented.[50] Medieval worship was not as uniform as it became at the Reformation. It was broadly similar in its pattern in all churches, but there were differences between the practices of the secular cathedrals and the various orders of monks and friars. The secular cathedrals were influential in setting standards for worship in parish churches. This came about for three reasons. They had high standing in the nine dioceses where they existed. Many of their vicars, chantry priests, clerks, and choristers became parish clergy, and their worship was more suitable for parish churches to follow than was the worship of the religious orders. A few cathedrals were particularly successful in spreading their 'use' or pattern of worship in their neighbourhoods: Bangor in Wales, Hereford and Lincoln in their dioceses, and York in the north of England. The most influential use of all was that of Salisbury Cathedral: the 'Use of Sarum' as it is known. This came to be widely followed in cathedrals and churches in southern England, and in 1543, towards the end of its history, its breviary containing the daily services in the choir was prescribed for the whole of the country.[51]

The services of the later Middle Ages followed traditional structures, but they were affected by changes in worship that evolved from the thirteenth to the fifteenth centuries. One was the increasing veneration of the mass which caused the proliferation of altars and chapels in cathedrals and the performance of daily masses within them. Another was the cult of the Virgin Mary expressed in the foundation of the Lady chapels. Here several clergy performed a daily cycle of services in her honour, including short versions of those said in the choir (the 'hours of the Virgin') with a dedicated Lady mass in the morning and an antiphon or anthem in the afternoon.[52] A third was the growing employment of polyphony in churches: music sung in harmony in several parts. This was used in the choirs of secular cathedrals on Sundays and festival days, and regularly, on a daily basis, in both secular and monastic establishments for the mass and anthem of the Virgin in the Lady chapel. By the fifteenth century, polyphony was written down, being known in this form as 'pricksong'. At first it was composed within two octaves for singing by a group of four men taking three or four parts in alto and tenor range. Later, during the 1450s, the octaves were extended to three and the number of parts increased to include boy trebles and adult basses. The number of singers rose from a small group to a large chorus of as many as two dozen.[53]

The leading role in the development of polyphony in the fifteenth century was taken by the private chapel of the monarch (the Chapel Royal) and those of the great nobility and higher clergy. They could afford to recruit composers and singers – clergy, lay clerks, and choristers – without the restraints of traditional customs and statutes. The cathedrals copied the chapels in this respect but had some problems in doing so. Because most of their daily worship was sung with fairly simple plainsong in the choir, it had not been usual to require monks or vicars choral to have more than basic singing abilities. By about 1450, however, cathedrals were making efforts to overcome this problem.[54] They appointed a new officer with the title of 'instructor of the choristers', 'master of the boys', or 'clerk of the [Lady] chapel' to compose polyphony, organise the Lady mass at which it was sung, and teach the singers. Men of this kind included Leonel Power of Canterbury (d. 1445), William Horwood (d. 1484) of Lincoln, and John Redford of St Paul's (d. 1547), some of whose works survive and who are among the first recorded cathedral composers.[55] More attention was given to finding at least some vicars choral and monks who could sing polyphony, and to supplementing the monks with lay singers if that was necessary. At Salisbury, for example, an original force of fifty-two vicars was reduced to more like thirty with greater skills, including four lay vicars chosen particularly for their vocal and musical talents. Similar changes happened elsewhere.

At the same time the organ, long present in cathedrals and major churches, came to be used as a musical instrument of greater refinement than before. One organ was often placed above the pulpitum and another in the Lady chapel. Its principal player was the musical instructor mentioned above, and he was expected to teach the art to his colleagues: boys and adults. The organist's role was not to accompany the singing, whether plainsong or polyphony, but to fill gaps in the sung service with improvisation on the appropriate chant (especially the offertory at high mass). He also variegated the performance of such repetitive and lengthy items of plainsong as the hymns and the Te Deum in the daily services, by substituting for the singers with improvisation on the chant at alternate verses. The organ was also played to mark and celebrate the formal entry of visiting dignitaries.

The wish for a wide range of voices meant that boys became more important in producing cathedral music. The choristers of the secular cathedrals began to receive training in polyphony as well as plainsong: it is significant that the new organiser of polyphony was often referred to as their instructor. In some places their numbers were increased to make their contribution more effective.[56] They began to acquire their modern function as an essential part of the cathedral's singing resources rather than the learners and assistants that they had previously been. The monastic cathedrals followed suit with some of their almonry boys, and a group of six or more of these would be given daily training in song alongside their other studies and duties. Almonry boys, however, did less singing than their counterparts in a secular cathedral. Their work was limited to the Lady mass in the morning and the anthem to the Virgin in the afternoon, and they were not usually referred to as choristers.[57]

The following description of a liturgical day reflects the changes of the later Middle Ages. It is based on the records of one secular cathedral, Exeter; the others would have done much the same but each with some variations.[58] There were three kinds of day: weekdays (usually Monday to Saturday afternoon), Sunday (beginning on Saturday afternoon), and holy days – the latter being ranked in importance and celebrated according to their rank. The timetable varied from summer to winter, the boundaries between them falling at Easter and Michaelmas (29 September) or All Saints' Day (1 November). Certain seasons – notably Advent, Christmas, Lent, and Easter – had their own observances, and so did vigils and fasting days which preceded the major holy days. The services on all days fell into three distinct blocks: one in the night-time, one from dawn to mid-morning, and one in the afternoon – or evening as it was known. The principal place of performance was the choir where the regular daily services took place, complemented by the Lady chapel with its own worship and the masses said there and at other chapels and altars within the church. Material was also said and sung in processions. These took place around the church (sometimes including the cloisters), and on certain days in spring they went outside the cathedral: circling its precincts or going through the neighbouring city.

The first block of observances consisted of two services: matins and lauds. These began at midnight in the choir, requiring the clergy to rise and dress for work after only a few hours of rest, although canons could depute the task to their vicars. During the eight weeks after Easter, matins was postponed until the end of the night so as to celebrate the dawn and allow a longer time of sleep beforehand. It was the lengthiest of the daily services (especially on festival days), the most important except for high mass, and took an hour or more to complete. The material consisted of psalms, hymns, and prayers, as did all the daily services, with the addition of lessons from the Bible or saints' Lives: three on ordinary days and nine on festivals. Matins was immediately followed by lauds, the second of the major daily services, and by the matins and lauds of Our Lady: short services in praise of the Virgin Mary. Together these four night services formed a block of devotions lasting up to two hours.

When they were over, some clergy went back to bed. Not everybody did so, however, at least not for long. At dawn the gates of the Close would be opened, followed by a cathedral door for lay people to enter. An early 'morrow mass' would then be celebrated at one of the lesser altars, perhaps in the nave so that pious folk could attend it before starting work. After this mass the second round of services began, lasting from six until ten o'clock. Not all the clergy were involved in all of them since there was some separation to do different things. At about six, one group of clergy would go to the Lady chapel to perform the short matins, lauds, and other 'hours' of Our Lady. This was followed later by the polyphonic Lady mass which lasted for an hour. From six o'clock onwards, the chantry priests each said their masses at the side altars, the last of these being fixed at ten o'clock. Also during this time or a little later, prime, the first of the daytime choral services, took place in the choir and lasted for about half an hour.

When prime was over, the clergy left the choir in procession and went to the chapter house for the chapter meeting. At this point canons were usually present as well. The meeting was partly a short service of prayers and partly a briefing for the following day. Since the liturgy varied so much with Sundays, great festivals, saints' days, vigils, and fasting days, everyone needed to be informed of what was to happen next. A chorister would read from the 'martyrology', which listed the saints throughout the year and also the names of the dead who were to be commemorated on the anniversary of their deaths. The rota of duties for the following day was announced, and on Saturdays the clergy were assigned their roles for the coming week. After this the dean and canons stayed to deal with chapter business. Errant members of the minor clergy might be called up at this point for warnings or penalties about their attendance or behaviour inside or outside church.

At about eight o'clock, most of the clergy gathered again in the choir for the rest of the morning services: terce (or undern), sext, none, and the high mass. The first three of these were short devotions made up mainly of psalms, and there was some variation in the arrangements for saying them. From autumn to spring the order was terce, sext, high mass, and none, all sung in turn in the choir. On Sundays and festivals, however, there was a procession of the clergy round the church between terce and sext, and if a sermon was preached, this too was placed between the procession and sext. The high mass was so called because it was the chief mass of the day, celebrated at the high altar with the greatest ceremony and with the largest number of clergy present. A priest, deacon, and subdeacon were appointed from the clergy in turn, wearing mass vestments coloured according to the season of the year instead of choir garments. On most days from autumn till spring, the morning services ended with none at about ten o'clock, but on fasting days (including Lent) they were extended. None was then said before high mass, and vespers was moved from the afternoon to follow high mass, which lengthened the services until eleven.

Morning service over, it was time for dinner. This was well in advance of modern custom, but it was common to dine at eleven o'clock or soon afterwards, reflecting the earlier start to the day. The meal was followed by a free period stretching into the first part of the afternoon. Then at about two or three o'clock the last block of services took place in the choir. First came two sets of prayers for the dead (*Placebo* and *Dirige*); next vespers (also known as evensong), a long service of about an hour, replaced in Lent by a service called 'collation'; then the shorter vespers of Our Lady; and finally compline. The afternoon sequence of services lasted for about two hours. Afterwards the minor clergy appointed to serve in the Lady chapel went there to say a final short round of services. This consisted of the vespers and compline of Our Lady and the anthem in her honour, sung at an image of her in the chapel or elsewhere.[59]

The clergy's work was now complete and they could go home to their suppers at about four or five o'clock. The gates of the Close would stay open for a few hours longer until eight or nine in the evening, by which time the clergy would go to bed for their first sleep until they were roused by the matins bell and the start of another day. How many hours had they spent in church? On a normal day the adult minor clergy – the vicars, chantry priests, and secondaries – might be there for seven or eight hours: the most on major festivals. The choristers worked for almost as long, partly in choir and partly in school. Less was expected of the canons, whose attendance may often have been limited to high mass and vespers. Nevertheless, as clergy they were still expected to say the daily round of services in private, and they were also responsible for supervising the running of the cathedral and its affairs.

The Setting of Worship

The worship, of course, cannot be divorced from the setting. It took place in a magnificent and highly decorated building. It used, and had done since the seventh century, the most costly materials that could be obtained. Altars were clothed in rich fabrics. Clergy, or at least the dignitaries and canons, wore magnificent vestments for mass or processions. Relics were enshrined in gold and crystal; chalices of gold or silver-gilt were used at mass. Inventories list hundreds of precious items. Lincoln, for example, possessed 'a great image of Our Lady sitting in a chair, silver and gilt . . . having upon her head a crown of silver and gilt set with stones and pearls and one bee [torque] with stones and pearls around her neck'. On the high altar stood two huge gold candlesticks 'embattled and buttressed like a castle', given by John of Gaunt. The Gospel of Matthew was read from a text 'covered with a plate of silver and gilt, having an image of [Christ in Majesty] with the four evangelists and four angels about the image'. Processions were led by 'a great processional cross of silver gilt' displaying 'a crucifix with Mary and John standing in the middle, with fleurs-de-lys at each end and the four evangelists engraved on it'. There were reliquaries containing bones of saints, thuribles for incense, bowls, cruets, and copes, and whole chests of vestments: red, blue, green, and black, often embroidered with gold or set with pearls.[60]

A service was a musical performance with singers and organs, a poetry recital based on psalms and hymns, and a history lesson read from the Bible or the Lives of the saints. It was a drama, with actors in costume, 'rulers' who acted as prompters, and a chorus, all of whom engaged in dialogue and movement full of symbolic meaning. The choir was a school as well, with the rulers as teachers and the clergy arranged in forms; indeed, about a quarter or a third of the clergy consisted of boys and youths in training. Worship took place in surroundings meant to be beautiful although not always well maintained. Above and beside the worship stood the art of the stonework, sculpted and sometimes painted, and walls adorned in places with paintings of Bible scenes and saints such as may still be seen at Durham and Winchester.[61] Light came in through windows of stained glass with similar scenes, of which some survive at Canterbury, Exeter, and York.[62] All this made it a place of intellectual stimulation. At its best, medieval cathedral worship must have been satisfying to offer and inspiring to watch and to hear.

Equally there could be much tedium in the routine. The hours in church were long and the work repetitive. Choir duties took up most of the day, and when meals and domestic activities were allowed for, there was not much time left over. Festival days, which for the laity were holidays, brought extra tasks for the clergy and absence was seldom allowed. Vicars and clerks would not have been human if they were always devout and well-behaved at services, or did not sometimes shirk their duties in church. In 1330 the bishop of Exeter, John Grandisson, complained that some had 'their bodies in the choir but their hearts in the market-place, or the street, or in bed'. They sang the services negligently and fraudulently, or were guilty of bursts of laughter and insolent behaviour. Worst of all, during matins when there were candles, the clergy at the back of the choir dropped hot wax on the heads of those below.[63]

In 1519 the vicars choral of York were equally critical about worship and their working conditions. They complained that the reredos behind the high altar was full of dust and cobwebs, and so were the walls and pillars. The side altar cloths were so ragged and torn that they would shame an upland village. Many of the white albs worn by the clergy under their vestments were torn as well, and so shrunk with washing that they could hardly be put on. The vestments themselves needed mending and no-one would take responsibility for this. The books in the choir were 'caduke' [corrupted] and so false that the vicars often sang discordantly. The gospel lectern had 'moistered' [rotted] away and fallen down. The vestry door was kept locked in the morning, so that the clergy could not get the bread, wine, and water that they needed for mass. There was a lack of towels in the vestry and the sink that supplied the water was blocked up, so that they had to wash their cruets in a bucket. The sacristans who should have patrolled the church were negligent in their attendance, letting dogs and 'bribers' [vagrants or thieves] into the church, which enabled the dogs to enter the choir itself where they urinated on the hangings.[64] We do not know that matters were always as bad as this but equally, given people's frailties and limitations, services were not always solemn and beautiful. It would be wrong to imagine a universal golden age of worship, even before the Reformation.

Culture and Learning

Cathedrals were centres of culture, both material and intellectual. Deans and resident canons were wealthy and often talented people. They lived in substantial houses that advertised their status with gatehouses, halls, and chapels. They had retinues of servants and their power extended into the countryside through the lands and churches belonging to their posts and benefices. The priors of the cathedral monasteries lived in equally grand surroundings away from their monks.[65] Prior William More of Worcester (1518–36) had a household of twenty-one servants comprising a marshal, chamberlain, six yeomen, seven grooms including a huntsman, and a gardener.[66] Such priors had great influence since they headed institutions with wide estates in their regions.

Thomas Dalby, who died in 1400, is a typical example of a rich cleric of a secular cathedral. He was archdeacon of Richmond supervising a huge territory in Lancashire and Yorkshire, a residentiary canon of York, and the incumbent of several parish churches as well. His house in York contained a hall for his household and a private chamber for himself, kept warm by a fireplace. Here he slept in a curtained bed beneath a coverlet embroidered with green chaplets or one of red displaying grey dragons. Nearby was a wardrobe, meaning a room for keeping clothes, where he could choose a gown of red, blue, or trimmed with fur, or a shorter riding gown for his journeys. Elsewhere he had a chapel, a basement for keeping his linen, a wine cellar, a kitchen, a stable, and doubtless other rooms for his retinue. They included three chaplains, two esquires (men of gentry rank) to attend him, a butler, a driver of his carriage, a porter, a cook, various valets and grooms, and a page. When he died his executors found £802 worth of cash in his possession along with quantities of silver and gilt plate – dishes, bowls, and cups – which they sold to other rich clergy and gentry for a further £300 or so. After a magnificent funeral, he was buried in the cathedral nave under a marble stone inscribed with his coat of arms because he was of noble rank, and a chantry priest was endowed to pray for his soul for ever.[67]

The lesser cathedral clergy lived far more modestly. Nevertheless, cathedral monks were well supported with generous food allowances, servants, medical care, and periods of rest at a rural manor, as well as the use of a good collection of books. The purpose-built lodgings and common halls of the vicars choral and chantry priests allowed them to gather possessions and funds. Robert Lyngham, for example, who died in 1428, was the clerk in charge of the cathedral exchequer at Exeter and the rector of a parish church in the Close. His will refers to several pieces of plate including a coconut cup mounted with gilt and topped by a cover displaying a griffin, two silver cups standing on three lions, a silver bowl with a cover, and another standing cup. His bed had hangings embellished with fleurs-de-lys, and his best clothes included a belt of blue silk bearing a silver image of St Christopher. He owned books as well: a prayer book, a text of canon law, and two of theology.[68]

This leads us to the intellectual life of cathedrals in the later Middle Ages. It differed from that of previous centuries because of the rise of universities: first Oxford, then Cambridge. Both were in existence by about the 1210s. University work was based on logic. Topics were debated and analysed using logical methods, and the topics were wider in scope than in education hitherto. The basic programme of study – the arts course – included grammar, rhetoric, logic, arithmetic, geometry, astronomy, and music, as well as philosophy, political science, and natural science. It took seven years to graduate in these, after which students could spend further years in the higher faculties of medicine, civil (Roman) law, canon (Church) law, or theology. Such long periods of study required personal wealth or backing by a patron. Organisations to provide support for students, in the form of colleges, appeared only slowly and at first catered chiefly for postgraduates rather than the undergraduates of the arts course.

The growth of the universities impacted first upon the secular cathedrals. Most students at universities were in effect secular clergy – clerks, not yet priests – who lived in the world and had personal possessions like cathedral canons and vicars. When they had graduated in arts or in the higher degrees they were skilled and knowledgeable men who had the influence through wealth and patronage to be given cathedral posts. Even if less wealthy, they were desirable employees for noblemen, bishops, and even the Crown. Accordingly, from the thirteenth century onwards deans, dignitaries, and canons were increasingly graduates. For example, all but four of the twenty-one deans of Hereford between 1300 and 1540 appear to have studied at university. Five probably held degrees as masters of arts, two as bachelors of canon and civil law, four as doctors of law, and six as doctors of theology.[69]

These studies could be put to practical use. Canon lawyers could work in the bishop's administration or in the Church courts which were based in all the cathedral cities, while theologians used their knowledge in preaching. A few produced works of pure scholarship. It is not always clear whether this was done while they were at a cathedral or at a university, but at least they deserve the credit for the achievement. Thomas of Chobham (Salisbury) wrote manuals on confession and preaching, Thomas Wilton (St Paul's) works of philosophy and theology, William of Wheatley (Lincoln) commentaries on Boethius, and Thomas Chaundler (Wells) and Robert Fleming (Lincoln) works of literature. St Paul's had a series of notable historians including the Renaissance Italian Polydore Vergil,[70] while Nicholas Hereford (Hereford) was a prominent disciple of John Wycliffe and a probable contributor to the first translations of the Bible into English.[71] Many of their colleagues continued to acquire books and keep up with their studies without creating original works (Fig. 33, p. 88).

The monks of the monastic cathedrals were slower to involve themselves with universities. Their dedication to worship and contemplation did not sit well with the public and argumentative life of Cambridge and Oxford. But as the thirteenth century continued, they found themselves left behind not only by the secular clergy but by the new orders of friars who appeared at this time and who embraced university life with enthusiasm. Very gradually the Benedictine and Augustinian orders to which the monastic cathedrals belonged began to accept that they needed to improve their educational standards. All monks should study grammar, logic, philosophy, and basic theology. Those who prospered should go to university and take degrees in theology, the arts course being deemed too secular.[72] In 1275 Canterbury appointed a lecturer in theology. Its leaders could

33. An initial from St Augustine's work, On the Assumption. *The book's owner, Canon Roger Waltham of St Paul's, watches the Assumption of the Virgin Mary.*

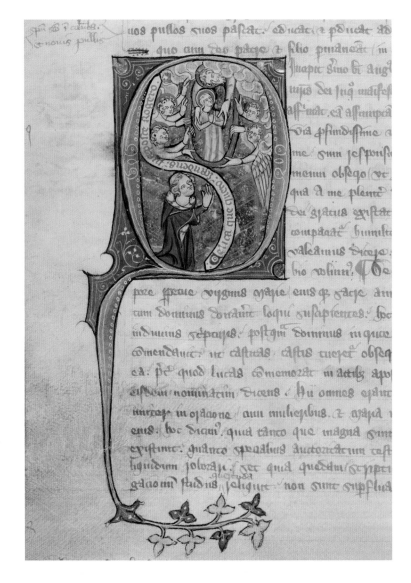

find only a friar for the purpose, and the monastic chronicler grumbled that 'this was unheard of in former times. What will be the result of this lecture and school the future will show, since novelties produce quarrels'.[73]

By 1291 Benedictine monks were beginning to study at Oxford, and in 1298 Gloucester College was established as a place for them to live: it has since become Worcester College. Meanwhile, Durham set up a house for its students in Oxford in the 1280s, which grew into Durham College (now Trinity College), and Canterbury established a hall for four monks in Oxford in 1331. This was eventually endowed as Canterbury College, now part of Christ Church. A third cathedral, Ely, opened a hostel at

Cambridge in the 1320s. Only a few monks even from these cathedrals were at university at any one time, but once they had studied sufficient theology they could return as lecturers in their houses. Both Canterbury and Worcester had monks able to do so from about the 1310s. By the fourteenth century, therefore, the life of a monk was more scholarly than it had been in the twelfth, and there continued to be individual monks who followed other interests. John Stone of Canterbury, John Washington of Durham, and Thomas Rudbourne of Winchester compiled histories of their houses.[74] Canterbury was also the home of Peter of Ickham, who composed a national history, Thomas Chillenden who wrote on canon law, and William Selling, a pioneer scholar of Greek in the early Renaissance.[75]

Meanwhile the books were piling up. At first monasteries had been centres of book production, at least for their own use, but by the thirteenth century the national demand was so great that it began to move into the hands of professional writers or scriveners in towns, especially London. There one could buy a popular title 'off the shelf' or pay for one to be written. As religious houses increased their stock, this had to be kept in a cupboard, book room, or treasury. Volumes that were frequently used

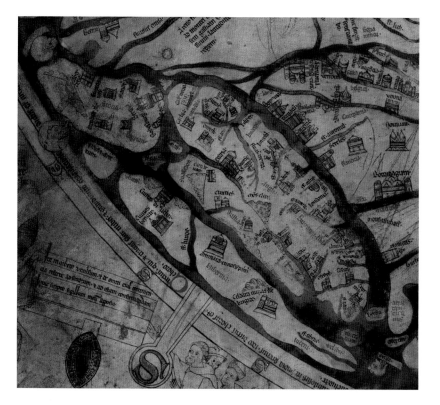

34. A medieval cathedral treasure: the Hereford Mappa Mundi, a diagram explaining the geography and history of the world and here showing the British Isles.

might be chained in the choir of the church or in the cloister. Eventually, in the fourteenth century, the modern library appeared in the form of a large room in which books could be both kept and studied.[76] This arrangement was adopted at most cathedrals in the early fifteenth century. The room would be long and narrow with desks at intervals placed at right angles to the outer walls, with shelves for books above or below the desks and sometimes both. At Salisbury and Wells the library was above the cloister; at Exeter it was in the north walk of the cloister, shut off by doors. Sometimes the books were chained to restrict their use to the nearest desk, and sometimes they were unchained. Exeter had 327 volumes in its library in 1506, and there were 293 at Canterbury two years later.[77] These were not libraries for public access, however. They had locks and a designated keeper, and may even have been reserved for canons or senior monks rather than for the whole community.

Cathedrals and the Public

Cathedrals might insist on their independence from local authorities, religious or secular. They might seclude themselves behind their walls and gates, but they wished to relate to lay people as long as they could choose the terms to do so. They advertised their presence with their grand west fronts, high roofs, and lofty towers. Nearly every cathedral had a spire on one or more of its towers, far more than have them today, and some like Chichester, Salisbury, and Worcester had an additional detached tower with a spire. Towers not only impressed passers-by but held clusters of bells whose ringing announced the times of services. These (with other church bells) allowed people to measure the course of the day. Chaucer's *Canterbury Tales* refers to its stages by the sequence of church services: matins, prime, and evensong. By the fourteenth century at the latest, cathedrals had clocks: at first marking time with bells rather than hands. This developed a more precise notion of clock time which became widely understood in the fifteenth century, so that cathedrals helped to form the modern habit of living the day by the twenty-four hours.

Many local people noticed and valued their cathedrals. In several places craftsmen or those devoted to particular religious cults formed guilds, which held their worship in a cathedral chapel or went in procession to the cathedral once a year. Six such guilds are known at Norwich and nine at St Paul's.[78] In London it is clear that the cathedral had a strong visual impact on those who saw it. It featured on the city's common seal. One fourteenth-century visitor drew a picture of its outline on a wall in the church of Ashwell (Herts.), where it may still be seen. Map-makers and artists of Tudor and Stuart London gave it a prominent place, emphasising the height of its spire.[79] Chroniclers in the city refer to it frequently: a lightning strike on the spire, the periodic repairs to the weathercock (evidently fascinating to watch), the royal marriages and funerals inside, and the sermons at Paul's Cross.[80] Its length and height were used as a yardstick against which to measure other buildings or geographical features. It even featured in proverbs: 'as old, or as well known, or as never finished, as Paul's'.[81]

All cathedrals encouraged visitors, if well behaved, in order to maintain their status and, if possible, to gain prayers and money. The secular cathedrals seem to have been liberal in this respect; the monastic cathedrals may have been less so because of monks' seclusion. Durham admitted women only to the Lady chapel known as the Galilee by the cathedral entrance and within a line traced at the very west end of the nave, although one wonders if that was enforced for royalty and nobility.[82] The cycle of services during the day, beginning with the 'morrow mass' and ending in the afternoon, allowed leisured people to enter to pray in the church and listen to the services from outside the choir, although only nobility, gentry, or leading citizens would be allowed in the choir itself. The masses at the side altars were likely to have their own devotees: one could watch one's favourite priest and meet one's friends at the time one preferred. For women, church worship was an acceptable way of leaving home and mixing with other people. Then there were children: babies and toddlers with their mothers, sick children brought to pray before a shrine or an image, and older ones in search of amusement and sometimes creating a nuisance.[83]

The shrines of saints remained attractive to visitors, and cathedrals went on acquiring them during the later Middle Ages. This was the case both in places that had no shrines and in those that did and, as in the twelfth century, the shrine was often that of a bishop regarded as godly and charitable (Fig. 35, p. 92). Men of this kind included Richard Wych at Chichester, Thomas Cantilupe at Hereford, Robert Grosseteste at Lincoln, and there were several others.[84] All drew local devotees to their tombs but none became a major national figure. This was partly because the popes now insisted on approving saints, which involved a long and tortuous process. Only Richard Wych and Thomas Cantilupe got through it, together with Osmund of Salisbury who was canonised in 1457, long after his death and at a cost of over £700. The rest were venerated without being canonised. Another factor was a gradual shift in people's devotion from relics of saints to images of Christ and the Virgin Mary. These were to be found in every church; some of them gained reputations for answering prayers, and the cathedral saints competed in an ever more crowded market.

Cathedral clergy went in processions around their cities on seven days of the year, between Palm Sunday in the spring and the feast of Corpus Christi in midsummer, followed by other local clergy and lay people. Some cathedrals had jollifications in their Closes at Midsummer, as Exeter did. There 'ridings' took place by the canons' servants, a bonfire was lit, and once a play is mentioned.[85] As well as those who came to cathedrals for worship, there were visitors in search of social pleasure. The nave of St Paul's was a well-known place for London citizens to walk and do business, and the naves and cloisters of other cathedrals probably served the same purpose. At Exeter the dean and chapter shut the cloisters in the 1440s because of damage caused by people playing at 'the top, queke, penny

35. Pilgrims venerating the relics of St William in York Minster, under the supervision of a member of the clergy.

prick, and worst [of all] at tennis'. 'Queke' was a board game while tops were merely noisy, but penny prick involved shooting arrows at a penny and tennis (then a game like modern fives) meant hitting balls against walls and buttresses, endangering windows and stonework. Later, in about 1490, we hear of two Yorkist conspirators meeting in the Exeter cloisters, one grasping the other by the thumb as a prearranged signal.[86]

Two people of this period have left records of their visits to cathedrals: the first of a series of travellers whom we shall meet. Both came from the same merchant class but they could hardly have been more different. Margery Kempe (c.1370–c.1440) was a wealthy married woman of King's Lynn. Passionately devout and restless, she spent much of her later life on pilgrimage, causing uproar with hysterical outbursts of crying when she was spiritually aroused. Her journeys took her to at least three cathedrals (Canterbury, Norwich, and York) and probably to three others (Ely, Lincoln, and St Paul's). At Norwich she made offerings to the Trinity before and after going to Jerusalem; here she was known and seems not to have triggered much comment. The opposite was true at Canterbury and York. At the first, on pilgrimage with her husband, she spent a whole day weeping in the cathedral, apparently noisily and to the annoyance of monks, priests, and lay onlookers. Her husband withdrew in shame and a crowd pursued her out of the building, shouting 'Thou shalt be burnt, false Lollard!' At York which she visited twice on pilgrimage to St William, she received communion on Sunday (a very unusual practice) which led to further 'boisterous sobbing'. Here views about her differed. One canon and a chantry priest were supportive. Others thought her irritating at best and heretical at worst. She was summoned to the chapter house, examined, sent to the archbishop, and ordered out of the diocese. It all made good copy for her autobiography: a record of heavenly visions received and earthly troubles patiently endured.[87]

Her fellow visitor was quite the opposite: methodical and rational. This was William Worcester (1415–c.1480), Bristol born and latterly living in Norwich. A former secretary to a knight, he was a hyperactive man with multifarious interests in history, geography, architecture, genealogy, and much else. In 1478–80, after retiring from work, he made three journeys across southern England, talking with people and looking at buildings. Passing through Exeter, Norwich, and Salisbury, he visited each cathedral and followed his custom of measuring its length and breadth, for reasons that are unclear. At Exeter he was shown round by a minor official and saw the cloister, the chapter house, and the shrine of Edmund Lacy. He admired the windows of the nave and the varied shapes of their lights. At Norwich he made detailed notes on the cloister and reminded himself to ask about the battering of the cathedral spire.[88] His note-taking was probably unusual, but he reminds us that many people must have visited cathedrals from curiosity as well as from piety like Margery.

More widely, there was a sense of the cathedral as the mother church of the diocese. It was where new bishops were enthroned and where they or their suffragans carried out many of the ordinations of clergy that took place four times a year, although these were sometimes held in other places. Its lands and churches extended its influence widely. In 1216 and periodically afterwards, copies of *Magna Carta* were sent to cathedrals for keeping and could presumably be consulted by important people. It was common for every household in a diocese to pay a farthing to their cathedral at Pentecost (Whit Sunday) for maintaining its fabric. At Chichester some parishes came to the cathedral in procession on Whit Monday, bringing the money and receiving the chrism and holy oil required for baptisms and anointing the sick.[89] It was also accepted practice for those who made wills to bequeath a token sum 'to the mother church of the diocese'. Some did so even in Buckinghamshire: a hundred miles away from their cathedral in Lincoln.[90] People would also respond to appeals on behalf of cathedral buildings, as we saw at Exeter.[91]

Cathedrals, then, were within people's consciousness, although it must be stressed again that they were not the only large and famous churches and had to compete for attention with the great monasteries. In the early sixteenth century several abbeys like Glastonbury, St Albans, and Westminster had larger incomes than the lesser cathedrals, buildings as splendid, and just as many relics, jewels, vestments, and books. Some of their abbots sat in Parliament alongside the bishops. So those who lived in the fourteenth or fifteenth centuries would not altogether have shared our concept of a cathedral as a very special church; for them it was one out of many great churches. As we have seen, the word 'cathedral' was not yet used in everyday speech.[92] People talked of 'Paul's' in London, 'Peter's' in Exeter, 'Andrew's' in Wells, or 'the minster' in Lincoln and York.

There were those, too, like city leaders who resented cathedral privileges. Lawless folk were happy to support them in a fight about the matter, to assault individual clergy, or to burgle cathedral property. Ely lost a large golden cross to thieves in 1324, although it was retrieved, and rings and jewels from a shrine in 1385.[93] At Exeter the pyx or box containing a consecrated wafer – the holiest object in the church – was stolen from above the high altar itself.[94] By the end of the fourteenth century we encounter people who disliked cathedrals for more cerebral reasons. Even Chaucer had a dig at clergy who preferred taking posts as chantry priests at St Paul's to doing God's work in the parishes.[95] More trenchant than him were the Lollards, the followers of John Wycliffe, who emerged in the 1380s and survived until the Reformation despite harassment and executions.[96] They disliked magnificent church buildings, elaborate worship, shrines, and relics, and must have linked cathedrals with all these.

In 1431 there was actually a riot at Salisbury Cathedral involving men with Lollard sympathies. The subsequent indictment of the participants claimed that they planned to destroy the building, its relics, and its ornaments as a prelude to a general religious uprising.[97] The leader of the riot was executed and the Lollards had little ability to affect the public understanding of cathedrals, but they were the forerunners of more powerful critics who would emerge in the middle of the sixteenth century.

Chapter
— 5 —

The Reformation
1530–1559

When Henry VIII became king in 1509, cathedrals were still at the height of their prosperity. No one could have foreseen the changes that would affect them during the next fifty years. Their churches were splendid and were still being added to in small ways like the erection of chantries. Inside they still fulfilled the complex round of services in the choir, with numerous masses there and at side altars in their chapels. Polyphony was performed in the choirs of the secular cathedrals on Sundays and festivals, and in all the foundations daily in their Lady chapels. There were still venerated shrines and collections of relics. Although no new saints had emerged anywhere since the late fifteenth century, there were often widely visited images of Christ, the Virgin, and other popular figures. Cathedral precincts were still guarded by gates (Fig. 37, p. 99), and their sub-communities of vicars choral, chantry priests, and choristers or almonry boys nearly always enjoyed their own accommodation and often their meals in common.

Alongside these apparent continuities, inconspicuous changes were in train that foreshadowed the Reformation. That event was a breach with the past but also grew out of it. One of the changes was a greater respect for monarchy than had been so before. There are signs of this in cathedrals in the royal coats of arms and emblems that were now appearing on structures like chantries. People had not felt the need to be so deferential in previous centuries. A strong monarchy seemed reassuring after the disruptive years of the Wars of the Roses, and that monarchy was developing greater ambitions to control its subjects, lay and clerical. Benefit of clergy – the privilege of clerics (including literate lay folk) to be tried for crimes in Church courts – was reduced by a series of statutes after 1489. Sanctuary – the right of criminals to take refuge in churches and sometimes in their precincts – was diminished as well. Taxation of the clergy began to increase, notably in 1523 and 1531 when the Crown compelled them to surrender sums of exceptional size.

Cultural changes were in progress too. Literacy was now common and the written word was more conspicuous in churches, including cathedrals. It appeared not only in the texts used by the clergy but in the prayer books brought in by lay people and by inscriptions placed on windows, walls, and tombs. These were traditionally in Latin but increasingly in English. Grammar schools, including those in the cathedral cities, were altering what they taught. From about 1480, the boys began to learn 'humanist' or classical Latin rather than the Latin of the Middle Ages. Most of the Christian works that had been read in school, including the hymns and sequences of the Church services, were abandoned in favour of classical authors. Schools remained Christian in ethos, but their studies were less close to the Church than before.[1] At a higher level, the study of classical Latin and Greek was leading to a new understanding of biblical texts and thereby of religion in the modern world. John Colet, dean of St Paul's from 1505 to 1519, was a reformer before the Reformation. He endowed the cathedral school, tried to reform the cathedral statutes, and revived the lectures in theology. Inspired by Paul's epistles before Luther was, he courted controversy by censuring the worldliness of the clergy, calling them worse than heretics in leading the people astray by their bad example.[2]

Such criticism, long embedded among ordinary people and Lollards, was moving from the edges of the Church to its centre. In 1526 the most famous scholar of the day, Erasmus of Rotterdam, published a lightly disguised account of a visit that he had made to Canterbury with Colet in 1512–14. With sly humour, he described the various relics that were produced for them to kiss. These included the 'sacred rust' of the sword point with which Becket was killed, his skull in the crypt, the bones of other saints including an arm with flesh still on it, and a box of rags that belonged to the martyred archbishop. Erasmus placed his criticisms in the mouth of his friend, now safely dead. Colet, he said, irritated the guide by suggesting that the gold and jewels on Thomas's reliquary would be better given to the poor. When the prior offered him a bit of rag to take away, he replaced it with a scornful look. Ten years before the rulers of the Church in England would

36. *Turner's depiction of the grand west front of Bath, the last cathedral to be rebuilt before the Reformation. It was still unfinished when it lost its status in 1539.*

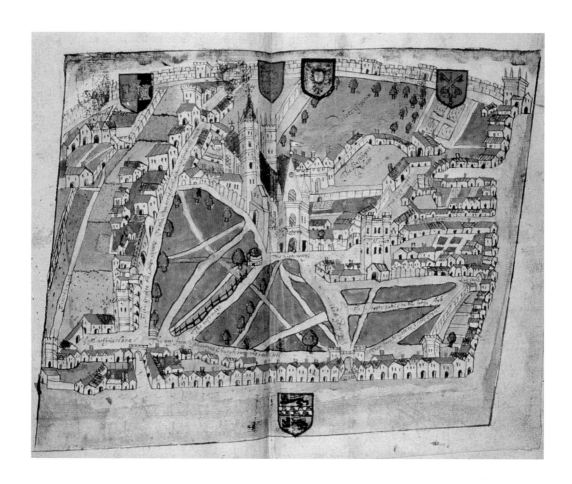

start to discourage the veneration of saints, senior clergy were starting to undermine it.[3]

Meanwhile a new technology had appeared that would play an important part in the Reformation. Caxton began to print at Westminster in 1476, soon followed by other printers and by the importation of printed books from the Continent. Manuscript books were already numerous but printing increased the supply, reduced the cost, and soon spread its products into cathedral libraries. At first there was no sign that printing would threaten the Church, but when the Reformation began in Germany in the 1520s it became easier for unorthodox literature to spread into England through this means. The Reformation of the Church in England was in part an outcome of printing and made much use of it. By the end of the 1530s every church would be required to have a printed Bible in English and later a series of English Prayer Books.

37. Exeter's gated cathedral Close in the sixteenth century. The plan omits the chantry priests' house, churchyard cross, and charnel chapel which were removed at the Reformation.

The Reformation under Henry VIII

The Reformation began for the English cathedrals in 1534 when their clergy – canons, monks, vicars choral, and chantry priests – were all required to sign a personal acknowledgement that Henry VIII was head of the Church of England, now separated from Rome (Fig. 40, p. 108). In the same year Thomas Cromwell, the king's chief minister, drew up a plan to increase the revenues of the Crown through partial disendowment of the Church. He proposed a reduction of the incomes of the wealthier bishops and greater abbeys, the dissolution of all monasteries with less than thirteen members, and heavier taxation on the clergy. These proposals affected not only the monastic cathedrals but the secular ones, to the extent that Cromwell planned to take half of the proceeds of their 'common funds' each year: the surpluses that were shared by the resident canons.[4] Much of the plan was achieved in the following years but the raid on the common funds did not go ahead.

The first proposal to be implemented was the taxation of the clergy. In 1534 Parliament authorised new, heavier rates for them along with the making of a new valuation of the Church's wealth on which to base the taxation. The valuation, known as the *Valor Ecclesiasticus*, was completed in 1535 and was more accurate than before. From now on, whenever a cleric received a new benefice, he had to undertake to pay a sum equivalent to one year's income from it, delivered in instalments ('first-fruits'). In every subsequent year he was charged 10 per cent of his income ('tenths'), and the common revenues of cathedrals and monasteries were taxed at this rate every year. The figures for the valuation survive, but they need to be used with care in the case of secular cathedrals. These had both general incomes and the specific ones of individual clergy, so that the total figures do not represent the disposable wealth of the whole organisation, and the dignitaries and canons had further incomes from their other benefices.

Of the secular cathedrals, Lincoln had the largest annual revenues: £3,426. Those of Exeter, St Paul's, Salisbury, Wells, and York were between £2,000 and £2,500. Lichfield had about £1,500, and Chichester and Hereford around £1,000. A few hundred pounds should be added in each case for vicars choral, chantry priests, and choristers. The monastic cathedrals were less well endowed. Only Canterbury matched the greatest secular foundations with about £2,500. Durham, Ely, Winchester, and Worcester had between £1,000 and £1,500; Bath, Coventry, and Norwich between £500 and £900; and Carlisle and Rochester a little under £500. To put this into perspective, three abbeys that were not cathedrals had incomes over £2,000, thirteen over £1,000, and thirty-three between £500 and £1,000. Within each cathedral, the amounts must be divided between the stipends of the dignitaries, canons, and lesser clergy, and these varied too from the £368 enjoyed by the dean of Lincoln down to the £58 of his counterpart at Chichester.[5]

In 1536 Parliament enacted another statute: dissolving smaller monasteries with incomes of less than £200 per annum. At this stage Henry had not decided to abolish every house, and he even reprieved and refounded a few of them. But the ease with which the smaller places were closed and the profits that resulted led to a creeping process in which the larger ones were required to surrender themselves and their property to the king. The last monastery to do so, Canterbury Cathedral, submitted on 4 April 1540. As that event shows, the process extended to the monastic cathedrals. The first to be dealt with was Norwich in May 1538, followed by Coventry and Bath in January 1539, and the remainder during the next fifteen months. Cathedral priors were given generous pensions for their compliance; their monks very basic ones. Other employees were allowed to apply for annuities if they had written contracts granting them salaries. But Henry, whose policies so often combined the radical with the conservative in an uneasy tension, was not hostile to cathedrals in general. The Crown did indeed put an end to Bath and Coventry. They were reckoned to be expendable because their bishops had a secular cathedral as well. Coventry was destroyed: the one great medieval cathedral of which nothing remains. Bath nearly disappeared too. It was offered to its citizens for a large sum of money, but they refused it. The lead was stripped from the roof, the glass from the windows, and it stood as a ruin until it was bought by the Colthurst family, given to the corporation of Bath, and restored in the reign of Elizabeth I to become the chief parish church of the city.[6]

These losses were exceptions, however. Henry could not conceive of a Church without bishops and cathedrals, although the Protestant Reformation in much of Germany abolished both. It would have been difficult to run the Church in England without bishops, but they could have operated without cathedrals. The king, however, valued cathedrals and their worship because it resembled that of his own chapel, and he personally intervened to protect them while the dissolution of the monasteries was in progress. On his initiative, a bill was taken through Parliament on a single day, 23 May 1539, to provide for the continuance of cathedrals and the creation of new ones. He actually wrote the bill's preamble in his own handwriting. Condemning 'the slothful and ungodly life' of those who had borne the name of 'religious folk', meaning monks, he argued that their resources ought to be employed in ways 'whereby God's word might the better be set forth, children brought up in learning, clerks nourished in the universities, old servants decayed to have livings, almshouses for poor folk to be sustained in, readers of Greek, Hebrew, and Latin to have good stipend, daily alms to be ministered, mending of highways, [and] exhibition of ministers of the church'. Accordingly, the bill, which passed into law, empowered the king to create new bishops, cathedrals, and collegiate churches, to endow them, and to make rules for their government.[7]

Henry VIII's New Cathedrals

The king's words had an optimistic ring about them, appropriate at a time when he held huge assets from the spoil of the monasteries. During the summer or

38. One of Henry VIII's six new cathedrals: the north transept and towers of the former abbey of Peterborough.

autumn of 1539 ambitious plans were drawn up to refound the monastic cathedrals as bodies of secular clergy and to turn some former monasteries into cathedrals. These plans probably reflected the king's views and certainly those of his conservative courtiers who wished to save as much Church property as possible. The existing monastic cathedrals that had to be reorganised were Canterbury, Carlisle, Durham, Ely, Rochester, Winchester, and Worcester. Norwich had been refounded individually in 1538.[8] Consideration was also given to the creation of new bishops, each with a seat in a former abbey. The places proposed included Bodmin, Bristol, Colchester, Dunstable, Gloucester, Guisborough (Yorks.), Osney (outside Oxford), Peterborough (Fig. 38, above), St Albans, Shrewsbury, Waltham (Essex), and Westminster Abbey. Burton-on-Trent and Thornton (Lincs.) were considered for collegiate churches.

Detailed and costed plans were drawn up for each new cathedral although these did not include estimates for the bishops, who would be an additional charge.[9] There was no attempt to reproduce the secular cathedrals of the Middle Ages. Their constitutions had grown up too gradually and individually to provide good models. Instead the planning was influenced by the collegiate churches which had been founded in England since the late thirteenth century. Some of these were university colleges, others foundations of priests endowed to perform daily worship and celebrate masses. Here the most important model was probably St George's Chapel (Windsor), the king's own collegiate church, parts of whose statutes were recycled in those of the new cathedrals. Colleges like St George's were more tightly organised than the secular cathedrals. They had comprehensive statutes, a head – dean, provost, or warden – with stronger powers of control, and clergy required to keep residence. Some included a grammar school, open to the public and often free of fees, and an almshouse for the poor and infirm.[10] These features were attractive to the Crown in about 1540, but only briefly. Within two or three years, the greed of the king and the court for religious property would extinguish most of the collegiate churches as it had done in the case of the monasteries.

The initial schemes for cathedrals were profuse, especially for Canterbury, Durham, and Westminster, which were to be the flagships of the scheme. The Canterbury plans (there were two) allowed for a dean, twelve canons or prebendaries, eight minor canons (priests similar to vicars choral) and twelve lay clerks to sing in the choir, ten choristers, a 'master of the children' to teach them to sing, and two clerks to read the epistle and the gospel. These clerks and the minor canons were copied from St George's (Windsor).[11] Ample resources were provided for education. Six clergy would be employed as preachers and provided with horses to ride round Kent proclaiming the doctrines of Henry's Reformation. Five 'readers' – lecturers of university standard – were to teach Greek literature, Hebrew divinity, Latin literature and divinity, civil (Roman) law, and medicine. A grammar school was to include a master and an assistant teaching Latin to all comers, free of charge, and sixty boys were to receive scholarships in the form of free board and lodging while they learnt Latin, Greek, and Hebrew. Twenty further scholarships would be available to support them at university, ten each at Cambridge and Oxford. An almshouse was to maintain twelve poor men who had served the king or been wounded in his wars, and the cathedral was entrusted with money for the upkeep of local highways. Eleven servants and administrators, eventually increased to twenty-one, were to guard the church, run the estates, care for the stables, buy food, and cook meals for those other than the dean and canons (who would have their own houses). The total cost of this would be about £2,000 per annum, not much less than the income of the former cathedral priory which had been about £2,400.

Thomas Cromwell, who was in charge of this project as he was of all Henry's affairs, sent the proposed scheme for Canterbury to Thomas Cranmer, the archbishop whose cathedral it was, in November 1539. Cranmer (Fig. 40, p. 108), who would eventually become one of the most radical reformers of the English Church, was not impressed.[12] He advised against the creation of prebendaries. In his experience, he said, the 'sect' of these men 'spent their time in much idleness and their substance in superfluous belly cheer', for 'commonly a prebendary is neither learner nor teacher but a good viander [i.e. diner]'. They vied for pre-eminence in the churches to which they belonged, and set a bad example to the young. He knew of learned men made prebendaries who had abandoned their studies and the practice of preaching and teaching. Instead the money should be spent on maintaining twenty theology students and forty students of Latin and Greek because, if there was no body of students at the cathedral, he could not see that the five proposed readers would have any audience. The prebendaries would not attend, and the grammar-school boys would be fully employed in their school.[13]

Cranmer's objections anticipated criticisms of cathedrals that would be made in years to come. In the meantime, they were ignored. Henry went ahead with his cathedral scheme even after Cromwell fell from power and was executed in July 1540. But it was greatly cut down in size, since the costs of the original plans were deemed unsustainable. The seven monastic cathedrals were re-established between March 1541 and January 1542 along with six additional ones based in other ex-monasteries.[14] These were Bristol, Chester, Gloucester, Oxford (based at Osney Abbey), Peterborough, and Westminster. Osney's life was brief. After four years it was closed and the cathedral was united with the king's new college of Christ Church in Oxford itself. Here the canons were given the former priory church of St Frideswide, which Cardinal Wolsey had begun to demolish but was now patched up: a church too small for a cathedral and too large for a college chapel (Fig. 41, p. 112). Westminster did not survive much longer. Its bishop was taken away in 1550 and its diocese reunited with that of London. It remained as a college of canons and other clergy until 1556 when Mary Tudor replaced the monks, and became a college again under Elizabeth I with the status of a royal chapel, which it retains today.

There was little symmetry about these foundations. Bristol was felt to need a bishop and cathedral because it was by far the largest town without them, but the only territory that could be found for its diocese was far away in Dorset. The diocese of Oxford covered only Oxfordshire, while Peterborough, which included Northamptonshire and Rutland, managed to split the old diocese of Lincoln in half. That diocese thereafter consisted of two northern counties, Lincolnshire and Leicestershire, cut off from three southern ones: Bedfordshire, Buckinghamshire, and most of Hertfordshire. There was still an imbalance between the number of dioceses and cathedrals in the two Church provinces (Fig. 39, p. 105). Canterbury now had eighteen in England and four in Wales. York's medieval three had grown only to five. Chester, whose territory came partly from Lichfield diocese and partly from York, was at first placed in Canterbury province but moved to York in 1542. The diocese of Sodor ('the southern isles'), which once stretched from the Isle of Man to the Hebrides, became divided into English and Scottish parts in the 1380s, each with a bishop, and the English part – Man itself – was regarded as part of York province by 1458. This diocese, later known as Sodor and Man, had a small cathedral at Peel which does not seem to have resembled its English counterparts and about which little is known.

The lack of consistency about the dioceses extended to the refounded cathedrals, which came to be known as those of the New Foundation. Canterbury, the grandest of them, was given a dean, twelve canons, six preachers, twelve minor

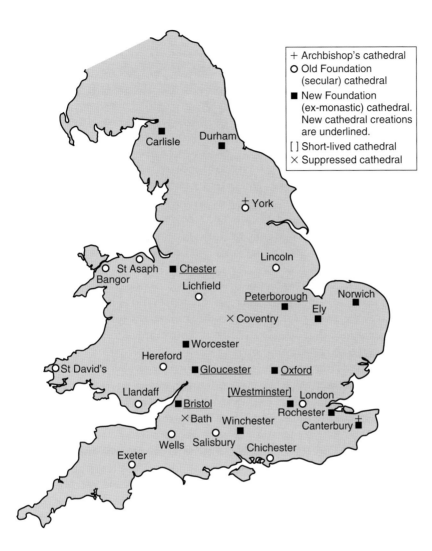

Legend:

+ Archbishop's cathedral
O Old Foundation
(secular) cathedral
■ New Foundation
(ex-monastic) cathedral.
New cathedral creations
are underlined.
[ ] Short-lived cathedral
✕ Suppressed cathedral

canons, twelve lay clerks, a master of the choristers cum organ player, ten choristers, two schoolmasters, fifty boarding grammar schoolboys, and twelve almsmen or 'bedesmen'. At the other end of the scale Bristol was awarded six canons and Carlisle four, with appropriately smaller numbers in the other categories. There was a good deal of continuity between the old monasteries and their replacements. The latter were housed in the former's buildings, of course, but they also kept some of its old lands, churches, and archives, and even certain of its personnel. The new deans of Carlisle, Chester, Durham, Ely, Norwich, Rochester, Westminster, and Worcester were the former heads of the monastery. The deans of Bristol, Gloucester, and Peterborough had been priors in houses elsewhere. Some ex-monks were retained as canons. This was not so much an expression of confidence in their abilities as a desire by the Crown to save money. The pensions awarded to the former monks – large ones in the case of their abbots and priors – were forfeited as soon as they gained new posts.

In 1544 statutes for most of the new cathedrals were drawn up by three royal commissioners: one more progressive, Richard Cox, and two more conservative, George Day and Nicholas Heath. The statutes varied slightly from place to place, as the cathedral establishments varied, but all followed much the same form.[15] Their nature can be seen by examining those for Winchester, which was one of the larger foundations.[16] Here and elsewhere the new cathedrals became more subject to the Crown than before. Previously canons had normally been chosen by the bishop and deans elected by the canons. Now both dean and canons were Crown appointments. The dean must be at least a bachelor of theology. He had no rival dignitaries and held large powers over the canons, lesser clergy, services, church goods, and lands, subject to some consultation with the canons in chapter. He was to keep residence, subject to an allowance of one hundred days of absence with pay. The twelve canons of Winchester had to be graduates too. They were allowed eighty days absence with pay, but four canons must always be in residence. During their residence they were to attend at least some of the services and to preach in turn on Sundays throughout the year.

The main work of the cathedral was to be done by twelve minor canons, a deacon and subdeacon, twelve lay clerks, ten choristers, and a master of the choristers. These were all subject to the dean and chapter: there was no separate college like those of the vicars choral. The minor canons were priests; the lay clerks were professional singers and might be young adults or older men. One minor canon was to be precentor and lead the choral singing, and another sacrist in charge of vestments, books, and ornaments. The lesser clergy and singers, apart from those married, were to live in the same premises and eat together as a collegiate body. There was a first serving of midday dinner at which the minor canons occupied the top table, the lay clerks a second, and the choristers a third. Afterwards the servants who had made and served the dinner ate by themselves. Twelve almsmen were chosen from the poor or broken in war.[17] They received accommodation and food, and the cathedral had to spend £66 13s. 4d. per annum on alms to other poor and on the maintenance of local highways.

Most of the New Foundations included a grammar master and sometimes an assistant 'usher'. These ran a school on the cathedral premises providing free education in Latin for boys from the city and neighbourhood: an improvement in so far that most cathedral schools had hitherto charged fees. Here too there were anomalies, however. Winchester did not get a school, the independent Winchester College being apparently regarded as a substitute. Oxford had one only briefly until about 1546–7, and Norwich was forgotten until 1547 when the Crown founded a school but placed it under the rule of the city council.[18] Seven cathedrals had an additional resource of scholarships for boys, enabling them to board on the premises and eat in the common hall with the minor clergy.[19] For a year or two some of the seven even had university awards to support their pupils at Cambridge and Oxford. In 1545, however, the Crown was short of money and, in the erratic manner of Henry's regime, it terminated most of the Oxbridge scholarships and reclaimed the endowments.[20]

That leaves the core business of cathedrals: to worship. How did Henry and his assistants expect them to do so in the new Church of England? Cranmer was interested in reforming the liturgy throughout England and began to draft plans for this as early as 1538–9.[21] His plans would eventually bear fruit but, until Henry died, Cranmer was obstructed by conservative opponents and an unpredictable king. Henry's own preference can be seen in the provision of minor canons, professional lay clerks, choristers, and a choristers' master in the New Foundations. This shows that he expected choral services in choirs and polyphony there and in Lady chapels to continue in their accustomed ways and to a high standard, like that in his own chapel. The statutes of 1544 included a chapter on worship so short and unspecific as to convey the same expectation. However, the chapter contained two interesting changes of a permissive nature. Services need not be said at night, which meant that matins and lauds could be brought forward to dawn and prefixed to the main block of morning prayers. And the lesser services of prime, terce, sext, and none could be said not sung to save time when a sermon was preached, as on a Sunday.[22] Both alterations chimed with Cranmer's views, and they surely indicate his influence at work: in the direction of simplifying things.

He also achieved three larger reforms. In 1542 a chapter of the New Testament in English was ordered to be read at mass each Sunday in parish churches, which affected cathedrals to the extent that a few of them had such churches within their walls. Next year the Sarum breviary was imposed on all clergy in the province of Canterbury, bringing closer a national system of uniform services.[23] Finally, in 1544, Cranmer achieved his greatest coup by getting Henry's permission to make a version of the litany in English. The litany was the material that was sung in processions on days of penitence and intercession. Its attraction to Henry was that he was currently at war, when such processions were customarily made. Having it in English would associate the population more closely with the war. In its medieval form the litany included intercessions to saints, but Cranmer left these out in another step away from the past. His hope was to abolish processions completely, and he would succeed in doing so once Henry died.[24]

While all this was in progress, a traveller was riding round England and describing what he saw. His name was John Leland and he had royal authority in the form of a warrant empowering him to search the libraries of religious houses for ancient writings. This led him to travel from Cumbria to Cornwall in the course of which he visited at least eleven cathedrals, but we only possess significant comments on seven.[25] His chief praise was given to Salisbury for its large and beautiful chapter house, its cloister ('one of the largest and most magnificentest in England'), and its central tower and spire ('a noble and memorable piece of work'). At Lichfield he liked the neat houses of the prebendaries and the west

40. The great
Reformers.
Henry VIII
and Edward VI
triumph over
the pope and the
monks, watched
by Protector
Somerset and
Archbishop
Cranmer.

front ('exceedingly costly and fair'). He noted the numbers of arches in the arcades of Salisbury, Wells, and York; recorded the clergy and benefactors who had built particular features; and made lists of the principal tombs. He was careful not to refer to the saints' shrines and images that were now being frowned on. For him cathedrals were fine buildings raised up to contemporary standards. Although he was aware of their history, they did not primarily speak to him of their ancientness or inspire romantic thoughts. In this respect he, and probably his contemporaries, were different from the travellers and tourists of later centuries.

The Cathedrals under Edward VI

Henry's Church policies did not survive his death in January 1547. He was succeeded by a regency government under the duke of Somerset acting on behalf of the young King Edward VI (Fig. 40, above). This was Protestant in sympathy and allowed Cranmer at last to realise his plans for the reform of the Church including its services. Soon after the old king's death, royal commissioners were sent out to each diocese with injunctions for its clergy to observe. Some commissioners visited the parish churches, others the cathedrals.[26] The cathedral commissioners, having scrutinised local conditions, gave further instructions for reforms where they judged it necessary.

The visitation of the cathedrals was significant for two reasons. It was the first occasion on which they were identified and addressed as a group; previously they had been treated along with the other religious houses. It also brought the Reformation to the secular cathedrals, those of the Old Foundation as they came to be called. These had remained untouched in their management while Henry was dealing with the monasteries. Some of the injunctions brought by the visitors were traditional ones. Canons were to give hospitality, especially to the poorer ministers of the church and to needy wayfaring people. Clergy were not to haunt taverns or drink, dice, play cards, hunt, hawk, or engage in other games but to give themselves to reading and studying holy scripture.

The main purpose of the injunctions, however, was to make substantial changes to what all cathedrals did. They were to keep their canons, vicars choral or minor canons, clerks, and choristers. But chantry priests were not mentioned, being already marked for abolition. A process was developed by which the vicars of the Old Foundations became a mixture of clergy and laymen.[27] This brought their cathedral choirs into line with those of the New Foundation with their minor canon priests and lay clerks. Next the injunctions began to alter the pattern of cathedral services. Matins was moved from midnight to six o'clock in the morning, the permission of 1544 now being made compulsory everywhere. The offices of prime, terce, sext, and none which happened later in the morning were to be discontinued if they got in the way of sermons. All the resident canons were to preach in turn on Sundays, and the dean at Christmas and Easter.[28] This was not necessarily a welcome duty. Up to the 1530s cathedral sermons had often been confined to Lent and Advent, and even then deputed to local friars. Meanwhile, in the injunctions for parish churches, but relevant to the cathedrals, the litany was ordered to be said kneeling not moving as in the past. This turned it into an ordinary static service, and in due course it became part of the weekly cathedral routine.[29]

One of the objects of the visitation was to increase the role of cathedrals in education, or rather the role of the Old Foundations since Henry VIII's statutes had already addressed this matter in the New. Each cathedral was ordered to place two Bibles in English in the choir for the clergy and ministers to read, and two in the nave for anyone else who wished to do so. Each was to establish a library (many already had them) and to ensure that it contained the Christian fathers like Augustine and Cyprian as well as the recent works of Erasmus. This was to encourage the clergy to study. Where there was no free grammar school in the cathedral Close or nearby, the cathedral was to maintain one, employing a schoolmaster and an usher with adequate salaries and accommodation. Choristers, who had not always been trained beyond the ability to read and sing, were now to be supported at grammar school after their voices broke. They were to receive scholarships of £3 6s. 8d. each for the next five years.

The following year, 1548, was a year of still greater changes. At the very end of 1547 an act of Parliament abolished all chantries and religious guilds in England with effect from Easter 1548. Their priests were awarded pensions like the monks, their communities were disbanded, and the masses at their altars came to an end. All their religious endowments were seized by the Crown but some cathedrals managed to retain or recover part of these, which was the case at Chichester and Exeter.[30] Early in 1548 a series of royal orders forbade most of the ceremonies previously enacted in churches including the lighting of candles at Candlemas (2 February), the dispensing of ashes on Ash Wednesday (the first day of Lent), the carrying of palms on Palm Sunday, and the crawling across the floor (the so-called 'creeping to the cross') on Good Friday. Worship was moving towards words alone, not performance. Finally, in the same year clergy were allowed to marry, which enabled deans and canons to bring wives into the Close if they and their spouses were brave enough to face its disapproving male society.

There was no abatement of change in the next year, 1549. In June a new liturgy was imposed by act of Parliament in the form of the Book of Common Prayer, for which Cranmer was chiefly responsible. This provoked popular risings, especially in Cornwall and Devon, but they were suppressed and did not prevent the measure's implementation. The Prayer Book made a clean break with the past in three respects. First, its services were in English not Latin: a great innovation and a confirmation that England now had its own Church rather than belonging to an international one. Secondly, it was a uniform text to be used throughout the kingdom, in place of the previous local 'uses'. Thirdly, it reversed the superiority of the cathedrals over the parish churches. Hitherto the secular cathedrals, each in its diocese and Salisbury and York more generally, had set the standard for local worship. Parish churches had followed this standard in a simplified way. Now the official liturgy in England was one designed for parish church worship, and cathedrals were expected to adjust themselves to its format.

The Prayer Book reduced the traditional eight daily services to two. These were matins, to be said in the first hours of daylight, and evensong in the mid-afternoon. The mass, renamed 'The supper of the Lord and the holy communion', changed too. It ceased to be a service that centred on a priest with an assistant or two and became a congregational one. A rubric attached to the service stated that 'in all cathedral and collegiate churches there shall always some communicate [i.e. receive the bread and wine] with the priest that ministereth'.[31] That meant that the canons and priest vicars could no longer celebrate private masses as they and the chantry priests had done in the past. Lest they attempted to do so, a royal order of 1550 required all stone altars in churches to be removed and the high altar to be replaced by a wooden table, so as to represent the Last Supper of Jesus in a more authentic way. The table was often placed in the choir rather than at the east end, to mark its difference from a Catholic altar.

The Prayer Book of 1549 was in use for only three years. In 1552 it was replaced by a new one of a still more radical kind, again chiefly due to Cranmer.

Matins and evensong were renamed morning and evening prayer. They became more disciplinary than before, beginning with prayers of confession, and a third service, the litany, was ordered to be used on Sundays, Wednesdays, and Fridays. This, as we have seen, was now a purely static service. At evening prayer, the well-known canticles of the Magnificat and Nunc Dimittis were provided with alternative psalms, because some Protestants disliked the canticles for their Catholic associations. Nearly all the remaining ceremonials of worship were abolished, such as the use of holy oil in baptism and the anointing of the sick. The communion service could now be held only if there were at least three people willing to receive the sacrament, and cathedrals were required to ensure that all priests and deacons did so every Sunday. The new table replaced the now absent high altar and the bread used had to be ordinary bread.[32] This was to express the Protestant belief that the communion was essentially a commemoration of Christ's Last Supper, not a sacrifice as it was in the Catholic Church. In due course cathedrals acquired large silver plates for administering the bread, and flagons instead of chalices for the wine, like the tableware of a domestic house.

Meanwhile, since the 1530s, another change had been in progress. Images of God, the angels, and saints, whether in the form of statuary or paintings, were being removed.[33] Official disapproval of images was first expressed under Henry VIII. Royal injunctions of 1536 permitted them to exist as reminders of holy things but urged that they be not venerated. In the following year Bishop Latimer of Worcester, an opponent of images, and his prior, Henry Holbeach, stripped one of their cathedral's chief figures, 'Our Lady of Worcester', of the clothing and jewels with which it had been beautified.[34] In 1538 more hostile royal injunctions forbade the donation of candles or small wax objects to images (people often hung up such objects as signs of prayers requested or granted), and ordered the removal of images that were 'abused' with offerings or pilgrimages.[35]

The same year saw the destruction of the greatest cathedral shrine, that of Thomas Becket in Canterbury. Its gold and jewels were taken away by the Crown in many cartloads, it was said, and the remains of the saint destroyed. Henry and Cromwell had a particular grudge against Becket. He had championed the rights of the Church against a previous King Henry, and the parallel was too close for comfort. In 1538 a royal proclamation forbade him to be commemorated. It included a revisionist account of his death, claiming that 'he gave opprobrious words to the gentlemen which then counselled him to leave his stubbornness', calling one of them 'bawd' and shaking another violently, so that he caused an affray in which he was slain by accident. His festival days were to be abolished, his statues removed, and his name expunged from all religious books.[36] The other cathedral saints fared no better. The veneration of Cuthbert at Durham, Hugh at Lincoln, and Osmund at Salisbury was suppressed as well. At Hereford the shrine of St Thomas Cantilupe was robbed of its gold and jewels in 1538, while those of St Hugh and John Dalderby at Lincoln were despoiled in 1540.[37] Meanwhile, from the late 1530s to the early 1550s, cathedrals and parish churches lost their treasures. Thousands

41. *England's only academic cathedral, Christ Church, Oxford, placed in the not quite complete church of the priory of St Frideswide.*

of ounces of gold and silver, jewelled crosses, candlesticks, chalices, incense burners, vestments, and altar cloths were carried off to London to be sold or turned into coin to fill the royal exchequer.[38]

During the early 1540s the destruction slackened because Henry VIII put a brake on reforms in the last years of his life, but Edward's government revived it vigorously. The royal injunctions of 1547 ordered venerated shrines, paintings, and other memorials to be destroyed, and all the images in St Paul's were pulled down in that year. The demolitions spread through London during the following winter and into the rest of the country in 1548. In 1552 Nicholas Ridley, the radical bishop of London, caused the removal of the reredos behind the former high altar of St Paul's. Even buildings disappeared. The cloister around the Pardon Churchyard at St Paul's, decorated with the Dance of Death, and the chapel of Thomas Becket in its midst were destroyed. The charnel chapels there and at Exeter were demolished, and so was the Lady chapel off the cloisters of Wells. All these had links with indulgences, prayers for the dead, or the worship of saints. In some places every trace of the past was obliterated by whitewashing paintings or leaving empty the niches where statues had stood. In others, statues that were part of the stone fabric had their heads broken off and were left disfigured. This turned them into records of the triumph of the Reformers over the superstitions of Catholic times.

Altogether, cathedral worship became much simpler, indeed starker, during Edward's reign. It was to resume most of this format with Elizabeth I and keep it for centuries afterwards. After 1549 the principal daily services were reduced to matins at about eight o'clock and evensong at about three o'clock in the afternoon. On Wednesdays, Fridays, and Sundays matins was followed by the litany with its prayers for forgiveness and requests for peace and security. On Sundays the communion service (or at least the first half of the service) came after the litany, including a sermon. All these were services of the word: to be heard, not enacted or watched. Ceremony, movement, and colour were virtually abolished. There was little more spectacle than the celebrant priest in a cope standing alone at the communion table on Sundays. The observance of time, once so complex, was now much abridged. The medieval Church had marked daily time (midnight, dawn, morning, and evening), seasonal time (Lent, Easter, and so on), and historic time (the days of many saints). The new Protestant one reduced these to morning and evening, a simpler pattern of seasons, and only about twenty saints' days – all saints of the New Testament.

Music too was greatly diminished. At St George's (Windsor) organ playing was discontinued in 1550. Plans were made to turn its singers' posts into scholarships for ordinands, and the number of its choristers was reduced.[39] In 1552 organ playing was forbidden at St Paul's and York, and Robert Holgate the archbishop of York, a strong Reformer, forbade any singing except for 'square note plain', meaning a simple setting that should be 'plainly and distinctly pronounced'. Protestants disliked elaborate music. It had too many Catholic associations. It needed specialised performers and so prevented lay people from participating. It intruded between the Word of God and the listener, making the Word less clear and more obscure. Cathedral music reached its least flourishing point under Edward, although later, as we shall see, it would revive.[40]

Nonetheless, even his regime still saw a place for cathedrals in national life. It seems to have envisaged them becoming rather like university colleges: communities dedicated to daily worship, study, and education. Since worship must be understood if it was to be devout, the clergy were to spend the time that they were not in church by reading and learning the Bible and hearing it expounded. The ideal seems to have been a daily lecture on the Bible after matins, given by the cathedral chancellor or another learned man and attended by all the clergy: canons and vicars. The Bible was to be read at meals in the vicars' hall, and they were urged to take advantage of the copies provided for them in the choir. Holgate even required the vicars to learn a chapter of St Paul's epistles in Latin every week, and the choristers a chapter of the gospels in English every week or fortnight. Both groups, he warned, would be tested on their knowledge![41]

Finally, changes were planned to two dioceses during Edward's reign. One has already been mentioned: the union of Westminster and London, which removed cathedral status from the Abbey. The other took place early in 1553 when an act of Parliament dissolved the bishopric of Durham so that the Crown could annex its substantial powers over local government. The act provided for the re-establishment of the bishopric along with a new one at Newcastle, thereby dividing the old diocese into two parts: County Durham and Northumberland. Provision was made for Newcastle to be given a cathedral with a dean and chapter, but the change had hardly been sanctioned when Edward died in July and it was never implemented.[42] An attempt to maintain a Protestant succession with Lady Jane Grey came to nothing, and Edward's Catholic half-sister Mary ascended the throne (Fig. 42, below).

42. Mary Tudor, who restored Catholic worship to cathedrals in 1553 but had too little time to undo her predecessors' changes.

Mary Tudor and the Catholic Restoration

Mary immediately began the restoration of Catholicism. This required a new relationship with the clergy, including those of the cathedrals. The governments of Henry VIII and Edward VI had moved change forward step by step, assuming that the clergy would follow their orders. Mary wished to reverse the changes quickly and she had to solve the problem of clergy who had committed themselves to the Reformation. Some were active Protestants. Others had merely taken advantage of the permission to marry, but this was impossible to reconcile with a return to the past.

Accordingly, Mary began a cull of cathedral clergy. In 1553–4 Cranmer and Holgate were expelled from their posts. So were seven bishops, eleven deans, and about seventy-five more dignitaries and canons. Others resigned before they were ejected. The expulsions were particularly numerous at Canterbury, Lincoln, Salisbury, Wells, and York, but in most other places only three or four clergy were ousted.[43] The measure was hard on the married men who had taken wives legitimately. They were eligible for reappointment to benefices elsewhere if they left their wives, and a few did so. What the wives thought, and how they would be provided for, were not matters with which Mary's regime was concerned. Even worse was the fate of those arraigned under the medieval heresy laws, abolished under Edward VI but restored in the winter of 1553–4, including the imposition of death by burning. Of about 280 people killed in this way under Mary, five were bishops (including Cranmer) and five cathedral canons. The latter included John Bradford, John Rogers, and Rowland Taylor, all of St Paul's, John Cardmaker of Wells (Fig. 43, p. 116), and Laurence Saunders of York.[44]

Mary's next task was to restore religion to its state in the early 1530s. The Crown gave up its headship of the Church. England submitted again to the pope's authority. Worship in Latin was reintroduced, including the whole daily round of services. This required the printing and purchase of fresh liturgical books. Most of those now published were of the Use of Sarum, including the most widely used: the breviary, missal, and manual. Only a few of the Use of York appeared, leaving Sarum as the chief model for worship in Mary's reign.[45] A harder task was to replace the traditional setting of the liturgy. High altars could be rebuilt or improvised, but the replacement of small chapel altars would take time. The chantry priests did not return and there were too few clergy to replicate the number of daily masses before the 1540s. Shrines had been dismantled and images destroyed.

Some attempts were made to reverse these losses. The Crown insisted that the 'rood' statues of Christ, Mary, and John should be restored above the pulpitum, and that of the patron saint in the choir. St Paul's had its rood back in time for Mary's visit there with Philip of Spain in October 1554. One of its canons left money to rail off the sanctuary and to build an altar or monument depicting the salutation of the Archangel Gabriel to the Virgin Mary. Exeter employed a foreign craftsman to restore some of the images. York repainted statues and re-erected those on the pulpitum. The new archbishop of Canterbury, Cardinal Pole, tried to encourage the restoration of the shrine of St Frideswide in Christ Church cathedral (Oxford), but it is not clear that this was achieved.[46]

In one respect the leaders of the Catholic Church under Mary were of the same mind as their Protestant opponents: cathedrals were vital in promoting education.[47] Each side wished to ensure that young people conformed to its views and, in the case of boys, provided a supply of devout and learned men to serve as clergy. Accordingly the medieval and Henry VIII cathedral schools remained in being. Efforts were made to appoint Catholic schoolmasters and to ensure the teaching of Catholicism in the schoolroom. Indeed, in the winter of 1555–6, Pole presided over a synod of the English clergy which ruled that schoolmasters should not teach in future until they had been examined and approved by their bishop. This was the first time that the Church had gained formal control over education. In addition the cathedral schools were told to recruit a number of boys from the age of eleven who would be tonsured, wear religious dress, learn Latin, and eventually qualify to be clergy. The scheme got close to being established at Lincoln and York, where plans were made to provide accommodation and scholarships for these boys. But Mary's reign, like Edward's, is a story of work in progress. The re-established Catholic Church was not securely bedded in when she died in November 1558, and nearly all her achievements were reversed under her sister and successor Elizabeth I (Fig. 44, p. 120).

43. The brutal side of Mary's regime: John Cardmaker, canon and chancellor of Wells, is burnt for heresy at Smithfield in 1555.

Elizabeth I and the Survival of Cathedrals

Elizabeth's accession in November 1558 brought a further round of changes for cathedrals. In the spring of 1559, Parliament enacted statutes that gave back the Crown its supremacy over the Church. The queen was awarded the more tactful title of 'supreme governor' and an English Prayer Book was restored, based largely on that of 1552. In June commissioners were appointed to carry out a visitation of the whole Church, including the cathedrals. They were ordered to enforce the statutes relating to the queen's supremacy and the Prayer Book, to remove and punish clergy who refused to obey them, and to restore clergy who had been unjustly deprived under Mary.[48] In contrast to her interventions, there was no wish to punish most of the clergy for what they had done or believed in the past. It was hoped that they would conform again to the law, although the threat of dismissal was used to persuade them.

In the event many clergy refused to recognise the new order of things and were removed from their posts in consequence. The archbishop of York (Pole of Canterbury had recently died), all thirteen English bishops still in office, twelve deans, and about 115 dignitaries and canons were deprived between 1559 and 1562. There were resignations too by some who expected that fate.[49] This was a bigger exodus than in 1553–4, reflecting in part the success of Mary's regime in stiffening the loyalty of the cathedral clergy and in part the merry-go-round of the previous twenty years. Deans and canons, most of whom were probably conservative in sympathy, had gone along with the changes of Henry VIII and Edward VI through necessity and had returned to Catholicism with relief under Mary. Some could not contemplate changing again, which allowed the Crown to make new appointments to replace them. Nevertheless, those leaving were in a minority. Most of their colleagues conformed once more to what the Crown required. Among the deans, for example, Nicholas Wotton, who held both Canterbury and York, Walter Phillips of Rochester, and Peter Vannes of Salisbury stayed stolidly in their stalls from Henry VIII to Elizabeth, and so did many canons.

The retention of cathedrals by Henry and each of his children meant that they survived the Reformation, which may be termed the third great crisis of their history. By 1559 two ancient ones had disappeared, seventeen had survived, and five had been added permanently, making twenty-two along with the four in Wales and one in the Isle of Man. This prompts the question why each Tudor regime of the mid-sixteenth century preserved them and, in Henry's case, even increased their number. It has sometimes been assumed that he was too concerned with other aspects of the Reformation to bother about them. That cannot be true. If Henry was capable of getting rid of several hundred monasteries, he could easily have dissolved the cathedrals. He took their valuables and, in a few cases, bits of their property. Lichfield gave up a prebend to the new diocese of Chester.[50] York lost six prebends and the endowments of the cathedral treasurer, the king decreeing that the latter post was unnecessary now that there was no treasure![51] Nevertheless, he allowed the cathedrals to retain the majority of their assets: lands, churches, and privileges. Even Cromwell's proposals of 1534 were lenient. Edward's regime too, radical though it was, took away cathedral status only from Westminster and planned to extend it to Newcastle.

What saved them, then? Some respect for their history and buildings, perhaps. A great kingdom should have great churches in its capital city and provincial centres, although antiquity and architecture did not protect most of the monasteries and collegiate churches, even some with tombs of the Tudors' ancestors. A liking too by the Tudor monarchs (excepting Edward VI) for cathedral worship and music as it had developed over the last hundred years. It was close to what they enjoyed in their chapels, and Henry in particular seems to have wanted cathedrals to reproduce the standards of St George's (Windsor) in these matters. There appeared to be scope for making cathedrals useful to society through education, learning, and poor relief. But the overriding factor in their survival was surely their possession of so many well-paid canonries, to which Henry added more. The silence that greeted Cranmer's objections to such posts is a telling one. The rulers of Tudor England needed deans and canons as much as their ancestors had done in the Middle Ages. Cathedral posts provided stipends for Church administrators, protégés of the Crown, relatives of the nobility and gentry, and senior scholars of the universities. No one could think of another way of supporting such people.

Chapter
— 6 —

Survival and Abolition

1559–1660

Visitors to a cathedral in Elizabeth's first years, the early 1560s, who had last seen it thirty years ago, would have found much that was familiar. Externally the place looked much the same. It was still a bishop's church where he would be enthroned, hold ordinations and perhaps confirmations, and be buried if he died in the vicinity. It was still administered by clergy, although the monks had gone. The New Foundation cathedrals of Henry VIII were less wealthy than their monastic predecessors, but those of the Old Foundation still held most of their properties. All possessed manors and churches, yielding them rents and tithes. All still had purchasing power in their community and patronage to dispense in terms of parish benefices for clergy, fees for stewards and auditors, and posts for servants.

Visitors as they approached the church still passed through a defensive perimeter. Old Foundation cathedrals were usually separated from their nearby cities by circuits of buildings and walls. The New Foundations, having been monasteries, were also shut off from the world. One entered precincts through gateways that would mostly survive until the late eighteenth or early nineteenth centuries. Within a cathedral Close, however, change would be noticeable. The charnel chapels had gone and the houses of the chantry priests had been turned to new uses (Fig. 37, p. 99). The ancillary buildings of the monastic cathedrals, once occupied by priors and monks, were now dwellings for deans, canons, and minor clergy, or used by grammar schools. In all the Closes wives and families had begun to appear. Clergy were free again to marry after 1559, and advantage was taken of this by bishops, canons, minor canons, and vicars choral, while lay vicars could do the same.

The cathedral arrangements of Henry VIII had expected the minor clergy to be unmarried and to live and eat together. Marriage led to the adaptation of cathedral accommodation for families or drove husbands and wives out to private houses, and this in turn caused the abandonment of common meals: at York in 1574, Canterbury in 1593, and Exeter in about 1610.[1] The choristers, the other beneficiaries of these meals, now had to come from local families and live at home. Elizabeth disliked married clergy and refused to allow her bishops to bring their wives to court, but she could not stop the gradual entry of women into Closes or into cathedrals themselves. The wives of canons acquired seats in the choir adjoining those of their husbands. Nor were these the only women now to be found in Closes, because the old exclusion of the laity ceased to apply. Gentry and wealthy citizens began to take leases of the well-placed and attractive dwellings no longer required by the clergy.

On entering the cathedral, more changes would be visible inside. The great structure looked the same in its dimensions, but much had happened to the detailing. The pulpitum still divided the nave from the choir, but the crucifix upon it, the images of Mary and John, and the lights before them, had gone. The queen herself was not opposed to images. She suggested that Christ, Mary, and John might be represented in a prominent part of the church, but her leading subjects – some of whom had been in exile in Protestant Europe – opposed the idea.[2] All other religious statuary had been removed or remained in a broken state. Wall paintings had been covered with whitewash, or would be so. Images of Christ and the saints survived only on corbels and roof bosses, where they were unobtrusive, or in windows that were too expensive to replace until they were broken. Side chapels were empty of their altars, chantries, and guilds. In 1560 the queen's attention was brought to the fact that tombs were being defaced and she forbade this to happen, but damage continued through vandalism.[3] Indeed, for the next three hundred years cathedral visitors enjoyed carving their names and initials on monuments, especially when these were made of soft alabaster.

The choir retained its seating, including the bishop's throne. But the high altar had gone and the reredos behind it had lost its statues. There was no focal point on which to fix one's thought or devotion. The Prayer Books of 1552 and 1559 required the replacement of the altar

44. The young Elizabeth I in about 1560, just after she presided over the Church Settlement of 1559 and the changes it brought to cathedrals.

by a moveable communion table. This was to stand in the choir or the nave, wherever the service beside it could best be heard. The Royal Injunctions of 1559 ordered that while out of use, the table should stand where the altar stood. When a communion service was held, on the other hand, it was to be moved into the chancel or choir in order to emphasise the difference between the Protestant and Catholic theologies of the service. In parish churches after 1559 communion usually took place only four times a year but cathedral practice was more frequent, which made moving the table irksome. In St Paul's it was at the east end of the nave from 1559 until 1564, when it was re-sited at the east end of the choir. That became a common place for it in Elizabeth's reign: at Durham and Gloucester, for example. The table was usually positioned there with its short ends pointing east and west to minimise its resemblance to an altar. The celebrant priest stood on its north side, and those receiving communion knelt round the table unless, as happened in some churches, they stayed in their seats and had communion brought to them. The table was meant to be covered with a silk or buckram cloth when out of use and a linen cloth when in use, but it had no other ornaments. Elizabeth kept the table of her own chapel permanently at the old altar site with a cross and candlesticks on it, for which she was often criticised. The leaders of her Church were as hostile to crosses as they were to images, and candlesticks hinted at veneration.

It is easy to grow accustomed to visual changes and to forget what existed before. But one elderly man of Durham in the 1590s could not free himself from the memory of what the cathedral had been like some fifty-five years earlier when he was young and it was still a house of monks. He wrote it down and we still possess it.[4] He recalled the great shrine of St Cuthbert in the church, embellished with marble and gilding, flanked by the flags of the nobility and the captured banner of the King of Scots, now all 'spoiled and defaced'. He remembered Maundy Thursday when the prior washed the feet of the poor in the cloisters, Good Friday when the monks crept on their knees along the cathedral floor to kiss the crucifix, and Eastertide when the great wooden candlestick was set up in the choir, rising almost as high as the vaulting. He thought of the busy life of the cloisters, with the porter sitting in the south walk to keep out intruders, the monks studying at their carrels or desks in the north walk, and the novices being taught in the west walk, sitting in a 'fair great stall of wainscot'. And he ended his memories with how, when the monks had left, the cathedral visitors of Edward VI came in 1547 to put an end to all the remaining rites and ceremonies. Dr Harvey, their leader, called for the portable shrine of Corpus Christi which had been carried around the streets every summer, and 'when it was brought before him, he did tread upon it with his feet, and did break it all in pieces'.[5]

Cathedrals and Their Critics

Alongside their losses and changes, cathedrals gained from the Reformation in one major respect. There were no longer competing churches in their cities in the form of monasteries or friaries, and no great abbeys elsewhere with wealthy incomes and abbots sitting in Parliament. The cathedrals were now the largest bodies in a much reduced group of religious houses in England that included the royal chapels of Westminster and Windsor, the university colleges of Oxford and Cambridge, the colleges of Eton and Winchester which were linked with the universities, and three collegiate churches that were suppressed under Edward VI but later re-established. These were Manchester and Southwell, revived by Mary, and Ripon by James I. Each of the latter three would become a cathedral one day, but not for three hundred years.

It is probably no accident that this new prominence coincided with the first recorded use of the word 'cathedral' on its own, in the late sixteenth century. The prominence, however, was not much of an advantage for a long time and gave cathedrals a profile that was often unwelcome. The Crown protected them but it saw them (like bishops) as fair game for exploitation. Some cathedral posts were given to royal lay servants. Sir Thomas Smith, the queen's secretary of state, became dean of Carlisle, his successor Thomas Wilson dean of Durham, and John Herbert dean of Wells. Courtiers were allowed to bully cathedrals into leasing them lands at reduced rates. The government of Edward VI obliged Chester to rent most of its estates to Sir Richard Cotton, comptroller of the royal household.[6] Elizabeth ordered Salisbury to lease the rich manor of Sherborne to Sir Walter Ralegh. Her favourite, the earl of Leicester, and her minister Robert Cecil both held leases of dean and chapter property, and only under James I did these pressures subside.[7] There were even suggestions in 1585, when a Spanish invasion seemed a real possibility, that cathedrals might be dissolved to find money for war. The archbishop of Canterbury, John Whitgift, wrote to the queen's chief minister, Lord Burghley, to head off the attack. He pointed to their value in providing livings for scholars and divines, their support of education, relief of poverty, and value to the local economy. He made a further, rather brief, recall of their worship of God and their music. The danger passed but it would return under Charles I.[8]

Attacks of a different kind, principled and rhetorical ones, came from Protestants who wished for further reformation of the Church and saw cathedrals as survivals from the old corrupt Catholic past. This view was shared at the very top of the Church and can be traced back to Cranmer's lukewarm response to Henry VIII's cathedral plans. John Hooper, the radical bishop of Gloucester, complained in 1552 of the lack of good men in cathedrals. His counterpart John Jewel of Salisbury wrote in 1559 that 'the cathedral churches were but dens of thieves'. A fourth bishop, Richard Cox of Ely, complained in 1576 that their activity 'now is only in singing and very little in edifying'.[9]

These comments reflected the fact that the leaders of the Elizabethan Church were often more radical than the queen herself. The refusal of so many Catholics to conform in 1559 had enabled the appointment of strong Protestants as bishops and deans, some of whom had been in exile on the Continent during Mary Tudor's reign. Their theology was strongly influenced by that of John Calvin

45. An
Elizabethan
cathedral
musician:
the memorial
to Matthew
Godwin, master
of the choristers
of Exeter, who
died aged only
eighteen in
1586.

and their idea of a working church by his city of Geneva. Services should centre on Bible reading, preaching, and extempore prayer, and churches become little more than lecture rooms for these purposes. Institutions and practices that were not sanctioned by the Bible or the early Church should be discontinued. Those who held such views were and are often known as Puritans. They were not a coherent group or identical in their opinions. Most were willing to put up with the traditions around them while hoping to move the Church in the direction of further reform. Bishops in particular had to moderate their views while they served a conservative queen, and it was difficult for them to change the habits of their cathedral clergy.

A minority of Puritans were more radical. They sought a Church that was independent of the Crown, self-governing, Calvinist in theology, and Genevan in practice. In consequence they detested cathedrals in all respects. When Parliament met in 1571, an anonymous Puritan pamphlet was published called *An Admonition to the Parliament*, urging its members to reform the Church, including the cathedrals. Its language was eloquent:

We should be too long to tell your honours of cathedral churches, the dens aforesaid of all loitering lubbers, where master dean, master vicedean, master canons or prebendaries the greater, master petty canons or canons the lesser, master chancellor of the church, master treasurer – otherwise called Judas the purse-bearer, the chief chanter, singing men – special favourers of religion, squeaking choristers, organ players, gospellers, epistolers, pensioners, readers, vergers, etc., live in great idleness and have their abiding. If you would know whence all these came, we can easily answer you that they came from the pope, as out of the Trojan horse's belly, to the destruction of God's kingdom. The Church of God never knew them, neither doth any reformed Church in the world know them.[10]

The authors, John Field and Thomas Wilcox, were discovered, arrested, and imprisoned for a year. But they were not alone.

A similar petition was made to the Parliament of 1587. This time it was, wisely, anonymous. It demanded that cathedrals 'be utterly destroyed':

These are indeed the very dens of thieves, where the time and place of God's service, preaching, and prayer is most filthily abused in piping with organs, in singing, ringing, and trolling of the psalms from one side of the choir to another, with squeaking of chaunting choristers disguised (as are all the rest) in white surplices, others in cornered caps and filthy copes . . . These unprofitable members [are], for the most part dumb dogs, unskilful sacrificing priests, destroying drones, or rather caterpillars of the Word. They consume yearly some £2,500, some £3,000, some more, some less . . . They are dens of lazy loitering lubberds, the very harbourers of all deceitful and time-serving hypocrites.

They should be pulled down, concluded the writer, or their loiterers turned out and four or five preachers put into their places.[11] Complainants like these might be vocal and witty, but they had no ability to make changes. Elizabeth and her successors were resolute in maintaining the Reformation of 1559, including the cathedrals. Not until the 1640s, when Civil War broke out and hostility towards them was much stronger, would cathedrals come into danger from such opponents.

Worship in the Elizabethan Cathedrals

The question arose in and after 1559 as to what services should take place in a cathedral, given that only the Prayer Book was sanctioned for worship. At first some Church leaders tried to keep as much as possible of the traditional pattern of services in a Protestant form. In 1559 John Jewel, who became Elizabeth's bishop of Salisbury, laid down instructions for Salisbury and Exeter as follows. Soon after dawn there was to be an early morning service replacing the old morrow mass. This included a confession, litany, New Testament reading, and two collects (set prayers). At a quarter to eight morning prayer (matins) would take place, using the Prayer Book, followed at nine o'clock by a divinity lecture three times a week and on the other weekdays a reading from Erasmus's *Paraphrases* which explained the epistles and gospels. At ten there should be a communion service, apparently every day. Jewel did not define the timetable after this point, but it is likely that he envisaged evening prayer (evensong) at about three o'clock, again from the Prayer Book, and a sermon in the communion service every Sunday morning, preached by one of the dignitaries or canons.[12]

In the long term it proved impossible to maintain such an ambitious scheme. Two elements were particularly unpopular. The new communion service required 'a good number to communicate with the priest'. But the English had traditionally communicated only at Easter or in grave sickness, and objected to doing frequently. The divinity lecture was disliked as well. The canons probably regarded it as inappropriate for their rank and learning, while the minor canons and vicars choral resented their enforced attendance, especially when they were threatened with periodic tests of what they had learnt. Accordingly, during Elizabeth's reign the daily worship shrank a little from what Jewel had suggested. An early service of morning prayer became common in cathedrals, either to employ their vicars or to cater for early worshippers. This was said at about six in the morning in a side chapel of the building, which came to be known as the 'morning chapel'.[13] Morning prayer in the choir, attended by some canons and by all the minor clergy, took place at about eight o'clock. This was choral and included the singing of the psalms and canticles. On Wednesdays and Fridays morning prayer was followed by the litany and sometimes by the 'ante-communion' or first half of the communion service, omitting the communion itself. Evening prayer was said and sung in the choir in the mid- or late afternoon before the cathedral grew dark. The divinity lecture was lessened to twice a week, on Wednesdays and Fridays too, chiefly for the benefit of the minor cathedral clergy but might be omitted during the Christmas, Easter, and summer holidays.[14]

Sunday worship consisted of the early morning service, morning prayer in the choir, the litany, and the communion service. Some bishops insisted that communion be held weekly, but others reduced its frequency to one Sunday every month along with the great festivals of Christmas, Easter, and Whitsunday (or Pentecost).[15] Parts of this service would also be sung. On a Sunday when there was no communion, the ante-communion alone would be performed with a sermon delivered by the dean and canons in turn. Communion, if celebrated, took place after the sermon. All then went home for midday dinner, after which the lesser clergy returned to read and sing evening prayer in the afternoon. These arrangements had the merit that vicars and minor canons were used to regular set services, while Protestant Reformers achieved part of their goal of making the services instructive and remedial. There would be six Bible readings on a Sunday: two in the morning, two in the afternoon, and the epistle and gospel at

46. Elizabethan vicars choral. The priest vicars of Wells, in surplices and hoods, receive privileges from a medieval bishop, Ralph of Shrewsbury, watched by their inferior lay colleagues in black gowns with ruffs.

communion. The litany reminded people of their sins and invited them to give thanks for their blessings, while the sermon explained the scriptures and gave directions for godly living.

Two contested issues in worship related to vestments and music. In the early years of Elizabeth's reign the Crown and the bishops laid down that clergy should dress in white surplices at all services and rites, and that the priest celebrating communion should wear a cope over his surplice.[16] The most fervent Reformers among the clergy disliked these, and wanted to wear the black gowns that they used in daily life. In 1564 the archbishop of Canterbury, Matthew Parker, ordered the use of the surplice at the queen's insistence. Twenty leading clergy, including the deans of Durham and St Paul's, petitioned against its enforcement, but they were not heeded. Some cathedral dissenters absented themselves from services, and a few were deprived of their posts. Most cathedral clergy thereafter wore surplices, although copes were probably rarer.

The dislike of vestments extended to traditional Church music because of its Catholic associations, its sometimes non-biblical content, and its exclusion of the congregation.[17] Puritans wished to limit music in church to the singing of psalms, since these were biblical texts, and preferred them to be sung in metrical verse, of which Psalm 100, 'All people that on earth do dwell', is now the best known. This made it easier for the congregation to join in than if the choral method was used. The queen, however, liked traditional music and had it in her own chapel. The injunctions of 1559 which her commissioners took round the country referred approvingly to 'the laudable science of music' in church, and ordered that it should be allowed to continue as long as it was 'modest and distinct' so that listeners could hear and understand the words that were being sung.[18]

This enabled cathedrals to keep to a more traditional style of worship. The words of the prayers would be said or intoned, and the psalms be chanted by the choir with simple melodies or some harmony. Psalms would be sung antiphonally, each side of the choir taking a verse in turn, hence the 'trolling of the psalms' mentioned in the attack of 1587. New composers came forward to set the words of the Prayer Book services.[19] The leaders in this respect held posts as 'gentlemen' of the Chapel Royal, notably Thomas Tallis (d. 1585), William Byrd (d. 1623), and Orlando Gibbons (d. 1625). Byrd, however, had previously been organist of Lincoln Cathedral, while Thomas Tomkins (d. 1656) combined work in the Chapel with the organist's post at Worcester, and Thomas Weelkes (d. 1623) held that position at Chichester. The works of all came to be sung in cathedrals. They included 'Short' and 'Full' Services, which might set the 'preces and responses' and the canticles at morning and evening prayer along with two parts of the communion service: the Kyrie and Creed but not the Sanctus and Gloria, perhaps from fear of copying Catholic practices. The injunctions of 1559 also allowed for the singing of a hymn or anthem 'in the best sort of melody and music that may be conveniently devised', at the beginning or end of morning or evening prayer.[20] This provided the opportunity to compose and sing texts of a more complex nature, generally at the end of one or both of these services. All the composers mentioned wrote such anthems, based now on biblical texts (such as psalms) or prayers and poems directed to God. In consequence the cathedrals, along with the Chapel Royal, Westminster Abbey, and some university colleges, maintained more elaborate music when it died away in most parish churches except for the singing of psalms to metrical tunes (Fig. 45, p. 125).

One musical change of the post-Reformation period is worth noting although it does not appear in any of the pronouncements about services. This led to the practice with which we are familiar, in which all the members of the choir sing in harmony in the choir stalls. In the Middle Ages most of the church music in the choir was plainsong, with polyphony on Sundays and festivals sung by groups of singers from a huge choirbook placed on a lectern in the middle of the choir. Polyphony in the Lady chapel was performed in the same way. Now there was no Lady chapel and the great choirbooks were out of date. All the polyphony that remained was performed in the choir and from individual music books, as it is today. This is the result of Elizabeth's musical conservatism combined with the determination of her Protestant Reformers to remove all centres of worship in a church except for the choir itself.

It remains to consider who attended cathedral worship after the Reformation. Deans and a few dignitaries and canons might be present, although they had liberal leave of absence during the year. The mainstays of the choir were the vicars choral or minor canons (Fig. 46, p. 128), the lay singers, and the choristers. The almsmen at the New Foundations were expected to attend all services, and the grammar master and his pupils might be present on a Sunday or festival day, or at the early dawn service if there was one.[21] Then there might be lay folk from the city. William Harrison, who wrote a description of England in 1577 and may have had London chiefly in mind, claimed that 'great numbers of all estates' of society resorted to cathedral sermons on Sundays and even to the theology lectures during the week.[22] As in the Middle Ages, there were arrangements to accommodate those of wealth and rank in additional fixed or moveable seating, while the common sort were likely to be left to sit on the stone benches or floors of the nave and the choir aisles.

Fabrics and Monuments

Although England kept its cathedrals, their building history now diverged from that of their sisters on the Continent. There, in Catholic Europe, cathedrals continued to be rebuilt as they had been in the Middle Ages. Gothic was replaced by the Baroque, as can be seen in southern Germany and Italy. In England cathedrals became frozen in time and this would last for most of the rest of their history. What they had been in 1530 would become what everyone expected them to be thereafter: with somewhat of a heavy heart in the eighteenth century.

There was more than one reason for this stoppage. Cathedrals were now too big for their needs. Their former chapels were redundant and some were turned to new uses. The Lady chapel at Hereford became the cathedral library. Bishops installed their 'consistory courts' (dealing with Church and moral matters) in chapels at Chester, Durham, and elsewhere. The nobility and gentry, as we shall see, used them as burial places. There were no practical reasons to rebuild and even aesthetic ones were not viable. The religious and social context had changed. While cathedrals were unpopular in some quarters, not only was there no impetus for development but potential opposition to it. Then again cathedrals were poorer. Despite keeping most of their property, their incomes were being reduced by taxation and inflation. Even the maintenance of their buildings was a problem. Many references survive to the ruinous state of cathedrals in the late sixteenth and early seventeenth centuries. Some of the sources of income for fabric repairs had disappeared with the ending of indulgences, saint cults, and will bequests. There may also have been greater negligence, but records of bishops' visitations of cathedrals after 1559 tell us more about dilapidations than we hear in the Middle Ages.

By the second half of the sixteenth century St Paul's had become the cathedral with the highest profile. Its size and its location in the capital city gave it a status not even enjoyed by Canterbury as a national institution. Contemporaries called it 'the queen of churches', the English equivalent of St Peter's (Rome) or St Mark's (Venice).[23] The defects of its building were consequently more obvious and criticised than those elsewhere. In 1561 lightning struck the spire, starting a fire that destroyed it and parts of the roofs of the church. Fund-raising was done, and Elizabeth herself contributed. The roofs were restored but the spire was not, to the queen's annoyance. By the 1620s the building seemed again in a parlous state. William Laud, the bishop, referred to its 'vast ruins'. A new appeal for funds began. Laud promised £100 per annum and the dean and chapter £50. Charles I assisted, as did peers, bishops, and universities. Over £100,000 was raised during the 1630s. Apart from general repairs, the money was used to fund a new west front of the cathedral, designed by Inigo Jones. This was modelled on Roman architecture and comprised a huge portico of Corinthian columns supporting a frieze and balustrade with statues of Charles and James. The work was unfinished when the Civil War began, but it embodied the first and only major attempt to update a cathedral's exterior between the Reformation and the 1660s.

The one kind of construction that flourished in all cathedrals after 1559 was that of church monuments.[24] Bishops, deans, and canons continued to be buried in their churches and effigies of bishops on chests were still being made in the early seventeenth century. These effigies were now usually placed alongside walls, the figures being sometimes recumbent but often lying on their sides with their heads supported on a forearm, or alternatively in a kneeling posture. There were far more tombs of nobility and gentry than before. The dissolution of the monasteries left the cathedrals as the most prestigious buildings in which to be buried. Redundant cathedral chapels, transepts, and aisles made plenty of spaces available for monuments, and the increasing power of the laity against the clergy made it easier to gain control of such spaces. Some of the monuments were huge, extending from the floor to the vault of an aisle or chapel. The dignitary himself would be represented with his wife or wives, and often children in submissive postures. Examples include the tombs of Sir Mark Steward (d. 1603) in Ely; Sir William Gee (d. 1611), secretary of the Council of the North, in York; and Edward Seymour, earl of Hertford (d. 1621), in Salisbury (Fig. 47, p. 132).[25]

There was also what critics called 'prophanation': the use of buildings for secular purposes and their misuse through disorderly behaviour. This was an ancient problem, as we observed at York in 1519.[26] St Paul's suffered most from its site in a crowded city.[27] Chimneys belched smoke from sheds in the churchyard. Parts of the crypt and cloisters were rented out to workmen. The nave was used as a thoroughfare and a gathering place (Fig. 48, p. 134). Wealthy men (it was less respectable for their wives) went there in search of company and to hear news. The poor, including women with babies in arms, sat round the pillars and the doors to the choir, no doubt in hope of alms. Children played until dusk,

47. A stupendous Jacobean cathedral tomb: that of Edward Seymour, earl of Hertford (died 1621) at Salisbury.

disturbing the sermons taking place in the choir. Pickpockets awaited their chance. Servants in need of employment gathered at a certain pillar and posted bills advertising their services: Falstaff hired Bardolph there.[28] Choristers pounced on any man wearing spurs and demanded a payment called 'spur money'. A countryman arrested for urinating against a pillar in 1632 said that he did not know he was in a church. For a payment, visitors could even climb the central tower. While at the top, they shouted, carved their names on the lead of the roofing, and dropped stones into the minor canons' garden.

The Arminians

Towards the end of Elizabeth's reign, the beginnings of a reaction are discernible against the Calvinist beliefs and dislike of traditional institutions held by many Church leaders and cathedral clergy. It was first memorably expressed by Richard Hooker, Oxford graduate, rector of Boscombe (Wilts.), and non-resident canon of Salisbury in his *Laws of Ecclesiastical Polity* published in the 1590s.[29] He argued that the Bible, which Puritans regarded as the sole basis for religion, should be supplemented by the use of reason to add that which was good and profitable in matters that the Bible did not cover. Book 4, which came out in 1593, defended the ceremonies of the Church, while Book 5 in 1597 validated the Prayer Book and the use of music in services.[30] Hooker wrote specifically to counter Puritan objections to English Church practices and his work helped to take the initiative away from them.

During the early 1600s, in the reign of James I, similar views spread in the Church and among some of its lay supporters. Puritans called the holders of such views 'Arminians' after Jacob Arminius, a Dutch Protestant theologian and critic of Calvinism. The English Arminians were such critics but they had a positive desire to make the Church of England more decorous and devout in its life and worship. An early exponent of this desire was Lancelot Andrewes (d. 1626), prebendary of St Paul's and later bishop of Winchester. After holding Puritan views in his young adulthood, he grew to value traditional ideas and practices such as confession, greater reverence for communion, and the observance of liturgical seasons and festivals. He disapproved of the casual treatment of communion tables, calling them 'more like oyster boards', and may have anticipated later practice in moving one such table at St Giles Cripplegate (London) to the east end and fixing rails around it.[31]

The evolution of these ideas into a movement came in the mid-1610s with the rise of Richard Neile, bishop of Durham (1617–28) and archbishop of York (1631–40).[32] Whereas Andrewes was a visionary, Neile was an organiser who began to implement Arminian policies in his dioceses and used his links with the king and the court to support and promote like-minded clergy in other places. In 1608 he chose as his chaplain William Laud (Fig. 49, p. 136), who duly became dean of Gloucester, bishop of London, and finally archbishop of Canterbury (1633–45).[33] The ruling monarch, James I (1603–25), was at first broad-minded in promoting clergy of different views, but after 1618 he leaned more towards the Arminians and began to favour them with posts. This royal patronage increased when Charles I became king in 1625 and a close alliance was forged between him and Laud. Laud became one of his chief ministers,

48. The nave of Old St Paul's Cathedral in the mid-seventeenth century. The vista does not include the visitors, traders, and thieves who crowded the place every day.

assisting in shaping royal policies and having the power to enforce his views on bishops and cathedrals throughout the kingdom.

Laud and Neile initiated changes at Gloucester and Durham as early as 1617. They aimed to recreate cathedrals as models of Christian life and worship for the parish churches, thereby returning to the strategy of the Middle Ages. At the same time they were not simply backward looking. Their aesthetic tastes anticipated those of the later seventeenth and eighteenth centuries. A cathedral should be a fine and spiritual building. The houses that often encroached on its exterior should be removed, whatever the annoyance of their owners. At St Paul's it was even proposed to demolish the church of St Gregory which abutted the south-west corner. Inside cathedrals the profane activities like those that disfigured St Paul's should be forbidden. The extra seating that had often been introduced into choir and nave for lay people should be removed and replaced by moveable chairs or benches. This too caused offence, since mayors and corporations often used such seating. Priests who celebrated communion in cathedrals should wear copes, as had been required since the reign of Elizabeth. Reverence should be shown by men removing hats in church and by everyone bowing at the name of Jesus and towards the communion table.

The position of this table now became a hotly contended issue. Hitherto official policy about its location had not been rigid. In 1604 a new code of canon law for the Church, approved by James I, required it simply to be placed 'within the church or chancel' where the priest could best be heard.[34] Laud preferred it to stand permanently at the east end of the choir where the high altar had been, placed 'altar-wise' with its short ends north and south. It was to have a fine covering, and often received more prominence by being raised on steps. Being permanent in this location, it could be made of marble although still in the form of a table rather than like the solid altars of the Middle Ages. It might have ornaments on its top in the form of candlesticks, an alms dish, or a Bible. The table area was to be fenced off with low rails, partly to protect it and partly to enable people to come to the rails to receive communion and kneel there resting against them. Hitherto they had often received it elsewhere in the choir or chancel, or at their seats, and not always kneeling but standing or sitting.

During the 1630s Laud did not insist that every table should be placed at the east end and railed, or that people had to kneel there for communion. But he was closely associated with these practices, which many people felt to be Roman Catholic in nature. This feeling was not really justified. Laud was indeed restoring a focus to each church, which it had not possessed since about 1550. The east-end table (not a solid medieval altar) provided a place or symbol that could be seen as representing God, yet it was not an image. Services in cathedrals and parish churches continued to be the Protestant ones of 1559. Laud and his associates beautified churches with altar cloths, hangings, and cushions, but when they introduced statues or paintings of religious figures, they kept to the patriarchs, prophets, and apostles of the Bible. Two cathedrals, Chichester and Exeter, placed texts of the Ten Commandments at their east ends, flanked by paintings of Moses and Aaron. These patriarchs had never been venerated in the Middle Ages; nor were they and other new images worshipped now.

In 1634 Laud dispatched commissioners to carry out a 'metropolitical' visitation of the province of Canterbury. Neile did likewise at York. The commissioners inquired into the conditions of buildings, the residence of clergy, the leasing of property, the conduct of worship, and the preaching of sermons. Many reports came back of unrepaired buildings, inadequate vestments, and lack of respect at services. In the following year Laud issued injunctions to the cathedrals concerned. In 1640 he helped prepare a new canon law for the Church

49. William
Laud, archbishop
of Canterbury
(died 1645), the
leading figure
in the reform of
cathedrals during
the 1630s.

of England to make his policies even more effective, and one of its sections addressed the issue of tables. It tried to defuse the issue by appealing to Elizabeth I's requirement that the table should stand at the east end, arguing that this did not make it an altar except in the sense that the word was used by the early Christian Church. However, it required all churches to follow cathedral practice in placing the table at the east, railing it off to keep it from being profaned, and administering communion at the rail rather than anywhere else in the church.[35]

Unfortunately for Laud the unpopularity of his religious policies with Puritans was now compounded by his involvement with the unpopularity of Charles I. The king had not summoned Parliament since 1629 and had attempted to raise revenues without parliamentary consent. When the Scots rose against Charles I's rule in 1640, the king was obliged to call Parliament again, and when the Irish did the same in 1641, the king and his parliamentary opponents were unwilling to trust each other with an army to suppress them. The authority of the Crown began to weaken in 1640, and by the late summer of 1642 there was Civil War.

Civil War and Abolition

On 26 December 1639 a storm lashed Canterbury Cathedral. A pinnacle bearing Laud's coat of arms was dislodged from a tower and crashed into the cloisters.[36] It was an omen of coming disaster. As soon as Parliament met in 1640, complaints were voiced about Laud's alleged Catholic services. On 16 December the House of Commons impeached him for high treason on various charges, including the alteration of 'true religion' and attempting to reconcile England and Rome. A few days later, after Christmas, popular resentment at Canterbury against the cathedral and its services led to a demonstration in the cathedral choir. Cries rang out of 'This is popery!' and 'Down with the altar!' When the singers attempted to chant the psalms in the normal way, the congregation drowned them out by singing the longest psalm of all, 119, in the metrical version used in parish churches.[37] In March 1641 Parliament sent Laud to the Tower of London. After an attempt to try him judicially failed, he was arbitrarily condemned to death by a parliamentary act of attainder and executed in January 1645.

During the 1640s there was a double assault on cathedrals: one legal, from the opponents of Charles I in Parliament, and the other physical, from local activists of one kind or another. The principal objects of attack were deans and chapters, their property, cathedral furnishings, and the current Laudian services rather than the churches themselves and their use for worship.[38] The first assaults were due to the outbreak of war. On Saturday 27 August 1642 Colonel Edwin Sandys, who was leading a parliamentary force to take control of Kent, arrived with soldiers at Canterbury Cathedral where, in the words of the dean, they 'began a fight with God himself'. A later account tells how they entered the church and overthrew the communion table. They tore off its velvet covering, broke the altar rails, and damaged the brass eagle lectern and the organ. In the vestry they ripped surplices and gowns, and tore up copies of the Prayer Book. Outside the church they discharged their guns at an old statue of Christ above the south gate of the cathedral. Eventually, Sandys restored order and led them off to Dover.[39]

Similar attacks took place elsewhere. Naturally, those men who joined the army of the London Parliament as we may call it (the king's supporters in the Lords and Commons having seceded to him) were the most strongly Puritan in temper and hostile to the established forms of religion. Acts of violence took place at Chichester, Exeter, Rochester, and Winchester in 1642, and later elsewhere.[40] There was also official iconoclasm. In August 1643 the London Parliament enacted an ordinance requiring the demolition and removal from cathedrals of all 'monuments of superstition and idolatry'. Communion tables were to be moved back into the church, their rails destroyed, and any altar platforms levelled. No ornaments were to be allowed on the table; no crucifixes, crosses, images, or pictures of the Trinity, the Virgin Mary, or saints within the church. The ordinance exempted coats of arms and funeral monuments, but these were sometimes damaged too through dislike of their imagery or aristocratic nature.[41] At Canterbury William Culmer, a radical Puritan preacher, climbed a ladder sixty feet high to smash figures of saints in the east window. Organs were often vandalised by soldiers and, if not, were later removed officially. So were vestments and Prayer Books: at Norwich those of the cathedral were burnt on a huge bonfire in the market place.

Meanwhile, in Parliament cathedrals were subjects of criticism and censure. In March 1641 the House of Commons started to frame charges against John Cosin, a prominent canon of Durham, for having allegedly set up images there and for introducing 'a holy consecrated knife, kept on purpose to cut the communion bread'. Shortly afterwards a committee of the House proposed the holding of a debate on 'the greatness of the revenues of deans and chapters, and the little use of them'.[42] There were two debates in May and June which represent one of the rare occasions in history when the merits and demerits of cathedrals have been discussed in public. The House invited Dr John Hacket, a senior clergyman of moderately Puritan views, to put the case in their favour. He argued that they advanced the glory of God, true religion and piety, learning, and the good of society. They maintained sermons, lectures, and grammar schools. The universities of Oxford and Cambridge (which sent MPs to the Commons) presented petitions on behalf of the cathedrals. These made similar points and added practical ones. Cathedral posts maintained younger brothers of good parentage. They benefited the economy of their cities by employing local people and attracting 'strangers' (i.e. tourists). They paid the king taxes. Such reasoning was no doubt meant to appeal to MPs, who were gentry or townsmen and all of them taxpayers.

Contrary views were put forward by Cornelius Burges, a more strongly Puritan cleric, and Sir William Thomas, MP for Caernarfon. Thomas entertained the house by claiming that deans had their origins as catering officers for monks. He recounted how a rich dean of St Paul's in the twelfth century had bequeathed his soul to the Devil, after which the king ordered his body to be thrown into a river. Present-day deans, he said, employed themselves about 'beggarly trifles'. He went on to attack Church music, which he asserted was introduced by a pope to usher in Antichrist, although he was happy with psalms if sung without organs, as long as people could understand them. Thomas Pury, MP for Gloucester, complained that deans and chapters were bound to reside, preach, teach, and provide hospitality. But these duties had not been observed in Gloucester for as long as he could remember. The cathedral there did nothing for the poor or for highways and bridges. The clergy had betrayed their mandate, and their possessions should be put into the hands of trustees to carry out the original pious and charitable purposes. The Commons agreed and on 15 June they resolved that deans and chapters should be 'utterly abolished'.[43]

This hostility grew in the Civil War. The unpopularity of cathedrals intensified through the sympathy of their clergy with Charles I and the support that they gave him financially. In March 1643 the London Parliament sequestrated the estates of all deans and chapters that had contributed to the king's war effort: potentially all of them.[44] In 1645 it forbade the use of the Prayer Book and in 1646 it abolished bishops, but another three years elapsed, until Charles I had been executed and a republic declared early in 1649, before an ordinance was passed to put an end to cathedrals as organisations. This was enacted on the following 30 April. All titles and posts of deans and chapters, canons, and prebendaries were dissolved. Their lands, churches, tithes, charters, and records were confiscated. Trustees were appointed to administer their properties, with power to sell or lease them. Payments to grammar schools, almshouses, and the repair of highways were safeguarded, but no pensions to the clergy were provided for, although a few received them as did some clergy widows.[45]

As a result most of the existing cathedral clergy forfeited everything: benefices, incomes, and houses. Their number has been estimated at about 668 deans, canons, and minor clergy, although when the number of non-resident canons is deducted, the losses in cathedral Closes were smaller.[46] Lay singers and choristers also lost their posts. Much cathedral property was subsequently sold along with that of the bishops, subject to the fact that the property was usually already leased to tenants. Bishops' palaces and canons' houses went the same way, often to be bought by gentry or citizens.

Cathedrals from 1649 to 1660

The abolition of cathedrals as bodies and their clergy did not satisfy the more radical Puritans. In February 1651 a parliamentary committee proposed the demolition of the buildings themselves where there were other churches available for worship. The materials should be sold and the proceeds used as funds to help the poor. In the following April it was agreed to begin with Lichfield and the lead was stripped from its roof. In July 1652 a new committee was appointed to select cathedrals for destruction, and a few weeks later it resolved to target Canterbury. But nothing was done, and although the issue was raised for a second time in December, there was again no outcome.[47]

In the end all the cathedrals survived as structures, albeit in a range of conditions. The worst affected was Lichfield, which endured sieges during the war, lost its spires, and was left in a ruinous and unusable condition. At Carlisle Scottish troops demolished most of the nave to get stone for repairing the castle and other fortifications (Fig. 50, p. 140).[48] Durham housed Scottish prisoners from 1650 to 1652, during which it was damaged and seems to have had little function thereafter. Soldiers and horses were quartered in the nave of St Paul's from 1648 till at least 1651 and again in 1657, but the eastern parts of the church remained in use and one chapel was allocated to a 'separatist' or sectarian congregation.[49] At Canterbury the church was largely abandoned and most of the worship moved to the former chapter house, now called the Sermon House. Parts of Rochester were used as a stable and carpenter's workshop.[50] Hereford lost its chapter house and Exeter its cloisters, but most of the cathedrals continued as places for services of a plain and preaching kind. Oxford was uniquely privileged. Universities were

50. *The damage of the Civil Wars: Carlisle Cathedral, robbed of most of its nave (left). Its truncated west end is propped by buttresses.*

exempted from the seizures of Church property, so it continued to maintain its former staff of clergy, albeit within the restrictions of Puritan worship.

In certain places Parliament provided stipends for Puritan ministers and gave them canons' houses to live in. These included the six preachers maintained at Canterbury since the 1540s, four at York, and three at Hereford.[51] Their duties included preaching in rural churches. Those buildings that stayed in use tended to fall under the control of the local municipal authorities, who managed the buildings and appointed ministers. At Norwich the corporation built seats for its members at the east end of the choir, where the Laudian table had been. The general effect was to convert cathedrals into civic churches, repeating what had happened to the abbey churches like Bath and St Albans that managed to survive the Reformation. In certain cities the Puritans divided into Presbyterians, who advocated a centrally organised church, and Independents who preferred giving power to individual congregations. At Worcester each party used the cathedral at different times, but at Exeter the cathedral was divided into two by a wall, the Presbyterians taking the choir and the Independents the nave.[52]

In 1645 the Prayer Book was replaced by a *Directory of Worship* which gives a rough guide to the services likely to have been staged in cathedrals for the next fifteen years. The *Directory* differed from the Prayer Book in providing only a structure for worship with a summary of the topics to be covered, allowing ministers to expound these as they wished. Morning and evening services began with a short prayer asking blessing on the readings from Scripture. One chapter from each Testament was to be read, working through the Bible in order. A psalm was sung, followed by a call to confession, a 'bidding prayer' inviting the congregation to pray for the needs of society, a sermon (advice was given on what it should aim to do), and a final prayer of thanksgiving.[53] Holy Communion, which was recommended to be celebrated frequently, should take place at a table 'decently covered' and placed so that communicants could sit around it, in other words on seats or benches and away from the east end of the choir.[54] No prohibition was made of vestments, but the likelihood is that ministers were envisaged as wearing black gowns. Worship was to take place only on Sundays and not on festivals or saints' days.

The period from 1649 to 1660 has become known as the Interregnum. During these years, in 1654, the diarist John Evelyn travelled through parts of England and visited six cathedrals.[55] All were apparently in use for Puritan services, which Evelyn (a Royalist) disliked and therefore omitted to mention. Three bore signs of injury. Oxford had suffered damage in its windows, presumably to remove saints' images. At Lincoln 'the soldiers had lately knocked off most of the brasses which were on the gravestones . . . . They went in with axes and hammers . . ., so hellish an avarice possessed them'. Worcester was 'extremely ruined by the late wars, otherwise a noble structure'. The other three were still largely unscathed. Evelyn thought Salisbury to be 'the completest piece of Gothic-work in Europe, taken in all its uniformity', and he admired its cloisters and 'remarkable monuments'. Gloucester, 'a noble fabric', had cloisters too, a whispering place, a new library, and monuments including Robert of Normandy. York 'alone of all the great churches in England had best been preserved from the fury of the sacrilegious'. Evelyn described it as 'a most entire, magnificent piece of Gothic architecture'. He praised the screen, carved with flowers and statues of old kings, and found the monuments still in place, 'many of them very ancient'. Even more surprisingly he was taken into the vestry to be shown a handsome Bible and Prayer Book with all the recent altar plate including chalices, patens, flagons, and basins.

Much therefore survived iconoclasm, wars, and hostile legislation. Indeed, it has been suggested that York Minster was now more fully integrated with city life than it had been before, and this may have been true elsewhere.[56] The corporation of York paid the government to acquire the cathedral's jurisdiction within the city and, with the disappearance of deans and chapters, it is likely that such jurisdictions became dormant generally.[57] Cathedral schools and almshouses were generally exempt from confiscation, and continued to serve their districts as before. There were even suggestions for improving the educational provision. The city of York petitioned for a grant of dean and chapter property to establish a college, presumably of a university kind. This was not successful, but in 1656 Parliament agreed that some of the cathedral revenues of Durham should be used for a similar purpose. In the following year the Lord Protector, Oliver Cromwell, issued letters patent founding a college of a provost, four professors, and four tutors, together with a free school of four masters with scholarships for students and boys. The letters named the men who were to hold the senior posts, but the college had not come into existence by the time that Charles II was restored to the throne, and with him the old cathedrals, in May 1660.[58]

Learning and Charity

The ancient role of cathedrals as centres of learning continued after the Reformation, but the context of learning had undergone much change. The evolution of the grammar school curriculum round about 1500 from the reading of medieval grammarians and poets to that of classical Latin and Greek authors made a huge difference to the understanding of history, geography, science, and literature. Developments in the understanding of biblical and patristic texts, along with the advent of Reformation theology, meant that most of the theological knowledge of the Middle Ages was discarded. The study of canon law, which had occupied so many medieval cathedral clergy, largely came to an end in 1535 because of its roots in papal decrees. The dissolution of the monasteries destroyed the system of education to which the monastic cathedrals had belonged since the thirteenth century. More positively, English had developed as a uniform literary language and printing as a means of disseminating it. This gave new opportunities for reaching the public through writing accessible works that people could understand.

For centuries cathedrals had possessed book collections and latterly libraries as a basis for study and writing.[59] After the Reformation these were left weaker because so much of their contents were out of date. The royal injunctions of 1547 set out to modernise them. As we have seen, all cathedrals were required to create a library and the injunctions went on to specify the inclusion of the works of the early Christian writers Augustine, Basil, Ambrose, Cyprian, and so on, as well as those of Erasmus 'and other good writers'.[60] But to order was not always to achieve. Exeter had none of the works of the early Church Fathers in 1559. At Winchester the bishop had to order a library to be set up in 1562, and Norwich 'had no convenient place for a library' six years later. The hundred years after 1560 did not see a widespread renaissance in the libraries; indeed they lost some of their holdings through gifts elsewhere or misappropriation. Donations of books were made by some deans and canons, but cathedrals had to compete in this respect with the two universities and their colleges to which greater generosity was often shown, perhaps from a feeling that they would use it more effectively.

Improvements were eventually made in some places. Salisbury's library was updated for modern study by a large bequest from the bishop, Edmund Guest, in 1577. This added sixty-five volumes of the early Fathers and Church councils in new editions, with texts and grammars in Hebrew and up-to-date dictionaries and commentaries. Hereford was revitalised in 1583, thanks to its precentor, Thomas Thornton, and given new bookcases and chains for the books. Durham underwent similar improvements in the 1620s, with the acquisition of nearly three hundred new volumes and the allocation of a regular income to the library. Finally, York benefited from a huge donation of three thousand items collected by Archbishop Tobie Matthew and given by his widow after his death in 1628. York's library was maintained by the corporation of York during the Interregnum, and Gloucester's corporation actually provided a better library at the cathedral there in 1648. Such resources were chiefly meant for deans and canons who alone could borrow books, but it seems likely that access could be gained by men of rank and learning from outside although it is not clear how many such people asked for the privilege.[61]

Some deans and canons continued to study, write, and preach as they had done in previous centuries (Fig. 51, p. 144). An analysis of those who lived in the seventeenth century has recorded 716 who left published writings to the extent of 4,265 separate works.[62] Not all these works were written while the authors held cathedral posts, and many such authors were non-residents whose links came merely from drawing an income. A large number of the titles concerned, 892, were political or controversial works, and another 414 works of theology. These were traditional topics for clergy to write on; the novelty of the period was the production of more popular works than before, aimed at intelligent general readers. So 958 items consisted of sermons, individually or collectively published, and even more, 1,083, of devotional literature about how to understand the Scriptures, pray, and lead a Christian life. This reflected the replacement of Latin

51. *One of the famous outdoor sermons at Old St Paul's in 1616. The Reformation emphasised preaching at cathedrals, and many sermons were published.*

by English in worship and Bible reading, which created a demand for religious literature among the public that clergy of all kinds were prompted to satisfy.

The most successful writers on religion were those who kept to the middle ground and did not take too extreme a stance as Arminians or Puritans. Lewis Bayly, treasurer of St Paul's and later bishop of Bangor, published *The Practice of Piety* in about 1612. Aimed at 'the very meanest readers' and printed as a little compact book, it gained immediate popularity and was reissued at least fifty times up to the middle of the eighteenth century. The book provided a series of prayers and meditations on the nature of God and on how to begin and end the day, Sunday observance, times of sickness, attending communion, and preparing for death. Its success was repeated in 1657 by another handy volume called *The Whole Duty of Man* by Richard Allestree, who became a canon of Oxford after the Restoration. This was directed more towards behaviour: the Christian's duty to God, the observance of his commandments, the cultivation of personal virtue, relationships with one's neighbours, and the obligations to avoid sin and give to charity. By 1690 it had gone into twenty-eight editions and was translated into six foreign languages.

The range of cathedral writings was very wide. There were works of history, geography, poetry, mathematics, and the sciences. William Camden, who wrote the first great survey of England's geography and antiquities, *Britannia* (1586), was a canon of Salisbury. His counterpart Richard Hakluyt, who published a comprehensive account of overseas explorations, *The Principal Navigations, Voyages, and Discoveries of the English Nation* (1589), held a prebend of Bristol. Another Salisbury canon, Thomas Fuller (d. 1661), was a prolific author of popular works including a history of the crusades, *The Church History of Britain*, and a biographical dictionary: *Worthies of England*. Joseph Hall, archdeacon of York, dean of Worcester, and bishop of Exeter and Norwich (d. 1656) wrote over a hundred popular works of devotion, controversy, satire, social comment, and poetry.

The two most famous cathedral authors of this period are John Donne and George Herbert. Donne (1572–1631) took holy orders in his forties after a secular career, and was dean of St Paul's from 1621 until his death ten years later.[63] In 1624 he published *Devotions upon Emergent Occasions*, which contains his famous reflection 'No man is an island'. His poems were first published in 1633 after his death, covering topics both secular and spiritual from the whole of his life. The latter category included some of his 'Holy Sonnets' including such well-known items as 'At the round earth's imagined corners', 'Death be not proud', and 'Show me, dear Christ, thy spouse so bright and clear'. They achieved seven editions by 1670. Eighty of his sermons were published in 1640 and another seventy-six later on.

Herbert (1593–1633) was another late entrant into the Church, in his early thirties. After this he secured a canonry of Lincoln Cathedral and the rectory of Fugglestone-with-Bemerton outside Salisbury.[64] He did not reside as a canon but exerted himself to restore the church of Leighton Bromswold near Huntingdon, which belonged to his prebend. Here he expressed his religious sympathies by building a reading desk (for the Prayer Book service) and a pulpit (for preaching) that were of identical height. His religious poems were printed posthumously in 1633 as *The Temple*, comprising such pieces as 'Let all the world in every corner sing', 'Love bade me welcome', and 'Teach me my God and King'. The poems, like Donne's, attracted many readers and were reissued twelve times down to 1709.

Cathedrals also supported learning through education. All continued to have a small group of choristers for whom they provided teaching in song, followed by a place at the free public grammar school which each foundation had to maintain after the 1540s. These grammar schools were important locally, but the only one with a national reputation – St Paul's – was no longer a true cathedral school. It continued to be sited near the cathedral and received some of the choristers, but John Colet, its re-founder in 1509, put it under the control of the Mercers' Company of London and when Laud, typically, tried to exert his authority over it, he was not successful.[65] Seven of the New Foundation grammar schools provided scholarships for some of the boys at the school, giving them maintenance allowances as well as free education.[66] A lack of university awards, however, which Henry VIII had briefly provided and then taken away, made the schools less attractive than those like Eton and Winchester that had such advantages.[67] A cathedral schoolboy who sought higher education had to be maintained by his family unless he could get a special grant from the dean and chapter or was at Canterbury, where Matthew Parker founded four scholarships to be held at Corpus Christi College, Cambridge.[68]

Charity was a further area of cathedral activity. Medieval clergy were expected to offer hospitality to travellers and alms to the poor, and this ethic was particularly strong at cathedrals where it was done institutionally at the monastic bodies and individually by the canons of the secular ones. Several of the secular cathedrals had an oversight of local hospitals and almshouses, including Exeter, Hereford, Lincoln, and Salisbury, although some of these houses disappeared at the Reformation.[69] We saw how Henry VIII established almsmen at all the New Foundation cathedrals in the early 1540s, who received accommodation and meals or an allowance.[70] The numbers ranged from four at Bristol and Gloucester to twelve at Canterbury and Winchester, with twenty-four at Oxford. As has been mentioned, they were often former royal servants or injured soldiers who had previously been farmed out to monasteries. The giving of hospitality and alms by individual canons tended to disappear during the seventeenth century in favour of donations made by deans and chapters collectively or by collections for good causes made at services. Nonetheless, the duty continued to be observed and applied to a range of needs including the local poor, Protestants in foreign countries, and (after the Restoration), captives of Turkish pirates, victims of the Great Fire of London, and the rebuilding of St Paul's.[71]

In the end cathedrals survived the Civil War and Interregnum, their fourth great crisis, to a greater extent than their fiercest opponents intended. They remained in their essential form as buildings. Disputes about how to use or replace these places, some local affection for them and their clergy, and memories of their role in supporting schools and almshouses may all have helped to preserve them. Most stayed in being as places of worship. When the Interregnum came to an end in 1660, it would not be too hard to revive them.

Chapter

── 7 ──

From Restoration to Romanticism

1660–1800

On 29 May 1660 Charles II entered London to enthusiastic crowds. The alternatives to monarchy tried between 1649 and 1660 had failed so completely, and the popular wish to return to the past was so great, that the restoration of the king was followed by the reappearance of most of what else had existed before the Civil War. The cathedrals had been swept away helplessly by the war and its consequences. Now they were swept back again with the turn of the tide.

Charles and his court, in exile in the Netherlands, had kept in touch with English affairs, including those of the Church of England.[1] Sir Edward Nicholas, secretary of state to the would-be king, kept lists of cathedral vacancies as far as he could and compiled a list of 86 men who would be suitable for promotion when the time came. There were many posts to fill because about 410 dignities, prebends, and canonries were vacant by 1660, out of a total of just over 600. Charles was anxious to appear as a moderate ruler. He promised religious toleration before his acceptance as king. Even after he regained the throne, he was willing to negotiate about Church matters and to include as many people as possible within the Church as long as they were loyal to the Crown. In October 1660 he issued the 'Worcester

House Declaration' in which he promised to give posts in cathedrals to the most learned and pious 'presbyters' of the dioceses. The word was chosen to appeal to those clergy who had been Presbyterians during the Interregnum, and he did indeed make offers of such posts to some of their leaders.[2]

In practice, matters worked out differently. Locally, the surviving clergy returned to their cathedrals and, with the support of the neighbouring gentry and urban leaders, they started to take possession of the buildings and to organise themselves. By July chapter meetings were being held at Canterbury, Chichester, Peterborough, and St Paul's, and other cathedrals followed suit in this respect, although Durham did not follow till November. The Prayer Book services were resumed as soon as copies of the book could be procured. Meanwhile the king found himself overwhelmed with candidates requesting cathedral posts or being proposed for them by courtiers. Between June and September Charles made 223 appointments of dignitaries, canons, and archdeacons in those cathedrals where he had the right or power to do so. Few of these men were old clergy. Most were newcomers with no cathedral experience and some had collaborated with the regimes of the 1640s and 50s. The Church of England thus re-established itself as much as it was re-established, and by the time that Charles got round to offering some leading Presbyterians posts as bishops or cathedral clergy, they refused his offers, probably perceiving that they would be isolated figures in an unsympathetic world. The cathedral preachers who had been appointed since 1645 might have survived to join the new order but they too were strong Puritans and refused to adjust themselves to it, so that they lost their places.

The ordinances and acts of Parliament to which the Crown had not assented lapsed in 1660. These included the acts of 1645 and 1649 abolishing bishops and cathedrals and appropriating their property, so that the new appointees could expect to recover their losses. In October Charles II sent letters exhorting bishops and cathedrals to be generous in their treatment of the purchasers of lands and of the tenants holding them. The king's first 'Convention' parliament, which sat from April to December, laid down principles for re-possession but did not legislate formally on the matter. It proposed that those who had bought property should be compensated, and a royal commission was established to arbitrate disputes. In the end the process of recovery was easier than one would expect. Many purchasers of lands were the former cathedral tenants. They could now surrender their deeds of possession and receive new leases on good financial terms. The system of leasing involved the tenant paying a large lump sum or 'entry fine' when the lease was agreed and a much smaller annual rent for the term of the lease. Cathedrals were lenient to purchasers willing to lease. York halved the fines and Winchester charged them at only six times the rent.

52. The Restoration: Exeter, with the 'Babylonish wall' removed from between the nave and chancel, and the new organ of 1665. The pulpitum windows are later insertions.

As a result there was a flurry of leasing in and after 1660. At Durham, for example, 65 new leases were agreed in November 1660 and another 270 during the next three years, bringing in £22,500 in entry fines.[3] Sometimes it was harder to acquire the former houses of deans and canons, where citizens and gentry had made themselves at home. This caused problems for returning cathedral clergy, who were obliged to rent or buy their own dwellings until the traditional residences could be recovered, which sometimes involved litigation or compensation. Gradually, however, the cathedrals regained all their former possessions: not only lands and houses but their jurisdictions over their city properties and over the parish churches that they owned. The windfalls of money from entry fines had an obvious use: they helped to make good the serious damage to many cathedral churches and to ancillary buildings such as canons' houses. At Winchester nine out of thirteen such houses had been demolished or damaged during the Interregnum, and these had to be rebuilt in brick at some expense.

The plight of the churches was often dire. Even York, which had been maintained by the city authorities, was reckoned to need about £2,000 for repairs. Lichfield had to resume its services in the chapter house, the only large roofed area. Its immediate restoration cost £9,092, and it was not re-dedicated until Christmas 1669. Lincoln's repairs were estimated at £3,054 plus £1,100 for furnishings, and Exeter's at £5,000, including the demolition of the 'monstrous Babylonish wall' which had divided it into two sections (Fig. 52, p. 148). Durham's costs were reckoned at £14,120 for the church, the deanery, and the canons' houses, and Worcester's at £16,354. Money was given, as of old, by bishops, by chapters corporately or canons individually, and by wealthy lay people. Another major appeal was launched at St Paul's. It received donations from the lord mayor and aldermen, since the political changes had extended to city corporations. By 1666, £6,051 had been raised and there were plans not merely for repairs but to raise a new classical cupola in place of the central tower and former spire. Events would shortly overtake these plans.[4]

Worship was re-established in its traditional forms during the summer of 1660.[5] Choral services were revived at Winchester by early September, with an organist, ten clerks, and six choristers. Here again there were difficulties. Lay posts as vicars, clerks, choristers, and masters of choristers were not too hard to fill, but there was a shortage of clergy to become priest vicars or minor canons. Durham had only five minor canons out of twelve posts in 1665, and after St Paul's was burnt in the following year, the dean of Durham wrote to London to invite such clergy to move to the North instead.[6] Furnishings, vestments, and ornaments had often disappeared, and organs in particular had been vandalised and removed. Many small items had been hidden or removed to safety during the 1640s and these were now returned. Other necessary objects were bought or donated. New organs were constructed. St Paul's commissioned one in 1661, Exeter's was completed in 1665 and Hereford's in 1686, the latter costing £720.[7] The royal almsmen reappeared as well, although from now on they usually lived privately in the city and merely received a pension. At Worcester, Charles appointed a former servant of his wine cellar and two men who had lost their property after fighting for the king in the siege of the city.[8]

The methods of worship returned to their former lines. Cathedrals reintroduced daily morning and evening prayer, with the litany, ante-communion, sermon, and sometimes communion on Sundays. In 1662 a revised version of the Prayer Book was produced and imposed by act of Parliament. This was preceded by discussions between the bishops and leading Puritan clergy to make the book more widely acceptable, but the two sides found no common ground and the 1662 Prayer Book was largely identical with those of 1552 and 1559. Clergy who refused to conform to the Prayer Book – effectively Puritan ministers in parish churches – were deprived of their benefices. Non-conformist sects, notably Baptists and Quakers, had already come into existence after the Civil War, and the ejected clergy now formed their own Presbyterian and Independent (or Congregational) churches. These groups did not gain toleration for their worship until 1689, but their departure from the Church of England removed some of the tensions that had existed up to the Civil War. It also facilitated the restoration of the Laudian furnishings. The communion table was re-established altar-wise at the east end of the church, given a fine covering, and decorated with candlesticks and a Bible. Rails were restored around it and congregations came to the rails to receive communion. When window glass was restored, it became customary to fill this with images of scenes from the Bible, representations of Christ, and figures of New Testament saints.

During the 1680s there were a few reprises of earlier clashes. Charles II had no legitimate children, making his heir his brother James II, who had become a Roman Catholic. A political opposition had formed against Charles which sought to exclude James from the succession in favour of Charles's illegitimate son, James, duke of Monmouth. For a time, Monmouth had a strong following of political and religious dissidents. In 1679 he visited Chichester Cathedral where the precentor put him into the dean's stall and an anthem was sung in his honour: 'He shall be like the tree that grows by the river side'. The local mob lit bonfires, and when the bishop refused to contribute fuel for the purpose, shots were fired at his house and stones thrown against it.[9] Three years later the duke was at Chester Cathedral, but by this time the Church establishment was firmly against him. Canon Fogg preached in his presence against disobedience with a pointed reference to Achitophel, the fomenter of rebellion in the reign of King David. Again there was a disturbing sequel: a mob of the duke's supporters burst into the cathedral, damaged the glass, the organ, and the font, and tore up surplices in the manner of the 1640s.[10] When Charles died in 1685, James succeeded peacefully but Monmouth led a rebellion in the West Country which got as far as Wells Cathedral before it was crushed. The duke's adherents included Non-conformists, and they did some injury to the furnishings in the church, including the organ. Horses were stabled in the building as they had

53. London in flames in 1666, the work of a probable eyewitness. The fire is engulfing St Paul's.

once been at St Paul's, and the precentor's wife paid £20 in protection money to save the canons' houses from being looted.[11]

Monmouth's defeat and subsequent execution left James with strong public support, which he soon proceeded to lose. He wished to encourage the revival of Catholicism so, realising that he could not get Parliament to pass legislation for this purpose, he issued two Declarations of Indulgence based on his prerogative powers alone. These suspended the laws against Catholics and granted freedom of worship to them and to Protestant Non-conformists. James planned to put Catholics into cathedral posts and achieved this at Oxford, where John Massey was made dean of Christ Church with a dispensation from the duties of the office![12] Massey's appointment, followed by others of Catholics at Magdalen College (Oxford), struck at the heart of the Church of England, while the use of suspending and dispensing powers threatened the laws made in Parliament. The result was the invitation by leading English noblemen to William of Orange in 1688 to intervene to restore the English constitution, and the subsequent flight of James to France at the end of the year.

In February 1689, Parliament, having ruled that James had abdicated, offered the crown to William and his wife Mary, James's elder daughter, to be worn jointly but with William having the sole exercise of royal power. This produced the last of the crises of conscience that had troubled the English clergy since the Reformation. Most accepted that the change in the royal succession was justified to save the Protestant religion and the constitution, and were willing to take oaths of allegiance to the new monarchs. A minority held to the belief that monarchy was a divine institution with which humans should not interfere and refused the oaths, regarding James as their lawful ruler. They were duly deprived of their posts, including the archbishop of Canterbury (William Sancroft), seven bishops, the deans of Durham and Worcester, and a couple of dozen canons, minor canons, and vicars choral.[13] The deprived bishops consecrated successors as well as new clergy, thereby establishing a small independent Church of the 'Non-Jurors', who continued to exist for about a century without, of course, holding any of the posts or buildings of the Church of England.

The Rebuilding of St Paul's

On Sunday evening, 2 September 1666, the Great Fire of London broke out at Thomas Farriner's bakery in Pudding Lane and spread through the city, fanned by a strong east wind. At first St Paul's seemed a bulwark against it and nearby booksellers moved their stock into St Faith's church underneath. Two days later, however, flying debris caught the cathedral alight, assisted by the wooden scaffolding in place for the restoration project (Fig. 53, p. 153). When John Evelyn ventured out on Friday, he found the building a ruin. Inigo Jones's portico was 'rent in pieces'. The lead of the roofs, which Evelyn reckoned to cover six acres, had melted. The vaults beneath them had fallen into St Faith's, and the books there were consumed and burnt for a week. Only the roof of the east end, over the altar, was still in place, and only one monument survived unscathed: that of the poet John Donne.[14]

At first there was a notion of contriving a temporary church within the walls of the nave, but these were found to be unstable and in 1668 the decision was taken to build a new cathedral.[15] Christopher Wren had already been co-opted to advise about restoring the medieval building, and the cupola had been his suggestion. He now became the preferred architect of the rebuilding project, funding for which was voted by Parliament in the form of a tax on coal. This produced a large annual sum of over £4,000. In 1669 Wren produced his first plan of a new building and in the following year he was appointed surveyor of the cathedral fabric. His plans (accompanied by models) went through a series of revisions until a definitive scheme was agreed in 1675. Meanwhile demolition went on – the task took several years – allowing rebuilding to start in the summer of that year. The final stone in the lantern over the dome was laid by Wren's son Christopher and the son of one of his master masons on 26 October 1708. Wren thus had the good fortune to live long enough to see the completion of the project. When he died in 1723, he was buried beneath his great work (Fig. 54, p. 156).

The rebuilding of St Paul's was an astonishing contrast to the difficulties and unpopularity that had beset cathedrals during the Civil War and Interregnum. Many factors combined to make it possible. The public mood in the 1660s was still that of the Restoration: in favour of cathedral renovation. Remedial work was going on in several other places. St Paul's had become the nearest thing to a national church, and England was entering a period of self-confidence in which London vied with other European cities to be a great centre of trade and culture. There was a wish for a 'design, handsome and noble, and suitable . . . to the reputation of the city and the nation'.[16] Wren had impeccable credentials. He was the son of a dean of Windsor and the nephew of a bishop of Ely.[17] He was a fellow of the new Royal Society and was building the much admired Sheldonian Theatre in Oxford. Charles II supported his involvement and his plans, and the dean of St Paul's, William Sancroft, was sympathetic too. The dean and chapter influenced Wren's designs, however, notably by rejecting one of his early proposals, a circular choir, because it had 'not enough of a cathedral fashion', meaning a conventional English one.

The new building stood on the site of its predecessor, but with a slightly different orientation to avoid the old foundations (Fig. 55, p. 157). It was a little shorter and a little wider than before. Much about its plan was traditional. There was a long nave and a slightly less long choir with continuous north and south aisles beside them. The west end of the nave formed a gathering area or vestibule. Between the nave and choir lay a large crossing area flanked by transepts with aisles of their own. All these areas were covered with stone vaults topped by a raftered and lead-covered roof, as in a medieval building, and there were two western towers. The choir was separated from the crossing by a pulpitum as in previous centuries, albeit a wooden one.

54. Sir Christopher Wren (d. 1723), painted in about 1695, the architect of the new St Paul's whose completion he lived to see.

SIR CHR: WREN.
Late Surveyor General of
the Royal Buildings .
He died the 25 of Feb: 1723, aged 91.

In other respects the building was new and Continental. Its elements were classical: an eastern apse, a two-storey western portico, frontages outside the transepts, round- and square-headed windows, the use of exterior classical columns, and most impressively the great dome over the central crossing (Fig. 57, p. 163). The balustrades around the roof line were added in 1717 and were not Wren's idea. Little was included by way of secluded spaces. There was a 'morning chapel' for early morning prayer and late evening prayer, a corresponding room for the bishop's consistory court, and vestries for the dean and canons, the minor canons, and the

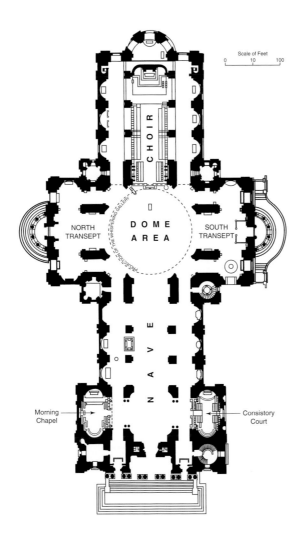

lord mayor of London. No chapter house was provided; a separate one was built in the precinct in 1714.

The choir offered the chance to solve the issues about seating that had arisen since the Reformation. There needed to be accommodation not only for the clergy but for lay people of status. This had been difficult to supply in the old cathedrals since Sunday worship now included a sermon as well as the prayers, and Laud had wanted both to take place in cathedral choirs rather than their naves. The potential congregation at St Paul's was large, since the lord mayor and aldermen were likely to attend as well as London's resident elite and its wealthy visitors. Wren's furnishings for the choir dealt with these problems through a traditional layout of two (rather than three) tiers of stalls for the clergy, containing 116 sittings (Fig. 56, pp. 158–9). Above and behind these tiers were two storeys of galleries

56. *A grand service of thanksgiving at St Paul's in 1706, attended by Queen Anne and both Houses of Parliament.*

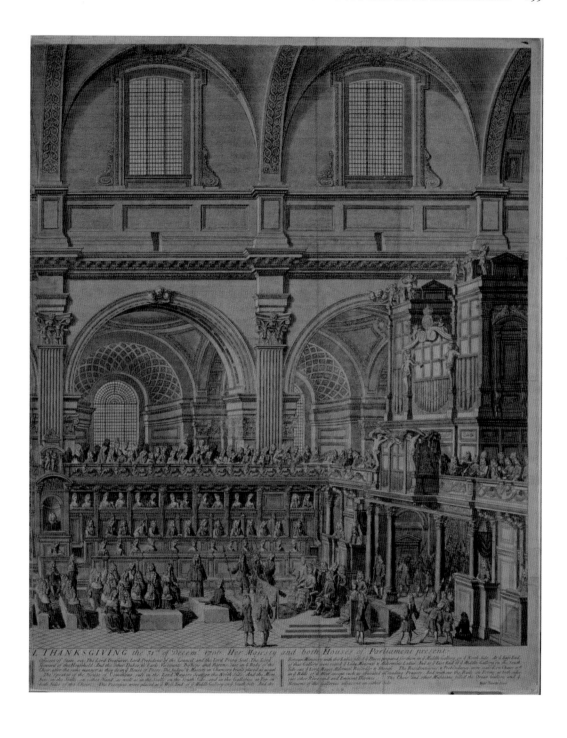

providing a further 300 places. The lower storeys were divided into boxes with seats and a bench behind, perhaps for servants. The upper storeys had three rows of seats. Benches were placed in front of the lower clergy stalls, while an ingenious device allowed others to be wheeled out from under the stalls to lie athwart the middle of the choir. It became possible to house large numbers in the choir, notably in 1702 and 1706 when the House of Lords and about 200 members of the Commons attended the cathedral for thanksgiving services.

The choir contained a tall pulpit for sermons, possibly moveable, and a large organ above the pulpitum to enhance the music. Tradition was observed with regard to the Laudian arrangements for the altar or communion table, with the placing of the altar in the eastern apse beyond the choir and inside a rail. Wren wished the altar to provide a prominent focus for worship by taking the form of a marble altar-piece with lofty columns above it supporting a hemispherical canopy. This was apparently deemed too Catholic and a plainer un-canopied altar was installed. Other former uses of the building, on the other hand, were abolished or modernised. A new crypt was built but the church of St Faith was not reinstated within it, nor St Gregory against the south-west wall, and their parishioners moved to nearby city churches. In St Paul's own congregation, there was more segregation by gender as was now common in churches in English towns. Ladies in particular sat in the galleries, and an engraving of 1736 suggests that they received communion separately from the men. The building lost the most blatantly secular activities that had previously taken place in the nave. Wren's early plans included the provision of exterior arcades or an enclosed portico at the west end for such purposes, but these ideas were abandoned. However, the cathedral remained a place where folk arrived to promenade in the nave, aisles, and huge crossing area. In 1724 the bishop complained about their presence during services, walking and talking, and they were still a problem in the nineteenth century.[18]

Deans and Chapters from 1660 to 1800

A period of about 170 years stretches between the Restoration and the great Church reforms that began in the 1830s. The Victorians, who were energetic reformers, liked to characterise this period as one of indolence and stagnation. Portraits of late Stuart and Hanoverian clergy seem to agree as they stare at us with placid expressions under their large white wigs. Yet while it is true that no political event affected the Church on the scale of the Civil War and Interregnum, those events cast a shadow for many decades. Bishops and canons worried about religion becoming heated again – the word they used was 'enthusiasm' – and equally about its cooling into Deism and rationalism. They feared public disorder, situated as some of them were in the largest towns of the kingdom where there was social and economic discontent. Indeed, mobs sometimes attacked cathedrals even during this era, as in the Monmouth years.[19] And the clergy of the period had one undeniable achievement. They refurbished their churches after the Restoration, preserved them, transmitted them to the Victorians, and thereby conveyed them to us.

The Church of England, bride of Christ, was in a close embrace with the Crown, and this was manifest in cathedral appointments. The Crown held the right to choose bishops, who were then formally elected by their cathedral chapters, and deans. In the case of the deans of the New Foundation cathedrals this was a statutory right. In those of the Old Foundation it had become customary by the sixteenth century and was made statutory in 1840. Canons or prebendaries were mostly appointed by the Crown in the New Foundations, although at Canterbury the archbishop had the control of three prebends. The Crown could also make appointments in the Old Foundations during vacancies of bishops and when canons moved up to be bishops. The majority of Old Foundation canonries were filled by the diocesan bishop, but even here the Crown was likely to make requests (as did other powerful people) and to propose which of the canons should be allowed to come into residence.

An analysis of the origins of 146 canons of St Paul's between 1714 and 1830 reveals that the largest contingent, 48, were the sons of knights or gentlemen, 35 of professional men (lawyers or doctors), 35 of clergy, and a handful each of peers, soldiers, tradesmen, or plebeians.[20] It was possible to arrive from origins in trade or even farming but unusual to do so, and equally so for the sons of peers. There was a common experience of having attended a public school and university, both with a strong Church of England ethos. All were graduates and at St Paul's two-thirds held doctorates. To gain a canonry, however, required not a qualification but patronage from a family member, the monarch, a courtier, or a politician. Bishops promoted their relations. At Lincoln, Richard Reynolds (1723–44) made one son, George, archdeacon of Lincoln and another, Charles, chancellor of the cathedral. His successor, George Pretyman (1787–1827), became notorious for his nepotism. Pretyman's sons George and Richard were given prebends and later dignities, George as chancellor and Richard as precentor. The bishop's brother John was appointed precentor and then archdeacon of Lincoln, and he made his two sons registrars of the archdeaconry.[21] At the New Foundation cathedrals, posts were filled through links with the Crown or with influential courtiers and politicians. Of the deans of Canterbury in this period, George Hooper and George Stanhope had been chaplains to William and Mary, John Potter to Queen Anne, and Elias Sydall to George I. Brownlow North was the half-brother of the prime-minister Lord North, and William Buller was one of North's protégés, while John Moore had been tutor to the sons of the duke of Marlborough who lobbied George III for his appointment.[22]

Cathedral posts all carried dignity and status but, as in the past, they were not all equal in their monetary value. Some of Henry VIII's schemes for new bishops were inadequately funded, particularly those of Bristol, Oxford, Peterborough, and Rochester, and this was true of most of the Welsh sees and that of Sodor and Man. Diocesan officials – archdeacons, vicars-general, and diocesan chancellors

– had only fees as their perquisites. The prebends of the Old Foundations varied greatly in income, from very little to very much. There was more uniformity in those of the New Foundations, but post-1660 clergy did not always have fixed and predictable stipends. Payments were sometimes in arrears: this was a particular problem at Rochester in the late seventeenth century.[23] On the other hand windfalls from leases allowed the canons in residence to share them in addition to the income of their prebends. The solution to unequal and inadequate pay was pluralism: the permitting of clergy to hold more than one benefice. This was a practice that went back to late Saxon times, and had become well established in the Middle Ages, as we saw in the case of Bogo de Clare.[24]

Pluralism was widespread. It was unusual for a dignitary or canon to hold that post alone, and he would have one or more further benefices: a canonry of another cathedral or a parish church or two. The custom became extended after the Reformation to include bishops who, in the Middle Ages, had been expected to give up their other benefices once they were promoted. Now the poorer sees were insufficient to maintain their occupant. He was, after all, a peer, required to attend Parliament to vote for the patron who had promoted him, keep a London residence and servants, and maintain a house in his diocese. In consequence many bishops continued to hold their earlier appointments or collected new ones while they were bishops. At Durham, for example, three eighteenth-century deans were bishops of Peterborough, Lichfield, and St David's when appointed and continued to hold both posts, making their lives triangular between the diocese, the cathedral, and London. Canonries of Durham were held at various times by bishops of Bristol, Gloucester, Oxford, London, and St David's.[25] Cathedral posts were even granted as endowments to other institutions. Three canonries of Oxford had long been reserved for professors, and between 1714 and 1718 three others at Gloucester, Norwich, and Rochester were annexed to college headships at Oxford and Cambridge. Their holders could only have kept their cathedral residence in the Long Vacation.[26]

Residence was another issue. The deans and all the canons of the New Foundations were bound to observe it for a designated number of days every year. In the Old Foundations, only the dean and a few of the canons kept residence. Since the end of the Middle Ages, such canons could not reside at will but had to wait for a vacancy and submit to the judgement of the dean or all the residentiary canons as to who should fill it. Only those who resided formed the chapter for normal purposes of government, although 'greater chapters' including all canons were occasionally held. The residentiaries alone shared in the 'common fund', meaning those revenues that did not belong to specific prebends. There were not many residentiaries in the Old Foundations. Exeter had the most, with nine, but four or five (including the dean) was more usual. However, even the residentiaries did not reside all the time. By the eighteenth century the chapters of most cathedrals, Old and New, had divided up the year so that each canon served for two months or even a month and a half, often leaving only one of them in full residence with the duty of attending the daily

services. A single canon's house might be kept for each to use in turn. The decline of residence was partly the result of pluralism, which meant that clergy might need to spend time on their other benefices. It was socially acceptable because it resembled the way of life of the richer gentry and aristocracy who moved between their London houses and their country seats. The other residentiaries needed to turn up for chapter meetings, however, so that periodically during the year there would be three or four of them at hand to transact the cathedral's business.

Non-residence, pluralism, and marriage were inclined to make cathedral clergy more individualistic and less corporate than they had been in previous centuries. A permanent problem was to make them observe their duties. Discipline was hampered by a gentlemanly ethic of tolerance, by the powerful patrons (including the Crown) possessed by many clergy, or by dispensations elicited from the Crown or the bishop. There were no arrangements for retirement and men held their posts till they died. In consequence it was difficult to get rid of an unsatisfactory dean or canon.

57. Canaletto's painting of the lord mayor's procession on the Thames. It portrays London as Europe's largest and richest city, with St Paul's as its pre-eminent modern building.

Thomas Wood, dean of Lichfield (1663–71), quarrelled with both his bishop and his chapter. He refused to call chapter meetings and claimed a right of veto on such meetings. When the bishop, John Hacket, tried to intervene, he refused to appear before him and locked the chapter house. Hacket excommunicated Wood but the archbishop of Canterbury, Gilbert Sheldon, absolved him. Wood was a thoroughly unsatisfactory dean, yet when Hacket died in 1670, Wood's connections at court got him the bishopric and he then ruled as an unsatisfactory bishop for twenty-one years.[27]

The lesser members of the cathedral staff tended to imitate their masters. Those of the choir consisted of clergy, lay singers (lay vicars, clerks, or singing men), and choristers. Numbers of clergy were not large: four or five priest vicars in most of the Old Foundations, and six minor canons in the New, although St Paul's had eighteen vicars some of whom held additional posts in the Chapel Royal or Westminster Abbey. In the Old, the priest vicars formed a separate corporation with their own property, but this did not include the lay vicars and the priests could share the surplus revenues as the canons did. In the New, the minor canons and others were salaried and more subject to the control of the dean and chapter. Priest vicars and minor canons were generally graduates and differed from canons chiefly in coming from families of lesser wealth and fewer connections with men of power. All were awarded a house in the cathedral Close, as were some lay vicars, but the stipends of both grades were generally low and changed little over the centuries. At Lichfield the clergy earned about £22 and their lay colleagues £18.[28]

In consequence priest vicars and minor canons were pluralists as well. They held small parish churches in the city or nearby countryside, which solved another problem of how to fill these equally modest benefices. On Sundays they juggled their appearances in choir with their duties elsewhere, and like canons, only one or two vicars or minor canons might be on duty on any particular day. Lay singers had other concerns as well, since they were often local tradesmen with musical talents who fitted in their work around their singing. Choristers were the most reliable in their attendance. Exeter and Salisbury led the field with fourteen while Lichfield and St Paul's had ten each, but Hereford still only seven. They received tuition in song and sometimes attended the cathedral grammar school or its equivalent. When their voices broke, the dean and chapter were likely to pay for an apprenticeship or some other kind of education.

Choir members, like canons, were not always satisfactory in their attendance or performance. The reasons were similar: recruitment through patronage rather than competition, tolerance from above, and lack of a provision for retirement. As in the Middle Ages, there were often cases of unauthorised absence and insubordination. At the same time it was possible for work as a vicar choral to be taken seriously. In 1769 William Richardson, a young curate in Yorkshire, visited York Minster and was highly impressed by a service. His neighbour, Mr Robinson, suggested he become a vicar choral and, when a vacancy was reported, wrote to the dean on Richardson's behalf. He was interviewed by the dean, the poet William Mason, who said that there were several candidates, one of whom was a bass which they most required whereas Richardson was a tenor. Nonetheless, the dean had the curate read prayers in the minster and sing an anthem, and when the bass candidate was selected, he wrote Richardson a 'polite and friendly' letter. The bass died of consumption six months later in 1771, and Mason then appointed Richardson. The new vicar wrote that he came to his post 'with fear and trembling, for I knew the arduous task that lay before me, and my own great unfitness for it'. He was in fact a highly conscientious cleric who rose to be succentor or senior priest vicar at York and stayed in his post until he died fifty years later.[29]

Cathedral clergy continued to include men of learning during the eighteenth century, although in view of their pluralism it is not easy to say where they did their study and writing. At Canterbury, for example, they included William Beveridge, historian of the early Church; Richard Farmer, Shakespearian scholar; John Hancock, writer against Arianism; George Horne, commentator on the Psalms; John Mill, editor of the Greek New Testament; and Samuel Shuckford, synthesist of the religious and secular history of the world.[30] Cathedrals re-established their libraries after the Reformation. Michael Honywood, dean of Lincoln, gave £780 in the 1670s for the fitting out of what is now called the Wren Library after its famous designer. By the eighteenth century, Canterbury and Exeter each had more than five thousand books in their collections.[31] As we shall see, the period from 1660 to 1820 was also one of growing interest in archives and buildings. Charles Lyttelton, dean of Exeter (1748–62), researched the history of Worcester and its cathedral.[32] His successor Jeremiah Milles (1762–84) made large collections of material for a history of Devon by sending questionnaires to the county's parish clergy.[33] Each man was elected as president of the new, national Society of Antiquaries of London.

Worship and Its Setting

Since St Paul's was the only cathedral to undergo total rebuilding, deans and chapters elsewhere had to make the best of their ancient surroundings. They tried to modernise these as far as they could, especially in the choir. Here they could furnish the area for the kind of worship they wanted and commission the fittings to follow the taste of the period. The prevailing wish was to use the choir for all purposes: liturgy, music, sermons, and communion. This was impeded by the limitations of some choirs to hold all the laity who wished to attend, especially sermons which were the most popular feature of the Sunday services. Such choirs included Chichester, Ely, Gloucester, and Salisbury, where it was the custom to move from the choir into the nave at sermon time.[34] But the problem was a powerful impetus to enlarge the choir. Accordingly, at Ely the choir area was moved from beneath the octagon further eastwards in 1769 (Fig. 26, p. 60), while at Lichfield and Salisbury the choir was extended in the same direction during the 1780s.[35]

The choir had to contain the altar as well as a pulpit which was sometimes portable and brought in for sermons. It also needed to house stalls for the clergy, seating for the public, and an organ. Choirs in this period were still shut off from naves by a solid pulpitum: usually the medieval one but occasionally a replacement as was so at Ely, Gloucester, St Paul's, and Salisbury.[36] The pulpitum carried the organ and, as we have seen, new or rebuilt organs of substantial size were re-installed in cathedrals after the Restoration. Some cathedrals kept the wall of the medieval reredos or screen behind the altar, modernising it with painting or other forms of art. At York two tapestries hung there depicting scenes from the life of Moses, given by Archbishop Lamplugh (1688–91). In other places the east end was reshaped in the classical style. This was done at Gloucester in 1717–18, at Hereford three years later, and in several other places. At Hereford the bishop, Philip Bisse, paid for the building of a wooden reredos behind the altar in the classical style with columns and a broken pediment, framing the Ten Commandments (Fig. 58, p. 167). Above this, the east window was surrounded by painted curtains which gave the ensemble a rather domestic appearance, and much of the choir was given rectangular panelling. One contemporary called the effect 'sumptuous and elegant'; by the nineteenth century it was condemned as 'wretched'.[37]

Not all cathedral furnishings were as classical as Hereford's. Some choirs kept their medieval stalls, especially those at the back where the canons sat, and modernised the seating in front of them in the form of square 'box pews' to accommodate the rest of the clergy.[38] Other such pews were placed east of the choir for lay people. The local mayor and corporation had designated places and insisted on these being appropriate to their dignity. At Exeter the mayor thought his seat 'was not high enough in proportion to the bishop's, nor sufficiently adorned', while his counterpart at Gloucester, on being evicted from the archdeacon's seat in 1738, refused to attend the cathedral until a proper alternative was provided.[39] Box pews had doors and could be assigned to particular people who paid rents to use them. The doors were useful in deterring people of low degree from taking seats above their station. Respectable visitors who had no pew would tip a verger to open one.[40]

Wren's extension of the seating at St Paul's by building galleries was copied in other cathedrals, including Hereford, Salisbury, and Wells where they occupied a similar position above and behind the clergy stalls.[41] At Hereford they accommodated the mayor and corporation, canons' families and households, and the boys of the cathedral school. Special seating might be provided for ladies, particularly single ones. York had ladies' pews in front of the pulpit, to which the occupants had keys and for which they paid fees. At Chichester they paid 2s. per annum for a seat in the galleries. Worcester allowed them into the choir but not the organ loft.[42] An unusual feature of Gloucester's east end was Mrs Cotton's private pew, installed in 1753 near the altar. This was curtained and held, besides

58. Hereford
Cathedral
choir, improved
and beautified
according to the
tastes of the
mid-eighteenth
century.

the seating, a corner cupboard and a bird cage since the lady believed that
her daughter's soul had transmigrated into a robin.[43]

Most cathedrals had a common structure of daily and weekly services.[44]
Early morning prayer was said in a side chapel, the 'morning chapel', at
six or seven o'clock, usually by a single vicar choral but at St Paul's by all
the minor canons. In a few cathedrals this practice fell into disuse during
the period.[45] The main services of the day took place in the choir with
morning prayer at any time between eight and ten o'clock and evening
prayer between three and half past four. St Paul's was unusual in having
a second service of evening prayer in the morning chapel, again said by
the minor canons, at six o'clock. York said morning prayer in Latin on
Wednesdays and Fridays in Advent and Lent.[46] Morning and evening

prayer were attended by the canon in residence and by the choir, including at least one vicar choral or minor canon, the lay singers, and the choristers. As in the past the prayers might be said or intoned. The versicles, responses, and psalms were sung to chants, the two sides of the choir alternating as before, and the canticles (or hymns as they were known) either to chants or more elaborate settings, with organ accompaniment. Anthems remained popular towards the end of one or both of the daily services. The organist might play a voluntary, and at two cathedrals this was specified to take place between the psalms and the first lesson.[47] On Wednesdays and Fridays morning prayer was followed by the chanting of the litany.

On Sundays the morning services took longer because morning prayer was followed by the litany, the ante-communion, the sermon, and sometimes communion itself. At Hereford an organ voluntary was played before morning and evening prayer on that day, and this was probably common elsewhere.[48] The frequency of communion varied, depending on the views of the bishop and the scruples of the dean and chapter. Some cathedrals, like St Paul's and York, celebrated it weekly while others, such as Lichfield, did so only once a month as well as on the three great festivals (Christmas, Easter, and Pentecost or Whitsunday). There remained a problem in getting enough people to receive communion, since although the cathedral clergy were expected to do so, it was claimed that vicars and minor canons were prevented by their need to get away to their parish churches. Still, monthly communions were more frequent than the quarterly ones of most of the parish churches.

Music remained an important component of worship.[49] The Chapel Royal still kept its place as the leading centre in this respect, and the most prominent English composers for the liturgy – Henry Purcell (d. 1695), William Croft (d. 1727), and William Boyce (d. 1779) – held posts there. Among cathedrals, St Paul's was probably the most important. Some of its choristers went on to successful careers elsewhere, and its adult staff comprised such notable figures as the vicar choral Jeremiah Clarke (d. 1707) and the organist Maurice Greene (d. 1755). The musicians of the provincial cathedrals were less prominent, but still included men whose compositions circulated widely such as Thomas Wanless of York (1691–1712) and James Nares (1735–56), one of his successors. As before, all these composers wrote settings for the Prayer Book services with the addition, by the early eighteenth century, of the Sanctus and Gloria at communion. They also composed many anthems, still usually based on biblical texts like psalms, in the Protestant manner. 'Lord, let me know mine end' by Greene was sung at Nelson's funeral in St Paul's, and 'Hear my prayer' by James Kent (d. 1776), organist of Winchester, at those of George III and George IV, with the latter of whom it was apparently a favourite. Collections of music from and for cathedrals were also made. One edited by Wanless, the *York Anthem Book* (1705), including seventeen of his own compositions, remained popular for over two centuries, while Boyce's three volumes of *Cathedral Music* (1760–73) had a wide circulation as well.

The quality of performance in the liturgy and music was variable. Comments about it survive in the diaries of the Hon. John Byng: son of a peer, a peppery ex-soldier, and officer in the Inland Revenue who travelled through England during the 1780s and 90s. Byng liked to attend cathedral worship when he was staying nearby and noted what he found, often unfavourably. He thought the service he went to at York was decently performed with some good voices, but considered the anthem 'tiresome'. Lincoln was better, with two canons in residence, five men in the choir, and ten boys, three of whom sang well, although the two lay vicars who chanted the litany had 'voices like bulls'. At the other extreme, the liturgy at Canterbury 'was as sadly slurred over as any Dissenter could wish'. Oxford's was 'miserably performed' and Winchester's 'more irregularly . . . than I ever remember to have heard it . . . .' The creed 'was chanted to a tune like "God Save the King"'.[50]

A contrary experience was that of William Richardson. His linkage with York Minster came about because, at the end of October 1769, he called at the church on his way home from being ordained priest by his bishop:

> In my return through York I strayed into the Minster. The evening service was then performed by candlelight. I had never before been in the Minster but in the middle of a summer's day. The gloom of the evening, the rows of candles fixed upon the pillars in the nave and transept, the lighting of the chancel, the two distant candles glimmering like stars at a distance upon the altar, the sound of the organ, the voices of the choir raised up with the pealing organ in the chaunts, service, and anthem had an amazing effect upon my spirits as I walked to and fro in the nave. The varied tones, sometimes low, sometimes swelling into a great volume of harmonious sound, seemed to anticipate the songs of the blessed and the chorus of praise round the Throne of God and the Lamb. I was greatly affected.[51]

Admittedly, Richardson was not a typical tourist but a cleric and musician, susceptible to the spell of a cathedral choir. Nevertheless, he shows the power of such music, at its best, to make a profound effect on the feelings of a listener and beholder.

Furnishings and music formed the chief decoration of cathedral services. Little remained in terms of vestments and ceremonial. Altars had candlesticks on them but these were lit only in darkness as at York. Clergy and singers wore surplices, or were supposed to since the bishop of Chichester had to issue an order to this effect in 1727.[52] Preachers also preached in a surplice, unlike their colleagues in parish churches who took it off to wear a gown instead. Copes were in use at Durham, and the traveller Celia Fiennes who visited the cathedral in 1698 thought it the only place in England where this was so. In 1760, however, the copes were abandoned because they had worn out and some of the clergy thought them popish.[53] Ely was quite unusual in burning incense at the three great festivals.[54]

When the choir was used for all purposes, the nave remained an empty space without seating. An exception to this was Exeter, where there was a pulpit in the choir but the demand for places at sermons was such that another was built in the centre of the nave with two 'grandstands' of seats facing inwards towards it on either side.[55] An empty nave was easily regarded as a place for perambulation, play for local children, or soliciting by beggars. Lincoln and Worcester had problems with both. Vergers or almsmen were assigned to keep order and the church doors were locked before worship began.[56] As for the rest of the church, one chapel would serve as the morning chapel: at Gloucester and Rochester the Lady chapel did duty for this purpose.[57] The others, as before, were used for the consistory court, a library, or vestries. If they were not needed for other purposes, they provided room for interments beneath the floor and the insertion of monuments.

Monuments continued to proliferate but changed their form.[58] The fully recumbent medieval figure disappeared, one of the last being that of Archbishop Frewen in York Minster (1664). Huge memorials of the Elizabethan and Jacobean type fell into disuse as well. The emergence of a standing army in the 1640s made a sharper difference between soldiers and civilians. Wealthy laymen who wished to be commemorated on a grand scale now opted for standing or sitting statues of themselves and their wives, wearing contemporary clothes or Roman costume. Wall tablets became very common, embellished with classical frames, cherubs, urns, and heraldry along with lengthy accounts of people's ancestry, curricula vitae, and admirable qualities (which sometimes included the avoidance of 'enthusiasm'). Such tablets partly reflected a larger population: there was less room for memorials than before. One cathedral long remained aloof from this practice. At first St Paul's rejected burials and monuments in the main church, making an exception only for Wren (interred in the crypt) and his family. The rule was not abandoned until 1792 in favour of statues of John Howard, the philanthropist, and Dr Samuel Johnson. By this time Britain was at war with France and more such figures soon arrived to honour admirals and generals, most famously Nelson and eventually Wellington.[59]

The First Cathedral Historians

During the period of this chapter, interest in the history of cathedrals grew significantly. Awareness of the past had existed among their clergy since at least Eadmer of Canterbury in the eleventh century. Throughout the Middle Ages cathedrals had celebrated their antiquity by holding the anniversaries of bishops, canons, and noblemen, and by displaying the relics and tombs of previous ages. By the fifteenth century Exeter provided a Latin chronicle of its past on a board for those who could read it, while Peterborough presented its early history in couplets of English verse along its cloister.[60] The Reformation discarded the anniversaries, the relics, and some of the tombs, but cathedrals continued to attract visitors. Accounts by such people confirm that guides (minor clergy or vergers) were available to show the marvels and monuments, no doubt for fees, and even to open up chapter houses, vestries, and libraries.

A good example of the visitor interest in cathedral history in the early seventeenth century is a certain Lieutenant Hammond of the Norwich militia. In 1634 he toured the north of England with two friends and next year he travelled through the south on his own.[61] Like William Worcester a century and a half before him, Hammond was an earnest collector of information; once he even paced out a building. He visited every cathedral that he passed and made detailed notes about them in the form of a diary. Laudian in sympathy, he attended worship wherever he went and wrote, usually appreciatively, about organs, singers, and choristers. He climbed the towers of Chichester and Salisbury, saw treasures in vestries, and heard local folklore. He had an appreciation for buildings as a whole, but he did not give much attention to architectural details. His chief interest was in monuments, and the majority of his notes are about their forms, the people they commemorated, and sometimes the inscriptions they carried.

Hammond made notes when the study of cathedrals was beginning to develop in a serious and systematic way. Its chief practitioners, like him, were mostly traditionalists who cherished cathedrals instead of deploring them as Puritans did. The first important writer was John Stow (c.1525–1605), whose great descriptive *Survey of London* in 1598 included several pages on the building, history, customs, and monuments of St Paul's.[62] The next was William Somner (1598–1669), a Laudian appointed by the archbishop as an official of the Church courts of Canterbury diocese.[63] His history of Canterbury was published in 1640 and dedicated to Laud.[64] Somner gave forty pages to the cathedral. He talked briefly about monasticism, told the history of the fabric with attention to its catastrophes and rebuildings, and then embarked on a tour of the church in the way that contemporary topographers made tours of English counties. He traversed the nave, transepts, choir, library, crypt, cloister, and so on, and spent six pages on the major monuments. A striking feature of his work is an understanding that the church was built in several phases and that these might be dated by comparison across the building or from archival sources. This was unusual in his day and even among writers as late as the middle of the eighteenth century.

Hard on the heels of Somner came William Dugdale (1605–86), a gentleman of private wealth and one of the royal heralds (Fig. 59, p. 172).[65] Dugdale is one of the great English historians. His deep research into archives, his careful editing of records, and the presentation of his work with illustrations and good indexes anticipate the skills of a modern scholar. His *Antiquities of Warwickshire* (1656) was the first real history of an English county to be published and the prototype of all the later ones. He started recording monuments in cathedrals and churches in 1641, foreseeing the problems that were about to arise. Five years later he formed an association with Roger Dodsworth, a Yorkshire antiquary who was collecting

59. Sir William Dugdale (d. 1686), the greatest English antiquary of the seventeenth century and author of the first volume wholly devoted to a cathedral history.

documents relating to monasteries, and in 1655 (after Dodsworth's death) he brought out the first volume of their joint work *Monasticon Anglicanum*.[66] This was the first attempt to list all the monasteries of pre-Reformation England with editions of their charters and other relevant documents. It was aimed at the learned since it was wholly in Latin, but it was a courageous enterprise. Many people still regarded such research as covert Catholicism and as likely to endanger the transfer of monastic lands at the Reformation.

The first volume included all the medieval monastic cathedrals, the five monasteries that Henry VIII had made into cathedrals, and the secular cathedrals of Exeter and Wells: the last two in the belief that they had been monasteries long ago. Along with the documents, the book provided one or more illustrations of the exterior of each cathedral, and these were published separately by the engraver Daniel King in 1656: the first ever cathedral picture-book.[67] A second volume (1673) dealt with the monasteries not hitherto covered, including Carlisle Cathedral, and a third of ten years later included the remaining secular cathedrals. By this time Dugdale had extended his documents to include some cathedral statutes and even medieval inventories of their ornaments and vestments: something that would once have been highly controversial.

Even this did not exhaust his energies. In 1658 he brought out the first book wholly devoted to a cathedral: *The History of St Paul's*.[68] It was a notable feat, although when compared with Somner's work it shows Dugdale to have been a better editor than an author. The arrangement is somewhat haphazard, beginning with a history of the cathedral but deviating into individual topics without a very clear logical or topographical order. Nevertheless, it provides invaluable material: lists of chantries, accounts of the major medieval shrines and images, descriptions of the church's subordinate parts such as the crypt, chapter house, and cloisters, and a detailed survey of the monuments. Any limitations that it has are massively outweighed by its providential composition just before the Great Fire, which makes it a unique and indispensable record of old St Paul's (Fig. 48, p. 134).

Dugdale brought cathedral history to public notice, and others built on this. John Le Neve (1679–c.1741), gentleman and later clergyman, undertook the huge labour of compiling *Fasti Ecclesiae Anglicanae* (1716), a list of 11,051 bishops, deans, dignitaries, and canons of all the English cathedrals down to that date. Twice updated in later times, it remains the standard guide for identifying cathedral clergy.[69] At about the same time a wealthy Buckinghamshire squire, Browne Willis, undertook something just as ambitious: accounts of all twenty-seven cathedrals in England, Wales, and the Isle of Man.[70] Willis was another 'high' churchman in the Laudian tradition. He famously bought a Non-conformist chapel near his house in order to demolish it, and wrote to bolster the status of the Church of England. Starting with the four Welsh cathedrals (1717–1721), he followed these with a history of the major abbeys including the medieval monastic cathedrals (1718–19), a 'survey' of ten secular and Henry VIII cathedrals (1727), and a similar account of the four remaining ones (1730). Eventually his writings about cathedrals were collected together in a three-volume work (1742).[71]

Willis, even more than Dugdale, was a collector rather than a writer, and his writing has a rather pompous air. He visited all the cathedrals except for Carlisle, but most of his information came from books and from information supplied by cathedral clergy, with whom he kept up a large correspondence. The latter feature is worth noting, because it shows that an interest in the past of cathedrals was now widely shared by deans, canons, and even vicars choral, although few of them would ever put pen to paper. However, most of Willis's work on cathedrals resembles a directory rather than a monograph. His treatment of York is typical. It begins with a floor plan and an elevation, after which it describes the diocese and the cathedral personnel before turning to listing monuments. Only then does it cover the building, and merely for three pages, before proceeding to the endowments of the bishop, dean and chapter, and vicars choral, including details of the sales of lands in 1647 (themselves now part of history). After this it provides lists of the archbishops, dignitaries, and canons in the manner of Le Neve, to whose work Willis claimed to have added many names. The final section is a list of the parishes of the diocese under their archdeaconries and deaneries, with details of their patrons and appropriators.

Willis went on to produce or contribute to the first directories of the Church of England, notably J. Ecton's *Thesaurus Rerum Ecclesiasticarum* ('treasury of ecclesiastical information') of 1742: the ancestor of later works like *Crockford's Clerical Dictionary*. In the meantime other authors were developing the Dugdale tradition by writing accounts of individual cathedrals. In 1680 Sir Thomas Browne, the well-known physician and author, made a list of the monuments in Norwich Cathedral and their inscriptions, which was published with additions after his death.[72] A more ambitious work was *The History of the Church of Peterburgh* (1686) by Simon Gunton, prebendary of that church, brought out after Gunton's death by the dean, Simon Patrick.[73] This provided a history of the abbey and cathedral arranged under abbots and bishops, a topographical tour through the church (inspired by Somner's method) and a description of the monuments. It ended with a long appendix of charters extending for over two hundred pages on the lines that Dugdale had laid down.

After 1700 cathedral histories began to appear at regular intervals. Samuel Gale produced one for Winchester in 1715, Richard Rawlinson for Hereford (1717) and Rochester (1723), John Dart for Canterbury (1726), Christopher Hunter for Durham (1733), Thomas Warton for Winchester (1750), an anonymous writer for Canterbury and York (1755), Francis Drake for York (1768), and James Bentham for Ely (1771). They all had much in common: aiming themselves at intelligent gentry and clergy who could afford to buy them and place them on their shelves. Their authors were strong on history, recounting major events and personalities, and on the monuments which visitors came to see. The major difference from modern works of this kind lies in the lack of architectural history, which was only just beginning to be studied. This would not become a major issue in cathedral studies, as we shall see, until the last few years of the century.

The Coming of Romanticism

On Easter Monday, 17 April 1786, at about six thirty in the afternoon, the west tower of Hereford Cathedral collapsed due to pressure from its central companion, further east. The whole west end of the nave fell with it, making the cathedral appear like one of the creatures of Hieronymus Bosch that is whole at one end and smashed at the other (Fig. 60, p. 175). Considering the magnitude of the disaster, it was greeted with remarkable equanimity. The vicars choral

were having a dinner party, and their servant did not tell them the news until the event was concluding. Even the *Hereford Journal* merely reported next week, 'We are happy to find that no person has received any hurt . . . The ruins, though awful, afford a pleasing view, especially to behold the statues of kings and bishops resting one upon the other.'[74]

60. Hereford Cathedral, showing the dramatic effects of the fall of the western tower in 1786.

After some delay the dean and chapter secured the services of James Wyatt to rebuild the west end of the nave. Wyatt was one of the most esteemed architects of the day.[75] He had begun as a master of the classical style, but he was turning his attention to the newly fashionable Gothic and had already been retained to make alterations to Lichfield Cathedral. Later he would be employed at Durham and Salisbury. His work at Hereford, carried out between 1788 and 1795, constituted the largest cathedral building project since those of Inigo Jones and Christopher Wren at St Paul's. Unlike theirs, however, Wyatt's reconstruction was in Gothic not in classical form. Seventeenth-century people could imagine a mixture of the two. By the end of the eighteenth century this was inconceivable.

In 1747 Horace Walpole had acquired an estate at Strawberry Hill in Middlesex, on which he erected a mansion with fanciful Gothic decorations such as pointed arches, battlements, pinnacles, and a

61. Hereford
Cathedral, the
west end rebuilt
by James Wyatt
in the style of
the early Gothic
revival, later
criticised and
replaced.

round tower and turret. This signalled a new vogue for Gothic in both architecture and writing. Landscaping schemes began to include ruined castles and churches. Literature started to generate Gothic romances like Walpole's own *Castle of Otranto*, ballads such as those in Thomas Percy's *Reliques of Ancient English Poetry*, and William Chatterton's mock medieval poems. Walpole's friend the poet Thomas Gray became a keen student of medieval architecture, and took a particular interest in York where his own friend William Mason was dean. He was enthusiastic about Gothic – its 'tall piqued arches, the light clustered columns, the capitals of curling foliage' – as opposed to the 'clumsy and heavy proportion' of earlier, Norman times. He disapproved of the introduction of 'Greek (or Roman) ornaments in Gothic edifices'. His ideal cathedral, in the words of his *Elegy Written in a Country Churchyard*, was one where 'through the long-drawn aisle and fretted vault, the pealing anthem swells the note of praise'.[76]

Wyatt had a good understanding of form and proportion. His new west end at Hereford was a picturesque piece of Gothic containing an impressive window filled with imagery designed by Sir Joshua Reynolds (Fig. 61, above). However, his Gothic was not based on a detailed knowledge of medieval architecture, which was also beginning to develop. Here the pioneer was the scholar John Carter, fellow of the Society of Antiquaries which published, between 1797 and 1809, a series of his measured plans, elevations, and sections of English cathedrals. Carter was a careful archaeologist who drew buildings as they were designed to be, rather than the weathered structures that they had become.[77] Along with other members of the Society, Richard Gough and John Milner, he began to attack Wyatt in the popular journal of the day, *The Gentleman's Magazine*, for engaging in needless destruction and poor quality replacement. In 1797 they blackballed Wyatt's admission to the Society, although he was re-nominated shortly afterwards and elected by a huge majority. The architectural historian John Britton was another opponent. Writing in 1805, he called the Hereford west front 'extremely incongruous to the principles of the style it pretends to imitate . . . . Whether it arose from the inadequacy of the funds or from the want of skill of the architect, its effects are certainly to be lamented'. When Britton came to publish a survey of Hereford Cathedral in 1831, he refused to illustrate the west front and railed anew against the architect's 'flimsy columns, poor mean mouldings; all the dressings equally insipid and wholly discordant to the original work'.[78]

Most people were not archaeologists. They were attracted to Gothic because of its quaintness, embodying time and mystery. From the late eighteenth century onwards, engravings of medieval buildings began to be produced for the wealthy public, either in books or as pictures for framing. *The Antiquities of England* by Francis Grose and *The Beauties of England and Wales* by John Britton and Edward Wedlake Bayley are good examples. Each traverses the English counties in a series of volumes, describing places of interest and illustrating some of them, including cathedrals. There is much stress on the picturesque. Hereford Cathedral appears in Grose's book at a distance from the river with small boats in the foreground; another engraving shows the ruined chapter house.[79] Britton and Bayley's view of Norwich has a dilapidated gatehouse in the foreground, and that of Winchester features ramshackle buildings as well.[80]

A little later, John Constable was to bring the romantic portrayal of a cathedral to perfection. In 1798 he got to know John Fisher, canon of Windsor and later chaplain of the Royal Academy.[81] When Fisher became bishop of Salisbury, Constable visited him there, made several oil sketches, and was commissioned to paint a view of the cathedral. He finished the picture, 'Salisbury Cathedral from the Bishop's Grounds' in 1823, and featured Fisher and his wife in the foreground (Fig. 62, p. 178). After Fisher's death, Constable painted the scene again from further away, 'Salisbury Cathedral from the Meadows' (1831). Both are masterpieces in the portrayal of a cathedral: steadfast and beautiful alongside stormy clouds, like the heroine of a Romantic opera.[82]

Wyatt, despite his detractors, was the first of a great series of Gothic cathedral architects. He was brought in by bishops and chapters to make improvements, but often discovered structural defects with which he dealt effectively. Like those who employed him, his commitment to Gothic went hand in hand with the tastes of the eighteenth century. He and his clients wanted a cathedral to be orderly and beautiful: neat outside and free of clutter within. This had its ancestry in Laud's wish to remove obtruding houses, and it had a practical value in making buildings easier to maintain. Several cathedrals in the eighteenth

62. Salisbury Cathedral, portrayed in the romantic style by John Constable in 1823.

century, for example, removed the spires from their towers. This was not understood but resented by local people. When removal was threatened at Lincoln in 1726, a mob attacked the cathedral and the cleric deemed to be responsible. Here and at Ely in 1748, the dean and chapter had to relent, and the spires survived until the end of the century.[83]

At Hereford, Wyatt shortened the nave and lowered the roofs to emphasise the central tower, the only one after the fall of its companion. At Lichfield he extended the choir to include the Lady chapel, walled off the choir to make it cosier, and replaced some of the stone vaulting with plaster to lighten the load from above. At Salisbury he also threw the choir into the Trinity chapel (its equivalent of a Lady chapel) and tried to enhance the building by removing its later accretions. These included two porches, two chantry chapels, and the cathedral's detached bell tower. He removed but replaced the pulpitum and relocated the major monuments in the church into two lines between the pillars of the nave, as if they were exhibits in one of the London museums. At Durham he was involved with schemes (which he said came from the chapter) to make the building more accessible by demolishing the Galilee chapel at the west end, and to extend the choir eastwards by removing the Neville screen behind the altar. Carter again led protests, and both proposals were eventually dropped.

Tidying up was also proceeding in Closes. That of Norwich, for example, was packed in the early seventeenth century with tenements, shops, and alehouses like the rest of the city. Very gradually, after the Restoration, the dean and chapter upgraded the area. They leased properties on condition that houses were built 'fit for gentlemen to live in'. The alehouses were reduced in number to five, all respectable places. Tradesmen left or were evicted (a mason's shop was closed because of noise), leaving only those who served the gentry like a fine hat-maker and a nurseryman.[84] The same process was in train elsewhere. Clergy and gentry houses were rebuilt or had their medieval cores concealed behind Georgian frontages. The Close at Salisbury is one of the best examples today with imposing buildings of the period such as Mompesson House (c.1680), Myles Place (1718), and the Walton Canonry (c.1719).[85] Landscaping here and elsewhere was improved. Burials on the open ground were forbidden, graves removed, and the terrain levelled and turfed as Wyatt did at Salisbury. Gravel paths were laid, lime trees were planted, and by the end of the eighteenth century railings were being installed around open areas, which served to regulate or exclude activities upon them.[86] Even those once cherished marks of distinction, the Close gates, now sometimes seemed redundant through better public order and disruptive of traffic and vistas. Lichfield demolished one gate in the middle of the century and another in 1800, while those of Exeter were taken away between 1812 and 1825.[87]

Reaching Out and Looking In

Every eighteenth-century cathedral remained involved with its surrounding area. As before, it recruited clergy from nearby families, especially in the choral posts. It employed local workmen and spent money in the cathedral city. Its Sunday services attracted congregations to hear sermons and listen to music. It gave out charity: £40 a year at Worcester to the local poor, ransoms again for captives of the Turks, and the establishment of an infirmary.[88] Cathedrals linked their neighbourhoods with the national government of Crown, Church, and Parliament. Mayors and councils came to Sunday worship; so did the judges when they held the assizes. Deans and chapters observed the fast-days proclaimed by Parliament in times of national emergency. They celebrated the anniversaries of the monarch's accession, the Gunpowder Plot, and the Restoration of 1660. Their bells rang out to commemorate victories in war: the Boyne, Blenheim, Culloden, Quebec, and Minden.[89]

There were, too, the modest beginnings of the cultural outreach undertaken by modern cathedrals. By 1719, and perhaps from ten years before, an annual musical 'meeting' began to rotate between the nearby cathedral cities of

63. Bristol
Cathedral, in
the days when
it lacked a nave.
Dismissed as
mediocre by
Celia Fiennes
and Daniel
Defoe, it is
here portrayed
appreciatively
by Turner (aged
sixteen) in
1791.

Gloucester, Hereford, and Worcester.[90] This event, now known as the 'Three Choirs Festival', consisted of choral services at the host cathedral and other kinds of music provided by music clubs in secular venues. Salisbury had a similar event by 1744, which took place annually up to 1787 and intermittently until 1828.[91] It took some time to accept that a cathedral itself could be the venue for anything other than liturgical music performed in the choir. When the festival's first performance of Handel's *Messiah* took place at Gloucester in 1757, the event was staged in a public hall. It was the huge popularity of Handel's work that caused a change of mind at Hereford two years later. No secular place was available to hold the large expected audience, and so *Messiah* was presented in the cathedral choir – a landmark in the history of cathedral usage.

Progress in this direction was nevertheless rather slow. Cathedrals were deeply associated with worship and, by the eighteenth century, with decorous Prayer Book worship. Although *Messiah* was repeated at the Three Choirs in nearly every one of the next two hundred years, it was not until 1837 that the performance took place in a cathedral nave (again at Hereford), which thereby became a kind of concert hall rather than a liturgical setting. In 1850 Beethoven's *Mass in C* was performed at the Gloucester festival. It was advertised as *Service in C* to conceal its Catholic nature, but many of the congregation walked out in protest at the departure from Protestant norms. As late as 1875 the dean and chapter of Worcester decreed that no festival music should be performed in the cathedral unless it was part of a religious service. Accordingly, only the three cathedral choirs took part in the festival, and merely in the liturgy. But by this time popular views of the matter had changed. There was public dismay, few came to the services, and the civic authorities in the three cities joined to express their concern. The restriction was never repeated.[92]

We can see how eighteenth-century people viewed cathedrals, as we have done before, through accounts by travellers. Celia Fiennes was an unmarried gentlewoman, granddaughter of a viscount. She made intrepid journeys all over England during the years around 1700, making notes of the places she saw. She visited every one of the twenty-three English cathedral cities and all their cathedrals except for Rochester, of which she seems to have been unaware. Guides were available to show her the features and rarities of at least some of the buildings: at Ely she was taken around by a woman. In some of them she climbed resolutely up the towers and looked at the views. Cathedrals, to her, were certainly places worth visiting, but her reactions were rather cool and unemotional. Bristol had 'nothing fine or curious in it', Norwich was 'fine' and 'lofty' but 'nothing remarkable for monuments'. At Wells she noted only the west front with its statues. She liked modernity as much as history: the fine tapestry hangings by the altar of Chester, the crimson damask and cloth of gold carpet of the bishop's throne at Durham, and the embroidered crimson altar cloth and cushions at York.[93]

Daniel Defoe toured most of Britain in the mid-1720s. His chief interest was in economic and social matters, and he disclaimed any deep concern with history or antiquities. He visited every cathedral, although he too thought Bristol 'very mean' (Fig. 63, p. 180) and said little about Carlisle, Durham, or Exeter. Again he had the services of guides and recounted, with appropriate scepticism, the tales they told to tourists. At Chichester a heron settled on the spire when a bishop was to die. After a local butcher shot it, news came of the bishop's death the following day. Chester claimed to have the tomb of the German Emperor Henry IV who had allegedly died there as a hermit. Defoe preferred cathedrals' exteriors to their interiors. He liked spires and external statuary, and was dissatisfied with Winchester, which had neither, but overwhelmed by Lichfield which had both. He thought it one of the most beautiful churches in England, but extended his praise to Peterborough (save for its lack of a fine tower and spire), and rated both inferior only to York and St Paul's. He particularly noticed the gentrification of cathedral Closes, approving the new houses being built for clergy and gentry and commending their occupants for creating a polite society in the locality. Here Lichfield scored again as 'a place of good conversation and good company'.[94]

A third and somewhat different commentator was John Byng, whom we met as a critic of choral worship during the 1780s and 90s. Caustic about small towns, inns, their food and stabling, fellow travellers, and barking dogs, he was equally forthright in his views on cathedral buildings. A fervent admirer of Gothic, he wanted them wholly, solely of that form without intruding styles from other times. Lincoln overwhelmed him: 'Gothic in the highest preservation . . . How superior to a lumbering Grecian St Paul's!' Gloucester was good and the tower very handsome and light, but he disliked the Romanesque nave whose pillars seemed 'gouty and immoderately swelled'. Winchester was 'venerable' apart from Inigo Jones's pulpitum with Le Sueur's statues of James I and Charles I which he thought 'entirely out of character and situation'. At York the new pavement designed by Lord Burlington 'might have been invented by a schoolboy for his kite'. Worcester was clean and neatly paved, its cloisters in better condition than usual. He liked Prince Arthur's tomb 'in the most beautiful state of Gothic magnificence', but his Romantic sympathies were disappointed by the 'total want of stained glass, so necessary for church grandeur to cast "a dim religious light"'. His account of Salisbury justifies most of Wyatt's later improvements. The building was kept 'in sad order'. The chapter house and cloisters were dilapidated, and the churchyard was 'like a cow common' with a boggy ditch stagnating through its centre.[95]

Byng's journeys reflected a system of roads in much better condition, with regular coach services for the use of wealthy travellers. Tours for enjoyment became more feasible. Dr Johnson claimed to have visited every cathedral except for Carlisle.[96] Guide-books began to be written for such people. One of the earliest was James Easton's *Salisbury Guide* (1769), addressed to 'residents in the county as well as to strangers who may resort to Salisbury, either on business or pleasure'.[97] Priced at a shilling, it gave brief accounts of the cathedral, the city, Old Sarum, and other nearby attractions such as Stonehenge, along with details of the local postal arrangements and coach services. Five years later William Gostling, MA and minor canon of Canterbury Cathedral, produced *A Walk in and about the City of Canterbury*, also for residents and strangers, and guides to Winchester, Chester, and York appeared in the next few years.[98] These, like Easton's, covered both city and cathedral, so that the earliest guide-book to a cathedral alone may be that of William Dodsworth, verger of Salisbury, who published it in 1792. As well as describing its ancient fabric, his title page promised 'a particular account of the late great improvements made therein under the direction of James Wyatt, Esquire'.[99]

These guide-books certainly found purchasers; some of them went into several editions. Gostling's and the *Chester Guide* laid out a perambulation so that their readers could inspect the city and cathedral with the book in their hand. Easton's *Salisbury Guide* advertised engravings of the cathedral, its organ, and the Hungerford chapel. But the most surprising work, perhaps, is George Millers's guide to Ely Cathedral (1805).[100] Unlike the others, which have little notion of architectural history, this modest booklet (67 pages) begins by describing the sequence of medieval English building styles. Millers distinguished Saxon, Norman, Early English, Ornamented, and Florid (i.e. Perpendicular), explained their features, and showed what Ely had of each of them. Five years into the nineteenth century, a visitor to one cathedral could already buy something akin to Pevsner's 'Buildings of England'.

Chapter
—— 8 ——

The Nineteenth Century

1801–1900

A New Reformation

William Cobbett, the farmer and radical journalist, was an early riser. On Wednesday 30 August 1826, while he was staying in Salisbury, he rose at seven o'clock and went to the cathedral. 'When I got into the nave of the church, and was looking up and admiring the columns of the roof, I heard a sort of humming. I wondered what it was and made my way towards it . . . and at last I turned into a doorway . . . where I found a priest and his congregation assembled. It was a parson of some sort, with a white covering on him, and five women and four men, so when I arrived there were five couple of us . . . .

'I wonder what the founders would say if they could rise from the grave and see such a congregation as this in this most magnificent and beautiful cathedral! I wonder what they would say if they could see the half-starved labourers that now [provide] the luxuries of those who wallow in the wealth of those endowments . . . For my part, I could not look up at the spire and the whole of the church at Salisbury without feeling that I lived in degenerate times. Such a thing never could be made now.'[1]

Cobbett can be faulted in one respect. The service he observed was that of early morning prayer in the 'morning chapel', then still provided at Salisbury and the lineal descendant of the 'morrow mass' of medieval times.[2] It had probably never attracted more than a few devout lay folk who liked to pray before they went to work. Still, he is a representative figure of his time in two other ways. First, he was incensed by what he saw as the wealth and indolence of cathedral clergy: keeping their buildings ill and doing little or nothing in return for large incomes – 'fellows in big white wigs, the size of half a bushel' as he called them. Secondly, and not altogether consistently, he was a Romantic. He had a vision of the Middle Ages as a world of humble clergy, caring gentry, and well-fed peasants, like that of Charles Kingsley and William Morris a few decades later. And as a Romantic, he was struck by the ancient beauty of Salisbury Cathedral. It was inspiring to him in a way that would not have been quite the same if he had lived fifty years earlier.

Many people in Cobbett's England believed that the country needed a thorough reform of both its Church and State. In 1820 John Wade, another radical journalist, published *The Black Book; or, Corruption Unmasked!* – an indictment of waste and privilege in the national institutions.[3] The Church, Wade claimed, observed the principle of 'pay without service; service without pay'. On the one hand, only the parish clergy appeared to perform any religious duty, many of whom were impoverished curates. On the other, bishops, archdeacons, deans, canons, and prebendaries were 'clerical sinecurists, filled with the Holy Ghost for no other purpose but to enjoy the loaves and fishes of the Church'. They numbered, he believed, 26 bishops and deans, 60 archdeacons, 544 canons and prebendaries, and about 300 minor canons and vicars choral. All, apart from the last 300, had large incomes, which he estimated, as best as he could, at £1,500–£12,000 for a dean and £400 for a canon; in truth some canons were far wealthier. Most were pluralists and non-residents. Gloucester's bishop was dean of Wells, Lichfield's dean of Durham, Lincoln's dean of St Paul's, and so on.[4]

Discontent was widespread at this time due to economic deprivation and the perceived inequalities of the political system, especially the unreformed House of Commons. Some of it crystallised in the quarrel between George IV and his queen, Caroline, who was wildly popular. When the queen died in 1821, the bells of Durham Cathedral did not toll. This led John Williams, another militant writer, to attack the cathedral clergy in the *Durham Chronicle* as un-Christian hypocrites who make 'our churches look like deserted sepulchres'; 'beetles who crawl about amidst its holes and crevices'. The clergy prosecuted Williams for libel but he was defended slashingly by Henry Brougham who had been the queen's barrister, and although found guilty, escaped any penalty.[5]

Cathedrals were coming into a dangerous period: the fifth great crisis of their history. At first, however, public attention was chiefly concerned

64. Worcester Cathedral by Turner: an almost Continental evocation with its colourful boats on the River Severn.

with political reform and, by 1831, with the Reform Bill that sought to modernise the franchise and constituencies of the House of Commons. When twenty-one of the twenty-six bishops helped to vote out the Bill in the House of Lords, public fury erupted against them. On 30 October, a mob in Bristol attacked the bishop's palace and set it on fire. Men broke into the cathedral chapter house where the library was stored, and carried out volumes with which to feed the flames. Some tried to enter the cathedral itself, but were prevented by the subsacrist, William Phillips, whose memorial stands by the cloister door that he slammed to keep them out.[6]

The Reform Act was passed in June 1832. Meanwhile Wade had revised the *Black Book* and now examined the Church in the opening chapter. Like Williams, Wade accused cathedral clergy of holding no services of interest to the public, acquiring multiple benefices where they could not possibly function, and spending their time – he imagined – hunting, playing cards, and staying in watering places. Two of his pages listed deans, canons, and their pluralities.[7] The *Black Book* went into several editions, selling 50,000 copies and ensuring that cathedrals remained in the public eye as places in need of reform. All this alarmed the canons of Durham: by far the wealthiest foundation because its lands were now enriched with coalfields. One of them confided to a friend in 1831 their fears that as soon as the Reform Bill was passed, a reformed Parliament would deal with deans and chapters, and 'Durham will be the first object'.

The chapter of Durham decided to 'ward off the blow' by a pre-emptive move.[8] In September of that year it resolved to found a university and began to transfer property with a capital value of £80,000 to endow it. The bishop, William Van Mildert (Fig. 65, p. 188), contributed further thousands and eventually handed over his palace, Durham Castle, to be the home of what became University College, Durham. The university was founded in 1837 with the dean and chapter as its governors and a requirement that its graduates should subscribe to the doctrines of the Church of England: the 'Thirty-Nine Articles'. This allowed Non-conformists to enter the university but ensured that only members of the Church might receive a degree.[9]

The Durham canons were right to expect cathedrals to remain an issue and for the reformed Parliament to take it in hand. Much was written on the subject in the early 1830s, notably by Robert, Lord Henley.[10] Henley was influential because he turned the criticisms of men like Wade into positive proposals and brought them from radicalism into the mainstream of politics. His *Plan of Church Reform* was published in 1832 and went into eight editions. He proposed, in effect, to disestablish the Church by putting the appointment of bishops into the hands of a commission of laymen and clergy, and by removing them from the House of Lords. Their salaries should be made more equal and they should not move from diocese to diocese except to be made an archbishop. Cathedrals should lose their dignitaries and canons to become parish churches. The money saved through this should be used to create new parishes and improve the incomes of poor clergy. A further pamphlet by him called for a re-organisation of diocesan

boundaries and the creation of new bishoprics to cope with changes in population and the growth of industrial towns.[11]

Henley's brother-in-law was Robert Peel, who became prime minister in January 1835. He began to move cautiously towards implementing the less controversial of these proposals. In February he set up a committee of politicians and lawyers, chosen by himself, and bishops selected by the archbishop of Canterbury, William Howley. This ensured that reform of the Church would be more acceptable by involving the clergy themselves. Peel lost power in April but his successor, Lord Melbourne, re-established the committee as the 'Ecclesiastical Commission'. It produced five reports in 1836–7 which proposed the adoption of much of Henley's programme. The incomes of the bishops should be rationalised and made more even. Diocesan boundaries should be redrawn to make them more consistent in size and population. All cathedrals should be staffed by a dean and four residentiary canons, some of whom should be archdeacons. All non-residentiary canonries should be abolished, while the deans and residentiaries of the Old Foundations should lose their own separate endowments and merely share their common revenues. Minor clergy should be reduced in numbers and have their salaries raised.[12]

The proposals were criticised but commended themselves by their practical advantages, and in the end they were enacted as statutes. The Established Church Act of 1836 equalised the stipends of the bishops with extra weighting for the holders of the five senior posts: the two archbishops and the bishops of London, Durham, and Winchester. Bishops were forbidden to hold other benefices in plurality. The money saved was given to the Ecclesiastical Commission, which now became permanent, to use for the benefit of the whole Church. The dioceses were reshaped on a more equal basis and two new ones were sanctioned, Manchester and Ripon, to serve the industrial areas of Lancashire and Yorkshire. The choice of these places was based on the survival of a collegiate church at each of them, with a dean, canons, buildings, and endowments, ready-made to turn into cathedrals.

Here a problem arose. There was a good deal of public hostility to the presence of bishops in the House of Lords and it was thought controversial to increase the current number of twenty-six. Equally, bishops outside the House might prompt the removal of all the bishops from it. So two dioceses must be abolished to make room for Manchester and Ripon: Bristol, to be united with Gloucester, and St Asaph with Bangor in Wales. In addition, the diocese of Sodor and Man, whose bishop had no seat in the Lords, would be joined to Carlisle. The bishop of Bristol was speedily moved to Ely, which enabled the union with Gloucester to proceed, although Bristol was allowed to keep its cathedral. The other amalgamations were resisted and never took place. This enabled Ripon to gain a bishop and cathedral in 1836 but Manchester did not do so until 1847, by which time it was conceded that since there was one bishop without a Lords' seat, there could be another, and that the most recently appointed bishop should wait until there was a vacancy in the Lords. This delay has since applied to all new English bishops apart from those in the five senior posts.[13]

Two further statutes were enacted in 1838 and 1840. The first, the Pluralities Act, limited to two the number of benefices that a single clergyman could hold – and these had to be within ten miles and under a certain value and population. The second, the Ecclesiastical Duties and Revenues Act, at last addressed the cathedrals. All were now to be staffed by a dean and four residentiary canons, except for Exeter and Winchester with five, Canterbury, Durham, and Ely with six, and Oxford with eight (due to its many professorial chairs).[14] Deans were to be appointed by the Crown and canons by the bishop, except that the Crown continued to fill canonries vacated through promotion as a bishop. Two of the Durham canonries were attached to chairs at its new university and two at Ely to chairs at Cambridge, while Oxford's three canonry-chairs were increased to five. All non-resident prebends were suppressed (about 360 of them), with the proviso that each bishop could appoint twenty-four non-stipendiary canons as honours. Dignitaries such as precentors, chancellors, and treasurers lost their statutory powers although they could informally be given their traditional responsibilities. The endowments of the non-residents and those that belonged to the dean and residentiaries personally all passed to the Ecclesiastical Commissioners. The deans and residentiaries kept only those estates and revenues that they had formerly held in common.

The Ecclesiastical Duties Act represented the most important change to cathedral finances and personnel since the Reformation, apart from the Interregnum. It relieved the cathedrals of a potential sum of about £360,000 a year for funding new parishes and improving poor clergy stipends. It made cathedral stipends more equal, with deans receiving £1,000–£3,000 and canons £500 or more. However, the change was more gradual than those of the 1530s and 1640s because existing clergy were allowed to keep their posts and revenues for life. Even the reduction in the number of residentiary canons was delayed to enable bishops to make new appointments, so that at Winchester, for example, where seven canons had to be lost, one place could be filled after two were abolished, which took eleven vacancies to complete the process. Henry Phillpotts, the pugnacious and Tory (yet reforming) bishop of Exeter, held on to his pluralities until he died in 1869. These included a prebend of Durham worth £2,683, while the treasurership and a canonry of Exeter Cathedral with a country parish in Devon brought him a further £1,300.[15] The very last prebend to fall in under the Act, that of Wiveliscombe in Wells Cathedral, did not do so until 1891.

The cathedrals therefore altered only slowly in terms of their clergy and these persons' endowments, and the transfer of property to the Ecclesiastical Commissioners was equally protracted. Deans and chapters continued to have estates, as did the colleges of vicars choral in the Old Foundations. Clergy liked having estates – it gave them the status of gentry – but the privilege was now of doubtful value because cathedrals could not keep any revenues above their allowable income: the surplus went to the Commissioners. Moreover, the old system of entry fines and low rents impeded the continuous flow of income needed for the new stipends. In 1852 York bargained with the Commissioners to hand over its remaining lands for an annual payment of £4,410.[16] Other cathedrals soon followed, and in 1868 Parliament gave legal status to the arrangement by passing the Ecclesiastical Commissioners' Act. This abolished entry fines, authorised transfers of lands to the Commissioners for annual payments of a similar value, and allowed deans and chapters to receive back a consolidated holding of lands instead of the payments if they so wished. The Act caused cathedrals to go in different directions. Three of them (Hereford, Manchester, and Oxford) held on to what they possessed. The rest surrendered their estates: some (Canterbury, Salisbury, and York) negotiating new consolidated properties, while others

(Exeter and Lichfield) chose to continue with payments.[17] Vicars choral made similar arrangements. Payments were reliable but fixed. Estate income could grow potentially but remained low during the late nineteenth century because of agricultural depression. On the whole, cathedrals were poorer towards the end of the century than they had been before.

The Creation of More Cathedrals

England in 1830 had the same number of bishops, dioceses, and cathedrals as in Elizabethan times. Some people thought this inadequate. The issue was not the lack of cathedrals, which seemed to need reforming not increasing, but, as Henley had urged, of bishops to minister to the new industrial areas. Reformers ranged between 'moderates', who thought in terms of a few new bishops and dioceses, and 'radicals' who wanted many more. Thomas Arnold, the headmaster of Rugby School, suggested a bishop in every major town.[18] Agreement about this issue and its implementation were slow because the Church of England was an established Church. Every decision about its constitution had to be taken in Parliament. In the end the government embraced the moderate policy of creating dioceses for Manchester and Ripon, but even this ran into the problems already mentioned, so that by 1847 Ripon was still the only place with an additional bishop and cathedral. In that year the prime minster, Lord John Russell, established a committee to advise on new dioceses. It proposed Cornwall (Bodmin or Truro), St Albans, and Southwell. The government sponsored a bill to allow the Manchester scheme to proceed without a compensatory merger and to implement the other three proposals, but the latter were rejected by the Commons so that only Manchester was authorised.[19]

In September 1850 the English Church and government were taken by surprise. Pope Pius IX established a new system of Catholic dioceses in England. Hitherto the Catholic Church had been organised as a series of districts: at first four, later eight, under bishops who did not have titles based in this country. Catholics had been growing in numbers for some time, due to conversions and to Irish immigration, and their ambitions had risen accordingly. The papal action turned the districts into an archbishopric and twelve bishoprics, recalling, perhaps, Pope Gregory's scheme for southern Britain in about AD 600 (Fig. 66, p. 192). Its announcement caused a shock to a still largely Protestant nation, increased by the florid proclamation of the new archbishop and cardinal, Nicholas Wiseman, that 'Catholic England has been restored to its orbit in the ecclesiastical firmament'. The proclamation's emphasis on the authority of the pope led to the charge that the act was one of 'papal aggression'.[20]

A parliamentary statute of 1829, when Catholics were granted civil rights, barred them from adopting any titles of bishops and deans which reproduced

66. New cathedrals 1836–1900.

those of the Church of England. The new Catholic bishoprics were obliged to take other names. The archbishopric was named after Westminster and the bishoprics after Beverley, Birmingham, Clifton (in Bristol), Hexham, Liverpool, Newport (Gwent), Northampton, Nottingham, Plymouth, Salford, Shrewsbury, and Southwark. Some of the titles indicate the heartlands of Catholic support, while others were convenient centres in large and still undeveloped areas, such as Plymouth and Shrewsbury. In 1878 the diocese of Beverley was divided into Leeds and Middlesbrough, Portsmouth was formed out of Southwark in 1882, and further creations were made in the twentieth century. Following this event the great Catholic convert, John Henry Newman, preached a sermon in 1852 in which he regretted the loss of the ancient religious sites in England, but hailed the new dioceses as a sign of resurrection. 'The Church in England has died, and the Church lives again. Westminster and Nottingham, Beverley and Hexham, Northampton and Shrewsbury, if the world lasts, shall be names as musical to the ear, as stirring to the heart, as the glories we have lost.'[21]

Inevitably it took longer for the Catholic Church to set up cathedrals than dioceses. There were nominal cathedrals from about 1852 but not all were fully established and some were temporary 'pro-cathedrals'. Westminster's pro-cathedral was at St Mary's (Moorfields), Hexham's cathedral was at Newcastle, and Northampton began with a 'collegiate church'. A site for Westminster's present cathedral was acquired in 1867 but the building was not constructed until after 1895. Nevertheless, the first issue of the *Catholic Directory* in 1856 proudly listed the cathedrals, each staffed by a provost and a chapter of seven to ten canons, one of whom was usually a 'canon theologian' and another a 'canon penitentiary'. These were largely honours bestowed on parish clergy who worked elsewhere in the diocese.[22] Both provosts and canons held the title 'Very Reverend', which was shared only by deans in the Church of England, but in the course of time most of the provosts were renamed deans except in places like Portsmouth and Westminster where there was a Church of England dean. One feature of Catholic cathedrals was that their bishops usually lived nearby and therefore had more authority over them than bishops of the Church of England – or Anglican Church as we may now permissibly call it.[23] Another was that they were all parish churches, deeply involved in mission and with priorities different from Anglican ones. Their public services took the form of a series of masses during the morning, they were centres for the hearing of confessions, they celebrated the cults of the saints, and they organised 'confraternities' or guilds of laity to venerate these cults or to promote the work of the Church.[24]

The Catholic initiative may have stimulated those who were calling for more cathedrals in the Church of England, but it took another twenty-five years for such calls to have an effect. In 1854 a Cathedral Commission was appointed to examine the role of cathedrals and made fresh proposals for additional bishops. These would be based at Bristol once again, St Columb Major in Cornwall (whose church was available for the purpose), Southwell, and Westminster.[25] The problem was how to finance these extra bishops and their activities since the Ecclesiastical Commission was committed to using its money in other ways. This, along with the need to gain parliamentary approval, held up matters for years while opinion gradually strengthened to favour such plans. Some existing bishops wished to divide their territories: Phillpotts of Exeter had always supported a Cornish see. The revival of a Church of England assembly, the Convocation of Canterbury in 1855, allowed Anglicans to voice their opinions outside Parliament. In 1865 its members asked for Cornwall, St Albans, and Southwell. Meanwhile, George, Lord Lyttelton, a peer and educationist, introduced a private bill to create more dioceses in 1860. It did not succeed, and when he tried again in 1867 on behalf of St Albans, Southwell, and Truro, he failed a second time.[26]

He made a third attempt in 1875 but this time his plans were overtaken by those of the home secretary, Richard Assheton Cross, who had the backing of the government. Cross sponsored a bill on behalf of St Albans, which Parliament approved, and one for Truro in the following year with similar success. The legal foundations took place in the opposite order: Truro in December 1876 and St Albans in the following May. Each diocese was created on the understanding that its bishop must wait for seniority to enter the Lords and that no costs would fall on the Ecclesiastical Commissioners. Neither project was to proceed until an income of £2,000 was secured. This sum was achieved at both St Albans and Truro through other bishops giving up part of their revenues, generous private benefactions, and public appeals. During the 1880s four more dioceses were sanctioned by acts of Parliament: Liverpool (1880), Newcastle (1882), Southwell (1884), and Wakefield (1888), followed by the restoration of Bristol (1897).[27]

It continued to be axiomatic that a bishop needed a cathedral. St Albans possessed a large abbey church (Fig. 67, p. 195) and Southwell an ex-collegiate church, both of appropriate size and both parish churches as well. Unfortunately, Southwell's chapter of clergy and their endowments had been abolished in the reforms of 1840 without regard for their possible long-term value. Newcastle and Wakefield each had a large parish church which became the cathedral, with little adaption at first. Newcastle only received new fittings in the choir: a screen, stalls, and a bishop's throne, and although Wakefield was eventually extended, this did not happen until after 1900. Greater problems arose at Liverpool and Truro where no suitable church was available. At Truro the decision was taken to build a new cathedral on the site of the parish church of St Mary, as we shall see. At Liverpool the bishop used the parish church of St Peter pending a search for a new site, which was not successful until 1901.

The new Anglican bishops had the problem not only of finding cathedral buildings but of staffing them. It was assumed that the new cathedrals should have a dean and a chapter of canons like their older counterparts, and the St Albans and Truro acts provided for this. However, only Truro had even a single endowed canonry, which Phillpotts had procured in 1840 with Cornwall in mind and which was now transferred from Exeter. Often the bishop doubled as the dean which he did at Liverpool until 1931 and Truro until 1960, allowing him power over the institution like that of the Catholic bishops. The incumbent of the parish church that became the cathedral might be renamed dean, as happened at St Albans, and an archdeacon might have some role. Any other clergy had to be supported from diocesan funds or be largely honorary post-holders based at other churches. It took a long time for the new cathedrals to evolve their chapters. Southwell was staffed by a rector and two curates as late as 1927, while St Albans did not acquire a residentiary canon until 1936.[28]

*67. St Albans,
a great existing
church in
almost rural
surroundings,
chosen to be the
seat and centre
of a new bishop
and diocese in
1877.*

Cathedral Worship

The State did not legislate about cathedrals to any great extent after 1840.
Parliament established two Cathedral Commissions: the first in 1852
and the second in 1879, and these gathered evidence from cathedrals.
Their data and opinions are a valuable source for historians but their
recommendations were not made into laws.[29] Deans and chapters were
largely left to improve themselves by themselves. How they did so is a
complicated story, unique to each place. Sometimes the lead was taken by

a reforming dean: Merewether at Hereford (1832–50), Peacock at Ely (1839–58), Alford at Canterbury (1857–71), and Duncombe at York (1858–80). At others the dynamic came from canons like W. H. Hale and Sydney Smith at St Paul's (1829–70, 1831–45), Walter Kerr Hamilton at Salisbury (1841–54), and John Pilkington Norris at Bristol (1864–91).[30]

The process of improvement was not straightforward because so many factors were involved. Bishops hovered at the side: more active now in visiting cathedrals but restricted in their powers of intervention. They could chiefly make suggestions and hope to move things on through the canons they appointed. Some cathedral clergy were members of the wider movements in the nineteenth-century Church, while others were antipathetic towards them. The Evangelical movement had arisen in the late eighteenth century and emphasised a devout life based on Bible reading and preaching, expressed in sober ways of living and loyalty to Reformation Protestantism. The 'high Church' movement, known as Tractarianism and later as the Oxford Movement, began in the 1830s. This drew inspiration from the whole history of the Church and sought to encourage devotion through more reverent services in more beautiful settings. Such dissimilar goals caused disputes like those of Puritans and Laudians in the seventeenth century. Both parties took over parish churches or built new ones, moulding their worship accordingly, but they had less effect on cathedrals. Individual deans and canons might be Evangelicals or Tractarians, but it was difficult for them to make alterations without the consent of their colleagues. The need for such consent, the traditional gentlemanly ways of running cathedrals, and the life interests of so many old-fashioned clergy protected by the Ecclesiastical Duties Act all slowed down the process of change.

Change ensued, however, and did so in four major respects: worship, buildings, education, and outreach, each of which will now be considered in turn. There was wide agreement by the 1830s that cathedral worship was poorly performed. The criticisms of Byng and Cobbett were echoed not only by onlookers but insiders: musicians and clergy. Music in particular seemed defective. In the outside world, festivals, concerts, operas, and even amateur music in private houses were setting standards against which cathedral singing and elocution sounded perfunctory and shoddy. Adam Sedgwick, canon of Norwich, complained in 1834, 'We have the shadow of Catholicism without its substance . . . . A cold empty cathedral and a set of unwilling hirelings singing prayers for an hour together.'[31] Matters seemed no better in 1849 to Samuel Sebastian Wesley, a leading cathedral organist and choirmaster. 'The cathedral choirs have long been in a state very far *below* one of *the least* "efficiency"'. 'No cathedral in this country possesses, at this day, a musical force competent to embody and give effect to the evident intentions of the Church with regard to music.' 'Our Church music [is] a source of grief and shame to well disposed and well instructed persons.'[32]

There were several reasons for the shortcomings. One was a lack of personnel. The custom had long been that only one of the chapter – dean or canon – was present at services, and often only one priest vicar or minor canon. More crucially, as Wesley pointed out, choral music was antiphonal, involving two groups of singers on opposite sides of the choir, and he regarded a minimum of twelve men as necessary for this, plus choristers.[33] Many cathedrals had fewer, either out of economy or because the singers – lay vicars or lay clerks – were local shopkeepers or craftsmen, frequently kept away by the trades that gave them their living.[34] Organists too were poorly paid and had to subsist by giving music lessons. In the Old Foundations, the priest vicars formed an independent body which chapters found hard to control. These vicars, and the minor canons of the new cathedrals, had their own long-standing practices and resisted changing them just as chapters contested changes by politicians. There was often little rehearsal of music and no arrangements were made for the retirement of members of the choir, so that they remained in their posts long after they were capable of serving them.

Gradually, deans and chapters exerted more control over their personnel. Firmer measures were taken to ensure attendance by choir members, with the threat of fines. Opposition from colleges of vicars choral was faced down and attempts were made to suppress them, although these were not successful until the 1930s. The Pluralities Act prevented vicars choral and canons from holding other benefices unless these were near the cathedral, and they became less able to justify absence from their duties. In 1862 the minor canons of Canterbury began to be paid proper salaries in return for full attendance.[35] At some places more lay singers – lay vicars or singing men – were recruited, their wages raised, and arrangements made for their retirement.[36] The numbers of choristers were increased and, as we shall see, more thought was given to their education. Organists were better paid and rehearsals of the choir became more common, enabling them to direct the music more effectively.[37] Music evolved to embrace Romanticism.[38] Anthems by Mendelsohn and Spohr made their appearance, and new generations of English composers wrote service settings and choral pieces, including Wesley himself, Sullivan, Walmisley, and later Parry and Stanford. Meanwhile, parish churches were imitating cathedrals: bringing their singers (previously in a gallery at the west end) into the choir and dressing them in robes. Cathedrals were again setting standards for the rest of the Church as they had done in the Middle Ages.

The core of cathedral worship continued to be the two daily services of morning and evening prayer in the choir: matins and evensong as they were now called again through love of the Middle Ages. Some cathedrals still had an early service in the 'morning chapel', but these seem to have lapsed in other places.[39] Weekday matins was at around half past ten and evensong at three or four o'clock, while times on Sundays varied from ten to eleven o'clock and four to half past four. The choir services were chanted and sung with an anthem, and there was always a sermon on Sunday mornings. Sunday afternoon sermons were introduced at Ely in 1837, Salisbury in 1841 (but only in the summer), and Canterbury and Chichester in the late 1850s. They came to be common although sometimes reforming deans were obliged to preach them or to bring in outsiders, since they were not statutory tasks for the canons.

Communion had long held a secondary place in cathedral services. It followed the Sunday morning sequence of matins, litany, ante-communion, and sermon, and most of the congregation did not stay for it. It was an adjunct and was not sung chorally. Nor did it always happen every Sunday. Many cathedrals held it only once a month in the early nineteenth century, but there was a gradual movement towards once a week, although this did not reach Salisbury until 1841, Canterbury and Chichester until about 1850, and Carlisle even later.[40] The Tractarians re-emphasised communion as the central rite of the Church, and this began to influence cathedrals towards the end of the century. One innovation was an early communion at eight o'clock on Sundays and sometimes major saints' days. This was provided at Durham and Lincoln from 1870 and subsequently at Chichester and Lichfield.[41] Another was to make the late Sunday morning communion into a more self-contained service with choral accompaniment. Lincoln and Wells did so towards the end of the nineteenth century, but matins remained the principal morning service in cathedrals well into the twentieth.[42] Daily communion was slow to establish itself because its popularity with Tractarians made it objectionable to many clergy. Chichester introduced it in 1896 but the dean of Wells forbade it in 1905, and it did not begin at Salisbury until 1915.[43]

There was a similarly slow response to other aspects of Tractarianism: ornate vestments, lighted altar candles, incense, and ceremonial procedures. Not only did some deans and canons dislike such things but many believed them to be illegal until, very gradually, law-courts and bishops allowed them. Cathedral clergy had once worn copes, but during the eighteenth century cathedral worship had become plainer and it was slow to recover its past. The normal dress in church throughout the nineteenth century remained a surplice with an academic hood for graduates. By 1871 St Paul's allowed the celebrant at communion to face eastwards towards the altar (the medieval position) rather than the Protestant one of standing at the north facing south, although the eastward position had recently been ruled as illegal.[44] Lincoln did not allow its altar candles to be lit in daylight until 1892, York until 1896, and several places only well after 1900. As for processional crosses and the use of communion wafers instead of ordinary bread, these were not embraced by most cathedrals until a decade or two after the century ended.[45]

A more speedy achievement was the reclaiming of naves for worship. Contemporaries bemoaned and engravings record their dim, cold, empty spaces, whose sense of abandonment encouraged loitering and disorder (Fig. 68, p. 199). In the 1850s and 60s, however, measures were widely taken to make naves fitting for worship. They began to be lit with gas and heated with huge anthracite stoves of Gurney's patent, supplied by the London Warming and Ventilation Company.[46] This made possible, or was meant to allow, the holding of a late evening service on Sundays at six or seven, aimed at the working classes who

68. *Wells Cathedral nave in the 1820s, evoking the vast, cold emptiness of such places before the introduction of heating, lighting, and nave services.*

were effectively excluded from the middle-class congregations at choral matins and evensong. The late service was usually evensong with a sermon and a hymn or two. Benches and hymnbooks were provided. This was the beginning of a process that would blossom during the twentieth century, in which cathedrals began to behave like parish churches and indeed to compete with them. The fact was noted and deplored by neighbouring parish clergy, who said that it drew away their congregations.[47] But the services succeeded in making naves into spiritual parts of cathedrals again, for the first time since the Reformation, which encouraged more respect for these areas and lessened disorder.

The reclaiming of naves was accompanied in three cathedrals by the removal of the parish communities that had occupied parts of their buildings. The congregation of St Peter the Great moved from Chichester to a new church in 1852, followed by those of St Mary (Carlisle) in 1870 and St Oswald (Chester) in 1881.[48] At the remaining cathedrals where such arrangements survived, Ely continued to house the congregation of Holy Trinity and Hereford that of St John in their Lady chapels well into the twentieth century.[49]

Buildings and Restorations

Buildings remained a constant source of concern. Their structures had to be maintained and there was a wish to bring their insides up to date, to suit contemporary tastes and larger congregations. To do so, deans and chapters employed a series of architects who were national figures and allowed them, to a large extent, to put their personal stamp on their work. This was an age of 'restoration', in which the aim was to recreate a cathedral in an ideal form rather than simply to conserve what survived.[50] Wyatt had been the first such architect. He was followed by Lewis Cottingham (1787–1847), Edward Blore (1787–1879), George Gilbert Scott (1811–78), J. L. Pearson (1817–97), and G. E. Street (1824–81), of whom Scott worked at nearly every ancient cathedral. Augustus Welby Pugin (1812–52) was important in building Catholic churches but, being a Catholic convert, was not employed by Anglican deans and chapters.[51]

The Catholic Church was re-establishing itself and therefore built new cathedrals. Pugin's first great creation was St Chad's (Birmingham), erected in 1839–41 as a grand church that might acquire cathedral status, which it did in 1850. Funds were limited, so it was constructed of brick yet boasted two impressive western towers as well as a nave, choir, and aisles. Pugin designed three other churches that duly became cathedrals: Southwark, Nottingham, and Newcastle.[52] Generally, however, Catholic resources did not afford the creation of specially large or impressive buildings, and the additional cathedrals of the Church of England were almost all existing churches for similar reasons. Only one and a half new buildings were planned by 1900. The half was Bristol, which, having lost its nave by the sixteenth century and its bishop to Gloucester in 1836, prompted the witticism 'half a bishop and half a cathedral' (Fig. 63,

p. 180). In 1866 local people began a campaign to improve the building and thereby the reputation of the city. Funds were raised through subscriptions and a large new nave was designed by Street and completed by Pearson, again with western towers.[53] The whole cathedral was Truro, where the first bishop of the new diocese was Edward White Benson, whom we shall meet again. His energy coincided with an Anglican revival in Cornwall, where members of the Church had become a minority by 1841 but were now increasing and determined (like all their countrymen) that Cornwall should have parity with England. Truro had been chosen for its centrality but its parish church was too small. A cathedral committee was formed in 1878 and Pearson was commissioned as the architect. He kept the south aisle of the parish church as a Lady chapel but planned a large cathedral north of it with three impressive towers. The foundation stone was laid in 1880 and the towers completed in 1910 (Fig. 69, p. 202).[54]

Rebuilding or restoring cathedrals could be controversial, as Wyatt had found. Architectural experts criticised the type of Gothic employed or the accuracy with which it was replicated. Objections were raised to the kinds of furnishings that the restorers introduced, on the grounds that these were Catholic in nature and fostered superstition. Cathedral restoration was a public matter, dependent on subscriptions and widely reported in newspapers. Organisations were formed to press particular causes. One such group was the Cambridge Camden Society, founded in 1839 and later renamed the Ecclesiological Society, with its journal *The Ecclesiologist*. Its members had scholarly views about the nature of medieval architecture and believed that it should reflect the liturgical and devotional practices of the medieval Church. The English Church Union (1859) defended the tenets of the Oxford Movement and the Church Association (1865) those of the Reformation. The Society for the Protection of Ancient Buildings (1877), founded by William Morris and others, opposed the very concept of restoring buildings to an imagined medieval state and campaigned for the conservation of what remained. Its point of view would eventually prevail in the care of cathedrals during the twentieth century, but the great restoring architects had their way for most of the nineteenth.

The cathedral reformers of the 1830s had not thought to provide resources for maintaining buildings. Some deans and chapters managed to elicit exceptional grants from the Ecclesiastical Commissioners. Carlisle got £15,000 in 1854, Salisbury £10,000 in 1861, and Lichfield £15,000 in 1876, but in the last two cases the grants were part of the negotiations in which the chapters gave up their estates in return for fixed payments.[55] Cathedrals usually had fabric funds, and when these were exhausted they had to make public appeals. Appeals produced substantial amounts, including significant gifts from rich people: Victorian England was wealthy, after all. The bulk of the money was spent on structural repairs. Many buildings were in a poor condition, a fact dramatically emphasised in 1861 when the spire of Chichester fell through the central tower into the crossing, luckily without loss of life.[56] Scott restored the tower and spire,

69. Truro's new cathedral in c.1905, still lacking the two western towers. It transformed the landscape of the town and gave the Cornish something to equal the English.

strengthened their counterparts at Salisbury, repaired the timber lantern at Ely, and did much remedial work at Lichfield. Alongside the repair of structures came the refurnishing of choirs. A reaction against Georgian fittings had begun at Lincoln as early as 1786 and at Gloucester by 1819.[57] By the 1840s it was spreading widely. Box pews, galleries, and reredoses were removed. Medieval Gothic stalls were repaired or recreated. In the place of the old reredoses, with their tables of the Commandments and sometimes the figures of Moses and Aaron, the restorers built new stone ones, often of marble and alabaster, and embellished with figure sculpture.

A major issue in restoring the choir was that of the pulpitum. All Anglican cathedrals had medieval ones or replacements. They fully shut off the choir from the nave and some had the organ above them. Their original purpose was to seclude the area where the clergy performed the liturgy from the rest of the church and to shield the choir from draughts in an unheated building. Some people wished to remove them. One consideration was the inadequacy of choir areas to accommodate congregations even with their eighteenth-century extensions. Abolishing the pulpitum would allow people in the nave to watch the service: that nave with new lighting and heating. Another impetus was the Victorians' 'lust for vistas'. They were lovers of the theatre in which one looked at a performance on a stage. The choir was a potential stage with its scenery of reredos, stalls, and columns, and its costumed actors. It should be opened up to have its full effect.

The restoration architects were familiar with medieval churches and doubted this. They understood that cathedrals had been designed in layout and proportions to be divided into sections. Moreover, some of the pulpitums were genuine medieval artefacts. The architects therefore resisted the integration of choir and nave, and when Pugin was building St Chad's he planned to include a partition between the two. Nicholas Wiseman, the bishop, dissented but Pugin insisted and designed a beautiful screen of metal and glass which, it has been well said, made the choir into a reliquary for the relics of St Chad which the church had recently acquired.[58] This was an elegant compromise: a division yet also a window. Scott erected similar screens of metal, wood, or stone at Durham, Hereford, Lichfield, Worcester, and elsewhere (Fig. 70, p. 204). When he came to work at Exeter, the dean and chapter wanted to remove the pulpitum, which dated from the fourteenth century, but Scott pleaded for its historic importance. A compromise was reached by which the structure was lightened with an open doorway and two new windows but otherwise left intact (Fig. 52, p. 148).[59] It gives the impression of visibility into the choir but supplies almost none. In the end most cathedrals emerged from restoration with a pulpitum or screen except for St Paul's, which dispensed with the former in 1860 and was then wholly open inside.

Furnishings were largely a matter of taste but their decoration raised religious issues. At first some Anglicans condemned even the display of a plain cross as illegal and 'Roman Catholic'. A legal judgment of 1857 permitted crosses, but as late as the 1860s two members of the Durham chapter objected to Scott's addition of one to the gable of his choir screen, although the modest feature survived in the end.[60] Sculptured images aroused hostility for the same reasons. Scott's reredos for Exeter featured Christ's Ascension, flanked by his Transfiguration and the Descent of the Holy Spirit (Fig. 71, p. 205). The archdeacon of Cornwall, W. J. Phillpotts, son of the redoubtable Henry, complained that it contravened Tudor legislation against imagery and had been erected without the bishop's permission. The bishop took legal advice and ruled that the reredos was unlawful, but the dean and chapter appealed and got the judgment reversed in 1875.[61] A row at Bristol in the following year had a different outcome. Street's rebuilding of the nave included a grand north porch embellished with images of the Virgin Mary and the Four Doctors of the Church. One, Gregory, was shown as a pope and another, Jerome, as a cardinal. There were public protests and the dean had the figures removed, to Street's vexation; they could, he complained, have been modified.[62]

A further issue was that of internal burials and monuments. Burials were becoming objectionable on hygienic grounds and most cathedrals came to prohibit them during the nineteenth century, except for a few important people. Monuments were a concern because they were overwhelming naves, aisles, and cloisters in the

70. The
choir screen
of Worcester
Cathedral
designed by
George Gilbert
Scott: an elegant
compromise
to demarcate
the choir while
making it more
visible.

form of mural tablets.[63] One writer accused these of 'blistering' the walls, another of 'grievously marring' the churchscape: complaints that reflected the Victorian love of images as against the Georgian liking for texts.[64] Effigy monuments, however, continued to be permitted for the great and the good. In the early decades of the century they were still classical, and often featured standing or seated figures like Bishop Van Mildert in Durham (Fig. 65, p. 188). Then, in the 1840s, Gothic taste caused the revival of medieval tombs with recumbent figures to honour important clergy. Most of the archbishops of Canterbury were commemorated in this way between Howley (d. 1848) and Davidson (d. 1930), and similar effigies were erected for their counterparts at Norwich, York, and elsewhere. The privilege was extended to an occasional dean and at Lichfield even to an archdeacon and a canon.[65]

A new addition to the monuments was the military memorial. In a sense this had long been present in the form of medieval, Tudor, and Jacobean knights, while St Paul's had become a mausoleum of heroes of the Napoleonic wars. The 1840s, however, saw the appearance of collective memorials to particular campaigns. Some of the earliest were those at Lichfield and Norwich to the local regiments who fought in the Afghan and Indian wars. Such memorials might honour officers alone and

71. The controversial reredos of Exeter Cathedral, also by Scott, which prompted an objection to its images but was finally ruled to be legal.

be subscribed for by their colleagues, while others extended the tribute to all the ranks. The Crimean war generated many more and its heroine, Florence Nightingale, eventually had one of her own in the crypt of St Paul's. Christian mission left its mark as well. Exeter's pulpit was erected in memory of the murdered John Coleridge Patterson, first bishop of Melanesia (d. 1871), while Truro's baptistery commemorated the city's hero Henry Martyn (d. 1812), a pioneering missionary in India and Persia.

Although we think of cathedrals as essentially local, they have always had links with a much wider world.

Some cathedrals sought to divert the building of monumental projects into the glazing of memorial windows. All filled or renewed their windows with glass in the nineteenth century.[66] Ely, for example, had a long project to this effect from the 1840s to the 1870s. The nave aisle windows were filled with Old Testament scenes, those of the choir aisles with New Testament ones, and those of the octagon with founders and benefactors of the cathedral including Queen Victoria and Prince Albert, the latter robed as chancellor of Cambridge University.[67] Window imagery seems to have been less controversial than figure sculpture. It accorded with the Victorians' love of costume drama, and many people now liked the idea of a church that, in the words of one of their favourite poets, was a place with 'storeyed windows, richly dight, casting a dim religious light'.[68]

Cathedrals and Education

Defenders of cathedrals pointed to their past and potential future as places of teaching and learning. Responding to Lord Henley in 1833, the Tractarian Edward Pusey praised the distinctly English theology that had grown up from the writings of divines based in cathedrals. Such places, he suggested, should become new centres of education where would-be clergy could spend two years of study before their ordination.[69] Five years later George Selwyn extended the proposal. Why might not cathedral song schools be opened to others, such as parish clerks; their grammar schools take in deserving scholars from lesser local schools; their libraries be used by parish clergy; and divinity lectures be re-established, as they had been in the time of Henry VIII?[70]

Cathedrals continued to provide homes for scholars in the traditional way, but much of their scholarship came out of their university careers rather than their cathedral residence. Henry Liddon and Joseph Lightfoot, canons of St Paul's in the 1870s, were distinguished theologians but retained their university chairs along with their canonries. So did Adam Sedgwick of Norwich (d. 1873), professor of geology at Cambridge. Robert Scott, dean of Rochester (d. 1887), had been master of Balliol College and co-author of Liddell and Scott's *Greek Lexicon*. Most research and writing that took place at cathedrals consisted of popular theology, such as the publication of sermons and tracts on matters of religious debate, or historical works. Arthur Stanley, canon of Canterbury and later dean of Westminster, wrote a history of the cathedral, *Memorials of Canterbury*, in 1854. St Paul's embraced a series of historians. Henry Hart Milman (d. 1868) had written surveys of Judaism and early Christianity as well as editing Gibbon before he was dean. He compiled a history of St Paul's which was published after his death, and his successor-but-one, R. W. Church (d. 1890), wrote one of the Oxford Movement. Their more antiquarian colleague, Archdeacon Hale

(d. 1870), made a pioneering collection of church court proceedings as well as editing episcopal and cathedral records.[71]

The education of the young, on the other hand, was not being managed well when Pusey and Selwyn wrote. Every cathedral had a group of choristers, ranging from six to fourteen and trained in song by a master who was also the organist. Sometimes they boarded in the Close but usually they lived at home, the sons of local tradesmen or artisans. Most cathedrals provided them with further teaching in reading, writing, and arithmetic. Some went to the cathedral grammar school as was the case at Chichester, Ely, and Hereford, while at Salisbury they had their own grammar master. When their voices broke, the dean and chapter paid for them to be apprenticed, and this was an attraction of their posts.

In 1810 Maria Hackett, a moderately wealthy woman in her late twenties, procured a chorister's place at St Paul's for her young orphaned cousin, where the boys boarded.[72] She found that they were not well housed, supervised, or educated, and were regularly hired out by their singing master to perform at concerts and dinners. Tracing their history in the cathedral archives and the British Museum, she learnt that they were denied their ancient entitlements. She wrote letters about this to the bishop and the chapter, receiving evasive replies. In 1813 she and her family instituted legal proceedings, and gained a court order restoring some of the relevant funds. Being unmarried, she made the cause her life-work. She printed her correspondence with St Paul's and became well known. She made regular visits to other cathedrals to see what they did with their boys. On her arrival she brought each one a book, a purse, and a new shilling. She gave treats to those of St Paul's, where she continued to worship, and lived to see the cathedral open a new school building in 1873. Maria did not succeed in bringing choristers' welfare and education up to standard in every place. At Salisbury the boys' school lurched from master to master, some inadequate, for most of the nineteenth century.[73] But she forced cathedrals to take them more seriously, and as musical and educational standards improved during the century, choristers became better accommodated, more highly trained in music, and more widely educated.

Most cathedrals still possessed the grammar schools established in the Middle Ages or by Henry VIII at the Reformation. Those of the Old Foundations had always been somewhat detached, and at Lichfield, Lincoln, and St Paul's they passed out of the control of the dean and chapter in Tudor times. Exeter let its school expire in the eighteenth century. That left five Old Foundations and ten New ones with grammar schools in 1800.[74] In the Middle Ages they had been important regionally and until the seventeenth century most had been of good quality, but latterly they had stagnated: to a large extent through lack of interest from the deans and chapters in charge of them. Meanwhile, endowed town grammar schools like Harrow, Rugby, and Shrewsbury had forged ahead to become big, successful boarding schools, thanks to enterprising headmasters and more supportive bodies of governors.

Most chapters still gave their master only a house and the stipend laid down by Henry VIII. Since this was now a tiny sum, the master needed a further income. He might hold a minor canonry, charge fees from pupils other than the statutory foundation scholars, and make extra money by boarding boys in his house. Henry had meant his schools to be free, but it was assumed that this applied only to Latin and Greek. He had provided stipends for the foundation scholars but these too were still at the ancient rates unless they had lapsed altogether. Most cathedral schools had a single master, perhaps with a deputy 'usher', causing standards and attendances to fluctuate wildly from one occupant to another. Some still occupied the original ancient classroom: the old almonry hall at Canterbury, the monastic refectory at Worcester. None was very large: even York had only twenty boys in 1819 and Canterbury only forty ten years later. Their pupils came mainly from gentry and professional families, but these were often tempted elsewhere by private schools with more effective masters. Some deans and chapters saw little value in secondary education. In about 1814 Peterborough considered requesting the Crown to change the grammar school to an elementary one, and Chester made the change without permission, reporting that its school did not teach classics and was 'appropriated to the education of the lower orders'.[75]

In 1842 the dean and chapter of Rochester appointed Robert Whiston as their schoolmaster, no doubt applauding themselves because he was a fellow of Trinity College, Cambridge, and ran a thriving private school in Rochester.[76] The previous master had flogged all the pupils away, except for his son. Whiston soon turned the school round, filled the twenty foundation scholarships, and adapted his dwelling, the Old Palace, into a boarding house at his own expense. He got the chapter to build a new schoolhouse but then demanded that it restore the maintenance grants to the foundation boys and upgrade the four university exhibitions to acceptable levels.[77] After getting no satisfaction from either chapter or bishop, he published a tract in 1849, *Cathedral Trusts and their Fulfilment*, showing how the New Foundations had deviated from their original charters and statutes, and attacking the Rochester canons specifically. The chapter dismissed him for libel and appointed a replacement. Whiston refused to go and continued teaching, supported by his pupils' parents. The case gained national attention. Money was raised to support him and questions were asked in Parliament. In the end, the case went to the bishop who deplored the libel but reinstated him. The chapter was obliged to raise the value of the scholarships, the exhibitions, and the wages of the minor officers in the cathedral. Whiston remained triumphantly in office until 1877: a tireless man who duly became a magistrate and an elected member of the new Kent County Council.

Not all deans and chapters were so unhelpful. At York they built a new schoolhouse in 1830 and, this becoming inadequate, bought a private school at Clifton in 1844 where they erected fresh buildings on a more spacious site. By that date there were a hundred boys, forming a viable school with boarding houses and playing fields.[78] At Canterbury numbers grew in the 1830s and the curriculum was widened. In 1863 the chapter built or acquired houses for the master, his deputy, and two groups of boarders; by 1896 there were eight masters and 143 boys in better accommodation.[79] Mitchinson, the head in 1869, helped found the Headmasters' Conference, and his colleague at Durham was one of its earliest members. There the chapter had moved the school from the Close in the 1840s to a larger site west of the river, enabling what had been a day school to develop boarding facilities with nearly a hundred boys by the end of the century. The Durham choristers' school was also improved with the teaching of a varied range of subjects and the playing of games.[80]

By the 1860s pressure on cathedral schools was coming from the State as it became more involved in education. In 1869 the Endowed Schools Act created commissioners with the power to change the objectives of such schools and to establish new governing bodies. They helped draw up a revised scheme for Chester in 1873 which enlarged the governors to include the mayor and representatives of the city council. The cathedral was released from its statutory duties in return for an annual grant.[81] At Rochester a similar plan in 1877 brought in governors from outside, and shortly afterwards the Ecclesiastical Commissioners gave money for new buildings.[82] In other places the chapter itself reformed its school, as at Hereford which appointed a better-paid headmaster during the 1870s whose coming was followed by new premises and eventually external governors.[83] Inevitably, as the schools grew, they turned into more independent bodies whose headmasters and staff controlled most matters and could begin to rival leading schools elsewhere as they had done in the remote past. Much the same happened to Durham University, where the cathedral gradually lost control as the century wore on. Like the schools, it became too big and diverse, and had to be left to itself.

Pusey's and Selwyn's calls for cathedrals to be involved in higher education were probably suggested in part by events at Durham, but elsewhere bishops rather than deans and chapters were the driving forces in this direction. William Otter, bishop of Chichester (1836–40), was an educationist who had been principal of King's College London, a new Anglican university. In 1839 he founded the Church's first theological college for training clergy at Chichester, and Phillpotts of Exeter established a 'Diocesan Training College' for schoolmasters in his cathedral Close. The following year saw a similar training college for men appear at Chichester, planned by Otter and founded in his memory, and a second college for clergy at Wells promoted by two archdeacons with the support of the bishop.[84] Similar foundations were made in several other dioceses. None of the colleges was joined to its cathedral constitutionally but the principal of the clergy college was sometimes (although not routinely) given a canonry by the bishop. Its buildings were often near the cathedral, and the students used the church for daily worship. The colleges for teachers tended to be more detached because they needed larger premises than could be found in a Close, while, in educational and social terms, they were inferior to those for the clergy.

Alongside these formal institutions there were ways in which cathedrals and their clergy contributed to education on an occasional or individual basis. Deans and chapters were obvious bodies to ask for donations to build and establish village schools where they held property or owned the church.[85] J. S. Howson, dean of Chester, was a major figure in the foundation of Queen's School, Chester, a school for middle-class girls to complement the revived King's School for boys in 1877. Its governing body came to include the bishop and members of the chapter.[86] At about the same time, in 1872, Bishop Wordsworth of Lincoln appointed Edward White Benson as chancellor of the cathedral.[87] Benson suffered from depression and found release in activity. His principal duty was to start the new theological college, but during his five years there he did much else. He preached on Sunday afternoons. He lectured on Church history during Lent in the chapter house. He organised 'University Extension Lectures' on the model of a scheme in Nottingham to bring university learning to popular audiences. He ran a Bible class for mechanics from local factories. He started night schools teaching reading, writing, and arithmetic, promising the return of the joining fee to those who finished the course. He led a Mission Week in a city church which was well attended by men of the 'artisan classes'. It is not surprising that in 1877 he was made the first bishop of Truro and rose to the throne of Canterbury only six years later.[88]

Cathedrals and Society

The political and religious reforms of the nineteenth century had a significant impact on the ties between cathedrals and society. Democracy eroded any political influence they once might have had. The removal of lands and tithes, either partly or wholly, weakened their ancient links with the countryside. Cathedrals ceased to be major property owners in their own cities and their relations changed with the local authorities. Up to the 1830s the arrival of the mayor and aldermen with their mace-bearers on Sundays, to sit in their privileged seats, proclaimed that Church and State were present together, joined in beliefs and policies. After the 1830s, city government was open to non-Anglicans, and although some ceremonial intercourse would remain, there was no longer such a common interest.

The public laws now gave the city authorities power over the whole of their territory. The privileges of the Close shrank to little more than the care of its landscape. A similar change took place in the spiritual sphere. A statute of 1836 enabled the Ecclesiastical Commissioners to transfer all peculiar jurisdictions to the bishop, and this was implemented during the next few years. Thereafter the cathedral alone remained outside the diocesan administration, and chapters kept only the right to nominate clergy to the churches in their patronage. Further laws of 1855–7 took away most of the powers of the Church courts. Hitherto some of these had been based in cathedrals, and people were obliged to attend them in cases of defamation, marriage, and wills. Now these matters came under the secular law, and the chapels where the courts had sat were eventually turned to other uses, although Chester's still survives.

These losses were partly offset from a direction that the cathedral clergy of the 1820s and 30s would not have expected and indeed fought hard against: the growing power of ordinary people. The population of England quadrupled during the nineteenth century, from 7,750,000 at the beginning to 30,000,000 by the end. Religious leaders often bemoaned the secularism of the age and the supposed decline of faith. Yet Victorian England contained large numbers of people, of all social ranks, who hungered for religious experiences, and many satisfied these at cathedrals in Prayer Book worship, sacred music, and sermons. Wider education and greater prosperity broadened horizons and gave more time for leisure. Railway travel made it easier to visit cathedrals on a day-trip or during a holiday. London got its first railway station in 1837 and Bristol in 1838. By the 1840s most cathedrals were linked to the national network, and even the last of them, Wells, acquired a station in 1859 only twenty-two years after London.

Cathedrals made themselves more accessible both to worshippers and tourists. A journalist who came to Bristol on a Sunday morning in the 1840s found some of the pews already occupied while the rest were locked. The verger ignored him until he produced a shilling, after which a pew was opened and he could sit down.[89] By that date other cathedrals like Norwich and Rochester were giving their vergers living wages and barring the taking of tips. Entry to services became easier and worship grew more attractive with better music, the addition of a sermon to evensong, and the heating and lighting of naves. True, congregations did not improve uniformly, and as late as the 1910s Hensley Henson, dean of Durham, complained of small attendances.[90] Yet, equally, there could be crowds, especially on Sunday evenings. Cathedrals then attracted working people who had had a day of rest, wanted somewhere to go, and did not need to fear arousing attention as they would in a parish church or chapel. By the late 1850s Canterbury's seating was filled for evensong on summer afternoons by holidaymakers from Ramsgate and Margate.[91] York's evening services from the 1860s brought in large audiences of 'labourers' and those of Wells in 1886 for 'working men' filled the nave and parts of the aisles.[92] As for St Paul's, which introduced them under the dome in 1858, it was said that ten thousand people competed for the two and a half thousand chairs that had been provided. By 1872 an afternoon service with a sermon by the popular chancellor, Liddon, was reckoned to attract six thousand.[93]

Cathedrals also reached beyond their regular supporters with special services. The Three Choirs Festival had long been a regular and popular event at three of them, as we have seen. York held similar festivals of sacred music from 1823 for the benefit of local charities.[94] In 1856 Lichfield organised a Diocesan Choir Gathering. Twenty-six parish choirs from the diocese joined the cathedral choir to accompany matins and evensong; the event was successful and reproduced widely elsewhere.[95] In 1869 Durham instituted a 'Mining Service', appropriately in view of its closeness to the coalfields. Communities of miners walked in procession with their bands and banners, and have done so ever since.[96]

Norwich, which was a garrison town and often had soldiers attend, staged 'Military Services' at about the same date.[97] Harvest Festivals were organised and in 1880 Edward White Benson invented what would be a runaway success in his temporary cathedral at Truro: a late evening service on Christmas Eve with nine lessons and carols.[98] Public events were celebrated too. Here St Paul's had a special role as the national cathedral. It held the funerals of Nelson and Wellington, gave thanks for peace in 1814 and for the recovery of the Prince of Wales from typhoid in 1872, and celebrated Victoria's jubilees of 1887 and 1897.[99]

Meanwhile, there was more provision for those who came merely as visitors. In the early nineteenth century cathedral buildings were often closed, even between Sunday services, and entry at any time might involve tipping a verger who could also provide a tour. St Paul's was the first to develop more formal arrangements because it had more sightseers. It restricted entry to most of the cathedral with barriers and charged 2d. to pass through them, except for certain hours on Sundays. The dome and library could be seen for 1s. 6d.: money which like the twopences went partly to the cathedral and partly to the poorly paid vergers. In 1837 the home secretary, Lord John Russell, supported by the young Queen Victoria, asked for more public access but the cathedral would only concede another free hour. In 1851, however, when huge crowds were anticipated because of the Great Exhibition, the Ecclesiastical Commissioners made a grant to pay the vergers proper salaries, on condition of free entry.[100]

Elsewhere there was a gradual opening up, although often with retention of some fees. In 1849 Salisbury allowed free admission to the nave but took 6d. to see the choir, cloisters, and chapter house.[101] Canterbury appointed special guides in 1870 for parties of up to thirty people, but not on Sundays. It charged as well but allowed free entry one day every month and at Whitsuntide.[102] Hereford was open in 1876 from nine to six o'clock and exacted no fees but asked for donations of 6d.[103] Durham stayed open in summer until six o'clock in the 1880s and allowed the climbing of the tower for 3d.[104] Peterborough was wholly free from 1853 to 1878 under a reforming dean, Augustus Saunders, and displayed printed cards explaining the objects of interest. Here too, however, charges were later imposed.[105]

Those who wished to prepare themselves for their visit, or wanted more information than vergers provided, could avail themselves of the handbooks to cathedrals and their cities that had begun to appear in the eighteenth century. These grew in number along with the tide of visitors. Books with 'Guide' in the title were produced by local publishers for York (by 1826), Chichester (1831), Peterborough (1846), Wells (1855), Canterbury (1857), Worcester (1863), Hereford (1865), and Gloucester (1867). At first they advertised themselves for 'strangers', which gave way to 'tourists' in the second half of the century, reflecting the change from individual visits to mass and sometimes organised sightseeing. In due course, national series of guide-books began to appear that included cathedrals. Murray's *Handbooks* was one of the first such enterprises in 1838, although its earliest volumes were for travellers to Europe: it started producing guides to English regions only in 1851. *Bradshaw's Handbook for Tourists* came out in 1858, including all the cathedral cities, and continued to appear until 1896. Later still, the firm of Ward and Lock published guide-books to popular holiday areas such as the coasts and the Lake District. In 1887 they extended these with a guide to Canterbury Cathedral and followed it with similar ones for most of its Anglican siblings. Similar but more learned was Bell's Cathedral Series which appeared from 1896 to 1905 and included a history of each cathedral's diocese.

Bradshaw's Handbook is a fair specimen of how cathedrals were viewed by organisers of Victorian tourism.[106] It was based on the railway lines, assuming that people would travel by train, and told them about the places along the routes. Cathedrals did not get undue treatment; indeed they were usually accorded only a few lines in an informal style that merely tried to suggest a few points of interest. The tone was generally respectful. Peterborough and York were 'noble', Lincoln 'splendid', and Gloucester even 'magnificent'. Ely was 'the longest cathedral in Europe and, taken as a whole, the most beautiful'. Chapter houses, cloisters, and libraries were mentioned, evidently because they could be visited. Victorian taste was present in the comment that Hereford had been 'spoiled' by Wyatt but 'finely restored' by Scott, and in the praises given to Ely's newly painted roof and Chantrey's sculpture, 'Sleeping Children', in Lichfield. In contrast Rochester got a mixed review: 'the cathedral has a half ruinous look outside, but contains some excellent Norman work'. That was better than poor Bristol which (still lacking a nave) was written off again as 'a plain, shapeless, early English church'. Visitors were advised to go to its neighbour, St Mary Redcliffe, as being 'more interesting'. As for the Catholic cathedrals, apart from a brief allusion to Pugin at Birmingham, there was no assumption that tourists would wish to see them.

People who liked to visit cathedrals liked to have pictures of them. Pictures, as we have seen, had been published as early as 1656, and were appearing by the end of the eighteenth century in books of the beauties of Britain and as prints for mounting or framing.[107] J. M. W. Turner produced several watercolours of cathedrals during his early career in the 1790s, including Ely, Bath, and Bristol (Figs 26, 36, 63, pp. 60, 96, 180). These were often meant for publication in the form of engravings on wood or copper, and Turner painted others for a printed edition of *Picturesque Views in England* (1827–38). The latter exhibit more of his mature style, including an impressionistic view of Durham and one of Worcester with boats on the River Severn that might have come from one of his European tours (Fig. 64, p. 184).[108] In this period even first-rate artists like Constable and Turner were willing to turn their hands to depicting cathedrals.

Victorian painters favoured human subjects, especially ones that told a story. Topography was relegated to be a more mundane and commercial branch of art. At the same time, it began to reach a greater audience through the introduction of engraving on steel plates during the 1820s. This gave a result that looked more like a painting and could be reproduced in much larger numbers (Figs 2, 28, pp. 3, 67). Images of cathedrals in books or as prints became cheaper to provide and

Ripon Cathedral from the River

72. An early postcard of Ripon Cathedral. Technology kept pace with rising numbers of visitors by offering them cheap souvenirs of their visits.

their circulation grew greater still with the invention of picture postcards. These were first permitted by the Post Office in 1894 and in 1902 they acquired the modern 'divided back' with sections for an address and a message. The rise of photography allowed local firms to publish cards of cathedrals costing a penny or two. Now people could take them home as souvenirs, post them to friends, or collect them, spreading knowledge of the buildings yet more widely (Fig. 72, above).

Cathedrals in Literature

That cathedrals were romantic places, yet places in need of reform, made it inevitable that they would become the subject of novels. One of the earliest such was William Harrison Ainsworth's *Old Saint Paul's* (1841), 'a tale of the plague and the fire', which is still in print. This was the English equivalent of Victor Hugo's *Notre Dame de Paris* written ten years earlier: a costume drama set in 1666. The plot is that of a Victorian melodrama with a sturdy apprentice hero, a blind piper and his beautiful daughter, an attempted clandestine marriage at the 'high altar', the priest who arranged the marriage struck down by the plague, and the prophet Solomon Eagle striding around with a pot of fire on his head proclaiming the vengeance of heaven. It culminates in the burning of St Paul's during which the hero is raised to the peerage by Charles II and the two villains, sheltering in the crypt, are overwhelmed by floods of molten lead.

Other cathedral novels were more realistic. Charles Kingsley was an Anglican clergyman and a supporter of Christian socialism. He wished to purge the Church of England of its wealthy, privileged clergy and to revive its mission to working people. These ideas permeate his story *Alton Locke*, published in 1850: a novel like those of Dickens and Mrs Gaskell that called for the reform of the nation's institutions. The hero of the title is the son of a small shopkeeper who becomes a tailor and joins the Chartists (political radicals), while possessing a questioning mind and spiritual sympathies that express themselves in the writing of poetry. Locke is befriended by the dean of an imaginary cathedral in the Fens who proposes to send him to a Church training college for teachers. He visits the dean and the cathedral but feels uncomfortable with both. The dean is kind yet remote from real life, living comfortably with servants and studying natural history. The men of the choir seem 'exceedingly ill looking', their 'faces bespoke principally sensuality and self-conceit', their function 'that of praising God on the sole qualification of good bass and tenor voices'. The cathedral is in a poor condition, its worship defective. Locke was 'appalled, rather than astonished, by . . . the unintelligible service – the irreverent gabble of the choristers and readers – the scanty congregation – the meagre portion of the vast building which seemed to be turned to any use'. 'Never more than that evening did I feel the desolateness, the doleful inutility, of that vast desert nave with its aisles and transepts – built for some purpose or other now extinct. The whole place seemed to crush and sadden me.'

Thus far, cathedrals are indicted for complacency, inefficiency, and irrelevance, but Kingsley marshals counter-arguments. The dean's daughter praises cathedrals for their art and spirituality. 'How those pillars, rising storey above storey, and those lines of pointed arches, all lead the eye heavenwards. It is a beautiful notion, that about pointed architecture being symbolic of Christianity.' Eleanor Staunton, a well-educated woman, defends cathedrals on social and economic grounds. 'You may sneer at monasteries if you will, Mr Locke [the cathedral is a converted one like Ely or Peterborough] . . . . The working classes would have been badly off without them. They were, in their day, the only democratic institution in the world, and the only socialist one too. The only chance a poor man had of rising by his worth, was by coming to the monastery. And bitterly the working classes felt the want of them, when they fell. Your own Cobbett can tell you that.' This causes Locke to rethink his position: 'it showed that there might be two sides to the question of the people's cause.' As a reformist, Kingsley disliked much about cathedrals and wished them to be reshaped in their economy and worship. Yet he valued them for their spiritual potential and because he believed, like Cobbett, that they recalled society to an older better world in which the Church reached everyone and fostered fairness, fellowship, and charity.

Anthony Trollope came to Salisbury in about 1852 and was inspired to write a story about a cathedral city that he called Barchester, for which he also drew on Winchester and Exeter. The story, *The Warden* (1855), tells how Septimus Harding, precentor of Barchester Cathedral and warden of Hiram's Hospital, becomes the target of a campaign to reform the hospital and resigns his post there as a consequence. The tension in the novel is that the hospital needs reforming, yet Harding is an admirable man. Two years later Trollope published *Barchester Towers* in which the action moved towards the cathedral. He was not wholly clear about how such places were governed and confused the two kinds of Foundations. Barchester has a dean, precentor, chancellor, and treasurer, so ought to be one of the Old. But it has both vicars choral (Old) and minor canons (New), while Harding's work in leading the choral singing looks like that of a New cathedral precentor. On the other hand, the book is correct in depicting the lingering presence of clergy with protected rights under the Ecclesiastical Duties Act. Notable here is Dr Stanhope, the non-resident prebendary and pluralist rector of Crabtree Canonicorum, Stogpingum, and Eiderdown, who is normally to be found in Italy engaged in the study of butterflies.

Barchester Towers has a theme of reform but a less serious one. A struggle takes place in the Church between old and new. The old are the cathedral clergy like Harding and his son-in-law Archdeacon Grantley. They are gentlemanly and hospitable. Cathedral services are well performed. 'The psalms were beautifully chanted, the Te Deum was magnificently sung; and the litany . . . has long been the special task to which Mr Harding's skill and voice have been devoted.' The new are the incoming bishop, Dr Proudie, his termagant wife, and their oily chaplain, Mr Slope. The bishop is a mediocre man who has risen in the Church as a token clergyman on commissions devised by politicians and civil servants. His wife is a sour Evangelical, obsessed by Sunday observance. The chaplain shares her views but is devious and self-seeking. When the bishop is enthroned in the cathedral, Slope preaches a sermon criticising its worship for the primacy of music over the Word of God, of art over understanding, in the manner of a post-Reformation Puritan.

Barchester Towers has become *the* cathedral novel. That is partly because of an array of varied characters and their interactions to which the cathedral is merely a background. But it is also because Trollope's view of cathedrals coincides with, and may even have helped to form, the public stance towards them since his day. His cathedral is a backwater, but he does not think that this matters. He gives a rosy, only slightly ironic, account of comfortable clergy and their families living in pleasant surroundings. He has no real wish to reform cathedrals except, perhaps, to reduce non-residence and over-generous stipends, and he makes clear his preference for the Barchester clergy over the would-be reformers. The book ends with the banishment of Slope and the appointment of a new dean, Mr Arabin: a moderate Tractarian who is likely to lead the cathedral onwards in sensible, gradual reform.

Dickens produced a cathedral novel too: his last work, *The Mystery of Edwin Drood*, published as a serial in 1870 (Fig. 73, p. 217). In his draft notes for the story, he wrote 'cathedral town running throughout', and underlined this twice. The

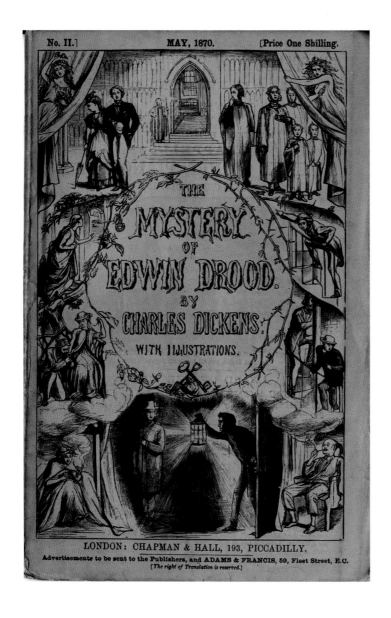

No. II.]   MAY, 1870.   [Price One Shilling.

THE MYSTERY OF EDWIN DROOD. BY CHARLES DICKENS. WITH ILLUSTRATIONS.

LONDON: CHAPMAN & HALL, 193, PICCADILLY.

Advertisements to be sent to the Publishers, and ADAMS & FRANCIS, 59, Fleet Street, E.C.

[The right of Translation is reserved.]

73. Cathedral fiction: the wrapper of an instalment of The Mystery of Edwin Drood *by Charles Dickens, with images of dark events in a gloomy building.*

town, called Cloisterham, was loosely based on Rochester. Dickens was a far more imaginative and dramatic writer than Kingsley or Trollope, and *Edwin Drood* establishes its character in its incomparable opening. The cathedral tower appears: not as it really is but as a vision shimmering behind processions of Turkish soldiers, dancing girls, and elephants in the drug-induced hallucinations of John Jasper, the unsavoury lay clerk. When Jasper arrives dishevelled for cathedral evening prayers and joins the procession of singers scuttling into their places, the opening words of

74. Canterbury Cathedral and its precinct at peace in the early twentieth century, as H. G. Wells portrayed it in The History of Mr Polly.

the service, 'When the wicked man . . .', 'rise among groins of arches and beams of roofs, awakening muttered thunder'.

At first sight *Edwin Drood* seems like another reforming novel, which would be odd in 1870 when cathedrals were raising their game. Cloisterham's building is ancient but unlovely. It attracts some visitors; sprigs of holly adorn the choir on Christmas Day. But it is not well cared for. The crypt windows are bare of glass; it is surrounded by graves and damaged by the storm on the night of Drood's disappearance. Inside it is dusty, its choirmen slovenly, its congregation 'small and straggling'. The dean is a bland evasive figure while the only attractive cleric is Septimus Crisparkle, a minor canon whose surname hints at 'Christ' and 'sparkle' and whose forename, perhaps, at Septimus Harding. But *Edwin Drood* differs from the novels of Kingsley and Trollope by being set in the past, about thirty years previously. Dickens's purpose was not to propose reform but to create a mystery, never explained because of his death halfway through the writing. He created a magnificent stage-set of a gloomy decrepit place, but it was not a place of the time at which he wrote.

By about 1900 cathedral reform, as a public issue, had run its course. Future cathedral fiction was likely to be Trollopian, in which the building would form a setting and its clergy the characters in a story that had no intention of calling for change. Canterbury Cathedral is briefly described in this way in H. G. Wells's genial novel, *The History of Mr Polly* (1910). Polly is a young unmarried assistant at an outfitter's shop in the city. He has a convoluted imagination and vocabulary which give him, when he visits the cathedral, 'the strangest sense of being at home – far more than he had ever been at home before. "Portly capons", he used to murmur to himself, under the impression that he was naming a characteristic type of mediaeval churchman.' He wanders about the precincts, speculating 'about the people who lived in the ripe and cosy houses of grey stone that cluster there so comfortably. Through green doors in high stone walls he caught glimpses of level lawns and blazing flower-beds; mullioned windows revealed shaded reading lamps and disciplined shelves of brown bound books. Now and then a dignitary in gaiters would pass him . . . or a drift of white-robed choir boys cross a distant arcade and vanish in a doorway, or the pink and cream of some girlish dress flit like a butterfly across the cool still spaces of the place'.[109]

Wells's book (it was a best seller) is a sign of how cathedrals had changed in public perception. He and his readers might not be Christians or believe that religion had any relevance now. But they were charmed by these ancient places and no longer felt that their occupants needed reform (Fig. 74, p. 218). Cathedrals had come through the last of their five great crises, and had survived.

Chapter
—— 9 ——

The Twentieth Century

1901–2000

Cathedrals are not always the first to engage with change. Just as they and their clergy kept much that was Georgian long into the nineteenth century, so they went on being Victorian well after the old queen died in 1901. Reforms of cathedrals continued in the accustomed ways with changes to their numbers, staffing, and endowments. Gothic remained the most popular style for cathedral architecture. Tractarian notions spread further in the adornment of churches and the ceremonies of worship. Cathedrals pursued the strategies that they had devised since the 1850s to attract worshippers to their services and visitors to their buildings.

The foundation of new Anglican dioceses and therefore cathedrals, which had accelerated after 1877, went on throughout the first quarter of the twentieth century. Twelve of each were created between 1905 and 1927: more than throughout the nineteenth. Up to 1919 the foundation of a diocese required an act of Parliament. Then, as we shall see, power was devolved to the Church to run its own affairs, allowing changes to be made more easily. The new dioceses were Birmingham and Southwark (1905), Chelmsford, St Edmundsbury and Ipswich, and Sheffield (1914), Coventry (1918), Bradford

(1920), Blackburn and Leicester (1926), and Derby, Guildford, and Portsmouth (1927). Sometimes the location of the cathedral was obvious, sometimes less so. In Suffolk one contender, Bury St Edmunds, received the cathedral while the other, Ipswich, got the bishop and the diocesan administration. Two churches vied for the honour in Bury and two in Leicester.[1] In Essex the best site was unclear. The outgoing bishop of St Albans invited suggestions and seven places proposed themselves, ranging from the great conurbation of West Ham to the deeply rural parish church of Thaxted. The parishes of the new diocese were asked to vote and the majority opted for Chelmsford, which had the advantage of a central location. Thaxted got a single vote: its own.[2]

The creations of 1927 completed the list of Anglican cathedrals in England (Fig. 76, p. 223). There could have been others. Some thought that Essex merited two dioceses. In Devon there were plans to found a diocese of Plymouth and in 1902 the suburban church of Stoke Dameral was enlarged to make it suitable as the cathedral. But no more schemes were approved. Bishops had to be funded and funding was limited. The Catholic Church established only two dioceses and cathedrals in the early twentieth century: Brentwood (1917) and Lancaster (1924), but it renewed the process later with Arundel (1965), East Anglia (based at Norwich, 1976), and Hallam (in Sheffield, 1980). One further Anglican cathedral has been designated on the Isle of Man, which, although not in England, is part of the province of York. Here the historic church of the diocese at Peel had long been a ruin. In 1895 the bishop consecrated the chapel of his palace as a pro-cathedral and instituted a chapter of canons with himself as dean. Finally, in 1980 the parish church of St German in Peel was chosen to be the cathedral.

As in Victorian times, it was easier to establish a diocese and bishop than a cathedral with the resources of its older siblings. Most of the new Anglican and Catholic cathedrals were sited in a major parish church. The Catholic Church continued to name their dioceses and cathedrals separately from those of the Church of England, hence East Anglia and Hallam, while Anglicans did not feel bound to do the same with regard to Birmingham, Portsmouth, and Southwark. The new creations extended the range of buildings belonging to the two Churches. The Church of England acquired two eighteenth-century cathedrals in the classical style – Birmingham and Derby (Fig. 91, p. 261) – while the Catholic Church gained two impressive Victorian Gothic ones, cathedral-like in grandeur, at Arundel and Norwich. In terms of their staffing, however, most new cathedrals of either Church had to subsist with little more than their previous single incumbent. In the Church of England bishops might act as deans, as before, while most of the incumbents did not gain titles of distinction until 1931. Instead, the new cathedrals developed their buildings. Some built or began new structures while others were enlarged to reflect their higher rank and larger needs.[3]

75. Westminster Cathedral: an ambitious building of cathedral proportions, yet quite distinctive from its Anglican counterparts.

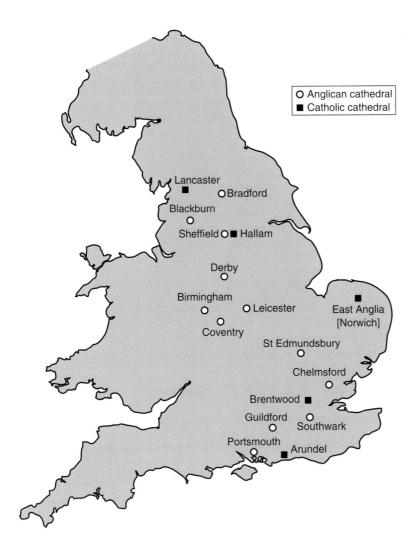

O Anglican cathedral
■ Catholic cathedral

The Catholic Church erected two cathedrals between 1900 and 1940, and started a third. The smallest and most traditional was Leeds where the need to change the site in 1900 produced a cathedral of modest size in the Gothic style of the 'Arts and Crafts' movement, popular at the end of the nineteenth century. A much greater project was that of Westminster Cathedral, created for what was then the only Catholic archbishopric in England and therefore to be the metropolitan church for the whole of the country. Cardinal Vaughan, the commissioner of the project, wanted a design that was not Gothic in order to distinguish it from the nearby Westminster Abbey. His architect, John Francis Bentley, made a tour in Italy where he was inspired by Byzantine models to produce a highly distinctive church by English cathedral standards. Built between 1895 and 1903, it has a bold appearance with candy stripes of red brick alternating with bands of stone, a profile with numerous domes and round-capped turrets, a Renaissance porch, and a slim high campanile like that of a church in Italy (Fig. 75, p. 220). Not only does it distance itself from the Abbey, it speaks of a Church that belongs to a wider world.[4]

The Church of England built two new cathedrals before the Second World War or, rather, began to build them. The first to be planned was Liverpool, which had become a diocese in 1880. The city of its home was prosperous, self-conscious of itself as a great imperial port, and a place where Protestant and Catholic identities were more pronounced than usual in England. The cathedral site was chosen in 1901 and a competition to design the building was won by Giles Gilbert Scott, grandson of George but himself a Catholic. The style was Gothic, the material stone, and the concept vast. The building would be larger than any cathedral in England: 600 feet long, more than Old St Paul's, with a central tower 80 feet higher than that of Canterbury (Fig. 77, p. 225). Such a building was necessarily lengthy in gestation. The foundation stone was laid in 1904, but the choir and east end of the building were consecrated only in 1924 and the cathedral was not regarded as finished and dedicated until 1978. By then its architect had been dead for eighteen years and Gothic had disappeared as an architectural fashion.[5]

The other new Anglican cathedral was more modest. This was Guildford, which like Liverpool stood on a virgin site and was not a parish church. It was commissioned in 1936 to a design by Sir Edward Maufe, still in the Gothic style but of a simpler kind and built in brick. Its progress was interrupted by the Second World War and it was finished only in 1966. Meanwhile, the Anglican activity in Liverpool had spurred the Catholics to plan a grand cathedral of their own. In 1930 they gave the task to another famous architect, Sir Edwin Lutyens, who produced a design in a massive, imperial, classical style that would constitute the biggest cathedral in the world with a larger dome than St Paul's or St Peter's in Rome. The Anglican cathedral was orientated north and south because of its site; the Catholic one followed suit so that the two buildings (only half a mile apart) would, as it were, go head to head. Work began on constructing a huge crypt in 1933 – itself a building partly above the ground – but this was suspended when the Second World War began. It was completed in a different form in the 1960s, but that we may leave till later in the chapter.

Most Anglican cathedral building in this period was far smaller in scale, and consisted of adapting the parish church foundations for their greater status and functions. Between 1900 and 1940 extensions were planned or built at Blackburn, Chelmsford, Derby, Portsmouth, Sheffield (Fig. 78, p. 228), and Wakefield. Some of these projects were not completed until the 1950s and 60s, by which time they had been joined by others at Bradford and St Edmundsbury. Most of the plans involved extending the east end of the church to make a larger choir and sanctuary. This reflected the fact that the new cathedrals increased their musical

resources with voluntary singers and choristers, and needed room to seat more people in the choir area: for example at diocesan and ordination services. At Portsmouth, where the site prevented an eastward expansion, the church was enlarged towards the west and the choir was moved in the same direction.[6] The most inventive reordering was done at Sheffield. This was a rich industrial city with enough civic pride and money to support ambitious rebuilding plans. In the 1930s the architect Sir Charles Nicholson began to enlarge the cathedral on a new north–south axis: another example of the vogue for ignoring the ancient direction. The plan was to build across the existing nave at a right angle, making the former chancel into an extended transept. He completed the northern end of the project but the Second World War intervened and the plan was abandoned in the 1960s. The church reverted to its east–west orientation, the nave was lengthened westwards with a south porch and narthex, and the northern part became a transept containing two chapels.

Cathedrals continued to acquire new stained glass windows and monuments, the former now taking precedence over the latter. In the 1930s and 40s several cathedrals acquired work by the brothers Christopher and Geoffrey Webb: attractive imagery set against clear glass, of a quality that deserves more respect than it gets.[7] The new Coventry cathedral,

77. Liverpool's huge Anglican cathedral, designed by Giles Gilbert Scott and planned on a bigger scale than all its sisters.

as we shall see below, contained striking windows by John Piper and others. More recently, Southwell has commissioned a fine one of the First World War by Nick Mynheer. Monuments, on the other hand, declined in numbers and profile throughout the twentieth century. Effigies became rare, apart from the archbishops of Canterbury named in the previous chapter. Even mural tablets diminished in size and ornamentation: for more than one reason. Burials no longer took place in cathedrals save in exceptional cases, and then usually in the form of interred cremations. The conservation of buildings ruled out adding large monuments, and shyness about pomposity reduced the encomiums of Georgian times to mere names, dates, and a scriptural text or the briefest of tributes: 'a man greatly beloved', a 'much loved Father in God'.

Reform and Evolution from 1900 to 1940

The creation of so many new Anglican cathedrals up to 1927 helped to prompt a re-examination of the roles of all those of the Church of England. This time the impetus came not from Parliament, which had long lost interest in them, but from the Church itself. During the second half of the nineteenth century it had evolved a framework of self-government, independent of Parliament. The ancient convocations of the clergy, one each for Canterbury and York, had been revived. Lay members were elected to them and in 1904 the two convocations met as 'The Representative Church Council': the first permanent body ever to embody the whole of the Church.[8] It came to be known as 'The National Assembly of the Church of England', and for short 'The Church Assembly'. In 1919 a parliamentary statute, 'The Church of England Assembly (Powers) Act', allowed it to bring laws called 'measures' to Parliament for approval, after which they possessed the force of statute law. This enabled the Church to initiate changes without waiting on Parliament, while remaining under the jurisdiction of the Crown in Parliament as it had been since the Reformation.

In 1924 the Church Assembly set up a commission like those of the Victorian era to inquire into the constitution and requirements of cathedrals. They were by this time a varied assortment of bodies. As well as the nine Old Foundations and the thirteen New, there were (or would shortly be) the twenty creations of the last ninety years.[9] All of the latter, apart from Guildford and Liverpool, were also parish churches, since even Manchester and Ripon had been parochial as well as collegiate. Truro possessed a statutory dean and chapter and St Albans a dean and a notional (but not a legal) chapter. The remaining cathedrals had a mere incumbent of the cathedral benefice, effectively a parish priest, assisted by other clergy with no status. The parish church cathedrals had even become more parochial through the establishment of parochial church councils throughout the Church in 1921. These councils were elected by parishioners, and at a parish church cathedral they had the right to be informed and consulted about its affairs.

The commission of 1924 reported three years later.[10] After deliberations, the Church Assembly passed and Parliament ratified the Cathedrals Measure of 1931.[11] This measure sought to bring about greater uniformity among cathedrals but in a more gradual way than Victorian reformers. It established a group of commissioners to create and revise cathedral constitutions and statutes through negotiation with each individual church. In the case of the older cathedrals founded up to Truro, the statutes were to provide for the existence of an administrative dean and chapter, as in the past, with a wider 'general chapter' of the dean and all the canons, including the honorary ones who had not hitherto been involved in cathedral affairs apart from having a stall in the choir. At the new parish church cathedrals (apart from Manchester, Ripon, St Albans, and Truro), the incumbent was to be styled 'provost', giving him dignity but denoting his different powers. Guildford too had a provost from 1930 until 1961 when, uniquely, his title became that of 'dean'. The commissioners were empowered to establish chapters at the parish church cathedrals that did not have them, but no resources were provided for the purpose. In the meantime these cathedrals were to have a 'council' consisting of the dean or provost with representatives of the chapter (if any), the parochial church council, and the laity of the diocese. This body had the chief administrative power, although any parochial church council continued to exist alongside it. Finally, the ruling was made that deans, provosts, canons, minor clergy, and their employees should retire at the age of seventy-five and arrangements be made for them to have pensions.

There were two other important changes. All cathedrals were required to transfer their remaining endowments of lands, tithes, and rents to the Ecclesiastical Commissioners in return for annual payments. This brought to an end the role of cathedral chapters as landlords of estates that had begun in the sixth century, although they retained their rights of patronage over parish churches. In addition the measure abolished the corporations of vicars choral in the Old Foundations and the additional one of minor canons at St Paul's. Any remaining lands they held passed to the Commissioners and their rights, premises, and other possessions to their deans and chapters. This was the fulfilment of a long-held wish among Victorian reformers, who found the corporations obstructive. They were by this time very small and sometimes consisted of only two or three clergy. Cathedrals continued to include one or two priest vicars and some had lay vicars but, like the minor canons of the New Foundations, these were now solely employees of their chapters.[12]

Meanwhile, cathedrals themselves were slowly evolving: indeed the cathedral commission was as much due to their own changing attitudes as an attempt to alter them from outside. Worship underwent a gradual but sure transformation. In 1956, R. C. B. Llewellyn, a former vicar choral of Exeter, recalled what services were like when he joined the choir in 1905 and how these had changed in his lifetime.[13] When he began his career, the singers consisted of four priest vicars, eight lay vicars, and fourteen choristers. The daily worship was still largely that of the post-Reformation era. An early service was said at a quarter to

78. Sheffield, one of the parish churches promoted to be a cathedral, before the ambitious rebuilding of the 1930s.

eight, consisting of matins on four days of the week and holy communion on Tuesday and Thursday, all this in the Lady chapel: the only cathedral chapel then in use. Choral matins was sung at half past ten and choral evensong at three o'clock, both in the choir. All the singers took part in both services except that the men sang by themselves on Wednesday afternoons when the choristers were allowed a half-holiday. On Sundays there was an early said communion at a quarter to eight, again in the Lady chapel, and the main morning service consisted of choral matins in the choir at half past ten. This was followed (without a break) by the litany and the ante-communion (including a sermon) up to the offertory and the prayer for the Church militant. The organist then played a voluntary, the singers and most of the congregation left, the doors of the choir were shut, and communion itself was celebrated by the clergy at midday for the few of the laity who remained. This was always a said service, and the clergy wore surplices, black scarves, and academic hoods.

Sunday matins was well attended. Since the choir was limited in its seating, some people had to sit outside it in the choir aisles where they could see nothing and only hear from afar. Sunday evensong at three o'clock was choral too and was locally regarded as a still more appealing service, drawing many worshippers. In view of their numbers it was held in the nave, where additional stalls were provided for the singers at the east end. At seven o'clock there was a second evensong of the kind that the Victorian reformers had introduced to reach out to working people. In 1905 this attracted the largest attendance of all. The congregation would fill or almost fill the seats in the nave and its aisles, and it was not uncommon for the vergers to open the choir so that people could sit there. As Llewellyn observed, there were few competing attractions on Sunday evenings.

During the following decades change crept slowly in. The weekday choral matins became less frequent, so that in the 1950s it was performed on only two days other than Sundays and by then, as Llewellyn noted, some cathedrals had abolished it altogether.[14] Choral evensong, however, continued to be maintained on most days of the week. In contrast, the communion service became more frequent and gained greater prominence. The early morning service on weekdays became a said communion instead of matins. On Sundays the communion at the end of the sequence of morning services began to be sung chorally on one and then two Sundays every month. But since the matins congregation was accustomed to leave before communion, it continued to do so despite the lure of the singing. Later still, the morning services were divided. Matins with a sermon took place at half past ten, and the litany was discontinued. Communion (called, as time went on, the 'eucharist') became a wholly separate choral service at midday, but the congregation still preferred matins and the attendance at communion was slow to increase.

Similar patterns and changes may be traced in most cathedrals.[15] By about the 1940s, the majority of their clergy had come to see communion as the desirable centre of worship. Accordingly it was widely moved on Sundays to a more popular time, such as ten o'clock. Choral matins with a sermon followed in the nave at eleven, a location that recognised its larger following. The long-term tendency was for communion to attract more people both to attend it and to 'communicate' by receiving the bread and wine, the bread now coming in the form of wafers not ordinary bread.[16] The service began to be done with more ceremonial. First the clergy exchanged their black scarves for coloured stoles. Next they wore copes which had been lawful for use in cathedrals since the Reformation. Finally (because copes are awkward garments meant for processions) they adopted the medieval eucharistic vestments, including a chasuble for the officiating priest. Lay male servers were recruited to assist the clergy, and liturgical colours were reintroduced so that the altar hangings and vestments changed according to the season of the Church year. Guilds of 'broderers' were formed to care for these fabrics and make new ones.[17] The emphasis on the eucharist revived an interest in cathedral chapels. They were brought back from emptiness or functions as vestries, and equipped with altars for use on occasional weekdays or saints' days.[18] Some chapels were assigned to regiments or organisations like the Mothers' Union. Others, later in the century, were dedicated to causes such as Christian unity at Coventry, and a few cathedrals introduced a special chapel for children to use or be remembered in.[19]

There was an increasing number of special services. Right back to the Middle Ages cathedrals had held prayers for national victory or relief in times of war and suffering. During the nineteenth century the concept developed of grand occasions marking great events. Coronations and royal funerals took place at Westminster Abbey, but St Paul's hosted the funerals of Nelson and Wellington, as we have seen, as well as Victoria's Diamond Jubilee service.[20] This practice grew in the twentieth century. St Paul's was chosen for another four royal jubilee events and the wedding of Prince Charles and Princess Diana in 1981.[21] Other cathedrals held their own versions on national occasions like coronations and the ends of the two world wars, as well as a wide range of events for local causes. Military and naval services, agricultural services, services for organisations and campaigns (the Mothers' Union, St John Ambulance, marches of the unemployed), Royal Maundy services (Fig. 89, p. 256), harvest festivals, and carol services all burgeoned, taking regular places in the calendar alongside the Christian festivals.[22] There is also the use of cathedrals for musical events and, in recent years, university graduations.[23]

Some Cathedral Personalities

The popularity of such services reflected changes in the understanding of what a cathedral was for. A pioneer in this process was Frank Bennett, dean of Chester from 1920 to 1939.[24] Bennett had been a parish priest for twenty-five years and brought strong pastoral gifts to his new post (Fig. 79, p. 231). Like the Victorian reformers, he wished to improve worship but he envisaged a cathedral with a wider spiritual and social mission. In a sermon preached as soon as he arrived, he expressed his wish to change Chester 'from a museum for curious visitors into a home for pilgrims'. As the dean of a New Foundation he had the power to do so. The first issue he dealt with was that of admission charges. These were still general at cathedrals: sometimes to enter the building itself, unless to attend a service, and sometimes merely to visit the choir and areas such as the chapter house, cloisters, or tower. The common price for this was 6d.: a sum sufficient to deter the poorest like Wells's Mr Polly, who liked to sit in the nave of Canterbury during services but never got beyond it because of the charge for admission.[25] Bennett did away with fees at Chester. Instead he sought to make a visit to the cathedral into a spiritual experience. Visitors were asked to be reverent, remain quiet at times of worship, say a prayer for themselves and one for the cathedral, and make a donation to maintain the building. The gratifying result was that the fees, which had produced £48 in the holiday season of 1919, rose through donations by a further £100 in the following year.

Bennett's sympathies lay with the Oxford Movement. He visualised communion as the main service on Sunday mornings, led by the dean wearing a cope (the least controversial of church vestments). A chapel was assigned for private prayer and a 'children's corner' made its appearance: a furnished space

79. Frank
Bennett, the
inventive dean
of Chester from
1920 to 1939, in
his cloisters.

for their use. Voluntary guides were recruited and a cheap booklet about the cathedral let people do tours by themselves. The monastic refectory was restored as a 'great hall' for the use of the cathedral, diocese, and local community, and the cloisters re-glazed as a place for walking and reflection. A common room was provided with magazines, notepaper, and freedom to smoke (the dean liked his pipe), and the cathedral undercroft was renovated to contain a self-service cafeteria: an idea taken from America. Bennett wanted the cathedral to be a pleasant as well as a sacred place, a centre of life in the city, and his innovations were influential. In 1924 *The Times* published an admiring account of Chester as unlike all others in the warmth of its welcome. The abolition of fees soon spread elsewhere, assisted by the higher receipts from voluntary giving, although (cathedrals being laws unto themselves) this was not so universally and charges continued at Lincoln and Norwich until the Second World War.[26]

One of the clergy influenced by Bennett was George Bell (1883–1958), whose career was a more exalted one.[27] The holder of an Oxford college post, he moved to be domestic chaplain to the archbishop of Canterbury and by consequent progression to the deanery of Canterbury in 1924. Previously, however, Bell had been curate in a working-class parish in Leeds and had absorbed the need to reach out to others. He consulted

Bennett after going to Canterbury and introduced some of the same reforms, with the difference that his cathedral had a higher profile and he himself more links with the world of the arts. He abolished fees and wrote guide-books. Knowing John Reith, the head of the BBC, he arranged some of the first radio broadcasts of cathedral services in 1925: a commemoration of the composer Orlando Gibbons, Remembrance Day, and a carol service at Christmas. The clergy had no experience of how to behave on the air. The precentor sat in the wrong seat and spoilt the Christmas transmission by coughing throughout.[28] A year later the BBC began regular broadcasts of 'Choral Evensong': at first only from Westminster Abbey but after ten years from cathedrals as well.

Bell made two other significant innovations. In 1926 he proposed the creation of a body of 'Friends of Canterbury Cathedral' to help maintain and beautify the church. The Friends were launched a year later and immediately attracted 750 supporters paying a subscription of 5s. each year.[29] York followed in 1928, Exeter and Norwich in 1929, and other cathedrals in turn although St Paul's delayed till 1952.[30] Numbers of subscribers, beginning in hundreds, often rose to a couple of thousand or more, with an aggregate of about 53,000 in 1992.[31] Next, Bell invited the poet John Masefield to write a religious play, *The Coming of Christ*, which was performed in the cathedral in 1928 with incidental music by Gustav Holst. This was said to be the first play in a cathedral since the Middle Ages but since medieval plays had other, usually secular, venues, it was perhaps the first ever. The success of the play led to an annual Canterbury Festival, centred upon the cathedral, with which Bell was associated after his promotion to be bishop of Chichester in 1929. In consequence he was involved in commissioning some of its later religious plays, including *Murder in the Cathedral* by T. S. Eliot (1935), *The Zeal of Thy House* by Dorothy Sayers (1937), and *Christ's Comet* by Christopher Hassall (1938).

A few cathedral clergy had a different kind of impact in the spheres of popular theology and social reform. There was an era from about the 1910s to the 1940s when many of the population still had religious interests yet were no longer tied to religious denominations. Clergy with distinctive views, and lay writers like G. K. Chesterton and C. S. Lewis, could satisfy these interests through the media of newspapers, novels, and (from about 1924) the radio. One such writer, William Inge, dean of St Paul's (1911–34), operated through the daily press.[32] A man of curiously mixed views – modernist theology, middle-class prejudice, and eugenics (to prevent the working classes from breeding too fast) – his romantic, iconoclastic, and somewhat unpredictable judgements on current issues formed the kind of provocative writing that editors like and readers react to. He wrote regularly for the *Evening Standard* on religious, political, and literary subjects, and his collected articles with titles such as *Outspoken Essays* (1919–22) and *Lay Thoughts of a Dean* (1926) were widely bought and read.

H. R. L. ['Dick'] Sheppard was more charismatic.[33] He made his name as vicar of St Martin-in-the-Fields in London, where he introduced daily communions and ministered to destitute people both in the church and by opening a hostel for their support. A compelling preacher irked by what he saw as the Church's preference for institutions over relationships, his book *The Impatience of a Parson* (1927) sold 100,000 copies. Sheppard became dean of Canterbury in 1929 and drew large crowds to his sermons, but had to resign because of ill-health in the following year. In 1934 he accepted a canonry of St Paul's but disliked the formality of cathedral life. Instead, having become a pacifist, he founded the Peace Pledge Union in 1936 as a movement of those opposed to war, wore himself out with his activities, and died in 1937. One hundred thousand people filed by his coffin in St Martin's church, crowds lined the route of his funeral procession to St Paul's, and the service was broadcast on the radio.

Hewlett Johnson, the 'Red Dean' of Canterbury (1931–63), was notorious rather than influential.[34] An unusual figure (a grammar-school educated, engineering graduate), he espoused the cause of the poor through Socialist politics. Not formally a Communist but rather a 'fellow-traveller', he believed that 'The communist . . . proves himself to be the heir of the Christian intention'. He chaired the board of the Communist *Daily Worker* and visited Communist countries, meeting and praising Stalin, Mao Zedong, and Castro. 'When he was in Canterbury', lamented his archbishop (Michael Ramsey), 'I wished fervently that he would go somewhere else. And when he went somewhere else, I wished even more fervently that he was back in Canterbury.' Johnson scandalised his cathedral colleagues and most of the media but it would be hard to show that he had any deeper effects.

Perhaps the last of such clergy to have such a public profile was John Collins, another canon of St Paul's (1948–1981).[35] Collins had been an air-force chaplain in the Second World War and was deeply disturbed by the dropping of the atomic bombs in 1945. He subsequently founded Christian Action to support radical causes such as the abolition of capital punishment, and in 1956 he began to campaign against apartheid in South Africa. Finally, in 1958 he helped to form the Campaign for Nuclear Disarmament, although he dissented when some of the campaigners turned to civil disobedience and resigned from his post in the organisation. Collins had a conscientious and respected career at St Paul's but he did not make the impact of Sheppard. He was perhaps a little too political, but the age of Sheppard had passed. The public and the media had lost interest in the clergy – unless they were caught up in scandals.

War

Cathedrals, as we have seen, are no strangers to war. At times in the past they suffered damage from it. They were long used to remembering it with monuments.[36] The wars of the twentieth century, however, differed in the enormity of their scale and their invasion of everyday life. The First World War, from 1914 to 1918, hit home forcibly. It affected cathedral staffing: some clergy and lay employees went off to war service. It prompted services to pray for peace or to remember the fallen. Certain events, like the loss of Lord Kitchener at sea in 1916, were widely marked. At Chelmsford the National Anthem was sung at the end of Sunday prayers. By 1915 there was a new issue: bombing from the skies by Zeppelin airships. York removed its ancient window glass and St Paul's gathered a force of 250 volunteers to deal with possible fires. Two years later Canterbury agreed to make its church available as a refuge to local people. In the event, although there was loss of life and property from aerial attacks, no cathedral was directly targeted. When the war ended, well-attended services were held on or around Armistice Day, 11 November 1918.[37]

The scale of casualties prompted a wish for memorials. Chelmsford was keeping a Roll of Honour by 1915. Eventually monuments were erected: usually collective rather than individual ones, although the heroine of the war, Nurse Edith Cavell, shot by the Germans in Belgium in 1915, received a personal one at Norwich four years later. A large stone cross on steps was built at Exeter, a statue of a rifleman at Winchester. In contrast, at Hereford and Wells, the cathedral clergy persuaded the community to sponsor monuments inside the church. A war memorial was placed in Hereford's Lady chapel and a commemorative reredos in the crypt. Two unused medieval chapels at Wells were furnished with altars and seating to honour the dead of Somerset. At Liverpool (Anglican) it was agreed to use the north-east transept for the purpose, then being built. An altar and reredos were installed along with a cenotaph to hold a book of remembrance. Regimental badges were incorporated into the stonework, two nearly life-sized figures of a soldier and a sailor installed, and military colours hung above the galleries.[38]

The Second World War, from 1939 to 1945, was unlike the First in the vastly greater danger from the air. The Civil War in Spain had shown how vulnerable cities were to bombers, and cathedrals hastened to remove their treasures. The ancient glass of Canterbury and York was taken away, the bishop's throne at Exeter, and Wren's model of his cathedral at St Paul's. These along with valuable ornaments, books, and archives were stored for safety in the countryside. Bodies of fire-watchers were organised. Once more there were disruptions of services and service times due to lighting restrictions and the disappearance of staff to war work or the armed forces. St Paul's choir school was evacuated to Truro but Durham's stayed, the boys being given beds in an undercroft. Chelmsford's hall became a hospital and Hereford's deanery a military headquarters.[39] The building of the new cathedrals at Guildford, Liverpool (Catholic), and Sheffield was suspended, although a little was done at Liverpool (Anglican) during the war. In two cases – Liverpool (Catholic) and Sheffield – the suspensions were fatal to the original plans which later gave way to others. Another abiding change was the removal of many outdoor railings for industrial purposes. This removed the barriers which cathedrals had erected since Georgian times to regulate activities in their precincts. Now precincts were open again: a consequence that was not intended yet curiously prophetic of how cathedrals would make themselves more available to the public in the second half of the century.

At least six cathedrals suffered damage to their churches or ancillary buildings from aerial assaults. The initial casualties were due to the bombing of industrial cities rather than attacks on cathedrals as such. Bristol and Liverpool (Anglican) were hit early on, in September 1940. At the first, a bomb destroyed part of the nearby cathedral school. In the second case, windows were blown in and some stonework was demolished. In 1941 a high-explosive bomb struck Liverpool as well but was fortunately deflected and burst outside the building.[40] The turn of St Paul's came on 10 October 1940 when a similar bomb penetrated the choir and shattered the high altar. Incendiary bombs were dropped on the building on the night of the following 29 December but were dealt with by the fire-watchers. This was the occasion when Herbert Mason took his famous photograph of the cathedral, with its silhouette apparently invincible above the smoke and flames of the burning city (Fig. 80, p. 236). Nevertheless, in April 1941 another bomb hit the north transept, reaching the floor, destroying the vault over part of the crypt, and blowing out much of the cathedral glass.[41]

The most serious damage in these first attacks was at Coventry. Here the city endured heavy bombing from German aircraft on the night of 14 November 1940 because it was a centre of aircraft production and other industries. As there were so many places to guard, the cathedral could muster only a small group of fire-watchers including the provost R. T. Howard, the stone-mason Jock Forbes, and two other men. Incendiary bombs began to fall on the cathedral roof at twenty minutes to eight and although the four of them fought bravely and successfully to extinguish the fires they caused, the dropping of more and more bombs at last set the roofs alight. The local fire brigades were busy elsewhere and when at last a force arrived from Solihull, its crew had difficulty accessing water. By eleven o'clock the roofs were beginning to fall in and efforts to save the place had to be stopped. The fire-watchers were able only to remove some crosses, candlesticks, communion vessels, and regimental colours. All the while there were people in the crypts which served as air-raid shelters; they were led to safety as the building above them collapsed. Two days later the king came to the site and stood in silence with the provost in the ruins (Fig. 81, p. 237).[42]

A second series of air attacks took place in May and June 1942. These are known as the 'Baedeker Raids' and aimed to disfigure historic towns in revenge for the British bombing of Lübeck. Three cathedral cities were targets. At Canterbury, many incendiary bombs fell on the church but were thrown off again by the watchers. More seriously, three high-explosive devices landed in the Close, destroying the cathedral library and four houses.[43] At Norwich the cathedral was showered with incendiary bombs, but the watchers were effective and the damage was limited to the roofs of the transepts where some lead melted and some timbers were burnt. Two old houses were gutted in the Close and one of the blocks of Norwich School. The worst experience was that of Exeter. Here a single high-explosive bomb struck the chapel of St James to the south of the choir and destroyed it along with three bays and two buttresses of the south choir aisle. The force of the blast shattered every window in the cathedral, damaging the

80. St Paul's apparently inviolable in the London blitz of 1940, in Herbert Mason's famous photo published in The Daily Mail.

sedilia in the sanctuary, the wooden medieval screens alongside the choir, the organ case over the pulpitum, and many mural tablets. The cathedral's vestments, housed in two oak chests in the chapel, were totally lost. Other bombs destroyed the cathedral school and the medieval hall of the vicars choral: the sole surviving building of their college. Immediate action had to be taken to secure the roofs and vaults, and services were transferred to the chapter house, the only large glazed room available.[44]

The bombing of Coventry Cathedral had very different results from that of the ancient foundations. In the latter the aim was to return the buildings to their former state, and damage was slowly repaired in the next ten years. Clergy and congregations then resumed their normal routines with relief. Coventry, out of the magnitude of its loss, experienced new life: indeed resurrection. In January 1941 the provost asked Forbes to build an altar out of rubble where the high altar had stood and to set up a cross behind it, made out of charred beams found among the ruins. The clergy and congregation stayed together, worshipping in a crypt chapel and

in the next-door church of Holy Trinity. A new bishop, Neville Gorton (1943–55), proposed the creation of a Christian Service Centre and a Chapel of Unity promoting outreach and worship in partnership with the local Free Churches. The Chapel was established in the crypt in 1945. In the following year contact was made with Germany: first with Hamburg, which had been damaged worse than Coventry, then with Kiel, and later with Berlin. Expressions of forgiveness were exchanged with symbolic gifts including small crosses of nails from the ruined church.[45] In due course a fresh cathedral was built that was not a copy of the old one but truly innovative, and the walls of the old were left beside the new, as if to quote the psalm that 'tears may linger at nightfall but joy comes in the morning'.[46]

As happened during the First World War, there were special services of prayer and remembrance in cathedrals during the Second, and many funerals in those that were parish churches. The end of the war in 1945 was marked by thanksgiving services to mark Victory in Europe and sometimes Victory in Japan. Thirty-five thousand people were reckoned to have joined in those at St Paul's on the first of these days. Once again the war was remembered with special monuments. St Paul's commissioned

81. King George VI talking to Provost R. T. Howard in the ruins of Coventry Cathedral, 16 November 1940. On the right is the Home Secretary, Herbert Morrison.

a new high altar from Stephen Dykes Bower to commemorate the war dead of
the Commonwealth. An American Memorial Chapel was created behind the
altar. Chelmsford turned its south-western chapel into a military memorial with
a book of remembrance, and built a porch in honour of American air forces.[47]
Another kind of tribute is to be found in four north windows of the nave of
Bristol Cathedral. These salute the auxiliary services of the Second World War:
nurses, fire-fighters, the police, air-raid wardens, and the home guard. Sixteen
auxiliaries are shown in their uniforms, which are already of historical interest.
Nine are women and seven men: a balance surely unusual in its day and, like the
railings, prefiguring changes to come.

Reform and Development from 1950 to 2000

The history of cathedrals in the second half of the twentieth century can be
divided, as usual, into the national and the individual, although the two were
not distinct and each affected the other. At the national level there were three
important constitutional changes in the form of measures of the Church
Assembly or, as it was renamed in 1970, the General Synod. As before, these
measures were ratified in Parliament. The first was the Cathedrals Measure of
1963: the result, like its predecessor, of an inquiry begun in 1958.[48] Once again
a commission was appointed to revise cathedral constitutions and statutes. The
revisions were intended to create more uniformity than before and, in particular,
to improve the staffing and government of the parish church cathedrals. These
were now to possess cathedral chapters consisting of a provost, canons, and
archdeacons. The Ecclesiastical Commissioners (who had been reorganised as
the Church Commissioners in 1948) would pay stipends to a dean or provost and
two residentiary canons in every cathedral. The residentiaries must be engaged
exclusively on cathedral duties. If one added archdeacons, any cathedral could
have a chapter of at least four clergy. The chapter was to be the administrative
body. There would also be a 'greater chapter' of the dean or provost and all the
canons, residentiary or honorary, and in the parish church cathedrals a cathedral
council consisting of the provost, residentiary canons, archdeacons, and members
of the parochial church council. Deans would continue to be appointed by the
Crown, as in the past, and provosts by the patron of the parish church cathedral
of which they were legally the incumbents. The patron was usually the diocesan
bishop, except at Bradford and Sheffield where the right belongs to trustees.
Parish church cathedrals became exempt from the jurisdiction of archdeacons
and rural deans, like their older counterparts. Further provisions were made,
if agreed, for parish church cathedrals to become dean and chapter ones, for
parochial church councils to be merged with parish cathedral chapters, and for
the creation of colleges of lay canons.

The next legislation was the Care of Cathedrals Measure of 1990. This was an
expression of the policy of conserving the past rather than reshaping it, which

had begun with William Morris and the Society for the Protection of Ancient Buildings. Research into archaeology and documentary records had greatly advanced the understanding of the history and value of ancient buildings and artefacts and of how to preserve them. At the same time, some cathedrals were altering their heritage without consultation and free of control. The removal of the Victorian screens at Hereford and Salisbury, for example, caused disquiet, as we shall see. A Cathedral Advisory Committee had been set up in 1949 to offer advice if requested, and this was upgraded to become a Commission of the General Synod in 1981.[49] Three years later, a Church of England report recommended that there should be a mandatory system of advice and supervision at local and national level.[50]

Moves were afoot to bring this into law when, in January 1988, the dean and chapter of Hereford decided to sell the *Mappa Mundi*: the great medieval chart of the world and its history which had belonged to them since about 1300 (Fig. 34, p. 89).[51] The motive was to raise money for repairs, provide better housing for the cathedral's chained library, and to endow the choral foundation, but the decision attracted national attention and aroused much criticism. In the end, fund-raising and donations – including a very generous one from Sir Paul Getty – enabled the sale to be cancelled. A body of trustees was created to care for the *Mappa Mundi*, and it and the chained library were enabled to go on display in a new building. The episode confirmed the need for the supervision of both cathedral fabrics and their historic contents, which was now implemented.

The Care of Cathedrals Measure created a system by which cathedrals must make formal proposals to carry out repairs or changes that affect the architectural, archaeological, artistic, or historic character of their buildings, of buildings that they own in their precincts, of the setting of the cathedral (its landscape), or of any archaeological remains. Similar proposals are necessary if they wish to sell, loan, or dispose of any object of importance in their possession, or to add one, and such proposals must be authorised. To do so, the measure re-established the Cathedral Advisory Commission as the Cathedrals Fabric Commission for England (CFCE) and ordered each cathedral to create its own Fabric Advisory Committee (FAC). FACs consist of experts from various fields chosen partly by the CFCE and partly by the cathedral involved. They are qualified to consider smaller issues and advise the cathedral accordingly. Major issues are considered by the CFCE, a body of national experts, and FACs or cathedrals may refer issues to the CFCE for final decision if there is no local agreement. In future all cathedrals must consult the CFCE before employing a cathedral architect or surveyor of the fabric (an appointment required by the Cathedrals Measure of 1963). They must also employ an archaeological consultant by a similar procedure unless the CFCE considers that the cathedral's significance does not merit such a post.[52]

The last of the three major pieces of legislation was the Cathedrals Measure, 1999. This too had some local origins. Since at least the 1980s the dean of Lincoln and his four canon colleagues had found it difficult to agree on the satisfactory running and development of their affairs.[53] There were personality differences and controversial issues, notably a project to take the cathedral's copy of *Magna Carta* to Australia in 1987, which led to a loss of £40,000. In 1989 when a new dean was required, the prime minister, Margaret Thatcher, was advised to appoint a strong person capable of bringing the canons to order. She was believed to have remarked, 'There will be blood on the carpet'. The Crown's choice was the provost of a parish church cathedral, where the office had considerable power, whereas Lincoln was an oligarchy of a dean and canons who needed to agree. His arrival caused further clashes of personality. He inquired into the Australian project, declared the canons incompetent, and briefed journalists who publicised the dispute. The canons complained to the bishop who made a visitation in which he was critical of the canons and particularly of the subdean responsible for the project. In 1990 the bishop asked the canons to resign and they refused. The situation remained unresolved until it was further complicated in 1994, when a former woman verger accused the dean of an inappropriate relationship with her. The bishop felt obliged to test the charge and cited the dean to the bishop's consistory court. This caused immense publicity but resulted in the dean's exoneration. The archbishop of Canterbury became involved. He pressed the dean and subdean to resign, and the dean eventually did so in 1997; the subdean did not and stayed until his retirement in 2003.

The problems of Lincoln showed that a small chapter in an ancient cathedral might not possess the abilities to run its affairs successfully. Yet it was effectively free from intervention because of its statutes and its clergy's rights of tenure which, at that time, extended until retirement. A better kind of management was needed. In 1992 the Archbishops' Council of the Church of England set up a committee led by Lady (Elspeth) Howe to examine cathedral government. It produced a report entitled *Heritage and Renewal* in 1994 which eventually led to the Cathedrals Measure of 1999.[54] The measure built on its predecessors which had outlined three possible bodies for the running of cathedrals: a 'greater chapter', a 'dean and chapter', and a 'cathedral council'. These were now updated and reformed. All cathedrals were to have a chapter led by a dean, a title now extended to all cathedral heads, replacing 'provost'. The chapter was to consist of the residentiary canons and not less than two and not more than seven other members (also styled canons), of whom at least two-thirds must be laity. The cathedral administrator might be one of these. The dean was to act as chair, with an extra casting vote, and to be a member of every chapter committee. His powers were increased so that he must consent to alterations of services, the settlement of the budget, and any decisions taken in his absence. The chapter was responsible for the administration of the cathedral, the planning of the budget, and the drawing up of accounts, and was required to meet at least nine times every year.

Next, every cathedral was required to have a 'council'. This was to be chaired by a lay person appointed by the bishop and to include the dean and representatives of the chapter, of the honorary canons, and of the cathedral community, with others who might be chosen from the locality, the diocese, or other religious denominations. The council was to meet at least twice a year, receive and consider the budget, accounts, and annual report, and raise or discuss any matter. Finally, the 'college' represented the old 'greater chapter', and included the dean, the residentiary and honorary canons, suffragan bishops, and archdeacons. By the 1990s some cathedrals included honorary lay canons, both men and women. The college was to elect the bishop, receive and consider the accounts and the annual report, and discuss whatever members wished to raise. All cathedrals were to retain a dean and two clergy canons, paid for by the Church Commissioners and engaged exclusively on cathedral duties. Any remaining parochial church councils at cathedrals were to transfer their powers to the new cathedral council. The result was to make all cathedrals uniform in their constitutions for the first time, while leaving space for their own traditions and characteristics in other respects.

Accompanying these developments was an unprecedented one: the opening of cathedral posts to women. They had always had a role in cathedral life as worshippers. The presence of wives of canons had been an issue in late Anglo-Saxon times. Even in the celibate world of the later Middle Ages women had been employed as seamstresses and laundresses. From the 1540s they reappeared as clergy wives and contributed invisibly yet indispensably to cathedral life. Very gradually during the twentieth century, as their political rights and employment opportunities grew, their status rose: but slowly. Until the 1970s, women worshippers were not offered seats in the choir of Durham.[55] The same was true at Oxford. The portly Hogarthian verger would lead men in jackets and ties to the choir, while he placed women, their companions, and men less formally dressed in the aisles. At Ely women were not invited to read lessons at services until 1975.[56] In these respects cathedrals lagged behind the rest of the world. Not only were women now established in positions of government and all the lay professions, but elsewhere in the Church of England they were fulfilling important roles as churchwardens and members of parochial church councils, diocesan synods, and the General Synod. They could lead worship and minister pastorally as deaconesses and readers.

Full equality in cathedrals came quite rapidly during the 1990s. First, in 1991, Salisbury admitted girls to be choristers and pupils of the Cathedral School. This was the inspiration of Dr Richard Seal, the organist and choirmaster, and was so successful than it soon spread elsewhere: to Exeter (1993), Wells (1994), Peterborough and York (1997), and rather more slowly to Durham (2009) and Canterbury (2014). The girls' and boys' choirs usually sing with the adults on different days of the week, which is helpful in balancing the work with the requirements of modern school life. Next, in 1992, the General Synod, after years of discussion, voted in favour of the ordination of women as priests. The resulting measure received the royal assent in 1993, and the first such ordination of thirty-two women was held by Bishop Barry Rogerson in Bristol Cathedral on 12 March 1994 (Fig. 82, p. 242). Meanwhile, as soon as the royal assent was given, Jane Hedges was appointed the first woman residentiary canon at Portsmouth,

82. *The first ordination of women priests in the Church of England, held at Bristol Cathedral in 1994.*

closely followed by Jane Sinclair at Sheffield, both in 1993. The next year saw June Osborne become the first such residentiary at an ancient cathedral, Salisbury, and in 2000 Vivienne Faull the first to lead a cathedral as provost (later dean) of Leicester. Osborne was raised to be dean of Salisbury in 1995, Faull of York in 2012, Hedges of Norwich in 2014, and similar appointments followed in other places. The first woman diocesan bishop, Rachel Treweek, was enthroned in Gloucester Cathedral on 19 September 2015.

Buildings and Worship from 1950 to 2000

In the early 1950s, a few years after the end of the Second World War, it became possible once more to create new cathedral buildings. Two parish church cathedrals in the Church of England set out to enlarge themselves as their sisters had done in the earlier part of the century. Bradford's extension, carried out between 1951 and 1965 by Sir Edward Maufe, produced a new east end with a choir and sanctuary, aisles, and a Lady chapel, as well as a song school, a chapter house, and a lantern tower.

St Edmundsbury's plans were more ambitious. Here the work, undertaken by Stephen Dykes Bower from 1960, made the usual eastward extension with a rebuilt choir, aisles, chapels, and transepts. But it also envisaged a four-sided cloister, the first to be built since the Middle Ages, of which the east and south walks have been finished, while a noble tower above the crossing between the nave and choir was completed in 2010. The tower is in the Gothic style and represents the latest expression of that style; perhaps the very last.

Meanwhile, a totally new cathedral had been built to replace the ruins of Coventry. Giles Gilbert Scott was approached but withdrew and the commission was won by Basil Spence. His building was constructed in the 1950s and consecrated in 1962, once again on a north–south axis at right-angles to the previous, ruined cathedral.[57] It caused a public sensation and queues of people formed for years to see it, both because it lies in the densely populated centre of England and because it was imagined to be a novelty: a new and modern kind of cathedral. In truth it was a mixture of old and new. The building plan was traditional in containing an oblong nave with a choir beyond it, albeit without a choir screen: an omission that would become a growing fashion (Fig. 83, p. 244). The nave was given aisles divided from it by slender piers.

The focus of the building was to be the high altar in the choir. Worshippers would go up to receive communion there in the time-honoured manner. Having done so, they would turn and see the great line of nave windows, arranged to be viewed from that point rather than further down the church. Bishop Gorton proposed that the altar should stand west of the choir stalls, close to the congregation: an idea that foreshadowed the 'Liturgical Movement' to be considered presently. His proposal did not find favour and the altar was located more traditionally at the east end of the choir, but it was placed so that the priest who celebrated communion could stand behind it to face the congregation. This was an innovation by both Anglican and Catholic standards. Later on, as we shall see, cathedrals would go further and, as Gorton had wished, bring the altar away from the east end of the church and into the centre.

Coventry's popularity came in part from the publicity given to the works of art commissioned to go inside it. Architecture and furnishings formed part of a single concept. Graham Sutherland's huge tapestry of Christ in Majesty with the beasts of the Four Evangelists dominates the interior from behind the high altar (Fig. 90, p. 258). Elizabeth Frink made the lectern and Jacob Epstein the statues of St Michael and the Devil outside the west entrance. The choir stalls with their asymmetrical clusters of wooden stars were Spence's own. Schemes of stained and engraved glass by Piper and others fill the windows. Since chapels had returned into fashion in cathedrals, Coventry included some attractive examples of these: the Chapel of Unity, the Guild chapel, the Gethsemane chapel. Some disappointment must be noted with the main part of the church, however: the nave and choir. The choir and its furnishings seem lost in a great void. Medieval architects strove to extend their space but gave it form, and that is lacking here. The canting of the windows so as to be seen only from the inner end of the nave

83. Coventry Cathedral, plan.

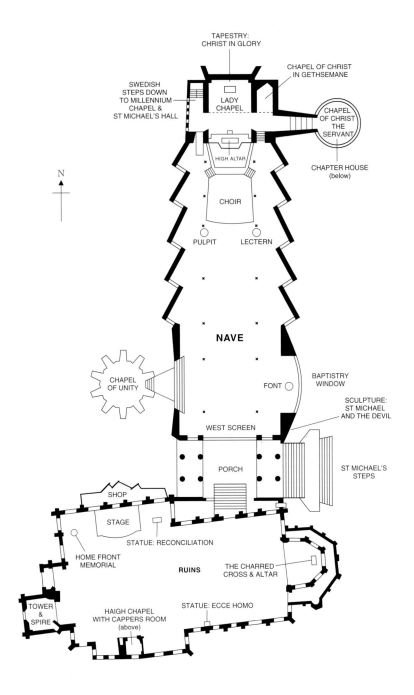

make the building look dark and gloomy as one enters. Perversely, only at that northern, inner end is one shown their magnificence.

The Catholic Church was equally active in building during the second half of the century. Its outstanding achievement was the completion

of the unfinished Catholic cathedral at Liverpool. The architectural commission was awarded to Frederick Gibberd in 1959 and the cathedral was built in 1962–7. It stands above the massive crypt that Lutyens had constructed, approached up a long staircase, and consists of a circular church surrounded by thirteen chapels with an entrance hall, the roof culminating in a great lantern with a crown of spikes (Fig. 84, above). The altar is in the middle with the seating around it (Fig. 85, p. 247). This was more innovative in layout than Coventry and its principles were repeated in two other new Catholic cathedrals. Clifton in Bristol, built in 1970–3, is a hexagonal building with a cluster of columns in place of a tower. The plan is contrived so as to include two chapels and a baptistery, and the church's high altar is almost central as well, with seating on three sides and an open sanctuary behind it. Middlesbrough, constructed in 1985–7, has a more traditional quadrangular shape, but here too the altar stands in front of the sanctuary and the congregation is located north, south, and west of the altar.

84. Liverpool Metropolitan Cathedral with its characteristic crown, emphasising (like Westminster) its difference from traditional cathedral design.

It is now appropriate to discuss the new developments in cathedral worship and the use of space which took hold in the 1960s and thereafter. The Liturgical Movement – the name that has been given to the ideas that produced these developments – was a view of worship rather than a movement to bring it about. It began in the Catholic Church and spread to the Church of England, now far less insular than it had been in previous centuries. The Movement regarded the eucharist (that is, the mass or communion) as the centre of Sunday worship, which had always been the case with Catholics and was becoming so among Anglicans. It further sought to make the laity fuller and more active participants in the eucharist by bringing the service closer to them in terms of language, space, and actions. New forms of services were produced: an English version of the mass in the Catholic Church (1973) and the successive experimental liturgies of 'Series 1, 2, and 3' in the Church of England, culminating in *The Alternative Service Book* (1980) and the final definitive *Common Worship* (2000). The last two provided services in both traditional and modern English. The Prayer Book of 1662 has also remained in use in Anglican cathedrals for choral evensong and for some weekday or early Sunday communions.

The symbolic change of the new approach (which in earlier times would have been a wonderful cause for disputes) was the placing of the priest at the eucharist. In medieval Catholic worship he stood on the west side of the altar facing east. The Church of England after the Reformation moved him to the north end of the altar facing south, with a return to the Catholic position among the Tractarians and gradually more widely in the Church. In 1964 the Catholic Church allowed the priest to stand behind the altar facing west towards the people, the practice already adopted at Coventry. This became general among Catholics after 1970 and later among Anglicans as well. The new position symbolised the aspiration of both Churches to reach out to congregations, an aspiration reinforced through the use of contemporary language and more modern music. Lay people were more involved than before in reading Bible lessons, leading prayers, bringing up the bread and wine (the 'offertory procession'), and even in helping to distribute the communion. Social interaction was encouraged. The 'exchange of the peace' was introduced during the eucharist, allowing handshakes and hugs, and coffee was served afterwards in the chapter house or some other convenient place.[58] There was a spatial dimension to these changes. Larger attendances at worship in the Anglican cathedrals made it more needful to use the nave to accommodate them, because the nave was bigger. The nave, which had begun to be used by the Victorians first for additional services and then for statutory ones, now came to be the favoured choice for the major services on Sundays.

The use of the nave brought up again the question of the relationship between the people sitting there with the service in the choir, if the high altar at the east end of the choir was to be used for communion. We have seen that some Victorians yearned for choir and nave to be brought closer together through the removal of the pulpitum or its replacement by an open screen. This desire increased in the 1960s. Most Catholic cathedrals lost their choir screens, Pugin's at Birmingham being removed in 1967. Anglican cathedrals were more inhibited, but even here pulpitums and screens became less universal than before. St Paul's had long gone while Guildford, Liverpool, and Truro never possessed them.[59] Salisbury and Hereford both had good open-work screens designed by Scott and made by Skidmore. Canon Ralph Dawson of Salisbury disliked both screen and reredos, and persuaded the chapter to remove them

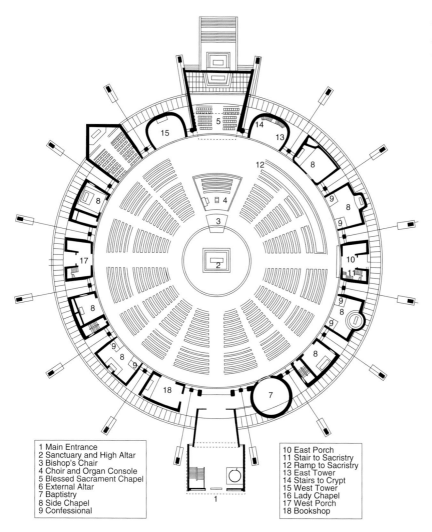

85. Liverpool
Metropolitan
Cathedral, plan.

1 Main Entrance
2 Sanctuary and High Altar
3 Bishop's Chair
4 Choir and Organ Console
5 Blessed Sacrament Chapel
6 External Altar
7 Baptistry
8 Side Chapel
9 Confessional

10 East Porch
11 Stair to Sacristy
12 Ramp to Sacristy
13 East Tower
14 Stairs to Crypt
15 West Tower
16 Lady Chapel
17 West Porch
18 Bookshop

in 1960. The screen was not preserved but sent for scrap. Hereford
followed suit in 1966, despite opposition, but here at least the screen
was not destroyed and survives, well restored, in the Victoria and Albert
Museum in London.[60]

Both actions may be regretted. Not only were the screens historical
objects of value but their absence spoils the proportions of the buildings.
It undoes the sense of an unfolding series of spaces that the medieval
builders meant to impart. The removals were unnecessary too because
a more radical, yet simpler, solution was available. In 1965 Westminster
Cathedral established a new altar close to the nave, while retaining the
older high altar.[61] Similar arrangements, with a second altar placed on a

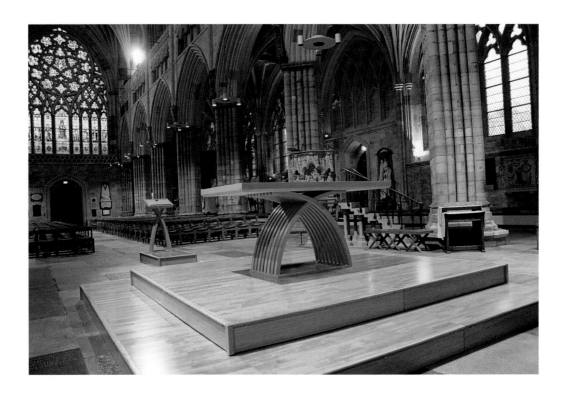

86. A typical
modern nave
altar in Exeter
Cathedral,
placed to be
close to a large
congregation in
that part of the
church.

platform at the east end of the nave, were introduced by all the Catholic cathedrals and most of the Anglican ones during the last decades of the twentieth century. The plan was adopted at Durham, Ely, and Norwich during the 1970s, at first experimentally then permanently, and was introduced even at Hereford in 1984.[62] It enabled the singers to be seated around the nave altar, and chairs for the congregation to be arranged on three sides of it, closer to and facing the altar (Fig. 86, above).

Cathedrals maintained their singers throughout the twentieth century, but the nature and tasks of the singers were not the same throughout. In 1900 an ancient Anglican cathedral had a choir consisting of three or four priest vicars or minor canons, some lay vicars or singing men whose modest salaries required them to have local jobs, and a group of choristers whose lessons in a small choir school were arranged around the hours that they were required in church. By the end of the century clergy in the choir had usually disappeared except for a single priest and it was harder to find lay adults able to leave their work to sing. In university cities, student choral scholars often took their places. Choristers remained but their duties had to be adjusted to the shape of a modern school day, rather than the other way round. These were the difficulties that led to the abandonment of weekday choral matins. They also caused the postponement of weekday choral evensong to a later time, after school or work, and for this to be said on at least one day or sung by the adults alone.

The history of cathedral music in the twentieth century is far too rich to be even summarised here, embracing as it did education, performance, commissions, and compositions. Cathedral organists not only trained the choristers (the composer William Walton was one such boy at Oxford), but they traditionally took articled pupils and still did so in the early part of the century. The students of Herbert Brewer of Gloucester (1896–1926) included Ivor Gurney, Ivor Novello, Herbert Howells, and Brewer's own successor, Herbert Sumsion. Some organists were notable composers, such as Edward Bairstow of York (1913–46) and Sumsion himself. Their settings of the Anglican services and those of others like Howells were widely adopted elsewhere. Naves have become places for orchestral concerts and cathedrals have commissioned a good deal of new Church music, with the advantage for composers of the availability of performers, appealing settings, and guaranteed audiences. The Three Choirs Festival, for example, featured the first performances of works by Elgar, Holst, Howells, and Finzi. Benjamin Britten's *Missa Brevis* was composed for Westminster Cathedral in 1959. At Chichester, where Dean Walter Hussey was an active patron of music in the 1950s and 60s, compositions were elicited from Walton and Lennox Berkeley, and the *Chichester Psalms* from Leonard Bernstein.[63]

Cathedral Life in the Late Twentieth Century

Anyone involved in running a cathedral in the twentieth century was faced by two permanent problems: the acquisition of a sufficient income and the vast cost of maintaining the building. Maintenance had always been a heavy charge, and the rising standards of conservation made it heavier. The story of every cathedral during the century was one of appeals to raise money for the building: stories too lengthy to tell. One can merely sum them up by saying that, through sterling efforts, all the buildings survived the century in reasonable condition. The damage of the Second World War was made good, and visitors by the 1960s would hardly have known it had happened.

Income has been a problem for the Anglican cathedrals ever since the reforms of 1840. In 1931, as we have seen, they lost their remaining landed endowments. Thereafter their revenues came from a range of sources and differed in amount and in proportion from one place to another. The sources and values are set out in *Heritage and Renewal* with respect to the year 1992.[64] Broadly speaking, there were two streams of income: external and internal. Externally, cathedrals were supported by the Church Commissioners through the payment of the dean and two canons. The poorer cathedrals, mostly the former parish churches, received further assistance with the salary costs of lay staff, such as administrators. In some cases a bishop and diocese added resources through paying for officers or functions based at a cathedral. In 1990 the government agreed to assist with some of the costs of repairs and maintenance. It made funds available for grants to cathedrals, both Anglican and Catholic, under the supervision of English Heritage. The grants had to be applied for and were limited to hundreds of thousands of pounds. Another scheme allowed the recovery of the Value Added Tax paid on repairs and approved alterations.

Next there were internal or local sources. Some of the older Anglican cathedrals still held endowments in the form of investments, buildings in their Closes that could be let, or windfalls received in the past. Otherwise cathedrals were dependent on money that they raised from the public. This included donations and bequests from their congregations and supporters, income from visitors, the proceeds of trading activities (shops and restaurants), and special public appeals. The latter, however, could usually be done only intermittently and needed an attractive purpose such as the maintenance of the choral foundation or a particular building project. The financial help of the Friends became more significant now than it was in the 1930s, due to rising membership and generous legacies. In about 1950 the Friends of Norwich even undertook the charge of looking after the cathedral fabric.[65]

Heritage and Renewal in 1992 divided the Anglican cathedrals into six groups in respect of their finances, which may be designated A–F. A consisted of Canterbury, St Paul's, Salisbury, and York, which far outstripped the rest in terms of income. B included the next most prosperous: all ancient foundations (Chichester, Durham, Ely, Gloucester, Hereford, Lincoln, Wells, Winchester, and Worcester). C consisted of seven less wealthy but still substantial institutions (Carlisle, Chester, Exeter, Lichfield, Norwich, Peterborough, and Rochester). D were the creations or re-creations of the nineteenth century, such as Bristol, Liverpool, and Truro; E the 'parish church' cathedrals with a tourist income of more than £10,000 per annum; and F their counterparts with less than £10,000. The sources of income in percentages of all the cathedrals are shown in Table 9.1.

Table 9.1 Sources of Income of Anglican Cathedrals in Percentages, 1992[66]

	A	B	C	D	E	F
Investment income	36	46	38	32	18	13
Church Commissioners and dioceses	6	17	25	26	25	28
Tourism	35	16	14	11	7	1
Voluntary giving	24	22	23	32	50	28

The most obvious features of the table are that the older cathedrals possessed the most in terms of investment income. The older were also best able to benefit from visitors, particularly those in the most popular tourist cities such as Canterbury, London, Salisbury, and York. The parish church cathedrals tended to be located in places where visitors did not go and had no ready way of attracting more. All cathedrals relied for about a quarter of their income on their local supporters and sometimes as much as half. The Church Commissioners provided a balancing mechanism, giving less aid to the richest foundations but more to the poorest which were greatly dependent upon it. Without such aid, it would have not have been possible for the latter to function like the others.

While congregations and Friends were valued and essential in their support, the financing of cathedrals was transformed in the twentieth century by the great increase in visitor numbers. The Victorian stream of local people and railway passengers (Fig. 87, p. 252) grew to a torrent: first through the growth of coach tours and car ownership, and then through that curious modern phenomenon that leads people to undergo the costs and cares of flights to distant countries in order to wander round buildings in dazed groups, be misled by guides, and take innumerable photographs that they will either never look at or understand if they do. Between 1992 and 2000 there were probably about ten to twelve million visits per annum to Anglican cathedrals.[67] St Paul's was said to be the fifth most visited English tourist attraction, while Canterbury and York ranked high on the list as well. Overseas tourists at St Paul's accounted for 70 percent of visitors, 50 percent at Salisbury and Exeter, and a third or more at Winchester, Canterbury, Ely, and Chester, although (as has been said) far fewer people reached the less famous cathedrals.[68] A further growth was that of school parties and university classes on educational visits. These were going on as early as 1950, and brought in hundreds of thousands of children by the end of the century.[69]

Visitors provided both an opportunity and a challenge. Since the 1920s some cathedrals had begun to offer refreshments and sell booklets and post-cards. These activities turned by the end of the century into well-provided restaurants and shops with large turnovers, at least at the most popular places.[70] Incomers brought needs as well, ranging from lavatories and signage to spiritual support. Bennett, Bell, and their successors were concerned that cathedrals should not become mere places of sight-seeing like stately homes and museums. Cathedral visits should offer visitors the opportunity at least for peace and reflection and, if desired, for prayer and counsel. During the century most cathedrals introduced lay guides and voluntary chaplains: retired clergy were helpful in this respect. Paid employees appeared, since while volunteers could run shops, restaurants required regular staff, and a full-time visitor officer became necessary along with a full-time education officer for visits by the young.

More widely there was a change in the number and character of the cathedral's lay employees. They had always been present as servants in canons' houses or workmen engaged on buildings; even in the Middle Ages these probably exceeded the clergy. They certainly did so by the end of the twentieth century. In 1992 it was estimated that there were about 190 cathedral clergy with residential posts as against 1,030 full-time paid staff, 800 part-time paid staff, and 9,900 volunteers.[71] A full-time administrator became necessary to direct

THE BOY KING HENRY III CROWNED
GLOUCESTER CATHEDRAL 28 OCT. 1216

GWR **GLOUCESTER CATHEDRAL** LMS

87. Cathedral tourism: a railway poster of the 1930s urging travellers to go by train to Gloucester.

each cathedral work force and to liaise with the chapter, whose meetings after 1999 he or she was allowed to attend. The costs and potential gains of tourism duly raised again the issue of admission charges. Bennett and Bell had abolished these in an age of lower costs and more local visiting; now running expenses and the demands of visitors were far greater. Some deans and chapters continued to hold to a policy of unrestricted access and voluntary donations, while others felt the need to reintroduce charges. In

1992 only Ely and St Paul's were doing so but by 2013 their number had grown to ten, all ancient foundations.

The provision of guide-books for cathedral tourists went on throughout the twentieth century.[72] Four new series were launched in and after the 1930s. The 'Shell Guides' to English counties, edited by John Betjeman and later John Piper, published from 1934 to 1984, targeted the rising numbers of motorists. They sought not only to list places of interest but to convey their atmosphere and appeal, sometimes provocatively. Betjeman himself described Exeter Cathedral as 'the most disappointing thing about Exeter' and praised its 'great black Norman towers' against its 'ill-proportioned west front'.[73] Probably closer to more people's taste were the county volumes of 'The King's England', edited by Arthur Mee, which came out between 1936 and 1952. These used a rich reverential language in their descriptions although, to be fair, they pointed out interesting things to see and featured famous people where appropriate.[74] Different again were the 'Buildings of England' volumes (1951–74) by Betjeman's bête-noir, the 'Herr Professor' Nikolaus Pevsner, including all the cathedrals from Southwell and Truro in the first two volumes to Oxford in the last. Their detailed descriptions, sometimes dry and mechanical but often perceptive and illuminating, made them companions of choice with serious visitors. For those who wanted easier fare, the short Pitkin guides to cathedrals began to appear with Coventry in 1962, providing an array of photographs with brief texts written by competent local authors. Similar guides or leaflets were produced in foreign languages.

Cathedrals continued their role as places of learning. As before, some of their leading clergy were scholars of note. The deans of York between 1932 and 1975, for example, included Herbert Bate, a former Oxford fellow; Eric Milner-White, fellow and dean of King's College (Cambridge); and Alan Richardson, professor of theology at Nottingham University.[75] As in previous centuries, however, cathedrals received men from the world of scholarship rather than providing a basis for continuing it. Cathedral posts were difficult places from which to match the growing erudition and resources of academic research, especially as the tasks of cathedral life grew heavier. The Victorian theological colleges, too, mostly disappeared from cathedral cities as the training of the clergy was concentrated in fewer centres or became a matter of part-time learning. On the other hand, cathedrals solved the long-felt problem of educating their choristers. In many places small choir schools taught by a single master grew into larger and more viable institutions taking in other pupils and providing a proper range of studies and activities. By 1992 twenty-five cathedrals had choir schools, and the rest sent their choristers to schools nearby.[76]

Meanwhile, there was a growing influx of scholars to cathedral archives and libraries. Up to the middle of the nineteenth century, little research was done in the archives which were not set up for strangers to use. Libraries existed as rather old-fashioned resources for cathedral clergy and fell behind the rising standards of their counterparts in cities and universities. Then, by the second half of Victoria's reign, the historical value of archives began to be realised and libraries

88. Marc Chagall's window, 'The Arts to the Glory of God', one of the commissions of Dean Walter Hussey for Chichester Cathedral.

to be reappraised as troves of rare books.[77] One pioneer, James Raine, librarian of Durham Cathedral (d. 1858), published numerous records of Durham and York in the volumes of the Surtees Society. Others followed, creating a 'golden age' of antiquarian cathedral clergy in the thirty years or so on either side of 1900.[78] Canon Wordsworth of Salisbury edited the medieval texts of the Use of Sarum. Canons Capes and Bannister of Hereford did likewise for the records of their cathedral and diocese. Canon Foster of Lincoln not only managed to be secretary, treasurer, and general editor of the Lincoln Record Society but published a dozen of its volumes on subjects such as wills, cathedral records, and *Domesday Book*.

Between the 1930s and the 1950s libraries and archives became more accessible to the general public with regular opening hours. A series of notable ladies presided over this process in some places, including Kathleen Major at Lincoln (later principal of an Oxford college), Elsie Smith at Salisbury, and Audrey Erskine at Exeter. They not only welcomed researchers but aided them through oral advice, published articles, and editions of records. The new accessibility coincided with the broadening of academic history from political and constitutional matters into religious, economic, and social affairs. Early researches of this kind included R. L. Smith's analysis of the medieval administration of Canterbury Cathedral (1943), Kathleen Edwards's work on the canons of Lincoln and Salisbury (1947), Edward Miller's study of the abbey and bishopric of Ely (1951), and thereafter a multitude of books and articles: too many to mention.[79]

There was also the growth of archaeology. As a study of standing buildings, it had begun with Carter and others in about 1800. Later on there were excavations: pioneering ones at Wells in 1894 and Old Sarum in 1912–15, the first of which revealed part of the Anglo-Saxon cathedral (although it was not then understood as such) and the second much of the church's plan and areas of its precinct.[80] The second half of the twentieth century saw huge advances in knowledge. The excavations at Winchester directed by Martin Biddle in 1961–9, those of Warwick Rodwell at Wells in 1978–93, and that of the Canterbury Archaeological Trust in 1993 brought to light much about the plans and character of the Anglo-Saxon cathedrals. Above ground, the careful correlation of standing remains with documentary evidence, the study of building stones, and the use of dendrochronology to date woodwork further extended knowledge of how and when cathedrals were built. At Exeter, for example, John Allan and others established the date and source of virtually every building stone, enabling reconstruction of the medieval decoration of the west front and the tracing of repairs and restorations across the centuries. These achievements were duly recognised by the Care of Cathedrals Measure with the requirement that cathedrals should appoint consultant archaeologists.

Meanwhile, cathedrals maintained their ancient role in the commissioning and presentation of art and culture. Festivals of music and drama proliferated. Canterbury's resumed after the Second World War with new plays by Laurie Lee and Christopher Fry.[81] Chichester became a centre of artistic creation to rival Coventry with the appointment of Walter Hussey as dean (1955–77) at the suggestion of the bishop, George Bell.[82] Hussey had been vicar of St Matthew in Northampton where he employed Henry Moore to sculpt a Madonna and Child and Graham Sutherland to design a Crucifixion. At Chichester he commissioned art as well as music. This included Sutherland's painting of Christ and Mary

89. Queen
Elizabeth II and
participants
in the Maundy
service at
Blackburn
Cathedral in
2014: an
example of
the use of
cathedrals for
great public
events.

Magdalene, *Noli Me Tangere*, as an altar-piece, a large tapestry designed by
Piper to back the high altar, and Marc Chagall's stained-glass window: 'The
Arts to the Glory of God' (Fig. 88, p. 254). Such works were not without
controversy. Cathedrals had become more exposed to public comment
during the nineteenth century. Hussey wryly observed that there was
greater disapproval of the tapestry than anything else at Chichester during
his deanship, and in 1961 a local woman attacked the Sutherland painting
with a biro, causing £50 worth of damage. Fortunately, since then the
public has become more used to innovative art.[83]

There was one further way in which cathedrals came to reach out
during the twentieth century: ecumenically. In this respect they mirrored
changing attitudes among the Christian Churches towards one another. In
November 1918 King George V and Queen Mary attended a thanksgiving
service for the end of the First World War in Westminster Abbey. It was
a wholly Anglican occasion. No representatives of other Churches were
invited, and the king and queen went to a separate Free Church service
a few days later. When Coventry announced its project with the Free
Churches in 1945, the fact provoked questions in the Church Assembly
and criticisms even from non-Anglicans.[84] By the 1960s, however, ancient
defences were being dismantled. The Second Vatican Council of the

Catholic Church opened its heart more fully to other Churches in 1963. Three years later the archbishop of Canterbury and the pope met cordially in Rome. Catholic clergy were invited to preach in Anglican cathedrals. National services began to include the leaders of other Churches as a matter of course. At St Paul's, for example, the moderator of the Church of Scotland, the cardinal archbishop of Westminster, and the secretary of the Methodist Conference all had roles in the 1980s. The Golden Jubilee service for Elizabeth II in 2002 included the reading of lessons by Welsh and Irish students, and prominent seats were allocated to leaders even of the non-Christian traditions.[85] In some cathedrals Catholic and Free Church leaders have been made honorary canons.

In this and other respects, particularly the ordination of women, the century ended in ways that could not have been imagined when it began. Indeed, it is fair to say that cathedrals underwent greater changes between 1901 and 2000 than they had done even during the great reforming century before. The extent of the changes, and the achievements made, stand as a reproof to those many scholars who assume that there was no Church history in the twentieth century.

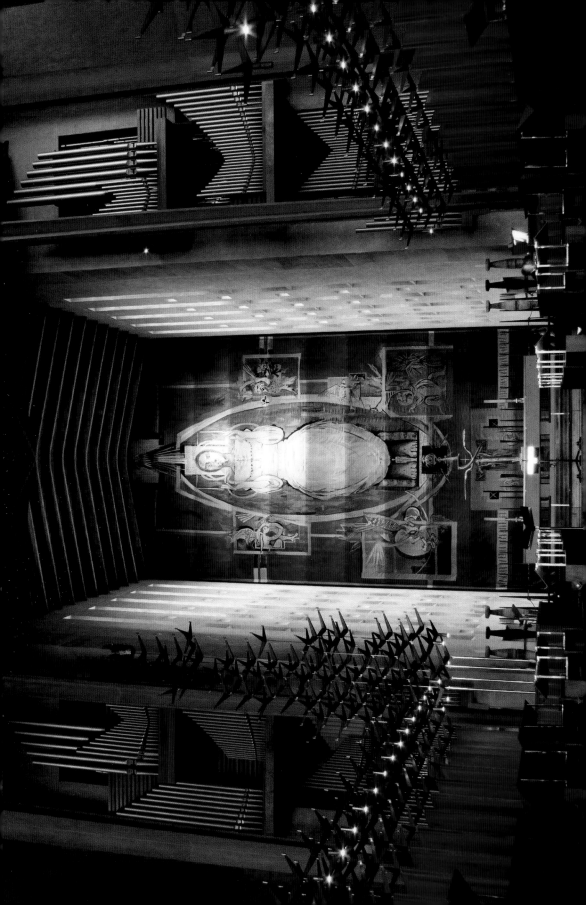

Chapter
— 10 —

Forwards and Backwards

Over the 1400 years since Augustine of Canterbury, the Church of England has gained forty-three cathedrals and lost about fifteen. The Catholic Church has acquired nineteen and lost one. The survivors are a remarkably varied collection. They are scattered unevenly, some in small places, some lacking from large cities. This stems from where the Anglo-Saxons placed them, the Viking age disrupted them, and Henry VIII and the Victorians rearranged them. Eighteen foundations have come down from the Middle Ages. Ten of these have always been secular cathedrals, staffed by canons. Eight were monasteries until Henry threw out the monks and put in canons. Five are his creations in what were previously monasteries. Twenty Anglican and nineteen Catholic ones come from the nineteenth and twentieth centuries. Four of the modern Anglican ones are in ancient monasteries or minsters. Four others have new purpose-built premises, as have five of the Catholic. The remainder are in parish churches with a greater or lesser amount of extension to help them to function as cathedrals.

Cathedrals continue to have a high profile nationally. In an age of apparently declining religious observance, the Anglican congregations have maintained their numbers and even grown, especially at mid-week services. An average estimate of 25,000 visits per week for worship in 2000 is said to have risen to 38,000 in 2015. The popularity of Anglican cathedrals with tourists shows no sign of weakening: in 2015 the number of visitors was estimated at about nine and a half million. The Churches to which cathedrals belong continue to value them. In 2010 the Church of England gave its attention to the mission of the Church in Yorkshire. This led to a proposal to unite three dioceses, the first such union since that of Bristol and Gloucester in 1836 and only the second since the Reformation. The final scheme, agreed by the General Synod and instituted on Easter Day 2014, joined together the former sees of Bradford, Ripon, and Wakefield into a new diocese named after Leeds, the principal city. Nevertheless, the union provided for the retention of the three cathedrals involved, and even authorised the bishop to designate the parish church of Leeds – now called Leeds Minster – as a further pro-cathedral. As with the survival of Bristol Cathedral in 1836, the reform prompts the thought that it is easier to abolish a diocese than a cathedral with its architectural embodiment and its many local (sometimes ardent) supporters.

Cathedrals go on developing too, as they did throughout the nineteenth and twentieth centuries. In 2014–16 Blackburn carried out a large building project to provide houses for the cathedral clergy and apartments for its staff. Other parts of the project include a library, refectory, conference centre, and offices, arranged around a quadrangle. More widely there has been a reintroduction of shrines, in sharp contradiction of what would have been acceptable before 1900. At Durham, the tomb of Cuthbert (once a place for storage) was honoured with candlesticks and a canopy in 1950–2. St Albans restored a shrine to Alban in 1993, Oxford one to Frideswide in 2002, and Hereford (a remarkably gaudy one) to Thomas Cantilupe in 2008. In 2015 Leicester even erected a tomb for a body conjectured to be that of Richard III and interred the remains with much publicity in the presence of bishops and archbishops. Some might have thought Richard unworthy of such an honour, in view of his somewhat unorthodox relationship with young people, but he too has a cult of a kind with its own devotees.

Inevitably, developments go hand in hand with problems. In 2011 the question of how to deal with a camp of protesters outside St Paul's caused disagreements in the chapter that led to the resignations of the dean and the chancellor. More widely there are still issues of governance and finance. In 2016 these led to interventions by the diocesan bishops at Peterborough and Exeter, followed by the departures of the deans and (at Exeter) the resignations of four canons. Peterborough's troubles required a loan from the Church Commissioners, and members of staff were made redundant. Durham, Guildford, and Ripon have also faced financial challenges, despite exertions to improve their sources of income. In April 2017, as this book went to press, the archbishops of Canterbury and York appointed a 'Cathedrals Working Group', chaired by the bishop of Stepney and the dean of York, to examine the

90. The Graham Sutherland tapestry at the east end of Coventry Cathedral. It shows Christ in Majesty and the symbols of the four Evangelists.

management of all the cathedrals. It was tasked with studying a wide range of matters: accountability, finance, safeguarding, buildings, and evangelism. The two chairs stated their wish to ascertain if the legislation and procedures governing cathedrals are fit for purpose in the twenty-first century.[1] Already matters are moving on from the twentieth.

91. Derby: one of the Church of England's two eighteenth-century cathedrals, with its elegant piers and railings.

This book is a history of cathedrals, however, not an account of what they are like today. It is more appropriate now to sum up this history and to try to identify some of its principal features. The basic one, the very 'reason for being', is the daily worship of God. Cathedrals have large buildings to provide a worthy setting for worship, and are fitted at their heart with furnishings for the purpose in the form of altars, stalls, and seating. This worship has hardly ever stopped, except perhaps for a few places in the Viking age and some others during the 1650s. Even the bombings of Coventry and Exeter did not prevent services continuing elsewhere on their premises. If we set aside social and economic institutions like the family and work, cathedrals (along with bishops and dioceses) are the oldest organisations to function in England, with records of continuous activity going back to about the year 600.

This history has been made possible in part by privilege. The Anglo-Saxon cathedrals were well endowed with lands and immunities. Later on came urban properties and tithes. These endowments (with contributions from the wealthy and the less wealthy) formed the resources from which the great buildings were made, their interiors filled with beautiful artefacts, and their senior clergy enabled to live in spacious dwellings. Cathedral privileges began to be dismantled in the 1830s and it is doubtful whether a modern dean and chapter, hard-pressed by financial restraints and multitudinous responsibilities, would consider that they still existed. Nevertheless, cathedrals still receive some distinctive treatment. In the Church of England they are not subject to the normal diocesan administration. They have access to some funding not available to parish churches. Five deans sit on the Church's governing body. It can be argued, of course, that such ancient and complex foundations could not survive without some special measures.

At the same time cathedrals have never been immune from the world outside them. They have absorbed and conformed to the values of that world and have changed as it changed. As has been previously observed, they have been Saxon, Norman, late-medieval, Tudor, Stuart, Hanoverian, and Victorian in character like those epochs. Their modern more democratic worship, the concerns of this worship, and the admission of both sexes to its participation and leadership, have mirrored the social and political changes of the twentieth century. As well as conforming to their surroundings, cathedrals have also been forcibly changed from outside. They have never been inviolable fortresses. Viking attacks, Norman reorganisations, papal provisions of clergy in the fourteenth century, the Reformation, the Civil War, and occasional mob violence have affected and often altered them in major respects. This has continued in modern times with the Victorian and post-Victorian reforms; with the Second World War. Cathedrals no longer have significant private endowments as they had before 1840. They depend for support on their congregations, Friends, visitors, and the national institutions of the Church and the state.

The most astonishing feature of cathedral history, when one has journeyed through its seventeen hundred years, is its immense and varied creativity. If we take buildings, there is the evolving history of their plans and construction, the sourcing of the materials, the labours of craftsmen, the elaboration of the decoration, and the successive layers of repair and restoration. There is the worship, complex in its calendar, its liturgical texts, the ways in which it is done, and the application of the worship to God, saints, or popular needs. There is the vast range of arts involved in producing worship and its setting: sculpture, painting, stained glass, metalwork, fabrics, singing, instrumental music, and chorography. There is the written and spoken word in prayer- and hymn-books, preaching, inscriptions, archives, libraries, guide-books, and service-sheets. Then, as we have seen, scholars have studied cathedrals since the sixteenth century, producing a vast amount of written history and revealing archaeological remains.

Next, there is the social history. The clergy have necessarily received the most attention in this book, yet they themselves have not been uniform but variously dignitaries, canons, monks, vicars choral, minor canons, chantry priests, and honorary chaplains. All these originated for particular reasons and have their distinctive histories. Then there have been far more laity than clergy: lay canons, lay singers, almonry boys, choristers, schoolmasters, sacristans and vergers, seamstresses and laundresses, masons and carpenters, and those who staff offices, shops, and restaurants. As the doors open in the morning, people come in, and they are worshippers, visitors, and occasionally nuisances whose social history has varied over the centuries in terms of their numbers, motives, and activities. Further out, beyond the cathedral and its Close, lie the properties that it owned and the churches with which it had or still has links, whose past and present may be understood through archives, landscapes, and buildings for which the church was once responsible.

For this reason alone, a history of English cathedrals could run into many volumes and even so would never reach an end. What one sees in a cathedral and its history, more concisely than anywhere else, is the amazing generative force of Christianity: never exhausted by what it has done across two thousand years, but tireless still, each year, inspiring more in human thoughts, relationships, or handiworks. To visit a cathedral is to become aware of something that transfigures human life and to take, from the past, a hope and a spur for the future.

Guide to Technical Terms

advowson – *see* **patronage**.

aisle – a corridor in a church, usually alongside and parallel with the **nave** or **choir**.

almsmen – also called 'bedesmen'. From the 1540s to about 1900, elderly or infirm men who received an annual pension at the **New Foundations** on condition of attending cathedral services and doing small tasks. They now exist only as voluntary workers.

altar – the place at which the **eucharist** (or holy communion or **mass**) is celebrated. In the Middle Ages it was a stone structure; at the Reformation it became a wooden table in the Church of England, but stone ones have gradually reappeared since then. The high altar is the principal altar in a church, at the east end of the **choir** or the centre of the church.

altarists – adolescent clerks at certain cathedrals in the Middle Ages; at others they were called **secondaries**.

Anglican – an adjective used since the nineteenth century to describe the Church of England.

Anglo-Catholics – *see* **Oxford Movement**.

anniversary – *see* **obit**.

annuellar – the original name for a **chantry priest**.

ante-communion – the first half of the communion service without the communion itself, often performed on its own from the sixteenth to the early twentieth centuries.

anthem – a religious text sung as a self-contained item during a service or as a devotion by itself.

antiphon – a piece of music sung before and after a psalm, or as an **anthem** in its own right.

appropriation – the procedure by which a cathedral or monastery became **rector** of a **parish** and could take **tithes** from the parish.

apse – a semi-circular projection from a church, often containing an **altar**.

arcade – a row of arches, usually separating a **nave** from an **aisle**.

archbishop – the chief cleric of a **province**, ruling over the **bishops** of that province.

archdeacon – the cleric in charge of an archdeaconry, a subdivision of a **diocese**.

bedesmen – *see* **almsmen**.

benefice – a Church post with an income.

bishop – the Church leader in overall charge of a **diocese** with the sole power to confirm and ordain, sometimes assisted by one or more **suffragans**.

breviary – a book containing the daily offices or services said by the clergy.

canon – a cleric following a rule of life, and the usual name for the senior clergy of the **secular cathedrals**. Up to the Reformation, Carlisle Cathedral was served by regular canons, similar in life to monks. Since 1999 Anglican cathedrals have also had lay canons: some acting as members of the **chapter** while others hold honorary posts. A canon's post and house are known as a canonry.

canon law – the law of the Church.

canticles – the Venite, Te Deum, and Benedictus said or sung at **matins**, and the Magnificat and Nunc Dimittis at **evensong**.

chancel – *see* **choir**.

chancellor – the cathedral dignitary in charge of documents and education.

chantry – the saying of a daily **mass** by a priest for the well-being of a living person or the soul of a dead one, either for a limited period or perpetually. The term is also used for the endowment that paid the priest and for the place where the masses were said, such as a chapel inside a cathedral.

chantry priest – the priest of a **chantry**, sometimes known as an **annuellar**.

chapel – an enclosed area within a cathedral or church containing an **altar**.

chapter – the meeting of the resident clergy of a cathedral, either secular or monastic, to take administrative decisions, held in the **chapter house**. The chapter is often referred to as 'the dean and chapter'. Since 1999 Anglican chapters have included lay members. *See also* **greater chapter** and **college**.

chapter house – a special building at a cathedral or monastery for meetings of the **chapter**.

chasuble – a close-fitting vestment worn by the priest at the **eucharist**.

choir – the eastern part of a cathedral where services are said, sometimes called the chancel although that is the usual term for the equivalent part of a parish church. Also the collective term for the singers who perform the service in that part of the cathedral. In this book it always has the first of these two meanings.

chorister – a boy singer in a **secular cathedral**. Similar singers in monastic cathedrals were usually called 'boys'.

Church Assembly – the governing body of the Church of England, established in 1919 and renamed the **General Synod** in 1970.

Church of England – the national Protestant Church in England since 1534.

civil law – Roman law, as distinct from **canon law** and English common law.

clerk – a term generally meaning a cleric who was not a priest but of lower status.

cloister – a covered walk beside a church, often in the form of three or four walks forming a quadrangle.

collation – *see* **institution**.

college – a word related to 'collection', meaning a group of **secular clergy** who served a church and also the buildings in which they lived, without implying academic functions. It was a popular name for some cathedrals (like Bristol) and for the organisations and dwellings of **vicars choral** in the **Old Foundation** cathedrals. Since 1999 the word has been used to mean the **greater chapter**: the body that comprises the cathedral **dean** and all the **canons**, including the honorary and the lay.

convocation – a meeting of the **bishops** and representatives of the clergy of a **province**. In England there were two: for Canterbury and York. In the late nineteenth century they acquired lay members, began to meet together, and eventually formed the **Church Assembly**.

cope – a vestment shaped like a cloak, originally worn in processions.

council – since 1999, a twice-yearly meeting at each Anglican cathedral of the **dean**, representatives of the **canons**, and lay representatives of various interests. It receives reports from the cathedral **chapter** and has the opportunity to discuss and comment on them.

crossing – the part of a church at the east end of the nave, between the **transepts**.

Crown – the government of England, led by the monarch until the eighteenth century and then increasingly by the prime minister and other ministers.

crypt – an area underneath a cathedral often used as a chapel or for burials.

dean – the title given to the chief dignitary of a cathedral (other than **monastic cathedrals**), except where that person was or is known as a **provost**.

Decorated – the style of **Gothic** architecture in use from about 1290 to 1360.

dignitary – one of the chief officers of a **secular cathedral** such as a **dean** or **precentor**.

diocese – the territory ruled by a **bishop**.

Early English – the style of **Gothic** architecture in use from about 1200 to 1290.

eucharist – the usual modern term for the celebration of holy communion or the **mass**, centring on the consecration of bread and wine in memory of the Last Supper of Jesus Christ.

Evangelicals – a term used since the late eighteenth century for those in the Church of England who emphasise the supremacy of the Bible and the importance of preaching, rather than of ceremonial worship.

evensong – in the Middle Ages the service of vespers said in the mid-afternoon, and since the Reformation the service of evening prayer said in the mid- or late afternoon.

Free Churches – Protestant churches distinct from the Church of England, such as Baptists, Methodists, and Congregationalists (later United Reformed Church).

General Synod – the governing body of the Church of England since 1970, previously the **Church Assembly**.

Gothic – the general name for architectural styles with pointed arches, built in England from about 1200 to about 1650 and again from about 1780.

greater chapter – the **dean** and all the **canons** of an Anglican cathedral, including both the residentiary and non-residentiary canons, the latter of whom may be (since 1999) either clergy or lay. Historically it has been responsible for electing the **bishop** of the **diocese**. Since 1999 it is known as the **college** of canons and also meets annually to receive and comment on reports of cathedral affairs.

high altar – *see* **altar**.

high Church – *see* **Oxford Movement**.

holy communion – the normal term in the Church of England after the Reformation for the **eucharist**.

indulgence (or pardon) – the remitting by a pope or a **bishop** of penance for sins in return for doing a good deed such as a crusade, pilgrimage, prayer, or contribution to a church or a hospital.

institution (or admission) – the act by which a **bishop** approves the appointment to a **benefice** of a clergyman or woman presented to him by a **patron**. When the bishop is himself the patron of the benefice and therefore both presents and institutes, the act is known as a 'collation'.

Lady chapel – a chapel in a cathedral, usually large, in which services are held in honour of the Virgin Mary.

lay canons – chiefly introduced in the Church of England in 1999: some of them as substantive members of the **chapter** to help in the administration of the cathedral while others are honorary and members only of the **college**.

ledger-stone – a flat stone laid over a grave in a church.

litany – a series of short prayers of penitence and requests to God for protection. Before the Reformation it was said or sung in processions, and after the Reformation as a stationary service following **matins**.

mass – the medieval and Catholic term for the service of the **eucharist** or holy communion.

matins – a service said soon after midnight in the Middle Ages but since the Reformation normally in the early or middle morning, also known as 'morning prayer'.

measure – since 1919 a law passed by the **Church Assembly** or **General Synod** which, if subsequently approved by Parliament, acquires full legal authority.

minor canon – a cleric of lower importance at St Paul's and the **New Foundation** cathedrals, with the duty of saying and singing the daily services.

minster – in Anglo-Saxon usage, any kind of church served by a community of clergy. Historians now use it to mean a church staffed by secular **canons**, **priests**, or **clerks**, rather than **monks**. Some of these were cathedrals, some not. In recent times some large town churches in the Church of England have been designated 'minsters' as an honorific title rather than a change of status.

missal – a book containing the service of the **mass**.

monastic cathedral – a cathedral served by **monks** or (in the case of Carlisle) regular **canons**.

monk – a cleric who lived in a monastery or cathedral that observed the Rule of St Benedict or another similar rule.

nave – the western part of a cathedral, also called the 'body'.

New Foundation – the term for the cathedrals founded or refounded by Henry VIII, as distinct from those of the **Old Foundation**.

Non-conformists – *see* **Free Churches**.

Norman – the architectural style of the period 1066–1200, also known as Romanesque.

obit – a **mass** celebrated on the anniversary of someone's death, also known as an anniversary.

Old Foundation – the term used after the 1540s for the **secular cathedrals** of the Middle Ages, as distinct from those of the **New Foundation**.

Oxford Movement – the modern term for those in the Church of England who, from 1833, emphasised the Church's continuity with ancient and medieval Christianity, its right of freedom from state control, and the value of beauty and ceremonial in church buildings and services. In the nineteenth century they were often called 'Tractarians' and then and since, 'Anglo-Catholics' or 'high Church'.

parish – the area of land served by a **parish church**.

parish church – a church that provides worship and other services for the inhabitants of a **parish**.

patron, patronage – the person or organisation with the right to appoint the clergyman (or nowadays a woman) of a **parish church**. The right is known as 'patronage' or as an 'advowson'.

peculiar, peculiar jurisdiction – a territory consisting of one or more parishes which had its own system of administration for Church purposes, separate from the normal administration of the diocese.

Perpendicular – the style of **Gothic** architecture in use from about 1335 until 1530.

pluralism – the practice of holding more than one **benefice** at the same time.

polyphony – music sung in harmony by voices taking different parts.

prebend – a share of the income of a church, equivalent to a **stipend** or salary; also in old-fashioned usage, a **prebendary**.

prebendary – a **canon** who holds a **prebend**. Properly 'canon' means the holder of the post or office and 'prebend' the endowment of the post. The term has been used of canons at both the **Old** and **New Foundation** cathedrals.

precentor – originally *cantor* or chanter: the dignitary responsible for the choral services in the cathedral and the choristers.

presbytery – the eastern part of a **choir** of a church, towards the high **altar**.

priest – a cleric with the power to celebrate the **eucharist**, baptise, and administer most other **sacraments**.

prior – the head of a **monastic cathedral** under the **bishop**.

pro-cathedral – a church that is the seat of a **bishop** on a provisional basis, pending the building of a full cathedral there or elsewhere.

province – a group of dioceses ruled by an **archbishop**. In the Church of England these are Canterbury and York.

provision, papal provision – an appointment of a **bishop**, abbot, **prior**, cathedral **canon**, **rector**, or **vicar** by the pope instead of by the **patron** normally responsible for making the appointment. Such appointments were common in fourteenth-century England but only superseded the rights of other clergy patrons, never challenging those of lay patrons.

provost – the title of the chief cleric of a cathedral in the Catholic Church, used from 1850 but later replaced by 'dean' in some places. In 1931 it was adopted by the Church of England for the clergy in charge of cathedrals that were previously parish churches; they were all retitled as 'dean' in 1999.

pulpitum – a solid stone **screen** between the **choir** and **nave** in many cathedrals.

rector – originally a cleric in charge of a **benefice** who had the right to all its profits including **tithes**, as opposed to a **vicar** who took only some of the profits. The rector's benefice and house were known as a rectory.

regular clergy – **monks**, regular **canons**, friars, and nuns, so called because they all followed written codes of rules.

reliquary – a wooden or metal container holding bones or other relics of Christ or the saints.

requiem – a **eucharist** including prayers for the soul of a dead person.

reredos – a stone screen behind the high altar at the east end of the cathedral, sometimes smooth, sometimes decorated with statuary, and now sometimes absent.

residentiary, residentiary canon – a **canon** at a **secular cathedral** who keeps residence and plays a full part in the chapter, as opposed to a canon who is allowably absent or honorary.

retrochoir – the area behind the high altar of a cathedral, similar to a choir **aisle**.

rood – a large image of Christ on the cross, once placed in a cathedral on the **pulpitum** between the **choir** and the **nave**.

rural dean – a cleric responsible for supervising a group of parishes.

sacrament – one of seven solemn rites of the Church: baptism, confirmation, marriage, confession, **eucharist**, ordination, and the anointing of the sick.

sacrist – a cleric in charge of a cathedral's goods such as vestments and ornaments.

sanctuary – the part of the cathedral around the high **altar** at the east end of the **choir**. Also a privilege by which people accused of a crime could take refuge in a church or on certain pieces of Church property.

Sarum, Use of – **breviaries**, **missals**, and other service books following the usages of Salisbury Cathedral, commonly used in southern England from the thirteenth to the mid-sixteenth centuries.

screen – a partition in a cathedral, usually allowing some view through it, between the **choir** and **nave**, around the edges of the choir, or closing off the individual **chapels** in the building. A solid partition between the choir and the nave is called a **pulpitum**.

secondaries – adolescent clerks at certain cathedrals; at others they were called **altarists**.

secular cathedral – a cathedral staffed by **canons**, comprising half of the cathedrals between the Norman Conquest and the Reformation and all of them afterwards.

secular clergy – clergy who did not follow the monastic life, including the **canons** and other clergy of **secular cathedrals** and also the parish clergy.

see – meaning 'seat', the office of **bishop** with its resources and responsibilities, as opposed to the **diocese** which is the area over which he has control.

stall – the seat of a canon in a cathedral **choir**, also used to mean his post or office, especially in the **New Foundation** cathedrals.

statutes – the regulations by which cathedrals are governed. In the Middle Ages only **secular cathedrals** possessed them and they grew up rather than being issued as sets or codes. After 1540 codes were drawn up for the **New Foundations**, and in recent centuries all Anglican cathedrals have received codes and these have been revised from time to time.

stipend – the salary of a cleric.

stole – a narrow coloured scarf worn with a surplice or a vestment.

succentor – the 'sub-chanter' or deputy of the **precentor** in supervising the choral singing and the choristers.

suffragan – an assistant **bishop** to the bishop of the **diocese**. Historically they had no role in cathedrals unless they were also a **canon**, but in modern times they have usually been given a **stall** and, since 1999, are members of the cathedral **college**.

surplice – a white wide-fitting linen garment with sleeves worn by clergy in church.

tithe – the obligation of all householders to pay the **rector** of their **parish** one tenth of the produce of their land, including all crops and young animals. It became a monetary payment alone in 1836 and was abolished in 1936.

Tractarians – *see* **Oxford Movement**.

transept – a wing of a cathedral extending laterally, usually at the east end of the **nave**.

treasurer – the dignitary in charge of the cathedral's moveable goods such as vestments and ornaments.

triforium – a gallery above the piers of a **nave** or **choir** arcade.

undercroft – an area underneath a cathedral, such as a **crypt**.

use – the prayers, readings, and ceremonies used in worship at a particular cathedral, such as **Sarum** (i.e. Salisbury), Hereford, and York.

vicar – the clergyman of an **appropriated** parish, who received part not all of its revenues. The vicar's **benefice** and house were known as a vicarage.

vicar choral – originally a cleric in a **secular cathedral** or **college** who deputised for a **canon** in saying the daily services. After the Reformation there were also lay vicars.

—— Notes ——

Abbreviations

BAA   British Archaeological Association, conference volumes.
ODNB   *The Oxford Dictionary of National Biography.*
VCH   *Victoria County History.*

Chapter 1: Why Cathedrals?

1 See, for example, Cannon, *Cathedral*; Pevsner and Metcalf, *Cathedrals of England*; Tatton-Brown, *Great Cathedrals*; Tatton-Brown and Crook, *The English Cathedral*; and the individual cathedral histories in the bibliography.
2 Stanford Lehmberg's history of 2005 stopped at 1900.

Chapter 2: Romans and Anglo-Saxons

1 It became customary to call English cathedral towns 'cities', even small ones like Wells. Since the mid-nineteenth century, however, the use of the word 'city' has been officially regulated, and towns that acquired cathedrals thereafter were not automatically re-titled cities. Some with Anglican cathedrals have become so, but Catholic cathedrals have not had such an impact.
2 *Concilia Galliae a.314–a.506*, ed. C. Munier, Corpus Christianorum 148 (Turnhout, 1963), 15.
3 For a map of possible Roman cathedral sites, see Tatton-Brown, *Great Cathedrals*, 24.
4 Bede, *Eccl. History*, 69–79, 114–15.
5 Ibid., 104–7.
6 On the Anglo-Saxon Church, see Blair, *The Church in Anglo-Saxon Society*.
7 Bede, *Eccl. History*, 558–61. For maps, see David Hall, *An Atlas of Anglo-Saxon England* (Oxford, 1981), 148.
8 Bede (*Eccl. History*, 190–1) calls *Dommoc* a *civitas*, meaning a Roman site. It is now usually identified with Dunwich, which may have had such a status, but some medieval writers preferred to place it at Felixstowe near the Roman fort of Walton, and other sites have been suggested (Atherton, *Norwich*, 4–5).
9 Above, p. 17.
10 There was another (South) Elmham (Suffolk) which may be relevant. For discussion of the issue, see Atherton, *Norwich*, 6–8.
11 Above, pp. 34–5.
12 *Dictionary of Medieval Latin from British Sources*, ed. R. E. Latham and others (London, 1975–2013), sub *cathedra, cathedralis*.
13 *Middle English Dictionary*, ed. H. Kurath, S. M. Kuhn, and others (Ann Arbor and London, 1956–2001), sub 'cathedral'; *Oxford English Dictionary*, sub 'cathedral'.

14 Bede, *Eccl. History*, 114–15.

15 Ibid., 80–1. On early Anglo-Saxon worship, see Billett, *Divine Office*, 78–132.

16 Brooks, *Church of Canterbury*, 87–91.

17 Ibid., 100–7; Collinson, *Canterbury*, 3–5, 12–13, 16; map on 34.

18 P. H. Sawyer, *Anglo-Saxon Charters: an annotated list and bibliography* (London, 1968). The early archives of most cathedrals have been lost.

19 Brooks, *Church of Canterbury*, 158.

20 Bede, *Eccl. History*, 186–7.

21 Ibid., 294–5. On the history of Lindisfarne, see Bonner, *St Cuthbert*.

22 Biddle, 'Excavations at Winchester', 277–326; Eddius, *Life of Wilfrid*, 36–7.

23 Eddius, *Life of Wilfrid*, 34–5.

24 Biddle, 'Excavations at Winchester', 319.

25 Bede, *Eccl. History*, 530–1; Eddius, *Life of Wilfrid*, 36–7.

26 Alcuin, 'History of the Church of York', in *The Historians of the Church of York*, ed. J. Raine, 3 vols (London, 1879–94), i, 349–98.

27 Brooks, *Church of Canterbury*, 40; Rodwell, *Wells Cathedral*, i, 55–126.

28 Aylmer and Cant, *York*, 113; above, p. 21.

29 Eddius, *Life of Wilfrid*, 32–7; Bede, *Eccl. History*, 204–5, 528–9.

30 On the Lindisfarne scriptorium, see Bonner, *St Cuthbert*, 125–212.

31 For bibliography, see *The Blackwell Encyclopaedia of Anglo-Saxon England*, ed. Michael Lapidge and others (Oxford, 1999), 213–16.

32 Bede, *Eccl. History*, 368–9; *The Anglo-Saxon Chronicle*, ed. Dorothy Whitelock and others (London, 1961), 130; Hugh the Chanter, *The History of the Church of York*, ed. Charles Johnson and others, 2nd ed. (Oxford, 1990), 2–3.

33 D. M. Hadley, *The Vikings in England* (Manchester, 2006), 44–54; Michael Lapidge, *Anglo-Latin Literature 600–899* (London and Rio Grande, 1996), 432.

34 Hadley, *Vikings in England*, 37–41; Brown, *Durham Cathedral*, 15–25.

35 *Anglo-Saxon Chronicle*, ed. Whitelock, 46; *Alfred the Great: Asser's Life of King Alfred and other contemporary sources*, trans. Simon Keynes and Michael Lapidge (Harmondsworth, 1983), 97, 264–5.

36 *VCH Wilts.*, ii, 27–8.

37 *VCH Cornwall*, ii, 127, 129.

38 No bishops of Lindsey are known after about 1011.

39 On what follows, see Blair, *Church in Anglo-Saxon Society*, 301.

40 Brown, *Durham*, 28–32; Yates, *Faith and Fabric*, 8.

41 On the revival of monasticism in the tenth century, see Knowles, *Monastic Order*, 16–56, and on its chief figures, Brooks, *Church of Canterbury*, 222–53; *St. Dunstan: his life, times, and cult*, ed. Nigel Ramsay, Margaret Sparks, and Tim Tatton-Brown (Woodbridge, 1992); *Bishop Æthelwold: his career and influence*, ed. Barbara Yorke (Woodbridge, 1988); and *St Oswald of Worcester: life and influence*, ed. Nicholas Brooks and Catherine Cubitt (London, 1996).

42 P. Barker, 'The Origins of Worcester', *Transactions of the Worcestershire Archaeological Society*, 3rd series 2 (1968–9), 28, 35; Engel, *Worcester*, 55–6.

43 Bede, *Eccl. History*, 156–9.

44 Barker, 'Origins of Worcester', 27.

45 Blair, *Church in Anglo-Saxon Society*, 368–425.

46 *VCH Yorkshire: City of York*, ed. P. M. Tillott (London, 1961), 397; Orme, *Churches of Exeter*, 150–2.

47 Derek Keene, *Survey of Medieval Winchester*, part i (Oxford, 1985), 107–9; Lepine, 'And Alle Oure Paresshens', 37; Aylmer and Tiller, *Hereford*, 79–80; Orme, *Exeter*, 19–22.

48 Orme, *Churches of Exeter*, 28–9.

49 The exceptions here were the 'parish church' cathedrals of the late nineteenth and early twentieth centuries, but these too have now acquired chapters to govern them (above, p. 240).

50 On what follows, see Tatton-Brown and Munby, *Archaeology of Cathedrals*, 33–5; Lepine, 'And Alle Oure Paresshens', 29–53; Weston, *Carlisle*, 9–10; Meadows and Ramsay, *Ely*, 84, 214; and Yates, *Faith and Fabric*, 35–6.

51 One may add Chester, briefly a cathedral 1075–1102 and again after 1541 (St Oswald), while Norwich and Ely (again) took in parish congregations shortly after the Reformation, respectively St Mary in the Marsh and Holy Trinity (Atherton, *Norwich*, 534, 663; Meadows and Ramsay, *Ely*, 153, 177, 214). Canterbury has had a French Protestant church in its crypt since 1576.

52 Lincoln's parish church, St Mary Magdalene, was moved out in the late thirteenth century; Ely's St Peter or St Cross in 1359–64; and Rochester's, St Nicholas, in 1423 (above, note 50).

53 Lepine, 'And Alle Oure Paresshens', 33.

54 Blockley, Sparks, and Tatton-Brown, *Canterbury Cathedral Nave*, 100–11 with plan on 105. H. M. Taylor, 'The Anglo-Saxon Cathedral Church at Canterbury', *Archaeological Journal*, 126 (1969), 101–30, prints the texts of Eadmer's descriptions.

55 Biddle, 'Excavations at Winchester', 277–326 at 317–21 with plan, 319.

56 Taylor, 'Anglo-Saxon Cathedral at Canterbury', 105–6, 128–9.

57 On worship in the ninth and tenth centuries, see Billett, *Divine Office*, 78–196.

58 *The Monastic Agreement of the Monks and Nuns of the English Nation*, trans. Thomas Symons (Edinburgh and London, 1953), 13–24.

59 Ibid., 2.

60 *The Old English Version of the Enlarged Rule of Chrodegang*, ed. A. S. Napier, Early English Text Society, original series, 150 (1916), 23–31.

61 Edwards, *Secular Cathedrals*, 9.

62 Eadmer, *History of Recent Events in England*, trans. G. Bosanquet (London, 1964), 15.

63 William of Malmesbury, *Gesta Pontificum Anglorum*, ed. M. Winterbottom and R. M. Thomson, 2 vols (Oxford, 2007), i, 314–15.

64 Hill, *Atlas of Anglo-Saxon England*, 152.

65 Bede, *Eccl. History*, 346–7, 354–5, 514–15.

66 Above, pp. 55, 91.

67 On education and learning in Anglo-Saxon England, see Lapidge, *Anglo-Latin Literature 600–899*, and idem, *Anglo-Latin Literature 900–1066* (London and Rio Grande, 1993).

68 *The Monastic Constitutions of Lanfranc*, ed. David Knowles and C. N. L. Brooke, 2nd ed. (Oxford, 2002), 162–4.

69 Edwards, *Secular Cathedrals*, 308–9.

70 Eddius, *Life of Wilfrid*, 44–5.

71 Bede, *Eccl. History*, 268–9.

72 Ibid., 332–5; Brooks, *Church of Canterbury*, 94–9; Lapidge, *Anglo-Latin Literature 600–899*, 141–68.

73 *Historians of the Church of York*, ed. Raine, i, 395–6.

74 Ibid., i, 349–98.

75 Lapidge, *Anglo-Latin Literature 600–899*, 381–98, 430.

76 Lapidge, *Anglo-Latin Literature 900–1066*, 1–48, especially 28.

77 *Monastic Agreement*, trans. Symons, 8, 13, 16, 18.

78 Lapidge, *Anglo-Latin Literature 900–1066*, 32–9, 183–223.

79 *The Exeter Book of Old English Poetry*, ed. R. W. Chambers and others (London, 1933).

80 Knowles, *Monastic Order*, 417–22, 634–5; Orme, *Medieval Children*, 213–16.

81 Above, p. 71.

82 Lepine and Orme, *Death and Memory*, 259–61.

83 Above, pp. 90–3.

Chapter 3: Normans and Angevins

1 *Councils and Synods I*, ii, 581. The reference may be to the moves from Crediton to Exeter and Ramsbury to Sherborne.

2 *Regesta Regum Anglo-Normannorum: the Acta of William I (1066–1087)*, ed. David Bates (Oxford, 1998), 587–9. The date of *c*.1072 looks likely because of the involvement of Pope Alexander II and the failure to mention Lincoln in the decisions of 1075.

3 *Councils and Synods I*, ii, 613. Compare William of Malmesbury's disapproving remarks about rural cathedrals in *Gesta Pontificum*, i, 276–7, 472–3, 314–15.

4 William of Malmesbury, *Gesta Pontificum*, i, 472–3.

5 Demidowicz, *Coventry's First Cathedral*, passim.

6 Eadmer, *History of Recent Events in England*, trans. Bosanquet, 19–21.

7 It is also noteworthy that Remigius of Dorchester-on-Thames, although a monk, was happy to found his new cathedral at Lincoln for secular canons.

8 Brown, *Durham*, 29, 32.

9 William of Malmesbury, *Gesta Pontificum*, i, 287.

10 Atherton, *Norwich*, 37.

11 Meadows and Ramsay, *Ely*, 51–2.

12 On the early history of Carlisle and its cathedral, see Henry Summerson, *Medieval Carlisle*, 2 vols, Cumberland and Westmorland Antiquarian and Archaeological Society, extra series 25 (1993), i, 32–7 and passim; Crosby, *Bishop and Chapter*, 105–13.

13 On this subject, see Crosby, *Bishop and Chapter*, e.g. 48–51, 174–7, 195–7.

14 On this change, see ibid., passim.

15 Above, pp. 62–6.

16 Edwards, *Secular Cathedrals*, 99.

17 On the medieval secular cathedrals, see Edwards, *Secular Cathedrals*, passim.

18 Ibid., 9.

19 Yates, *Faith and Fabric*, 27, 31.

20 *ODNB*, article by M. J. Franklin.

21 An alternative name was Chester, where the bishop had briefly been based beforehand. His house in London was known as Chester Inn.

22 Greenway, 'The False *Institutio*', 77–101.

23 Edwards, *Secular Cathedrals*, 8–19. Few secular cathedrals had a code of statutes, but rather a collection covering different subjects delivered by bishops at various times.

24 Ibid., 136–7.

25 Ibid., 137–55.

26 Ibid., 148–228.

27 Ibid., 243–50.

28 Tracy, *Episcopal Thrones*, passim.

29 Edwards, *Secular Cathedrals*, 169–72, 194–7, 223–8.

30 An anomaly at several secular cathedrals was the assignment of one or two canonries to local monasteries, but it is unlikely that the monks concerned took much part in cathedral affairs (e.g. Aylmer and Cant, *York*, 53).

31 Exeter was an exception: its prebends all had the same value and were not given individual names.

32 Edwards, *Secular Cathedrals*, 39, 41.

33 Ibid., 234–43.

34 Ibid., 50–6.

35 Le Neve, *Fasti Ecclesiae Anglicanae 1066–1300*, passim; *ODNB*, article by Henry Summerson.

36 Edwards, *Secular Cathedrals*, 70–83.

37 Ibid., 252–73.

38 Ibid., 307–17.

39 Orme, *Medieval Children*, 188–9, 232–3.

40 Edwards, *Secular Cathedrals*, 303–7.

41 For a good summary of Norman rebuilding, see Tatton-Brown, *Great Cathedrals*, 49–74.

42 *Gesta Stephani*, trans. K. R. Potter (London, 1955), 72.

43 Brown, *Durham*, 131–41; Pevsner and Metcalf, *Cathedrals of Midland, Eastern and Northern England*, 71–103.

44 For Canterbury in general, see Pevsner and Metcalf, *Cathedrals of Southern England*, 50–81.

45 For Wells in general, see ibid., 292–323.

46 For Salisbury in general, see ibid., 261–86; quotation at 270.

47 On what follows, see *ODNB*, article by Frank Barlow, and his larger study, *Thomas Becket* (London, 1986), 251–75.

48 The early miracles are listed in *Materials for the History of Thomas Becket*, ed. J. C. Robertson, vol. ii (London, Rolls Series, 1876), 37–117.

49 For an overview of the cult, see Collinson, *Canterbury*, 135–51.

50 *A Relation . . . of the Island of England*, ed. Charlotte A. Sneyd, Camden Society, old series, 37 (1847), 30–1.

51 C. E. Woodruff, 'The Financial Aspect of the Cult of St. Thomas of Canterbury', *Archaeologia Cantiana*, 44 (1932), 13–32. However, the figures are incomplete and may not include gifts of objects like rings.

52 *The Riverside Chaucer*, ed. Larry D. Benson, 3rd ed. (Oxford, 1987), 795–7.

53 *The Tale of Beryn*, ed. F. J. Furnivall and W. G. Stone, Early English Text Society, extra series 105 (1909), 1–24. John Lydgate's *Siege of Thebes* is another sequel to the *Canterbury Tales* but gives no details of the pilgrimage to the cathedral.

54 Others were Herfast at Thetford (d. 1084), Remigius at Lincoln (1092), Robert de Béthune at Hereford (1148), William of Blois at Worcester (1236), and Roger Niger at St Paul's (1244). On these saints see Farmer, *Oxford Dictionary of Saints*, passim; Worcester, *Itineraries*, 165 (Herfast); Aylmer and Tiller, *Hereford*, 72, 77; London, Lambeth Palace Library, MS 99, ff. 187r–194v (William of Blois); and Keene, *St Paul's*, 119–20.

55 Farmer, *Oxford Dictionary of Saints*, passim.

56 Above, pp. 80–5.

57 *The Rule of St. Benedict*, ed. O. Hunter Blair, 5th ed. (Fort Augustus, 1948), 55, 123–7.

58 On this subject, see Knowles, *Monastic Order*, 487–527.

59 On these and the names that follow, see Sharpe, *Latin Writers*, passim, and *ODNB*.

60 On what follows, see Orme, *Medieval Schools*, 190–2.

61 Ibid., 47–8, but the source – a charter – exists only in a version that seems to have been rewritten in 1200.

62 Above, p. 71.

63 Orme, *Medieval Schools*, 63–4.

64 Ibid., 191–2, 197. In Exeter and Worcester the archdeacon supervised the grammar school, rather than the chancellor or bishop.

65 Edwards, *Secular Cathedrals*, 185–92, albeit with more evidence for study than teaching.

66 Orme, *Medieval Schools*, 79–83.

67 Ibid., 84–5.

68 Ibid., 209–12.

69 Ibid., 351, 353, 358–9, 370.

70 Above, pp. 103–6.

71 Above, p. 109.

72 On this subject, see Nicholas Orme, 'For Richer, for Poorer? Free Education in England, c.1380–1530', *Journal of the History of Childhood and Youth*, 1 part 2 (2008), 171–87.

Chapter 4: The Later Middle Ages

1 Collinson, *Canterbury*, 117.

2 Meadows and Ramsey, *Ely*, 63; Yates, *Faith and Fabric*, 51–2.

3 Orme, *Exeter*, 52–3.

4 Collinson, *Canterbury*, 117.

5 Meadows and Ramsay, *Ely*, 63.

6 Orme, *Exeter*, 54

7 Yates, *Faith and Fabric*, 51–2.

8 Edwards, *Secular Cathedrals*, 127–35.

9 Above, p. 210. For maps of peculiars, see Humphery-Smith, *Atlas of Parish Registers*.

10 Orme, *Exeter*, 31–4; Keene, *St Paul's*, 42; *VCH Wilts.*, vi, 73, 75.

11 On what follows, see Gervase Rosser, 'Conflict and Political Community in the Medieval Town', in *The Church in the Medieval Town*, ed. T. R. Slater and Gervase Rosser (Aldershot, 1998), 20–42.

12 Atherton, *Norwich*, 255–80, especially 259–60, 262–6.

13 Edwards, *Secular Cathedrals*, 135–50; Lepine, *Brotherhood of Canons*, 183–91.

14 Lepine, *Brotherhood of Canons*, 91–2.

15 The most detailed accounts of provisions are in W. E. Lunt, *Financial Relations of the Papacy with England to 1327* (Cambridge, Mass., 1939), and *Financial Relations . . . 1327–1534* (Cambridge, Mass., 1962).

16 Edwards, *Secular Clergy*, 303–7.

17 Ibid., 307–17.

18 *Dean Cosyn and Wells Cathedral Miscellanea*, ed. Aelred Watkin, Somerset Record Society, 56 (1941), 98–109.

19 Edwards, *Secular Clergy*, 258–85.

20 Hall and Stocker, *Vicars Choral*, passim.

21 Edwards, *Secular Cathedrals*, 285–303.

22 On St Paul's, see Rousseau, *Saving the Souls*, passim.

23 Edwards, *Secular Cathedrals*, 299–301.

24 On these cathedrals in the fifteenth century, see Dobson, 'English Monastic Cathedrals', 151–72. Their monks are listed (apart from Durham) in Greatrex, *Biographical Register* and discussed by her (including Durham) in *Benedictine Cathedral Priories*.

25 David M. Smith, *Guide to Bishops' Registers of England and Wales* (London, 1981), 216–224, 269, 271, but on Durham, compare Brown, *Durham*, 101.

26 Collinson, *Canterbury*, 77–8.

27 On disagreements at Canterbury, see ibid., 71–4.

28 Orme and Cannon, *Westbury-on-Trym*, 26–31.

29 Collinson, *Canterbury*, 145–6, 569.

30 Brown, *Durham*, 438–41.

31 On Norwich and almonry schools, see Bowers, 'Almonry Schools', 177–222.

32 Above, p. 81.

33 Bowers, 'Almonry Schools', 200–2; Brown, *Durham*, 441–3.

34 Tatton-Brown and Munby, *Archaeology of Cathedrals*, 19–30.

35 Pevsner and Metcalf, *Cathedrals of Southern England*, 103–23.

36 On what follows, see Erskine, *Accounts of the Fabric*, ii, pp. ix–xxxvi.

37 Collinson, *Canterbury*, 424.

38 On access in a medieval cathedral, see Orme, 'Access and Exclusion', and on screens in particular, Peter Draper, 'Enclosures and Entrances in Medieval Cathedrals', in Backhouse, *English Medieval Cathedral*, 76–88.

39 Collinson, *Canterbury*, 414.

40 Orme, *Exeter*, 38.

41 Brown, *Durham*, pp. 143–7.

42 McNeill, 'The Medieval Cloister', passim.

43 Joseph Hunter, *Ecclesiastical Documents*, Camden Society, 8 (1840), 19.

44 McNeill, 'The Medieval Cloister', 55.

45 On church monuments in the later Middle Ages, see Kemp, *English Church Monuments*, 20–57, and Saul, *English Church Monuments*, passim.

46 In addition Edward II was buried in Gloucester which was then an abbey.

47 On the dynamics of cathedral Closes, see Orme, *Exeter*, 19–35, and Gilchrist, *Norwich*, 40–65, 236–61.

48 On charnel chapels, see Orme, 'Charnel Chapel', 162–71.

49 Orme, *Exeter*, 31, 194; Keene, *St Paul's*, 49.

50 On the sources of medieval liturgy, see Pfaff, *Liturgy in Medieval England*, and for an outline of its elements and performance, Harper, *Western Liturgy*. The works of Roger Bowers, listed in the bibliography and notes, are also fundamental.

51 D. Wilkins, *Concilia Magnae Britanniae et Hiberniae, 446–1717*, 4 vols (London, 1937), iii, 861; above, p. 107.

52 Nigel Morgan, 'Marian Liturgy in Salisbury Cathedral', in Backhouse, *English Medieval Cathedral*, 89–111.

53 Bowers, 'To Chorus from Quartet', 1–47; idem, 'Reform of the Choir', 167. I am grateful to Dr Bowers for further advice in the paragraphs that follow.

54 On what follows, see Bowers, 'Reform of the Choir', 157–73.

55 On these and other composers, see Grove, *The New Grove Dictionary of Music and Musicians*, ed. Sadie, 2nd ed. (London, 2001).

56 E.g. from five to seven at Hereford (Aylmer and Tiller, *Hereford*, 381) and six to twelve at Lichfield (*VCH Staffs.*, iii, 164).

57 Bowers, 'Almonry Schools', 208–13.

58 I am grateful for the advice of Professor John Harper in this section. The monastic cathedral day in the later Middle Ages is discussed by Knowles, *Religious Orders*, i, 280; ii, 238–9, and the general issues involved with medieval liturgy are well explored in Sally Harper, *Late Medieval Liturgies*.

59 At Exeter the anthem was sung in the chapel of St Paul, at least in the fourteenth century.

60 C. Wordsworth, 'Inventories of Plate, Vestments, &c. belonging to the Cathedral Church of . . . Lincoln', *Archaeologia*, 53 (1892), 1–82; compare idem, *Ceremonies and Processions of the Cathedral Church of Salisbury* (Cambridge, 1901), 160–84; G. Oliver, *Lives of the Bishops of Exeter and a History of the Cathedral* (Exeter, 1861), 297–366.

61 Rosewell, *Medieval Wall Paintings*, 244, 255–6.

62 Marks, *Stained Glass in England*; Sarah Brown, *Stained Glass of York Minster* (London, 1999); C. Brooks and D. Evans, *The Great East Window of Exeter Cathedral: a glazing history* (Exeter, 1988). There are three other detailed volumes on the York glass by Thomas W. French.

63 Orme, *Exeter*, 154.

64 James Raine, *The Fabric Rolls of York Minster*, Surtees Society, 35 (1859), 267–9.

65 On cathedral priors, see Heale, *Abbots and Priors of Late Medieval England*.

66 *Journal of Prior William More*, ed. Ethel S. Fagan, Worcestershire Historical Society (1914), 72.

67 *Testamenta Eboracensia*, ed. James Raine, vol i, Surtees Society, 4 (1836), 261–4; vol iii, ibid., 45 (1865), 9–22.

68 *The Register of Edmund Lacy, Bishop of Exeter, 1420–1455*: Registrum Commune, ed. G. R. Dunstan, vol iv, Devon and Cornwall Record Society, new series 16 (1971), 12–14. For Lyngham's biography, see Orme, *Minor Clergy of Exeter Cathedral, Biographies*, 178–9.

69 Le Neve, *Fasti Ecclesiae Anglicanae 1300–1541*, vol. ii, 2nd ed., ed. Lepine, 5–8.

70 Keene, *St Paul's*, 151–6.

71 Anne Hudson, *The Premature Reformation: Wycliffite Texts and Lollard History* (Oxford, 1988), 241–2.

72 Orme, *Medieval Schools*, 266–75.

73 Ibid., 267.

74 On these writers, see Sharpe, *Handlist of Latin Writers*, passim.

75 On Canterbury, see Collinson, *Canterbury*, 99–115.

76 *Cambridge History of Libraries*, ed. Hoare, i, 28–50.

77 Evidence about the contents of medieval libraries is being collected in the Corpus of British Medieval Library Catalogues. Vol. 4, *English Benedictine Libraries: the shorter catalogues*, ed. R. Sharpe and others (London, 1996), includes information about Ely, Norwich, Rochester, Winchester, and Worcester.

78 New, 'Fraternities', 35–45.

79 Keene, *St Paul's*, 128–31. On the medieval history of St Paul's see also Schofield, *St Paul's before Wren*.

80 *The Great Chronicle of London*, ed. A. H. Thomas and I. D. Thornley (London, 1983), 494–5.

81 Keene, *St Paul's*, 67.

82 *Rites of Durham*, ed. Fowler, 35, 43.

83 Nicholas Orme, 'Salisbury Cathedral and Education', *Wiltshire Archaeological and Natural History Magazine*, 104 (2011), 142–50 at 142; see also above, pp. 131–2, 170.

84 Other cathedral bishop-saints were Walter Suffield (d. 1257) and John Salmon (d. 1325) at Norwich, William Bitton II (d. 1274) and William of March (1302) at Wells, Robert Winchelsey (1313) at Canterbury, James Berkeley (1327) at Exeter, John Dalderby (1320) at Lincoln, Simon Sudbury (1381) at Canterbury, Richard Scrope (1405) at York, and Edmund Lacy (1455) at Exeter (Farmer, *Oxford Dictionary of Saints*, passim; Atherton, *Norwich*, 275, 304, 470 (Suffield, Salmon); Worcester, *Itineraries*, 79, 81 (Bitton); Orme, *Exeter*, 64–7 (Berkeley, Lacy); Collinson, *Canterbury*, 471–2 (Sudbury)).

85 Orme, *Exeter*, 168–9.

86 Ibid., 30, 132.

87 *The Book of Margery Kempe*, ed. S. B. Meech and H. E. Allen, Early English Text Society, original series 212 (1940), passim; Anthony Goodman, *Margery Kempe and her World* (London, 2002).

88 *ODNB*, article by Nicholas Orme; Worcester, *Itineraries*, 51, 117, 235, 367, 397.

89 *VCH Staffs.*, iii, 150 (Lichfield); Hughes and Larkin, *Tudor Royal Proclamations*, i, 269–70 (Exeter); Hobbs, *Chichester*, 11–12.

90 E.g. *Somerset Medieval Wills 1383–1500*, ed. F. W. Weaver, Somerset Record Society, 16 (1901), 15–16, 22, 24, 30, etc.; *The Courts of the Archdeaconry of Buckingham 1483–1523*, ed. E. M. Elvey, Bucks. Record Society, 19 (1975), 12, 24–6, 30–1, 35, etc.

91 Edwards, *Secular Cathedrals*, 318; New, 'Fraternities', 34; Lepine, 'And Alle Oure Paresshens', 43–6.

92 Above, p. 12.

93 Meadows and Ramsay, *Ely*, 67–8.
94 Orme, *Exeter*, 132.
95 Chaucer, *The Canterbury Tales*, General Prologue, lines 509–10.
96 On Lollard views of churches, see for example Hudson, *The Premature Reformation*, 321–3.
97 J. A. F. Thomson, *The Later Lollards 1414–1520* (London, 1965), 58–60; The National Archives, KB 9/227/2 m. 23.

Chapter 5: The Reformation

1 Orme, *Medieval Schools*, 118–27.
2 *ODNB*, article by J. B. Trapp; *The Sermon of Doctor Colete made to the Convocation at Paul's* (London, c.1530; STC 5550).
3 *The Colloquies of Erasmus*, trans. Craig R. Thompson (Chicago and London, 1965), 304–9.
4 Lawrence Stone, 'The Political Programme of Thomas Cromwell', *Bulletin of the Institute of Historical Research*, 24 (1951), 1–18 at 10.
5 For summaries of figures, see Lehmberg, *Reformation of Cathedrals*, 26–8, 46.
6 Kenneth Hylson-Smith, *Bath Abbey: a history* (Bath, 2003), 116–26.
7 Cole, *Henry VIII's Bishoprics*, 75–6; *Statutes of the Realm*, iii, 728.
8 Thompson, *Statutes of Durham*, pp. xxvi–xxi; Atherton, *Norwich*, 507–10.
9 Cole, *Henry VIII's Bishoprics*, 1–74.
10 On late-medieval collegiate churches, see *The Late Medieval English College and its Context*, ed. Clive Burgess and Martin Heale (York, 2008), and Paul Jeffery, *The Collegiate Churches of England and Wales* (London, 2004).
11 Roger Bowers, 'The Music and Musical Establishment of St George's Chapel in the 15th Century', in *St George's Chapel, Windsor, in the Late Middle Ages*, ed. Colin Richmond and Eileen Scarff (Windsor, 2001), 200–1.
12 On Cranmer, see *ODNB*, article by Diarmaid MacCulloch, and his definitive study, *Thomas Cranmer*.
13 Thomas Cranmer, *Miscellaneous Writings and Letters*, ed. J. E. Cox, Parker Society, 18 (Cambridge, 1846), 396–7.
14 Thompson, *Statutes of Durham*, pp. xxxi–lii; Lehmberg, *Reformation of Cathedrals*, 81–3.
15 Thompson, *Statutes of Durham*, pp. xxi–lii. No statutes were issued for Oxford, Norwich, or Westminster, and none has survived for Durham until 1555.
16 *Documents Relating to the Foundation of the Chapter of Winchester A.D. 1541–1547*, ed. G. W. Kitchin and F. T. Madge, Hampshire Record Society, 1 (1889).
17 On the history of cathedral almsmen, see Atherton et al., 'Pressed Down by Want'.
18 Orme, *Medieval Schools*, 306.
19 The cathedrals and numbers of scholarships were Canterbury (50), Chester (24), Durham (18), Ely (24), Peterborough (20), Rochester (20), and Worcester (40).
20 The university awards were certainly withdrawn from Durham, Ely, and probably Canterbury, but four survived at Rochester (above, p. 208).
21 On Cranmer's liturgical work under Henry, see MacCulloch, *Cranmer*, 221–6, 328–34.
22 E.g. W. T. Mellows, *Peterborough Local Administration, Part 2: The Foundation of Peterborough Cathedral*, Northants. Record Society, 13 (1941), 97.
23 Brightman, *English Rite*, i, p. lviii.
24 Roger Bowers, 'The Vernacular Litany of 1544 during the Reign of Henry VIII', in *Authority and Consent in Tudor England*, ed. G. W. Bernard and S. J. Gunn (Aldershot, 2002), 151–78.

25 These were Canterbury, Durham, Exeter, Lichfield, Salisbury, Wells, and York (Leland, *Itinerary*, passim).

26 Frere and Kennedy, *Visitation Articles*, ii, 135–70.

27 Already anticipated at Salisbury (above, p. 81).

28 As had been required in the New Foundations since 1544.

29 Brightman, *English Rite*, i, pp. lxii–lxviii.

30 Lehmberg, *Reformation of Cathedrals*, 107–8.

31 Brightman, *English Rite*, ii, 716.

32 Ibid., i, 129–33, 159–61; ii, 715–17.

33 On what follows, see Lehmberg, *Reformation of Cathedrals*, 69–76 (Henry VIII), 109–12, 117–19 (Edward VI); Aston, *England's Iconoclasts*, 223–46 (Henry VIII), 246–77 (Edward VI); and idem, *Broken Idols*, passim.

34 Aston, *England's Iconoclasts*, 173.

35 Frere and Kennedy, *Visitation Articles*, ii, 37–8.

36 Hughes and Larkin, *Tudor Royal Proclamations*, i, 275–6.

37 Aylmer and Tiller, *Hereford*, 89; Wordsworth in *Archaeologia*, 53 (1892), 38–9.

38 Aylmer and Cant, *York*, 200.

39 On cathedral music under Edward VI, see Le Huray, *Music and the Reformation*, 24–6.

40 Above, pp. 128–9.

41 Frere and Kennedy, *Visitation Articles*, ii, 246–52, 311–20.

42 D. M. Loades, 'The Dissolution of the Diocese of Durham, 1553–4', in *The Last Principality*, ed. D. Marcombe (Nottingham, 1987), 101–16 at 105–6.

43 Le Neve, *Fasti Ecclesiae Anglicanae 1541–1857*, passim. Exact numbers are difficult to estimate.

44 Lehmberg, *Reformation of Cathedrals*, 133–4.

45 A. W. Pollard and G. R. Redgrave, *A Short-Title Catalogue of Books Printed in England . . . 1475–1640*, 2nd ed. (London, Bibliographical Society, 1967–91), ii, 72–86. In 1555 Sarum was ordered to be used at Durham Cathedral (Thompson, *Statutes of Durham*, 159).

46 Lehmberg, *Reformation of Cathedrals*, 127–30; The National Archives, PROB 11/42A/114 (will of Gabriel Donne of St Paul's); John Foxe, *Acts and Monuments*, ed. J. Pratt, 4th ed., 8 vols (London, 1877), viii, 500 (Exeter); Aylmer and Cant, *York*, 202; Aston, *England's Iconoclasts*, 292.

47 On what follows, see Orme, *Medieval Schools*, 330–3.

48 Henry Gee, *The Elizabethan Clergy and the Settlement of Religion 1558–1564* (Oxford, 1898), 41–102, especially 89–93; Frere and Kennedy, *Visitation Articles*, iii, 1–29.

49 Le Neve, *Fasti Ecclesiae Anglicanae 1541–1857*, passim. Again, numbers are approximate.

50 *VCH Staffordshire*, iii, 166.

51 Aylmer and Cant, *York*, 197.

Chapter 6: Survival and Abolition

1 Lehmberg, *Reformation of Cathedrals*, 189–90; Collinson, *Canterbury*, 438; Lega-Weekes, *Cathedral Close, Exeter*, 65; Rogan, *Bristol*, 44; Atherton, *Norwich*, 637.

2 Aston, *England's Iconoclasts*, 303.

3 Hughes and Larkin, *Tudor Royal Proclamations*, ii, 146–8.

4 *Rites of Durham*, ed. Fowler.

5 Ibid., 108.

6 Burne, *Chester*, 24–5.

7 Lawrence Stone, *The Crisis of the Aristocracy 1558–1641* (Oxford, 1965), 405–8.

8 Collinson, *Canterbury*, 156–7.

9 Lehmberg, *Reformation of Cathedrals*, 267–71.

10 *Puritan Manifestoes*, ed. W. H. Frere and C. E. Douglas (London, 1954), 32.

11 *The Seconde Parte of a Register*, ed. Albert Peel, 2 vols (Cambridge, 1915), ii, 211.

12 Frere and Kennedy, *Visitation Articles*, iii, 31–3, 41–3.

13 Above, pp. 156, 167, 186.

14 Frere and Kennedy, *Visitation Articles*, iii, 79–365 passim.

15 Ibid., e.g. iii, 79, 116, 135, 148, 319, 347.

16 On what follows, see Lehmberg, *Reformation of Cathedrals*, 145, 156–9.

17 On cathedral music under Elizabeth and the early Stuarts, see Le Huray, *Music and the Reformation*, 157–402.

18 Frere and Kennedy, *Visitation Articles*, iii, 12–13.

19 On what follows, see Fellowes and Westrup, *English Cathedral Music*, 50–89, and the articles on the composers in Grove, *The New Grove Dictionary*.

20 Frere and Kennedy, *Visitation Articles*, iii, 12–13.

21 Ibid., iii, 33, 322.

22 William Harrison, *The Description of England*, ed. George Edelen (Ithaca, NY, 1968), 23–4.

23 On what follows, see Keene, *St Paul's*, 57–60, 171–82.

24 On monuments in this period, see Kemp, *English Church Monuments*, 58–107.

25 For lists of monuments, see Pevsner and Metcalf, *Cathedrals of England*, 2 vols. Most of the individual cathedral histories also have chapters devoted to them.

26 Above, p. 85.

27 On what follows, see Hughes and Larkin, *Tudor Royal Proclamations*, ii, 177–9, and Keene, *St Paul's*, 52–3, 57–8. There is a good comic description of visitors at St Paul's in *The Non-Dramatic Works of Thomas Dekker*, ed. A. B. Grosart, 5 vols (London, 1884–6, repr. New York 1963), ii, 229–37.

28 Shakespeare, *Henry IV Part II*, I.ii.52.

29 *ODNB*, article by A. S. McGrade.

30 Richard Hooker, *The Laws of Ecclesiastical Polity*, book 4; book 5 sections 15, 25–39.

31 *ODNB*, article by P. E. McCullough.

32 Ibid., article by Andrew Foster.

33 Ibid., article by Anthony Milton.

34 J. V. Bullard, *Constitutions and Canons Ecclesiastical 1604: Latin and English* (London, 1934), 86.

35 *Constitutions and Canons Ecclesiasticall* (London, 1640), section 7.

36 Lehmberg, *Cathedrals under Siege*, 22.

37 Collinson, *Canterbury*, 190–1.

38 For a general account of what follows, see Lehmberg, *Cathedrals under Siege*, 22–56, and for local ones, those in the individual cathedral histories.

39 *Mercurius Rusticus . . . Sacrileges . . . on the Cathedral Churches of this Kingdom* (London, 1685), 116–32.

40 Ibid., 133–63.

41 *Acts and Ordinances of the Interregnum*, ed. C. H. Firth and R. S. Rait, 3 vols (London, 911), i, 265–6.

42 John Rushworth, *Historical Collections: the third part*, 2 vols (London, 1691), i, 203, 206.

43 Ibid., i, 269–73, 285–90.

44 *Acts and Ordinances*, i, 106–17.

45 Ibid., ii, 81–104.

46 Keene, *St Paul's*, 63–4.

47 S. R. Gardiner, *History of the Commonwealth and Protectorate, 1649–1656*, 4 vols (London, 1903), ii, 22–3, 187, 211.

48 Weston, *Carlisle*, 19.
49 Brown, *Durham*, 95.
50 Yates, *Faith and Fabric*, 77, 141.
51 Aylmer and Cant, *York*, 214; Aymer and Tiller, *Hereford*, 106.
52 Erskine, Hope, and Lloyd, *Exeter*, 60–1.
53 *A Directory for the Public Worship of God* (London, 1645), 9–32.
54 Ibid., 40–6.
55 *The Diary of John Evelyn*, ed. E. S. de Beer (London, 1959), 340–50, 824.
56 Aylmer and Cant, *York*, 214–15.
57 Ibid.
58 Brown, *Durham*, 94–5.
59 On what follows, see *Cambridge History of Libraries*, ed. Hoare, i, 363–99.
60 Frere and Kennedy, *Visitation Articles*, ii, 136.
61 Lehmberg, *Reformation of Cathedrals*, 250–3.
62 On what follows, see ibid., 111–38.
63 *ODNB*, article by David Colclough.
64 Ibid., article by Helen Wilcox.
65 M. F. J. McDonnell, *A History of St Paul's School* (London, 1909), 187–94.
66 Above, p. 278, note 19.
67 Above, p. 107.
68 Lehmberg, *Reformation of Cathedrals*, 297–301; idem, *Cathedrals under Siege*, 247–50
69 These included St John Baptist and St Katherine (Exeter), St Ethelbert (Hereford), St Giles (Lincoln), and St Nicholas (Salisbury).
70 Atherton et al., 'Pressed Down by Want', 11–34.
71 Lehmberg, *Cathedrals under Siege*, 244–7.

Chapter 7: From Restoration to Romanticism

1 On what follows, see Green, *Re-establishment of the Church of England*, 61–79.
2 *English Historical Documents 1660–1714*, ed. Andrew Browning (London, 1966), 365–70.
3 Brown, *Durham*, 97–8.
4 Keene, *St Paul's*, 66.
5 On the re-establishment of cathedral music and its history to 1714, see Spink, *Restoration Cathedral Music*, especially 193–406.
6 Brown, *Durham*, 100.
7 Keene, *St Paul's*, 66; Erskine, Hope, and Lloyd, *Exeter*, 66; Aylmer and Tiller, *Hereford*, 120.
8 Noake, *Worcester*, 595; Atherton et al., 'Pressed Down by Want', 21. By 1660 almsmen lived out in nearly all cases except at Oxford which had an almshouse for some of them. They received small pensions from some New Foundation cathedrals until the early twentieth century (e.g. Crook, *Winchester*, 335). At Chester they have remained in being as volunteer workers, provided for in the cathedral statutes of 1935 (Cheshire Archives and Local Studies, EDD 2/38, /52/2).
9 Hobbs, *Chichester*, 106.
10 Burne, *Chester*, 153.
11 Colchester, *Wells*, 167–8.
12 *The Life and Times of Anthony Wood*, ed. Andrew Clark, vol. iii, Oxford Historical Society, 26 (1894), 201.
13 Lehmberg, *Cathedrals under Siege*, 79–80.

14 Evelyn, *Diary*, 496, 498.

15 On what follows, see Keene, *St Paul's*, 186–232.

16 Ibid., 187, 195.

17 *ODNB*, article by Kerry Downes.

18 Keene, *St Paul's*, 353.

19 The character of the period is well summarised in Collinson, *Canterbury*, 204–8.

20 Keene, *St Paul's*, 74.

21 Owen, *Lincoln*, 224–6.

22 Biographies in *ODNB*; Collinson, *Canterbury*, 217–18.

23 Yates, *Faith and Fabric*, 78.

24 Above, pp. 43–4.

25 Brown, *Durham*, 102–3.

26 Welander, *Gloucester*, 395–6 (Pembroke, Oxford); Atherton, *Norwich*, 586 (St Catharine's, Cambridge); Yates, *Faith and Fabric*, 98 (Oriel, Oxford).

27 *VCH Staffs.*, iii, 177–8.

28 Ibid., iii, 185.

29 Almira Gray, *Papers and Diaries of a York Family 1764–1839* (London, 1927), 13–14.

30 Collinson, *Canterbury*, 221–5.

31 *The Cambridge History of Libraries*, ii, 125–6, 313–18.

32 *ODNB*, article by Bernard Nurse. See also Lyttelton's anonymous work *Some Account of the Cathedral Church of Exeter* (London, 1797).

33 *ODNB*, article by Peter W. Thomas.

34 Hobbs, *Chichester*, 253; Meadows and Ramsay, *Ely*, 203; Welander, *Gloucester*, 389; *VCH Wilts.*, iii, 200.

35 Meadows and Ramsay, *Ely*, 204; *VCH Staffs.*, iii, 188; *VCH Wilts.*, iii, 200.

36 Meadows and Ramsay, *Ely*, 221; Welander, *Gloucester*, 411–12; *VCH Wilts.*, iii, 200 (the screen was replaced after removal).

37 Welander, *Gloucester*, 389; Aylmer and Tiller, *Hereford*, 249–50; cf. Rogan, *Bristol*, 44–5.

38 Yates, *Faith and Fabric*, plate 12.

39 Erskine, Hope, and Lloyd, *Exeter*, 69; Welander, *Gloucester*, 402.

40 Above, p. 211.

41 Aylmer and Tiller, *Hereford*, 250, 585; *VCH Wilts.*, iii, 200; Colchester, *Wells*, 186.

42 Aylmer and Cant, *York*, 257, 262; Hobbs, *Chichester*, 121; Noake, *Worcester*, 595.

43 Welander, *Gloucester*, 420–1.

44 On what follows, see *VCH Staffs.*, 180; Keene, *St Paul's*, 223, 353.

45 E.g. Lincoln (Owen, *Lincoln*, 218), Peterborough (Byng, *Torrington Diaries*, iv, 122); and Rochester (Yates, *Faith and Fabric*, 144).

46 Aylmer and Cant, *York*, 237.

47 Hobbs, *Chichester*, 255; *VCH Staffs.*, iii, 181.

48 Aylmer and Tiller, *Hereford*, 412.

49 On what follows, see Fellowes and Westrup, *English Cathedral Music*, 179–219.

50 Byng, *Torrington Diaries*, i, 79–80, 165; ii, 345–7; iii, 36, 171.

51 Gray, *Papers and Diaries*, 13.

52 Hobbs, *Chichester*, 254.

53 Brown, *Durham*, 320–1.

54 Meadows and Ramsay, *Ely*, 256.

55 Erskine, Hope, and Lloyd, *Exeter*, 69.

56 Owen, *Lincoln*, 221; Noake, *Worcester*, 597.

57 Welander, *Gloucester*, 408; Yates, *Faith and Fabric*, 144.

58 On monuments in this period, see Kemp, *English Church Monuments*, 107–41.

59 Keene, *St Paul's*, 271–92.

60 Orme, *Exeter*, 70; Gunton, *History of the Church of Peterburgh*, 104–12.

61 Northern tour in British Library, Lansdowne MS 213, summarised by Lehmberg, *Cathedrals under Siege*, pp. xxiii–xxviii; southern tour in L. G. Wickham Legge, 'A Relation of a Short Survey of the Western Counties', in *The Camden Miscellany XVI*, Royal Historical Society, Camden 3rd series 52 (1936), pp. iii–128.

62 John Stow, *The Survey of London*, ed. C. L. Kingsford, 2 vols (Oxford, 1908), i, 324–38. Stow's work was actually anticipated by John Hooker's *A Catalog of the Bishops of Excester* (London, 1584), which includes a short and not very accurate account of Exeter Cathedral (sigs Bi^r–Bii^v). Hooker was a moderate Puritan with cathedral links.

63 *ODNB*, article by Peter Sherlock.

64 William Somner, *The Most Accurate History of the Ancient City and Cathedral of Canterbury* (London, 1640), 150–90.

65 *ODNB*, article by Graham Parry.

66 Dodsworth and Dugdale, *Monasticon Anglicanum*. On Dodsworth, see *ODNB*, article by Graham Parry.

67 [Daniel King,] *The Cathedrall and Coventuall Churches of England and Wales* (London, 1656).

68 Dugdale, *History of St Paul's*.

69 *ODNB*, article by Nicholas Doggett. The most up-to-date editions are listed in the bibliography.

70 *ODNB*, article by Nicholas Doggett.

71 Willis's works are listed in the bibliography.

72 'Repertorium: or the Antiquities of the Cathedral Church of Norwich', pp. 1–80, in *Posthumous Works of the Learned Sir Thomas Browne* (London, 1712).

73 *ODNB*, article by W. J. Shiels.

74 Aylmer and Tiller, *Hereford*, 137–8.

75 On Wyatt, see J. M. Robinson, *James Wyatt (1746–1813): architect to George III* (New Haven and London, 2012), especially 225–30.

76 *Correspondence of Thomas Gray*, ed. Paget Toynbee and Leonard Whibley, 3 vols (Oxford, 1935), ii, 576–7, 795–6, 862–6.

77 *ODNB*, article by J. Mordaunt Crook.

78 Britton and Bayley, *Beauties of England and Wales*, v, 461; Aylmer and Tiller, *Hereford*, 262–3.

79 Francis Grose, *The Antiquities of England and Wales*, 2nd ed., 8 vols (London, 1783–97), ii, 238.

80 Britton and Bayley, *Beauties of England and Wales*, vi, 50; xi, 114.

81 *ODNB*, articles by Judy Crosby Ivy (Constable) and Nigel Aston (Fisher).

82 Graham Reynolds, *The Later Paintings and Drawings of John Constable*, 2 vols (New Haven and London, 1984), i, 56–8, 117–19, 225–8.

83 Owen, *Lincoln*, 212; Meadows and Ramsay, *Ely*, 203.

84 Atherton, *Norwich*, 634–45; Gilchrist, *Norwich*, 199–235.

85 *VCH Wilts.*, vi, 78.

86 There is a good depiction of the railings at Exeter on Caleb Hedgeland's model of Exeter, 1824 (Exeter, Royal Albert Museum).

87 *VCH Staffs.*, iii, 189; Lega-Weekes, *Cathedral Close, Exeter*, 26.

88 Noake, *Worcester*, 601–5.

89 Burne, *Chester*, 138–223; Noake, *Worcester*, 605–6.

90 Aylmer and Tiller, *Hereford*, 460–9; Welander, *Gloucester*, 398–9.

91 Henry Hatcher, *The History of Modern Wiltshire: Old Sarum or Salisbury* (London, 1843), 585–6.

92 Aylmer and Tiller, *Hereford*, 466.
93 Fiennes, *Journeys*, 77, 149, 178, 213–14, 237, 241.
94 Defoe, *Tour*, passim.
95 Byng, *Torrington Diaries*, i, 17, 45, 79–80, 106, 127, 165; ii, 345–7; iii, 36. The quotation is from Milton, 'Il Penseroso'.
96 James Boswell, *Life of Johnson*, sub 4 April 1777.
97 James Easton, *The Salisbury Guide* (Salisbury, 1769), p. viii.
98 William Gostling, *A Walk in and about the City of Canterbury* (Canterbury, 1774); *The Winchester Guide* (Winchester, 1780); *The Chester Guide* (Chester, 1781); *The York Guide* (York, 1787).
99 William Dodsworth, *A Guide to the Cathedral Church of Salisbury* (Salisbury, 1792).
100 George Millers, *A Guide to the Cathedral Church . . . at Ely* (Cambridge, 1805).

Chapter 8: The Nineteenth Century

1 William Cobbett, *Rural Rides*, 2 vols (London, 1912), ii, 58–9; compare ibid., ii, 229–30. Much additional information on nineteenth-century cathedrals will be found in Chadwick, *Victorian Church*, especially ii, 366–400, and in the excellent detailed account of Barrett, *Barchester*.
2 The morning chapel was the double chapel of the north-east transept.
3 *ODNB*, article by Philip Harling.
4 Wade, *The Black Book*, 272–331, especially 287–328.
5 Best, *Temporal Pillars*, 247–8.
6 Rogan, *Bristol*, 52–7.
7 Wade, *The Extraordinary Black Book*, 1–80.
8 Best, *Temporal Pillars*, 275–6.
9 Brown, *Durham*, 107–9, 113.
10 *ODNB*, article by G. B. Smith and V. Markham Lester.
11 Best, *Temporal Pillars*, 283–90; Chadwick, *Victorian Church*, i, 41–2.
12 Best, *Temporal Pillars*, 296–305.
13 Recently special arrangements have been made for women bishops of any diocese to enter the Lords more quickly.
14 Oxford's eight was later reduced to six.
15 Best, *Temporal Pillars*, 404.
16 Aylmer and Cant, *York*, 292; Best, *Temporal Pillars*, 459.
17 Best, *Temporal Pillars*, 457–60.
18 Burn, *Diocesan Revival*, 192–3.
19 Ibid., 194–6.
20 *The English Catholics 1850–1950*, ed. G. A. Beck (London, 1950), 86–115; Edward Norman, *The English Catholic Church in the Nineteenth Century* (Oxford, 1984), 96–109.
21 J. H. Newman, *Sermons and Discourses (1839–57)* (New York and London, 1949), 356.
22 *The Catholic Directory* (1856); *The English Catholics*, ed. Beck, 116–50.
23 The word 'Anglican' came into wide use in the nineteenth century. This reflected the growth of other churches in England and the creation of branches of the Church of England in other countries.
24 *The Catholic Directory*, passim.
25 Burn, *Diocesan Revival*, 149–50, 198.
26 Ibid., 202, 204; *ODNB*, article by Peter Gordon.

27 Burn, *Diocesan Revival*, 205.

28 Runcie, *Cathedral and City*, 94.

29 *Reports of Her Majesty's Commissioners* (Parliamentary Papers, 1854–5; 1882–5). The first commission received detailed evidence from cathedrals and made general recommendations; the second made recommendations for each cathedral separately.

30 Biographies in *ODNB*.

31 Atherton, *Norwich*, 605–6.

32 S. S. Wesley, *A Few Words on Cathedral Music and the Musical System of the Church with a Plan of Reform* (London, 1849), 5–6.

33 Ibid., 6–8.

34 Barrett, *Barchester*, 166–7.

35 Collinson, *Canterbury*, 263.

36 Aylmer and Tiller, *Hereford*, 159; *VCH Staffs.*, iii, 192–3.

37 Meadows and Ramsay, *Ely*, 334; Hobbs, *Chichester*, 259.

38 On this subject, see Fellowes and Westrup, *English Cathedral Music*, 220–58, and Gatens, *Victorian Cathedral Music*.

39 Welander, *Gloucester*, 450; Owen, *Lincoln*, 258; *VCH Wilts.*, iii, 202.

40 E.g. Weston, *Carlisle*, 141; Yates, *Faith and Fabric*, 148; *VCH Wilts.*, iii, 202; Hobbs, *Chichester*, 129.

41 Brown, *Durham*, 114, 323; Owen, *Lincoln*, 258–9; Hobbs, *Chichester*, 137; *VCH Staffs.*, iii, 192.

42 Owen, *Lincoln*, 258–9; Colchester, *Wells*, 196.

43 Hobbs, *Chichester*, 138; Colchester, *Wells*, 196; *VCH Wilts.*, iii, 206.

44 Keene, *St Paul's*, 90.

45 Hobbs, *Chichester*, 138; *VCH Staffs.*, iii, 196; Owen, *Lincoln*, 269; Colchester, *Wells*, 196, 198; Aylmer and Cant, *York*, 420.

46 Aylmer and Tiller, *Hereford*, 276; Owen, *Lincoln*, 252; Atherton, *Norwich*, 604–5; Yates, *Faith and Fabric*, 125–6; *VCH Wilts.*, iii, 204; Aylmer and Cant, *York*, 299–300;

47 Collinson, *Canterbury*, 275; Hobbs, *Chichester*, 134–6; Owen, *Lincoln*, 267–8;

48 Hobbs, *Chichester*, 129; Weston, *Carlisle*, 29–30; *VCH Cheshire*, iii, 193.

49 Meadows and Ramsay, *Ely*, 293; Aylmer and Tiller, *Hereford*, 163–4.

50 On restoration generally, see Cobb, *English Cathedrals*, passim.

51 Biographies in *ODNB*; David Cole, *The Work of Sir Gilbert Scott* (London, 1980).

52 Phoebe Stanton, *Pugin* (London, 1971), 56–65, 97–100, 113–24, 133–5.

53 Rogan, *Bristol*, 59–61.

54 Barham, *Creation of a Cathedral*, passim; H. Miles Brown, *A Century for Cornwall* (Truro, 1976), 30–3, 67.

55 Barrett, *Barchester*, 232; Hobbs, *Chichester*, 203; *VCH Wilts.*, iii, 203; *VCH Staffs.*, iii, 190–1.

56 Hobbs, *Chichester*, 130–2.

57 Owen, *Lincoln*, 222; Welander, *Gloucester*, 446; Aylmer and Tiller, *Hereford*, 267.

58 Pevsner and Metcalf, *Cathedrals of Midland, Eastern and Northern England*, 35–8.

59 Cole, *Work of Gilbert Scott*, 170.

60 Brown, *Durham*, 114–15, 363.

61 BAA, *Medieval Art and Architecture at Exeter Cathedral*, ed. Kelly, 212–13.

62 Rogan, *Bristol*, 55; Cobb, *English Cathedrals*, 49.

63 On nineteenth-century monuments, see Kemp, *English Church Monuments*, 142–59.

64 Collinson, *Canterbury*, 535; Colchester, *Wells*, 186.

65 Pevsner and Metcalf, *Cathedrals of Midland, Eastern and Northern England*, 195–6.

66 On nineteenth-century stained glass, see Brown, *Stained Glass*, 127–44, and Virginia C. Raguin, *The History of Stained Glass* (London, 2004), 168–95.

67 Meadows and Ramsay, *Ely*, 285.

68 Milton, 'Il Penseroso'.

69 E. B. Pusey, *Remarks on the Prospective and Past Benefits of Cathedral Institutions* (London, 1833), 55–111.

70 G. A. Selwyn, *Are Cathedral Institutions Useless?* (Eton, 1838), 15–28.

71 Biographies in *ODNB*.

72 *ODNB*, article by William J. Gatens; Keene, *St Paul's*, 81, 85.

73 Robertson, *Sarum Close*, 258–330.

74 The New Foundations of Oxford, Norwich, and Winchester did not get grammar schools.

75 *VCH Northants.*, ii, 215–16; *VCH Cheshire*, iii, 231–2.

76 *ODNB*, article by M. C. Curthoys; Yates, *Faith and Fabric*, 120–3.

77 Rochester, unusually, had managed to retain Henry VIII's university scholarships (above, p. 107).

78 Angelo Raine, *History of St Peter's School: York* (London, 1926), 109–23.

79 Collinson, *Canterbury*, 553–61.

80 Brown, *Durham*, 452–5.

81 *VCH Cheshire*, iii, 231–2.

82 Yates, *Faith and Fabric*, 120–3.

83 Aylmer and Tiller, *Hereford*, 588–91.

84 Hobbs, *Chichester*, 138–40; Colchester, *Wells*, 192–3.

85 Brown, *Durham*, 115.

86 *VCH Cheshire*, iii, 233.

87 *ODNB*, article by Mark D. Chapman.

88 Owen, *Lincoln*, 259–61.

89 *The Church-Goer: being a series of Sunday visits to the various churches of Bristol* (Bristol, 1845), 5–10.

90 Brown, *Durham*, 118.

91 Collinson, *Canterbury*, 272–3.

92 Aylmer and Cant, *York*, 299; Colchester, *Wells*, 196.

93 Keene, *St Paul's*, 89, 91.

94 Above, pp. 179–81; Aylmer and Cant, *York*, 273–4.

95 *VCH Staffs.*, iii, 192.

96 Brown, *Durham*, 117.

97 Atherton, *Norwich*, 619.

98 Brown, *Century for Cornwall*, 33.

99 Keene, *St Paul's*, 381–6.

100 Ibid., 87–8.

101 *VCH Wilts.*, iii, 202.

102 Collinson, *Canterbury*, 282, 285.

103 Aylmer and Tiller, *Hereford*, 165.

104 Brown, *Durham*, 115.

105 On this and on fees in general, see Bruce, *The Cathedral Open and Free*, 77–86.

106 First published as *Bradshaw's Shilling Handbook* (London, 1858–64). The edition used was that of 1875.

107 Above, pp. 173, 177.

108 On Turner's cathedral work, see Luke Herrmann, *Turner Prints: the engraved work of J. M. W. Turner* (Oxford, 1990), 11, 133, 136; *The Oxford Companion to J. M. W. Turner*, ed. Evelyn Joll and others (Oxford, 2001), passim; and Eric Shaner, *Young Mr Turner: the first forty years 1775–1815* (New Haven and London, 2016), passim, with numerous illustrations.

109 H. G. Wells, *The History of Mr Polly* (London, 1910), chapter 3.

Chapter 9: The Twentieth Century

1 St James won against St Mary in Bury, and St Martin against St Margaret in Leicester.

2 Tuckwell, *Coming of Age*, 55–80.

3 On the buildings that follow, see Pevsner and Metcalf, *Cathedrals of England*, 2 vols. There are good photographs in Tatton-Brown and Crook, *English Cathedrals*.

4 Rogers, *Westminster Cathedral*, passim.

5 Cotton, *Liverpool*, 1–38; Kennerley, *Liverpool*, passim.

6 Quail and Wilkinson, *Forever Building*, 121–42.

7 It is to be found at Canterbury, Chichester, Manchester, and Worcester as well as many Anglican and Catholic churches.

8 Chadwick, *Victorian Church*, i, 309–25; ii, 359–65.

9 Bristol is counted here as a New Foundation cathedral.

10 *Report of the Cathedrals Commission*.

11 *Cathedrals Measure, 1931*.

12 It took a few years for the corporations to be wound up, but this had generally been achieved by about 1935.

13 On what follows, see *Twenty-Seventh Annual Report of the Friends of Exeter Cathedral* (1957), 14–22.

14 Thomas, *English Cathedral Music*, 38–9.

15 On what follows, see Collinson, *Canterbury*, 311; Brown, *Durham*, 120, 325–7; Meadows and Ramsay, *Ely*, 296; *VCH Staffs.*, iii, 196; Atherton, *Norwich*, 756–6; Keene, *St Paul's*, 97; Crook, *Winchester*, 339, 342.

16 After the Reformation, communion bread was usually white bread. Wafers were due to the influence of Tractarianism. Lichfield changed in 1918 because of the poor quality of war-time bread, and Ely in 1936 (*VCH Staffs.*, iii, 196; Meadows and Ramsay, *Ely*, 296). As a result, cathedrals went back to using patens like medieval ones, rather than plates.

17 E.g. at Winchester in 1931, Exeter in 1933 (called 'tapisers'), and Guildford in 1936.

18 Brown, *Durham*, 325; Atherton, *Norwich*, 747; Colchester, *Wells*, 200, 202; Crook, *Winchester*, 339; Aylmer and Cant, *York*, 547.

19 Coventry had a children's chapel up to 1940 (Howard, *Ruined and Rebuilt*, 11) but this was not replaced in the new cathedral of the 1950s. Others have been established at Chester, Guildford, and Liverpool.

20 Above, p. 212.

21 Keene, *St Paul's*, 381–91.

22 E.g. Collinson, *Canterbury*, 320–1; Brown, *Durham*, 325; Meadows and Ramsay, *Ely*, 367–8; Aylmer and Tiller, *Hereford*, 177, 182–3; Owen, *Lincoln*, 290, 292; Aylmer and Cant, *York*, 550–2, 556.

23 Durham, being a cathedral foundation, held its graduations therein, but most universities from 1200 to 1990 deliberately provided their own buildings for the purpose to emphasise their independence. The use of cathedrals has developed among universities founded since 1990: sometimes due to an Anglican foundation (as at Canterbury, Chester, and St John York) and sometimes perhaps to a wish for an attractive venue.

24 On what follows, see Bruce, *Cathedral Open and Free*, especially 1–7, 74, 105–6.

25 Wells, *History of Mr Polly*, chapter 3.

26 Bruce, *Cathedral Open and Free*, 89–92.

27 *ODNB*, article by Andrew Chandler.

28 Collinson, *Canterbury*, 312.

29 Ibid., 314.

30 Aylmer and Cant, *York*, 551; *Friends of Exeter Cathedral, First Annual Report* (Exeter, 1931).

31 *Heritage and Renewal*, 111.

32 *ODNB*, article by Matthew Grimley; Keene, *St Paul's*, 94–6.

33 *ODNB*, article by Alan Wilkinson; Keene, *St Paul's*, 97–8.

34 *ODNB*, article by Natalie K. Watson; Collinson, *Canterbury*, 318–30.

35 *ODNB*, article by Trevor Beeson; Keene, *St Paul's*, 101–6.

36 Above, pp. 170, 204–5.

37 Collinson, *Canterbury*, 305–6; Tuckwell, *Coming of Age*, 98–127; Aylmer and Tiller, *Hereford*, 171–2, 432; Owen, *Lincoln*, 295–6; Keene, *St Paul's*, 95; Crook, *Winchester*, 338.

38 Tuckwell, *Coming of Age*, 103, 127; Aylmer and Tiller, *Hereford*, 172; Cotton, *Liverpool*, 65–9; Colchester, *Wells*, 200.

39 Collinson, *Canterbury*, 323; Tuckwell, *Coming of Age*, 179–86; Brown, *Durham*, 456; Aylmer and Tiller, *Hereford*, 175, 434; Owen, *Lincoln*, 307; Keene, *St Paul's*, 427; Aylmer and Cant, *York*, 532, 545.

40 Cotton, *Liverpool*, 9–10; Kennerley, *Liverpool*, 141–50.

41 Keene, *St Paul's*, 98–100.

42 Howard, *Ruined and Rebuilt*, 10–15.

43 Collinson, Canterbury, 325.

44 *Annual Report of the Friends of Exeter Cathedral, Thirteenth–Twenty-Fourth Reports* (1942–54).

45 Howard, *Ruined and Rebuilt*, 21–34, 87–9.

46 Psalm 30 verse 5.

47 Tuckwell, *Coming of Age*, 228, 302; Keene, *St Paul's*, 100, 103.

48 *Cathedrals Measure, 1963.*

49 For the 1949 date, see London, Church of England Record Centre, CATH/CONST/1.

50 *The Continuing Care of Churches and Cathedrals*, 123–38, 148.

51 On what follows, see Aylmer and Tiller, *Hereford*, 190–6.

52 *Care of Cathedrals Measure, 1990.*

53 There is a full account of the Lincoln affair in *Church Times*, 7015 (25 July 1997), 11–16.

54 www.legislation.data.gov.uk/ukcm/1999/1999-06-30 (accessed 1 June 2016).

55 Brown, *Durham*, 125.

56 Meadows and Ramsay, *Ely*, 298.

57 For the architect's own account, see Spence, *Phoenix at Coventry*.

58 Coffee was introduced at Durham in the 1970s (Brown, *Durham*, 298).

59 Pearson planned one at Truro but only its base was built and this was removed in 1961 (Barham, *Creation of a Cathedral*, 70).

60 Aylmer and Tiller, *Hereford*, 179–80.

61 On changes in Catholic furnishings, see Robert Proctor, *Rebuilding a Modern Church: Roman Catholic church architecture in Britain 1955 to 1975* (Farnham, 2014), chapter 7.

62 Brown, *Durham*, 327; Meadows and Ramsay, *Ely*, 298; Aylmer and Tiller, *Hereford*, 197; Atherton, *Norwich*, 745; Keene, *St Paul's*, 110.

63 For surveys of twentieth-century music, see Thomas, *English Cathedral Music*, 21–246, and Gant, *O Sing unto the Lord*, 329–72.

64 *Heritage and Renewal*, 153–72.

65 Atherton, *Norwich*, 750.

66 *Heritage and Renewal*, 160.

67 *Heritage and Renewal*, 136, suggested 14 million in 1992, probably an overestimate. Later statistics suggest a range of 9.5–12 million up to 2015, to which attendances at services could be added. See *The Church of England Year Book*, e.g. (2016) p. lv.

68 *Heritage and Renewal*, 135–51.

69 Ibid., 41–9. Attendances of 3,000 to 17,000 were recorded locally in 1992 (ibid., 43), and 300,000 estimated totally in 2015 (*The Church of England Year Book*, p. lv).

70 *Heritage and Renewal*, 129–34.

71 Ibid., 101.

72 One should also mention the 'Little Guides' to counties, published by Methuen from 1900.

73 John Betjeman, *Devon: Shell Guide* (London, 1936), 24–5.

74 Wells, for example, was 'the crown of Somerset'; 'a matchless place'; 'its glory will not pass away', and so on (*Somerset: county of romantic splendour*, ed. Arthur Mee (London, 1940), 417–18).

75 Aylmer and Cant, *York*, 548.

76 *Heritage and Renewal*, 53; Brown, *Durham*, 455–6; *VCH Staffs.*, iii, 196–7; Atherton, *Norwich*, 753; Robertson, *Sarum Close*, 331–69.

77 It is consequently amusing to note that *The Cambridge History of Libraries* totally ignores cathedrals in its modern volume.

78 On what follows, see E. L. C. Mullins, *Texts and Calendars: an analytical guide to serial publications* (London, 1958).

79 The reader is referred to the on-line edition of the *Royal Historical Society Annual Bibliography of British and Irish History*, published by Brepols. Edwards's work will be found in her *Secular Cathedrals*.

80 Tatton-Brown and Munby, *Archaeology of Cathedrals*, 13, 115–16.

81 Collinson, *Canterbury*, 329.

82 *ODNB*, article by Giles C. Watson.

83 Hobbs, *Chichester*, 271–9.

84 Howard, *Ruined and Rebuilt*, 32–3.

85 Keene, *St Paul's*, 390–1.

Chapter 10: Forwards and Backwards

1 Church of England Media Centre, press release, 10 April 2017.

Select Bibliography

Works cited only once or twice are excluded unless of general importance.
They are listed fully in the notes.

Aston, Margaret, *England's Iconoclasts*, vol. i: *Laws against Images* (Oxford, 1988).

Aston, Margaret, *Broken Idols of the English Reformation* (Cambridge, 2016).

Atherton, Ian (ed.), *Norwich Cathedral: church, city and diocese 1096–1996* (London, 1996).

Atherton, Ian, McGrath, Eileen, and Tomkins, Alannah, 'Pressed Down by Want and Afflicted with Poverty . . . : cathedral almsmen in England 1538–1914', in *Medicine, Charity and Mutual Aid: the consumption of health and welfare in Britain, c.1550–1950*, ed. Anne Borsay and Pater Shapely (Farnham, 2013), 11–34.

Aylmer, G. E., and Cant, Reginald (eds), *A History of York Minster* (Oxford, 1977).

Aylmer, G. E., and Tiller, John (eds), *Hereford Cathedral: a history* (London and Rio Grande, 2000).

Backhouse, Janet (ed.), *The English Medieval Cathedral: papers in honour of Pamela Tudor-Craig* (Donington, 2003).

Barham, Fisher, *The Creation of a Cathedral: the story of St Mary's, Truro* (Falmouth, 1976).

Barlow, Frank, *The English Church 1066–1154* (London and New York, 1979).

Barrett, Philip, *Barchester: English cathedral life in the nineteenth century* (London, 1993).

Bede, *Bede's Ecclesiastical History of the English People*, ed. Bertram Colgrave and R. A. B. Mynors (Oxford, 1991).

Best, G. F. A., *Temporal Pillars: Queen Anne's Bounty, the Ecclesiastical Commissioners, and the Church of England* (Cambridge, 1964).

Biddle, Martin, 'Excavations at Winchester, 1969', *The Antiquaries Journal*, 50 (1970), 277–326.

Billett, Jesse D., *The Divine Office in Anglo-Saxon England 597–c.1000* (London, 2014).

Blair, John, *The Church in Anglo-Saxon Society* (Oxford, 2005).

Blockley, Kevin, Sparks, Margaret, and Tatton-Brown, Tim, *Canterbury Cathedral Nave: archaeology, history and architecture* (Canterbury, 1997).

Bonner, Gerald, Rollason, David, and Stancliffe, Clare (eds), *St Cuthbert, his Cult and his Community to AD 1200* (Woodbridge, 1989).

Bowers, Roger, 'To Chorus from Quartet: the performing resource for English church polyphony, c.1390–1559', in *English Choral Practice 1400–1650*, ed. John Morehen (Cambridge, 1995), 1–47.

Bowers, Roger, 'The Almonry Schools of the English Monasteries, c.1265–1540', in *Monasteries and Society in Medieval Britain*, ed. B. Thompson (Stamford, 1999), 177–222.

Bowers, Roger, 'The Reform of the Choir of Salisbury Cathedral, c.1450–1549', in *Late Medieval Liturgies Enacted: the experience of worship in cathedral and parish church*, ed. Sally Harper, P. S. Barnwell, and Magnus Williamson (Farnham, 2016), 157–73.

Brightman, F. E., *The English Rite*, 2nd ed., 2 vols (London, 1921; repr. Farnborough, 1970).

British Archaeological Association, volumes of essays on cathedrals:
    Medieval Art and Archaeology at Worcester Cathedral (No place, 1978).
    Medieval Art and Archaeology at Ely Cathedral (No place, 1979).

Medieval Art and Archaeology at Durham Cathedral (No place, 1980).

Medieval Art and Archaeology at Wells and Glastonbury (No place, 1981).

Medieval Art, Archaeology and Architecture at Canterbury before 1220 (No place, 1982).

Medieval Art and Archaeology at Winchester Cathedral (No place, 1983).

Medieval Art and Archaeology at Gloucester and Tewkesbury (London, 1985).

Medieval Art and Architecture at Lincoln Cathedral (London, 1986).

Medieval Art, Architecture and Archaeology in London, ed. Lindy Grant (No place, 1990).

Medieval Art and Architecture at Exeter Cathedral, ed. Francis Kelly (London, 1991).

Medieval Archaeology and Architecture at Lichfield, ed. John Maddison (London, 1995).

Medieval Art, Architecture and Archaeology at Hereford, ed. David Whitehead (Leeds, 1995).

Medieval Art and Archaeology at Salisbury Cathedral, ed. Laurence Keen and Thomas Cocke (Leeds, 1996).

Southwell and Nottinghamshire: medieval art, architecture, and industry, ed. Jennifer Alexander (Leeds, 1998).

Alban and St Albans: Roman and medieval architecture, art and archaeology, ed. Martin Henig and Phillip Lindley (Leeds, 2001).

Carlisle and Cumbria: Roman and medieval architecture, art and archaeology, ed. Michael R. McCarthy and David Weston (Leeds, 2004).

Medieval Art, Architecture and Archaeology at Rochester, ed. Tim Ayers and Tim Tatton-Brown (Leeds, 2006).

Coventry: medieval art, architecture and archaeology in the city and its vicinity, ed. Linda Monckton and Richard K. Morris (Leeds, 2011).

Medieval Art, Architecture and Archaeology at Canterbury, ed. Alixe Bovey (Leeds, 2013).

Norwich: medieval and early modern art, architecture and archaeology, ed. T. A. Heslop and Helen E. Lunnon (Leeds, 2015).

Britton, John, *The History and Antiquities of . . . .*, 14 vols of cathedral descriptions and histories (London, 1814–35).

Britton, John, and Bayley, E. W., *The Beauties of England and Wales*, 18 vols in 21 (London, 1801–15).

Brooks, Nicholas P., *The Early History of the Church of Canterbury: Christ Church from 597 to 1066* (Leicester, 1984).

Brown, David (ed.), *Durham Cathedral: history, fabric and culture* (New Haven and London, 2015).

Brown, Sarah, *Stained Glass: an illustrated history* (London, 1994).

Brown, Sarah, *Sumptuous and Richly Adorn'd: the decoration of Salisbury Cathedral* (London, 1999).

Bruce, Alex, *The Cathedral Open and Free: Dean Bennett of Chester*, Liverpool Historical Studies, 17 (Liverpool, 2000).

Burn, Arthur, *The Diocesan Revival in the Church of England c.1800–1870* (Oxford, 1999).

Burne, R. H. V., *Chester Cathedral: from its founding by Henry VIII to the accession of Queen Victoria* (London, 1958).

Byng, John, *The Torrington Diaries*, ed. C. Bruyn Andrews, 4 vols (London, 1934–8).

The Cambridge History of Libraries in Britain and Ireland, ed. Peter Hoare, 3 vols (Cambridge, 2006).

Cannon, Jon, *Cathedral: the great English cathedrals and the world that made them* (London, 2007).

Cannon, Jon, and Williamson, Beth (eds), *The Medieval Art, Architecture and History of Bristol Cathedral: an enigma explored* (Woodbridge, 2011).

Care of Cathedrals Measure, 1990 (London, Parliamentary Papers, 1990).

Cathedrals Measure, 1931 (London, Parliamentary Papers, 1931).

Cathedrals Measure, 1963 (London, Parliamentary papers, 1963).

Cathedrals Measure, 1999: see www.legislation.data.gov.uk/ukcm/1999/1999-06-30 (accessed 1 June 2016).

The Catholic Directory, Ecclesiastical Register, and Almanac (London, 1856–).

Chadwick, Owen, *The Victorian Church*, 2 vols (London, 1966–70).

The Church of England Year Book (previously *The Official Year-Book of the Church of England*) (London, 1883–).

Cobb, Gerald, *English Cathedrals, the Forgotten Centuries: restoration and change from 1530 to the present day* (London, 1980).

Cocke, Thomas, and Kidson, Peter, *Salisbury Cathedral: perspectives on the architectural history* (London, Royal Commission on Historical Monuments, 1993).

Colchester, L. S. (ed.), *Wells Cathedral: a history* (Shepton Mallet, 1982).

Cole, Henry, *King Henry the Eighth's Scheme of Bishopricks* (London, 1838).

Collinson, Patrick, Ramsay, Nigel, and Sparks, Margaret (eds), *A History of Canterbury Cathedral* (Oxford, 1995).

The Continuing Care of Churches and Cathedrals: report of the Faculty Jurisdiction Commission (London, 1984).

Cotton, Vere E., *The Book of Liverpool Cathedral* (Liverpool, 1964).

Councils and Synods I: A.D. 871–1204, ed. Dorothy Whitelock, M. Brett, and C. N. L. Brooke, 2 vols (Oxford, 1981).

Crook, John (ed.), *Winchester Cathedral: nine hundred years 1093–1993* (Chichester, 1993).

Crosby, Everett U., *Bishop and Chapter in Twelfth-Century England: a study of the Mensa Episcopalis* (Cambridge, 1994).

Dalton, Paul, Insley, Charles, and Wilkinson, Louise J. (eds), *Cathedrals, Communities and Conflicts in the Anglo-Norman World* (Woodbridge, 2011).

Defoe, Daniel, *A Tour Thro' the Whole Island of Great Britain*, 3 vols (London, 1724–6).

Demidowicz, George (ed.), *Coventry's First Cathedral: the cathedral and priory of St Mary* (Stamford, 1994).

Dobson, R. Barrie, 'Cathedral Chapters and Cathedral Cities: York, Durham and Carlisle in the Fifteenth Century', *Northern History*, 19 (1983), 15–44.

Dobson, R. Barrie, 'The English Monastic Cathedrals in the Fifteenth Century', *Transactions of the Royal Historical Society*, 6th series 1 (1991), 151–72.

Dodsworth, Roger, and Dugdale, William, *Monasticon Anglicanum*, 3 vols (London, 1655–83).

Dugdale, William, *The History of St Paul's Cathedral in London* (London, 1658).

Eddius Stephanus, *The Life of Bishop Wilfrid*, ed. Bertram Colgrave (Cambridge, 1927).

Edwards, Kathleen, *The English Secular Cathedrals in the Middle Ages*, 2nd ed. (Manchester, 1967).

Engel, Ute, *Worcester Cathedral: an architectural history*, trans. Hilary Heltay (Chichester, 2007).

Erskine, Audrey M. (ed.), *The Accounts of the Fabric of Exeter Cathedral, 1279–1353*, 2 parts, Devon and Cornwall Record Society, new series 24, 26 (1981–3).

Erskine, Audrey M., Hope, Vyvyan, and Lloyd, John, *Exeter Cathedral: a short history and description*, 2nd ed. (Exeter, 1988).

Farmer, David, *The Oxford Dictionary of Saints*, 5th ed. (Oxford, 2003).

Fellowes, E. H, and Westrup, J. A., *English Cathedral Music*, 5th ed. (London, 1969).

Fernie, Eric, *An Architectural History of Norwich Cathedral* (Oxford, 1993).

Fiennes, Celia, *The Journeys of Celia Fiennes*, ed. Christopher Morris (London, 1947).

Forster, Bill, *Ripon Cathedral: its history and architecture*, 2nd ed. (Ripon, 2010).

Frere, W. H., and Kennedy, W. McN. (eds), *Visitation Articles and Injunctions of the Period of the Reformation, 1536–1575*, 3 vols, Alcuin Club Collections, 14–16 (1910).

Gant, Andrew, *O Sing unto the Lord: a history of English Church Music* (London, 2015).

Gatens, William J., *Victorian Cathedral Music in Theory and Practice* (Cambridge, 1986).

Gilchrist, Roberta, *Norwich Cathedral Close: the evolution of the English cathedral landscape* (Woodbridge, 2005).

Gostling, William, *A Walk in and about the City of Canterbury* (Canterbury, 1774).

Greatrex, Joan, *Biographical Register of the English Cathedral Priories of the Province of Canterbury, c.1066–1540* (Oxford, 1997).

Greatrex, Joan, *The English Benedictine Cathedral Priories: Rule and Practice, c.1270–c.1420* (Oxford, 2011).

Green, I. M., *The Re-establishment of the Church of England, 1660–1663* (Oxford, 1978).

Greenway, Diane E., 'The False *Institutio* of St Osmund', in *Tradition and Change: essays in honour of Marjorie Chibnall*, ed. Diane E. Greenway, C. J. Holdsworth, and Jane E. Sayers (Cambridge, 1985), 77–101.

[Grove, George.] *The New Grove Dictionary of Music and Musicians*, ed. Stanley Sadie, 2nd ed., 29 vols (London, 2001).

Gunton, Simon, *The History of the Church of Peterburgh* (London, 1686; reissued Peterborough, 1990).

Hall, Richard, and Stocker, David (eds), *Vicars Choral at English Cathedrals: Cantate Domino, history, architecture and archaeology* (Oxford, 2005).

Harper, John, *The Forms and Orders of Western Liturgy from the Tenth to the Eighteenth Century: a historical introduction and guide for students and musicians* (Oxford, 1991).

Harper, Sally, Barnwell, P. S., and Williamson, Magnus (eds), *Late Medieval Liturgies Enacted: the experience of worship in cathedral and parish church* (Farnham, 2016).

Heale, Martin, *The Abbots and Priors of Late Medieval and Reformation England* (Oxford, 2016).

Heritage and Renewal: report of the archbishops' commission on cathedrals (London, 1994).

Hobbs, Mary (ed.), *Chichester Cathedral: an historical survey* (Chichester, 1994).

Howard, R. T., *Ruined and Rebuilt: the story of Coventry Cathedral 1939–1962* (Coventry, 1962).

Hughes, Paul L., and Larkin, James F. (eds), *Tudor Royal Proclamations*, 3 vols (New Haven and London, 1964–9).

Huitson, Toby, *Stairway to Heaven: the functions of medieval upper spaces* [in churches] (Oxford and Philadelphia, 2014).

Humphery-Smith, Cecil (ed.), *The Phillimore Atlas and Index of Parish Registers* (Chichester, 1984).

Jeffery, Paul. *England's Other Cathedrals* (Stroud, 2012).

Keene, Derek, Burns, Arthur, and Saint, Andrew (eds), *St Paul's: the cathedral church of London 604–2004* (New Haven and London, 2004).

Kemp, Brian, *English Church Monuments* (London, 1980).

Kennerley, Peter, *The Building of Liverpool Cathedral*, 4th ed. (Lancaster, 2008).

Knowles, David, *The Monastic Order in England, 943–1216*, 2nd ed. (Cambridge, 1963).

Knowles, David, *The Religious Orders in England*, 3 vols (Cambridge, 1948–59).

Lega-Weekes, Ethel, *Some Studies in the Topography of the Cathedral Close Exeter* (Exeter, 1915).

Lehmberg, Stanford E., *The Reformation of Cathedrals: cathedrals in English society, 1485–1603* (Princeton, 1988).

Lehmberg, Stanford E., *Cathedrals under Siege: cathedrals in English society, 1600–1700* (Exeter, 1996).

Lehmberg, Stanford E., *English Cathedrals: a history* (London, 2005).

Leland, John, *The Itinerary of John Leland*, ed. L. Toulmin Smith, 5 vols (London, 1907–10).

Le Huray, Peter, *Music and the Reformation in England 1549–1660* (Cambridge, 1978).

Le Neve, John, *Fasti Ecclesiae Anglicanae, 1066–1300*, ed. C. N. L. Brooke and others, 11 vols (London, 1968–2012).

Le Neve, John, *Fasti Ecclesiae Anglicanae, 1300–1541*, ed. H. F. King and others, 12 vols (London, 1962–7); vol. ii, 2nd ed., ed. David Lepine (London, 2009).

Le Neve, John, *Fasti Ecclesiae Anglicanae, 1541–1857*, ed. Joyce M. Horn and others, 13 vols (London, 1969–2014).

Lepine, David, *A Brotherhood of Canons Serving God: English secular cathedrals in the later middle ages* (Woodbridge, 1995).

Lepine, David, 'And Alle Oure Paresshens': secular cathedrals and parish churches in late medieval England, in *The Parish in Late Medieval England*, ed. Clive Burgess and Eamon Duffy (Donington, 2006), 29–53.

Lepine, David, and Orme, Nicholas, *Death and Memory in Medieval Exeter*, Devon and Cornwall Record Society, new series, 46 (2003).
McAleer, J. Philip, *Rochester Cathedral, 604–1540: an architectural history* (Toronto, 1999).
MacCulloch, Diarmaid, *Thomas Cranmer: a life* (New Haven and London, 1996).
McNeill, John (ed.), 'The Medieval Cloister in England and Wales', *Journal of the British Archaeological Association*, 159 (2006; a collection of articles).
Marks, Richard, *Stained Glass in England during the Middle Ages* (London, 1993).
Meadows, Peter, and Ramsay, Nigel (eds), *A History of Ely Cathedral* (Woodbridge, 2003).
New, Elizabeth, 'Fraternities in English Cathedrals in the Later Medieval Period', in *Social Attitudes and Political Structures in the Fifteenth Century*, ed. Tim Thornton (Stroud, 2000), 33–51.
Noake, John, *The Monastery and Cathedral of Worcester* (London, 1866).
Orme, Nicholas, *The Minor Clergy of Exeter Cathedral, 1300–1548* (Exeter, 1979).
Orme, Nicholas, 'The Charnel Chapel of Exeter Cathedral', in *Medieval Art and Architecture at Exeter Cathedral*, ed. F. Kelly, BAA, 11 (1991), 162–171.
Orme, Nicholas, *Medieval Children* (New Haven and London, 2001).
Orme, Nicholas, *Medieval Schools* (New Haven and London, 2006).
Orme, Nicholas, 'Access and Exclusion: Exeter Cathedral, 1300–1540', in *Freedom of Movement in the Middle Ages*, ed. Peregrine Horden (Donington, 2007), 267–86.
Orme, Nicholas, *The Cathedral Cat: stories from Exeter Cathedral* (Exeter, 2008).
Orme, Nicholas, *Exeter Cathedral: the first thousand years* (Exeter, 2009).
Orme, Nicholas, *The Churches of Medieval Exeter* (Exeter, 2014).
Orme, Nicholas, *The Minor Clergy of Exeter Cathedral: Biographies, 1250–1548*, Devon and Cornwall Record Society, new series 54 (2013).
Orme, Nicholas, and Cannon, Jon, *Westbury-on-Trym: monastery, minster and college*, Bristol Record Society, 62 (2010).
Owen, Dorothy (ed.), *A History of Lincoln Minster* (Cambridge, 1994).
The Oxford Dictionary of National Biography, ed. C. Matthew and B. Harrison, 60 vols (Oxford, 2004); electronic edition (including revised and further biographies): http://www.oxforddnb.com
The Oxford English Dictionary, ed. J. A. Simpson and E. S. C. Weiner, 2nd ed., 20 vols (Oxford, 1989).
Pevsner, Nikolaus, and Metcalf, Priscilla, *The Cathedrals of England: Midland, Eastern and Northern England* (Harmondsworth, 1985).
Pevsner, Nikolaus, and Metcalf, Priscilla, *The Cathedrals of England: Southern England* (Harmondsworth, 1985).
Pfaff, Richard, *The Liturgy in Medieval England: a history* (Cambridge, 2009).
Quail, Sarah, and Wilkinson, Alan (eds), *Forever Building: essays to mark the completion of the cathedral church . . . of Portsmouth* (Portsmouth, 1995).
Reilly, Lisa A., *The Architectural History of Peterborough Cathedral* (Oxford, 1997).
Report of Her Majesty's Commissioners . . . to Inquire into the State and Condition of the Cathedral and Collegiate Churches in England and Wales, 3 reports (Parliamentary Papers, London, 1854–5).
Report of Her Majesty's Commissioners for Inquiry into the Condition of Cathedral Churches in England and Wales, 2 reports in several parts (Parliamentary Papers, London, 1882–5).
Report of the Cathedrals Commission Appointed in Pursuance of a Resolution of the National Assembly of the Church of England, 2 parts (London, 1927).
Rites of Durham, ed. J. T. Fowler, Surtees Society, 107 (1903).
Robertson, Dora H., *Sarum Close . . . the History of the Choristers for 900 years* (London, 1938).
Rodwell, Warwick, *Wells Cathedral: excavations and structural studies, 1978–93*, 2 vols (London, 2001).
Rogan, John (ed.), *Bristol Cathedral: history and architecture* (Stroud, 2000).
Rogers, P., *Westminster Cathedral: an illustrated history* (Westminster, 2012).

Rosewell, Roger, *Medieval Wall Paintings in English and Welsh Churches* (Woodbridge, 2008).

Rousseau, Marie-Hélène, *Saving the Souls of Medieval London: perpetual chantries at St Paul's Cathedral, c.1200–1548* (Farnham, 2011).

Runcie, Robert (ed.), *Cathedral and City: St Albans Ancient and Modern* (London, 1977).

Saul, Nigel, *English Church Monuments in the Middle Ages: history and representation* (Oxford, 2009).

Schofield, John, *St Paul's Cathedral before Wren* (London, 2011).

Schofield, John, *St Paul's Cathedral: archaeology and history* (Oxford, 2016).

Sharpe, Richard, *A Handlist of the Latin Writers in Great Britain and Ireland before 1540, with Additions and Corrections* (Turnhout, 2001).

Spence, Basil, *Phoenix at Coventry: the building of a cathedral* (London, 1962).

Spink, Ian, *Restoration Cathedral Music 1660–1714* (Oxford, 1995).

The Statutes of the Realm, from Magna Carta to the end of the reign of Queen Anne, 10 vols (London, Record Commission, 1810–24).

Tatton-Brown, Tim, *Great Cathedrals of Britain* (London, 1989).

Tatton-Brown, Tim, and Crook, John, *The English Cathedral* (London, 2002).

Tatton-Brown, Tim, and Munby, Julian (eds), *The Archaeology of Cathedrals*, Oxford University Committee for Archaeology, Monograph 42 (Oxford, 1996).

Thomas, Hugh M., *The Secular Clergy in England, 1066–1216* (Oxford, 2014).

Thomas, Martin, *English Cathedral Music and Liturgy in the Twentieth Century* (Farnham, 2015).

Thompson, A. Hamilton, *The Cathedral Churches of England* (London, 1925).

Thompson, A. Hamilton. *The Statutes of the Cathedral Church of Durham*, Surtees Society, 143 (1929).

Tracy, Charles, and others, *Britain's Medieval Episcopal Thrones* (Oxford and Philadelphia, 2015).

Tuckwell, Tony, *Coming of Age: the life and times of Chelmsford Cathedral 1914–2014* (Chelmsford, 2013).

Valor Ecclesiasticus tempore Henrici VIII auctoritate regia institutus, ed. J. Caley, 6 vols (London, Record Commission, 1810–24).

The Victoria History of the Counties of England.

Darlington, R. R., 'Anglo-Saxon Wiltshire', in *A History of Wiltshire*, vol. ii, ed. R. B. Pugh and Elizabeth Crittall (London, 1955), 1–34.

Edwards, Kathleen, 'Cathedral of Salisbury', in *A History of Wiltshire*, vol. iii, ed. R. B. Pugh and Elizabeth Crittall (London, 1956), 156–210.

Harris, B. E., 'Chester Cathedral', in *A History of the County of Chester*, vol. iii, ed. B. E. Harris (London, 1980), 188–95.

Kettle, Anne J., and Johnson, D. A., 'The Cathedral of Lichfield', in *A History of the County of Stafford*, vol. iii, ed. M. W. Greenslade (London, 1970), 140–99.

Leach, A. F. 'Schools', in *A History of the County of Northampton*, vol. ii, ed. W. Page (London, 1906), 201–88.

Orme, Nicholas, 'Religious History to 1560', *A History of the County of Cornwall*, vol. ii (London, 2010), 1–110, 126–335.

Wade, John, *The Black Book; or, Corruption Unmasked!* (London, 1820).

Wade, John, *The Extraordinary Black Book* (London, 1831).

Welander, David, *The History, Art and Architecture of Gloucester Cathedral* (Stroud, 1991).

Weston, David, *Carlisle Cathedral History* (Carlisle, 2000).

Willis, Browne, *A History of the Mitred Parliamentary Abbies and Conventual Cathedral Churches*, 2 vols (London, 1718–19).

Willis, Browne, *A Survey of the Cathedrals of York, Durham, Carlisle . . .*, 2 vols (London, 1727).

Willis, Browne, *A Survey of the Cathedrals of Lincoln, Ely, Oxford . . .* (London, 1730).

Willis, Browne, *A Survey of the Cathedrals of York, Durham, Carlisle . . .*, 3 vols (London, 1742).

Worcester, William, *Itineraries*, ed. John H. Harvey (Oxford, 1969).

Yates, Nigel (ed.), *Faith and Fabric: a history of Rochester Cathedral 604–1994* (Woodbridge, 1996).

Credits to Copyright Holders

Index

Medieval, early modern, and modern refer to the periods up to 1500, 1500–1800, and since 1800. Illustrations are in bold type.